Inscape

Inscape

The Christology and Poetry
of Gerard Manley Hopkins

James Finn Cotter

University of Pittsburgh Press

Library of Congress Catalog Card 73-189857
ISBN 0-8229-3247-4
Copyright © 1972, University of Pittsburgh Press
All rights reserved
Henry M. Snyder & Co., Inc., London
Manufactured in the United States of America

To E.K.C.

What none would have known of it, only the heart,
  being hard at bay,

Is out with it!

Jésus-Christ est l'objet de tout, et le
centre ou tout tend. Qui le connaît,
connaît la raison de toutes choses.

Pascal, Pensées

Art is the Tree of Life. God is Jesus.

William Blake, The Laocoön Group

Now tell me, tell me, tell me then!
   What was it?
    A. . . . . !
    ?. . . . . O!

James Joyce, Finnegans Wake

Jesus, teach me the gesture that reveals Omega.

Pierre Teilhard de Chardin
Retreat notes, 1940

Contents

Acknowledgments

A GRANT from the National Endowment for the Humanities made it possible for me to write the first draft of this study in the summer of 1968. I am grateful to Oxford University Press and to the English Province of the Society of Jesus for permission to quote from the published and unpublished writings of Gerard Manley Hopkins. I would particularly like to thank the Jesuits of Campion Hall, Oxford, for their kindness and cooperation while I worked on the Hopkins manuscripts there. The staffs of the Bodleian Library, Oxford, the Mount Saint Mary College Library, Newburgh, the Vassar College Library, Poughkeepsie, and the New York Public Library were always most helpful and resourceful in obtaining books and periodicals for me. Father Anthony Bischoff, S.J., graciously answered my queries on points of Hopkins's biography and the manuscripts. I wish to thank him and also the two journal editors who have kindly allowed me to use material I first had published, in quite different versions, in *Papers on Language and Literature* and *Renascence*. Finally, I have the pleasure of thanking the editors of the University of Pittsburgh Press who kept faith in a study that elicited a range of responses from its various readers. I hope this book will offend few and help many who care, as I do, about Christianity and literature or who share, in a wider sense, the desire to know more about them; and I hope that students of Hopkins will learn as much in reading as I have from writing *Inscape*. I would like this study to be, rather than the last word on the subject, the first of many investigations on the influence, say, of Origen or the *Nicomachean Ethics* on the shaping of Hopkins's myth. With increased awareness of the ground of his creative thought, we can become more perceptive readers of his poetry. We already owe a great debt to the many critics who have written on these poems with insight and regard for detail. My book is also intended as payment in part to them.

Abbreviations and Texts Used

D, G, M   Hopkins manuscripts at Campion Hall, Oxford. See D. Anthony Bischoff, S.J. "The Manuscripts of Gerard Manley Hopkins." *Thought*, 26 (1951), 551-80, or *Journals*, appendix IV (abridged list).

J   *Journals and Papers of Gerard Manley Hopkins.* Ed. Humphry House and Graham Storey. London, 1959. (Here and in the next three books, numbers indicate pagination.)

L1   *Letters of Gerard Manley Hopkins to Robert Bridges.* Ed. Claude Colleer Abbott. 2d ed. London, 1955.

L2   *Correspondence of Gerard Manley Hopkins and Richard Watson Dixon.* Ed. Claude Colleer Abbott. 2d ed. London, 1955.

L3   *Further Letters of Gerard Manley Hopkins.* Ed. Claude Colleer Abbott. 2d ed. London, 1956.

P   *The Poems of Gerard Manley Hopkins.* Ed. W. H. Gardner and N. H. MacKenzie. 4th ed. London, 1967. (Numbers refer to poems.)

S   *Sermons and Devotional Writings of Gerard Manley Hopkins.* Ed. Christopher Devlin, S.J. London, 1959. (Numbers indicate pagination.)

Other texts quoted and not individually noted include:
The Holy Bible: The Old Testament, Confraternity-Douay Version, and The New Testament, Confraternity Edition. New York, 1953. (This is one of the last translations made of the Vulgate version which Hopkins used. I have occasionally reworded the text in the light of present biblical research and of Hopkins's own interpretations and practice. In the reworded quotations the notation "adapted" follows the reference citation.)

The Ante-Nicene Fathers. Ed. Alexander Roberts and James Donaldson. Rev. by A. Cleveland Coxe. 10 vols. New York, 1884-86.

Introduction:
Myth and Gnosis

What are works of art for? to educate, to be standards.
Education is meant for the many, standards are for public
use. To produce then is of little use unless what we
produce is known, if known widely known, the wider
known the better, for it is by being known it works,
it influences, it does its duty, it does good. We must then
try to be known, aim at it, take means to it. (L1, 231)

GERARD MANLEY HOPKINS wrote these words in a letter to Robert Bridges in 1886. He was forty-two at the time and
had but three more years to live. The Jesuit priest himself had
written poems, but these remained unpublished and unknown
until Bridges, thirty years later, edited the first edition of Hopkins's poetry. Why then did he urge others to become known,
yet make no efforts to educate and form standards through his
own works of art? Instead, he had burned his own verses before
entering the Society of Jesus and afterward took little care to
preserve the manuscripts of later compositions. Hopkins guarded
his obscurity, yet knew himself to be—as his letters clearly show
—an original genius in shaping new forms of poetry and rhythm.
Certainly the words of St. John Chrysostom in a homily on
Christ's humiliation and glory, which the priest read and cherished, help explain the paradox: "For it is not possible to obtain
glory any other way than by fleeing from glory, for as long as we
pursue it, it flees from us; but when we flee from it, then it pursues us. If you would be glorious, do not desire glory. If you
would be lofty, do not make yourself lofty."[1] But expressive as
they are of a Christian tenet Hopkins stanchly adhered to, the
words do not explain everything about his secrecy and unwillingness to publish.

Today Hopkins stands alone as the best-known and most intensely studied poet of the late Victorian period. His poems are subjected to exacting analyses and appear in increasing bulk in anthologies of English verse. What he produced "is known," in the sense that some are famous and praised. But they are not "known" as Hopkins used the word—five times in one sentence quoted above. "Gnosis," knowledge of the poems' unifying meaning, of the private coinages "inscape" and "instress," and of the enigmatic poet-priest himself, still escapes his audience. Despite excellent individual commentaries in books and numerous articles, readers search the poems and glossaries but find no one sure thread to lead them through the labyrinth.[2] This study attempts to provide that mythic thread which winds around many inner passageways and corners. Emerging, however, we find the way possesses a unity and direction that are astonishingly simple and consistent. "By being known," the poet's "new skeinèd score" (P35) "works, it influences, it does its duty, it does good."

Modern literary criticism has rightly recognized and explored the individual poet's need to create a personal myth as a framework for his ideas and values. With the breakdown of accepted sets of communicating images, the author, it has been found, must now build his own interior nest of meaning from the scattered pieces of tradition. William Butler Yeats is the classic example, with his cyclic vision of history and art, but William Blake had already laid the pattern before him by shaping a Christian creed peculiarly his own. Hopkins, on the contrary, is generally regarded as a poet who accepted without question a ready-made myth, Roman Catholicism with its established ritual and dogma. Such an assumption, I believe, needs urgent reexamination.

A reappraisal of Hopkins's theology is necessary not only for an understanding of his poetry but for the sake of clarifying the wider relevance of Christianity to today's literary culture. Threatened by similar enemies of ignorance and indifference, both literature and religion may expire without a realistic encounter with one another. While such a cataclysm is unlikely, Hopkins appears to me to offer a proper meeting place to hold initial peace talks between contemporary Catholic theology and secular poetry. On their side of the table, the theologians themselves would profit from a study of his Christian *poesis*.

If Hopkins the priest were as unthinking in his religious acceptance of his Church's teachings as he has often been pictured, his poems would certainly have lacked the strong texture, rhythm, and structural complexity readers immediately sense in them. Each poem possesses a tough rind whose meat is not readily yielded. Some of the major poems seem particularly impenetrable because of the unique religious insights they express. Bridges, complaining of the troublesome oddities of *The Wreck of the Deutschland*, summarily dismissed it. Hopkins answered: "Granted that it needs study and is obscure, for indeed I was not over-desirous that the meaning of all should be quite clear, at least unmistakeable, you might, without the effort that to make it all out would seem to have required, have nevertheless read it so that lines and stanzas should be left in the memory and superficial impressions deepened, and have liked some without exhausting all" (L1, 50). Bridges's problem and prejudice were both theological and poetical. The ode is most obscure precisely in its religious meaning. One recent interpretation of the poem argues that the event which propels the narrative and the poet's high pitch of prayerful enthusiasm is nothing less than a miraculous appearance of Christ to the shipwreck victims.[3] When such suppositions win wide acceptance, one wonders at the gap that separates the thinking of the two disciplines and cultures.

Hopkins fashioned a myth of his own making. "Myth" here has nothing of the make-believe or farfetched about it. Hopkins echoed the pre-Socratic philosopher Xenophanes in his denunciation of the misusage of mythology by the Greeks. In his letters to Bridges and Canon Dixon he pictures the behavior of the gods as unnatural and pointless nonsense (L1, 212; L2, 144-47). From his Oxford years until the end of his life, however, the poet showed a deep interest in world mythologies: Egyptian deities; the Eleusinian mysteries; Greek, Roman, and Celtic myths. Myth, moreover, has a meaning quite applicable to Hopkins's own writings and in a letter to Dixon he provides this definition himself: "But mythology is something else besides fairytale: it is religion, the historical part of religion" (L2, 146). Years earlier, in an undergraduate essay on "Mythology and Philosophy" (see Appendix I), he attempted to trace the historical and psychological process by which man seeks through mythology the unity, rhythm, and ultimate personality behind the world. Mythology, according to Hopkins, provides the groundwork and scheme of this inquiry. In these pages, then, "myth" expresses the system of related ideas and images that make up a poet's vision of historical and created reality which religion encompasses, orders, and reveals.

Myth in this connotation is not logical discursive thought, but intuitive knowledge.[4] This mythopoeic gnosis in Hopkins attains the universal in the concrete, the whole in its parts, reality within appearance, and being in change. Father Walter Ong correctly and perceptively finds an open-end, evolutionary view of time in Hopkins's poetry;[5] but the poet, on the other hand, did not see mythology as a mere escape from the temporal, as his own definition of its historicity demonstrates. Through myth the unknown is momentarily made known, while yet remaining the unknowable, and is expressed in the language and imagery of man. The mythopoeic mind is of its nature humanistic, as well as religious, for it looks toward God and speaks to man. It intuits and proclaims "the historical part of religion." The eternal cycle from Alpha to Omega, from "the first outstress of God's power" in Christ to the Parousia and coming of the kingdom, is a linear procession of the entire human race from and to the Word made flesh who reveals in himself the mythic meaning of the real world. True myth is Christ whom others "fable and miss." Yet what reality mythology possesses, like all created things, it receives from him.[6] "God," Plato observed in his *Laws*, "as the old tradition declares, holding in his hand the beginning, middle and end of all that is, travels through the cycle of nature in a straight line towards the accomplishment of his end" (4. 715e).[7]

"What the poet says and undertakes to be," writes Martin Heidegger, "is the real," and poetry itself is "the act of establishing being by means of the word."[8] Hopkins rightly regarded himself as a realist: lambs are lambs and trees are trees in his poetry. A falcon is not a symbol of something or someone other than itself, it is a falcon being and acting out its *self*. His poems never slip into that facile borrowing of Christian symbolism which one finds in lesser writers. He shuns analogy and the allegory born of abstractions. For Hopkins, being is univocal, everywhere uttered one and the same way; each mortal thing "deals out that being indoors each one dwells" (P57). As we shall see, that "being" is Christic, a created expression of the creating Word or, additionally in man, an uncreated actuation of the redeeming Word. Both Words are, of course, Jesus. Bread and wine *are* the body and blood of Christ through his atonement, but lambs and trees are Christ-beings too in the totality of the Father's design of the universe.

The realist alone—as poet and "translator"—opens up the realm of mystery, for only he is probing and unearthing what is within and beyond our grasp. The *mysterium Christi*, as Hopkins discovered and articulated it in his concept of inscape, is the subject of this book. I ask the reader, believer and unbeliever alike, not merely to attempt a suspension of old disbeliefs but to aim at a new exploration of gnosis. For gnosis, which is the evolving theme of this study, has wide implications in our reading of Hopkins's poetry and in the meeting of the two cultures. As Nicholas Berdyaev argues in *Freedom and the Spirit*, gnosis as a Christian principle can now be freed and safeguarded from the aberrations of the past. The term, here devoid of the dualistic sense found in the Gnostic religions, is described by Clement of Alexandria, the first Christian humanist, in the *Stromata*, book 7, chapter 10. He says:

> For knowledge (*gnosis*), to speak generally: a perfecting
> of man as man, is consummated by acquaintance with
> divine things in character, life and word, accordant and
> conformable to itself and to the divine Word. For by it
> faith is perfected, inasmuch as it is solely by it that the
> believer becomes perfect. Faith is an internal good, and
> without searching for God, confesses His existence,
> and glorifies Him as existent. Whence by starting from
> this faith, and being developed by it, through the grace of

God, the knowledge respecting Him is to be acquired as far as possible.[9]

"The very term 'Gnostic,'" Cardinal Newman points out, "has been taken by Clement to express his perfect Christian."[10]

Gnosis is contact with divine mystery which results in natural fulfillment of the mind and heart of man as man. "For the image of God is the divine and royal Word, the impassable man; and the image of the image is the human mind" (*Strom.* 5. 14). Through his mind man is drawn into communication—indeed into identification—with God himself: "The Word of God became man, that you may learn from man how man may become God" (*Protrepticus* 1). Thus Clement summed up the guiding aim and goal of gnosis. Because all men are one man, the human form is made divine through kinship with the God-Man. "Over again I feel thy finger and find thee," Hopkins confessed in the opening stanza of *The Wreck of the Deutschland*. In the Christian view, man has been reborn with new perceptions and with new tidings to tell. At rare intervals a herald emerges from the wilderness of general agnosticism and, "touched in [his] bower of bone," utters the truth of his vision and ushers in a new way of knowing: "For I greet him the days I meet him, and bless when I understand."

Neither unexamined belief nor textbook restatements of familiar dogmas will suffice for a knowledge of Hopkins's quest for truth and the poetry which emanated from his search. His readers need to become explorers of his thought and growing vision. Hopkins scholarship has labored too long under the burden of stereotypes for and against his Catholic doctrines. Most explications that touch on the theology of his verse are either misleadingly rudimentary or Scotistically formidable; neither, I feel, does justice to the poet's own purpose and myth. One of the aims of this work, therefore, is the acquisition of gnosis as it developed within Hopkins himself. A full treatment of the subject is, for this reason, left to the final chapters.

The idea of writing this study came after reading numerous interpretations of "The Windhover" and concluding that, in the last analysis, the sonnet's secret code had not yet been broken since its inscape, I felt, was still undeciphered. Every attempt at solving the riddle from within the text itself had apparently been tried and basic questions remained: How was Christ identified with the kestrel or was he meant to be so identified? How was Christ hidden in the poet's heart? What, in a word, was the relationship between the octave and the sestet of this sonnet? No one critical approach seemed to hit on the right answer. I then turned to the sources Hopkins himself had studied and tried to retrace his mental steps as evidenced in his personal writings. A pattern began to appear—or, rather, a unifying point of converging images and ideas, the inscape of the myth he had fashioned.

In this book I have allowed the great voices of the past, from Parmenides to Newman, to speak as much as possible for themselves, for this is how they spoke to Hopkins. These are the sources the poet read and loved; he was a careful and catholic listener. His custom was to concentrate on an essential passage, gloss it exhaustively, and focus on a word or phrase that acted as key to the whole scene or meaning of the author. Translating and interpreting Thucydides or St. Paul, he approached the text with systematic concern for the author's original intention and subject matter.[11] The same method is followed in this study in order to re-create the poet's process of thought and the conclusions he reached. This procedure is necessarily conjectural, but so single-minded and inner-directed was Hopkins's search that once he caught an inscape he repeatedly employed it in the body of his myth. Gnosis of his method is neither guesswork nor gamble, it marks out the trail he previously blazed.

Indeed, Hopkins was well aware of the nature and importance of his ideas, even if he never gave them a final, set formulation in writing. In 1887 he informed his friend, the poet and Church historian Canon Richard Dixon: "What becomes of my verses I care little, but about things like this, what I write or could write on philosophical matters, I do; and the reason of the difference is that the verses stand or fall by their simple selves and, though by being read they might do good, by being unread they do no harm; but if the other things are unsaid right they will be said by somebody else wrong, and that is what will not let me rest"

(L2, 150). Objectively, through quotation and explanation, this work attempts to let Hopkins say the thing "right," through his own imagery and in his own words. According to his fashion, in poetry as well as prose, he framed "the vision splendid" and left it, monumental and new, on "ancient mounds that cover bones, / Or rocks where rockdoves do repair" (P15). Alchemist and architect of the religious imagination "in hiding," he addresses us still with his own clear response to the Word.

And how does Victorian Hopkins speak to us? It is, after all, the poet with a vision to share, and not the systematic philosopher-theologian he might have been, whose voice we hear today and shall hear again tomorrow. So be it. However solid or insubstantial may appear "the cloud capp'd towers, . . . the solemn temples, the great globe itself" unveiled in the following pages, it will be the knowledge gained of the poems themselves that finally matters. "If known widely known, the wider known the better." The poet "with aim / Now known and hand at work now never wrong"—the parent of immortal song—outlives our lagging explanations.

Christology

What is exegesis? In its traditionally accepted form, exegesis investigates the meaning of a text. This meaning can find expression in the ascertainable *scopus*. The *scopus* then states the object at which the text was aiming. If our progress is more limited, we must be content to ascertain at least the "intention" of the text. For this work there are various aids: the furthering of the history of word meanings with the aid of lexicons, grammar, literary and style criticism and parallel materials; research into historical circumstances which produced the text; comparative examinations of the history of ideas and of the history of religion, etc. In all this the text itself is understood as a part of intellectual work, and this intellectual research is understood as a contribution to the discovery of truth.

Ernest Fuchs
Studies of the Historical Jesus

1
The Making
of a Myth

"ALL thought is of course in a sense an effort at unity," Hopkins wrote in an Oxford essay entitled "The Origin of Our Moral Ideas" (1865). The sentence sums up the driving force and direction of his life and search for gnosis. The whole of being as an object of thought and attainment absorbed him. Nature and man in all their variety and individuality drew him only as facets of totality. In each object—cowslip, waterfall, or cloud—he sought out the mark and *telos* of unity that connected each with everything else. For this controlling and incorporating energy and end, the poet coined the word *inscape*. For the origin, impact, and grip of that inscape when it fused in man as being and thought, he coined a second word, *instress*.[1]

From its first stirrings in him, Hopkins's quest for oneness was a spiritual odyssey and adventure. Philosophy took its place there at his side but only as a ready squire to aid and support the Christian knight setting forth "to conquer the whole country." Indeed, armed with his hornbook of alphabet and prayers, the young man, like the bugler boy he later dubbed "God's own Galahad," already knew the Alpha and Omega of his *chivachie*. Months before converting to Catholicism, he spelled out the lesson clearly in a letter to his friend, E. H. Coleridge. On January 22, 1866, he had written:

> It is one adorable point of the incredible condescension
> of the Incarnation (the greatness of which no saint can

3

> have ever hoped to realise) that our Lord submitted not
> only to the pains of life, the fasting, scourging, crucifixion
> etc. or the insults, as the mocking, blindfolding, spitting
> etc, but also to the mean and trivial accidents of humanity.
> It leads one naturally to rhetorical antithesis to think for
> instance that after making the world He shd. consent
> to be taught carpentering, and, being the eternal Reason,
> to be catechised in the theology of the Rabbins. (L3, 19-20)

But a world of knowledge and suffering stretched between this
first statement of the myth of Christ the creator-redeemer and his
last poetic resolution in "That Nature is a Heraclitean Fire and
of the comfort of the Resurrection."

Nature and man, for Hopkins, were not the whole of reality;
God was the ultimately real. But how was he known and experienced in being and truth? How was the incarnation to be even
partially realized by man? And if Christ has united the divine
and human natures in his person, how does man know this change
within himself? These were mysteries the poet made personal in
his moral choices and in his incessant reflection and studies. Hopkins found the sources and responses he required in his reading
of the New Testament and the fathers of the church, in his expansive faith, and in his absolute commitment to the Catholic
Church and to his vocation as a Jesuit. He found the framework
in which to express his discovery in the pre-Socratic philosophers
and Holy Scripture. To Parmenides and Paul of Tarsus he owed
the pith and marrow of his myth.

At Highgate School the young Hopkins was remembered for
his tenacious and faithful reading of the New Testament; it is
one of the earliest recollections of him and is significant and typical.[2] When he matriculated to Balliol College, Oxford, in the fall
of 1863, Hopkins was swept up in an atmosphere of earnest intellectual and practical concern for the Christian religion. True,
the Oxford movement had blazed and passed away, but the figure
of John Henry Newman still burned in men's hearts and minds.
Newman had left Oxford and Anglicanism, but neither was to
be the same again. Orthodoxy had carried the day: fasting, medi-

tation, religious lectures, even confession and the mass, were the normal avenues of expressing piety and fervor. Edward Pusey, a founder of the original movement, became the young poet's adviser, confessor, and friend. From the earliest entries in his diaries and journal, Hopkins constantly notes his visits to chapels and churches, his strict fasting and abstention from "all beauty."

The central focus of the religious renascence at Oxford was the person of Christ. As God-Man and as real presence in the Eucharist, he ruled the lives of those who turned to him in faithful acceptance. Ritual and fasting were meant only to make closer contact by imitation of him. The Rev. Henry Parry Liddon, the influential Anglican apologist and divine, seems to have been Hopkins's chief spiritual mentor at this time. Hopkins attended his New Testament lectures, and we are fortunate to have nine pages of his notes for Liddon's course on the First Epistle to the Corinthians. In these notes, now reserved at the Bodleian Library (Eng. poet. Ms. e. 90), we find the first mention of gnosis, here defined as "superior enlightenment," a knowledge that "St. Paul allows" while warning the Corinthians against "resting on this superior enlightenment" when eating food already sacrificed to idols (1 Cor. 8:1-13). The central truth of the poet's Christology is also expressed here for the first time. Commenting on verse 6 of chapter 8: "For us there is only one God, the Father from whom are all things, and we unto him; and one Lord, Jesus Christ, through whom are all things, and we through him," Hopkins writes: "This is one of the passages shewing the co-equal divinity of Christ, proving Him (when compared with Col. 1, 14-16) the creator and end of all things, against the Arians who reduced Him to the ὀργανον and subordinate of the Father. If approached in an Arian state of mind these passages read like Arianism, but to a Catholic they present no real difficulty." In his commentary on the Pauline texts, Liddon directed his student to the wider questions of orthodoxy and morality implied in man's newness of life in Christ.

In a series of public discourses in this same period, Liddon lectured to overflow audiences on "The Divinity of Our Lord and Saviour Jesus Christ." As the titles of these eight Bampton lectures, delivered in the spring of 1866, indicate, Liddon's treatment of his subject was intended to be authoritative and exhaustive:

1. The Question before us
2. Anticipations of Christ's Divinity in the Old Testament
3. Our Lord's Work in the World a Witness to His Divinity
4. Our Lord's Divinity as Witnessed by His Consciousness
5. The Doctrine of Christ's Divinity in the Writings of St John
6. Our Lord's Divinity as Taught by St James, St Peter and St Paul
7. The Homoousion
8. Consequences of the Doctrine of Our Lord's Divinity.

Throughout the course, Liddon called for a unified vision of Christianity centered in the person of Christ: "The Word unveils Himself to the soul through the mediation of objects of sense in the physical world, and He also unveils Himself immediately. . . . The Word Who creates is also the Revealer."[3] Hopkins, who attended the lectures, noted in his journal on May 13: "7th Bampton, in which the most beautiful sentence I ever remember hearing of Liddon's " (J, 136). In "The Homoousion," the poet's spiritual confessor and friend traced the patristic teaching of Christ in history and dogma, and then called for one's own intellectual and active dedication to a "higher knowledge" and adoration. One "beautiful sentence" sums up man's response to the Ideal: "The adoring soul bends thought and heart and will before the footstool of the One Self-existing, All-creating, All-upholding Being; the soul wills to be as nothing before Him, or to exist only that it may recognise His Glory as altogether surpassing its words and thoughts."[4] Liddon insisted on a knowledgeable faith; "religion is practically inseparable from theology," he wrote. Although much revised before publication and overabundantly apologetic, his work is an indispensable aid in following Hopkins's own theological development. Like many of his contemporaries, he found in it a master plan for life.

As a counterbalance to the dogmatism of Liddon (who accused Hopkins of leaving the Church of England because of a "personal illumination"), Benjamin Jowett's liberal Christian views, which laid stress on sincerity and humanitarianism, appealed to another side of the poet's tolerant nature. Under Jowett he studied the New Testament Epistles, as well as Plato's *Republic*—two great influences on his thought—and from him he learned that respect for detail and freedom of spirit which characterized his approach to his studies.

Indebted as he was to both men, however, Hopkins was already finding his own distinctive expression for his Christian insights. Poetry above all else attracted him as a vehicle of self-knowledge and prayerful aspiration. His verses of this Oxford period are Christocentric in their use of eucharistic and penitential themes; they draw from traditional imagery to express his personal effort to make contact with Christ. A sonnet, number 16, concludes:

> No *better* serves me now, save *best*; no other
> Save Christ: to Christ I look, on Christ I call.

His Oxford world not only brought him to revere Plato and Aristotle, but led him to love Augustine and Origen as well. The West was the curriculum in which he studied Christ.

On October 21, 1866, John Henry Newman received the twenty-two-year-old Hopkins into the Roman Catholic Church. The conversion exacted a heavy price in personal estrangement from his family and in loss of a university career. The "Star of Balliol," as his friend and mentor Jowett once dubbed him, had taken a double first in Greats, top honors in both classical and modern *literae humaniores*. This he had done after his conversion, in the Trinity term of 1867, and he might have seemed otherwise to be one destined for a distinguished future as clergyman, professor, and author. His father's pained cry on hearing of his son's conversion: "O Gerard my darling boy are you indeed gone from me?" is tragically prophetic. Years later, as a Jesuit priest in Dublin, the poet mourned:

> To seem the stranger lies my lot, my life
> Among strangers. Father and mother dear,
> Brothers and sisters are in Christ not near.   (P66)

Then he was "at a third / Remove"; the first remove to Catholicism was even more drastic than the second to the Jesuits: from it the others followed. In terms of family and success, the young convert, like other English Catholics, paid dearly for his conviction of the historical truth of Christ's founding the Church of Rome. Never again would he be easily welcome or completely at home in the world that had formed him. Old ties and friendships remained, but weakened by cross-purposes and separation. "I count everything loss," St. Paul reflected, "because of the excelling knowledge of Jesus Christ, my Lord" (Phil. 3:8). But "loss," nonetheless.

By education and temperament, Hopkins was religiously oriented, bent on a Christian trust and commitment. There is no question here of a purely "natural" development that later became spiritualized; his life was one from the start. "All thought is . . . an effort at unity," he wrote in the essay quoted earlier. He continued: "It seems also that the desire for unity, for an ideal, is the only definition which will satisfy the historical phenomena of morality" (J, 83). Personal integrity is the root of right conduct. But there will also be no integrating action without knowledge and insight. Man needs to know wholeness before he expresses it in deeds. Hopkins sought knowledge of the One before finding the myth that embraced the ideal and ordered his own life. In an Oxford notebook, he made this translation of Plato's *Philebus* (15D [16D]): "Everything which was ever said to *be* has Being from unity and from multiplicity and contains the finite and the infinite as innate in itself. This being the order reigning in all things we have always one idea to presuppose in everything and in each case to look for that; for it is there and we shall find it" (D6, 7).

In a journal entry made the spring before his conversion, the poet observed: "To see the long forward-creeping curls of the newly-leaved trees, in sweeps and rows all lodged one with another down the meadow edge, beautiful, but distraction and the want of the canon only makes these graceful shapes in the keen unseasonable evening air to 'carve out' one's thought with painful definiteness" (J, 136). A week earlier he had also complained:

"But the warm greyness of the day, the river, the spring green, and the cuckoo wanted a canon by which to harmonise and round them in—e.g. one of feeling" (J, 135). Hopkins felt "out of joint" with nature's unity and unable to relate being and thought in one lasting impression. "The want of the canon" must refer to this lack of a body of principles and rules that comprehended the hidden law of the universe; he missed the framework that offered a center and focus for seeing and communing, intellectually and emotionally, within himself and with reality.

Finding beauty, Hopkins noted, "is almost synonymous with finding order, anywhere" (J, 139). And he found this order step by step by studying the inner law of individual kinds of trees, flowers, rocks, and even of the crowd in a theater. "I have particular periods of admiration for particular things in Nature," he stated as early as 1863; "for a certain time I am astonished at the beauty of a tree, shape, effect etc. then when the passion, so to speak, has subsided, it is consigned to my treasury of explored beauty, and acknowledged with admiration and interest ever after, while something new takes its place in my enthusiasm" (L3, 202).

In July of 1866, for example, the poet studied:

> Oaks: the organisation of this tree is difficult. Speaking
> generally no doubt the determining planes are concentric,
> a system of brief contiguous and continuous tangents,
> whereas those of the cedar would roughly be called hori-
> zontals and those of the beech radiating but modified
> by droop and by a screw-set towards jutting points. But
> beyond this since the normal growth of the boughs is
> radiating and the leaves grow some way in there is of
> course a system of spoke-wise clubs of green—sleeve-
> pieces. (J, 144)

The observer focuses in closer and discovers the key: "However the star knot is the chief thing: whorled, worked round, a little and this is what keeps up the illusion of the tree: the leaves are rounded inwards and figure out ball knots" (J, 144-45). But Hopkins has not finished his study. A week later he returns to a detail:

> I have now found the law of the oak leaves. It is of
> platter-shaped stars altogether; the leaves lie close like
> pages, packed, and as if drawn tightly to. But these old
> packs, which lie at the end of their twigs, throw out now
> long shoots alternately and slimly leaved, looking like
> bright keys. All the sprays but markedly these ones
> shape out and as it were embrace greater circles and the
> dip and toss of these make the wider and less organic
> articulations of the tree. (J, 146)

Hopkins brought to his glossing of the oak tree the same thoroughgoing methodology he employed in explicating a text.

The oak's secret is its star knot, the center which acts as a vortex in which the whole tree has its movement and being. Throughout the journal, details of nature are reduced to geometric design—the eye of the beholder owes more to Pythagoras than to Ruskin. One pattern emerges from point, radius, and curve: the circle, captured in word and in sketch (often enclosed by a tondo framed by the artist), in myriad "Catherine-wheel forms," not perfectly symmetrical or static, but bearing a radiating center that controls the whole. Horizontals and verticals mark and measure the direction inward toward that center, everything converging in the One. The myth was not yet formulated. For order was not inscape nor was pattern itself the point where being and thought were one.

Hopkins himself clearly defined the gist of the problem in a verse fragment (from *Floris in Italy*) written in this period. Both the outer arc and the inner center must be somehow fused:

> Beauty it may be is the meet of lines,
> Or careful-spacèd sequences of sound,
> These rather are the arc where beauty shines,
> The temper'd soil where only her flower is found.
> Allow at least it has one term and part
> Beyond, and one within the looker's eye;
> And I must have the centre in my heart
> To spread the compass on the all-starr'd sky. (P102, iii)

How was the "beyond" to be experienced within? Where was the compass that would point true center and trace out the whole sky? Another early poem cryptically pictures what form the final answer will take:

> It was a hard thing to undo this knot.
> The rainbow shines, but only in the thought
> Of him that looks. Yet not in that alone,
> For who makes rainbows by invention?
> And many standing round a waterfall
> See one bow each, yet not the same to all,
> But each a hand's breadth further than the next.
> The sun on falling waters writes the text
> Which yet is in the eye or in the thought.
> It was a hard thing to undo this knot.   (P91)

In water, eye, and thought, the sun inscribes the same curling hieroglyph which knots the three together: matter, sense, and mind. Sunlight words a bond between the world and the soul: the cipher is "the looker's eye" which catches the wording fire in acts of inscape. But the poet had yet to coin that word and to discover the true nature of this seeing. Patiently he searched the many texts of gnosis before arriving at the vantage point that enabled him to view the whole expanse and to set foot on the road ahead. One thing he knew: not structure but the drive toward structure was the cosmic wedge where reality and the mind converge and where the "effort at unity" thrusts home.[5] Having found the circle he had now to find his way out of it, through a center that was an exit as well as an entrance. The rainbow had yet to reveal its full meaning.

Nearly two years after finding the law of the oak leaves, Hopkins, in the early spring of 1868, shaped the myth with which to know and live existence. While teaching at Newman's Oratory School in Birmingham, he struggled with the question of his vocation to the priesthood and religious life; but within this choice lay the more profound problem of the integrity of his own selfhood in action and thought. Two essential breakthroughs occurred at this time: the discovery of a conceptual framework with which to relate to the whole of reality and a field of dedicated activity in which to funnel his talents and dreams. The first door opened through Parmenides; the second through Ignatius of Loyola.

"An interest in philosophy is almost the only one I can feel myself quite free to indulge in still," Hopkins wrote to his friend A. W. M. Baillie on February 12, 1868. In a notebook dated three days earlier, he entered his translations and reflections on Parmenides.[6] Here for the first time in his writings appear the words "inscape" and "instress." He opens his observations with a note on Parmenides' visit to Athens in Socrates' youth and then proceeds:

> His great text, which he repeats with religious conviction, is that Being is and Not-being is not—which perhaps one can say, a little over-defining his meaning, means that all things are upheld by instress and are meaningless without it. . . . His feeling for instress, for the flush and foredrawn, and for inscape / is most striking and from this one can understand Plato's reverence for him as the great father of Realism. (J, 127)

Parmenides' "great text" is a philosophical poem, the first of its kind, written in heroic measure, and now extant only in fragments. It is divided into three parts: "Prologue," "The Way of Truth," and "The Way of Opinion." The poem begins with an apocalyptic description of the poet-philosopher's conversion from error to truth. An unnamed goddess, probably his muse, promises him: "Thou shalt inquire into everything: both the motionless heart of well-rounded Truth, and also the opinions of mortals, in which there is no true reliability. But nevertheless thou shalt learn these things (*opinions*) also—how one should go through all the things-that-seem, without exception, and test them."[7] Hopkins begins his quotations of the Greek with "The Way of Truth." Translated, it reads:

> Come, I will tell you—and you must accept my word when you have heard it—the ways of inquiry which alone

are to be thought: the one that IT IS, and it is not possible
for IT NOT TO BE, is the way of credibility, for it follows
Truth; the other, that IT IS NOT, and that IT is bound
NOT TO BE: this I tell you is a path that cannot be explored;
for you could neither recognise that which IS NOT, nor
express it. (*Ancilla*, p. 42)

"Being," which was the accepted translation in Hopkins's time
for "IT IS," actually exists. The statement is not tautological;
rather, it marks a major philosophical intuition in the exploration
of human knowledge and has become the cornerstone of metaphysics. Parmenides affirmed that the "is" used so casually in
speaking and judging has existence of its own, is alone real and
the sole object worth our study in the "Way of Belief."

Hopkins responded to the poet's insight with his own recasting originality and need: "But indeed I have often felt when I
have been in this mood and felt the depth of an instress or how
fast the inscape holds a thing that nothing is so pregnant and
straightforward to the truth as simple *yes* and *is*" (J, 127). *Instress*
is man's *yes* in response to Being felt and known; *inscape*, the *is*
that marks not individuality but Being itself: it "holds" each object whole within the plenitude of IS. The divine name of Scripture, for both the old and new covenants is, as Hopkins knew,
I AM. The Lord of Abraham, Jacob, and Isaac greeted him in the
pre-Socratic poem. Philosophy "was a schoolmaster," wrote
Clement of Alexandria, "to bring 'the Hellenic mind,' as the law,
the Hebrews, 'to Christ.' Philosophy, therefore, was a preparation, paving the way for him who is perfected in Christ" (*Strom.*
l. 5).

To elucidate his meaning, Parmenides contrasted "IT IS" with
"IT IS NOT." Hopkins translates and comments:

"Thou couldst never either know or say / what was not,
there would be no coming at it." There would be no bridge,
no stem of stress between us and things to bear us out
and carry the mind over: without stress we might not and
could not say / Blood is red / but only / This blood is
red / or / The last blood I saw was red / nor even that,

for in later language not only universals would not be true
but the copula would break down even in particular
judgments. (J, 127)

Stress is the ictus of being flowing from the world of objects,
their knowability as projectiles of thought; it is the bridge or juice
through the stem of things, which impels us to acknowledge
Being. Parmenides writes: "One should both say and think that
Being Is; for To Be is possible, and Nothingness is not possible"
(*Ancilla*, p. 43). Using one of his favorite commands, Hopkins
nexts translates: " 'Look at it, though absent, yet to the mind's
eye as fast present here; for absence cannot break off Being from
its hold on Being: it is not a thing to scatter here, there, and everywhere through all the world nor to come together from here and
there and everywhere' " (J, 128). I AM is everywhere present to
the mind that knows how to see, present in no other way than
as One, self-existent, entire. Being is never less than a whole
holding fast to a ubiquitous center.

Not only does Being exist, but Being is knowable; it both
causes things to be known and is, in fact, itself the act of knowing. Hopkins notes: "To be and to know or Being and thought
are the same. The truth in thought is Being, stress, and each word
is one way of acknowledging Being and each sentence by its
copula *is* (or its equivalent) the utterance and assertion of it"
(J, 129). The mind, *nous*, intuits Being in no haphazard or confused fashion, but in direct and dynamic contact with reality, in
the act of judgment itself. Man intuits Being, in other words, in
the act of knowing himself asserting existence, not in the abstract,
but in the concrete world of objects that he knows. This intuitive,
judgmental contact with Being as the coalescing plenum of the
universe is inscape, the IS of all things that are, which leads back
directly in turn to instress, the foredrawing or ingathering act
of recognition: the giving back of being to Being. Intuition ends
in union, inscape in instress. Thus Hopkins concludes: "The
mind's grasp—νοεῖν, the foredrawing act—that this is blood or
that blood is red is to be looked for in Being, the foredrawn,
alone, not in the thing we named blood or the blood we worded

as being red" (J, 129). Gnosis, then, is knowledge of Being when Being is what is known: an independent, all-inclusive whole, "brim, in a flash, full" with intelligible energy and aim.

The greater part of "The Way of Truth" is taken up with descriptions of the qualities of Being: it is "one, only-begotten, motionless, eternal." Remarkable concepts here receive their first expression, and, if Parmenides' terms seem at times contradictory, we must remember he had to create the philosophical categories for his ideas. The vocabulary he needed did not exist. Hopkins too was driven to find new words as his mythmaking expanded. Despite his verbal handicaps, Parmenides proceeds with intense poetical control and feeling to the climax of his inquiry: "Nor is Being divisible, since it is all alike. Nor is there anything here or there which could prevent it from holding together, nor any lesser thing, but all is full of Being. Therefore it is altogether continuous; for Being is close to Being" (*Ancilla*, p. 44). In annotating the original, Hopkins translated "from holding together" as "from foredrawing" and the last phrase as "Being draws-home to Being." The same Greek word, to anticipate a little, is used by St. Paul to describe how "the love of Christ" foredraws all men to share in his death and resurrection (2 Cor. 5:14-15).

The philosophy of Parmenides is one of absolutes and opposites: Being and Nothing, Truth and Opinion, Yes and No, the very polarities that play an important role in Hopkins's thinking. For the Greek poet there is no place for becoming or change: "How could Being perish? How could it come into being? If it came into being, it is Not; and so too if it is about-to-be at some future time. Thus Coming-into-Being is quenched, and Destruction also into the unseen" (*Ancilla*, pp. 43-44). Becoming and change have been driven away; they "are beside the question," as Hopkins interprets the passage: " 'unerring faith puts such things by'—shewing the mixture of real with logical in the thought—'and it lies by itself the selfsame thing abiding in the selfsame place; so it abides, steadfast there; for strong Necessity has it in the bonds of that bound that guards it all about' " (J, 128). The distinction made here between the real and the logical is noteworthy; for Hopkins, the insights of Parmenides are not merely conceptual, but involve acts of faith in Being that "bodes but abides" (P28, 32). Man gives a real assent, his "yes," to "is."

The most significant contribution the pre-Socratic philosopher made to the Victorian poet's mythogenesis is hinted at in the passage under consideration. Being is in bonds that hold it fast in itself; it possesses "limits" and is complete on every side. Being, in short, is "like the mass of a well-rounded ball, equally balanced from its centre in every direction." Neither more extended in this direction than in that, nor less extended, since "Being is an inviolate whole. For in all directions equal to itself, it reaches its limits uniformly" (*Ancilla*, p. 44). Being is the perfect sphere in which oak trees and all else have their imperfect totality. Despite Hopkins's demurrer—he felt that Parmenides "may very well mean this as an analogy merely, especially as the comparison is to the outline and surface rather than to the inner flushness, the temper and quality of weight"—his debt to this figure of the "mass of a well rounded ball" is pervasive and profound. Being is globe-shaped, repeated throughout the universe, in stars, fruit, the earth itself, charged with expectant, immanent stress, "the flush and foredrawn." Being possesses a center of thrust and source of energy; everything radiates from this point and is drawn back to it.

What Hopkins wrote of Parmenides is true of himself: "His cosmology was a system of concentric . . . spheres or cylinders, ranging between fire and night, governed by a spirit (δαίμων) in the midst, also called Justice or Necessity. This spirit was the cause of the gods, creating Love first" (J, 130). One notes the similarity here to the Spirit of Love who fills creation and renews the face of the earth: "Because the Holy Ghost over the bent / World broods" (P31). In some unpublished notes on "Plato's Philosophy," Hopkins finds an image of the Trinity in the Platonic creation myth: "In the Timaeus he [Plato] says [that] in [the] beginning the Demiurgus made the world and like himself as being good—spherical—and set it moving, but mechanically, until he put in νοῦν. But νοῦς and matter are heterogeneous; therefore he made a tertium quid—ψυχήν" (D8). Father, Word, and Spirit are revealed in pre-Christian myths, Greek, Egyptian,

Welsh and even Hindu, as Hopkins carefully remarked. In a letter to Baillie from Dublin, for example, he wondered of Egyptian prototypes of Greek and Roman gods: "It seems likely that there was a Greek Trinity of the same gods as the Trinity of the Capitol at Rome, which was of Jove, Juno, and Minerva" (L3, 260). Just as the Three Persons are one Being, so is the One reflected in man's images of God prior to Christianity as a "forepitch" of his real Self. Among Hopkins's papers are quotations from the *Rig-Veda*, taken from Max Müller's *Chips from a German Workshop*, which note the triune nature of Hindu beliefs. One extract connects Being with the circle and the Self: "Self is the Lord of all things, Self is the King of all things. As all the spokes of a wheel are contained in the nave and the circumference, all things are contained in this Self; all selves are contained in this Self. Bráhman itself is but Self" (D7).[8] Wherever he found confirmation of the thought, the poet made its expression his own— whether from books or from experience, for "conditioned as man is he yet can unweave the web of his life for himself" (D8). One of his Jesuit superiors many years later was to observe that Hopkins's own mind moved "in concentric circles." Like Dante's "well-balanced wheel," his reflections and desires turned on the axletree of his crucified Master and Love. He wrote in 1865:

> Let me be to Thee as the circling bird,
> Or bat with tender and air-crisping wings
> That shapes in half-light his departing rings,
> From both of whom a changeless note is heard.
> I have found my music in a common word,
> Trying each pleasurable throat that sings
> And every praisèd sequence of sweet strings,
> And know infallibly which I preferred.
> The authentic cadence was discovered late
> Which ends those only strains that I approve,
> And other science all gone out of date
> And minor sweetness scarce made mention of:
> I have found the dominant of my range and state—
> Love, O my God, to call Thee Love and Love.   (P19)

Hopkins also found his music in an uncommon word: *inscape*; it intoned the dominant note of his range and state, his philosophical quest and practical response.

Inscape is the One "in the midst" that generates and shapes the whole and each of its measureless, finite convolutions; it is also man's intuition of the One through individual concrete existences. Of the many things written about the poet's most famous coinage, surprisingly little mention is made of its etymology beyond associating it with "landscape" and the archaic "scape": "a stem or stalk." Hopkins, I am convinced, derived the word from the Greek σκοπός and "the School-Latin *scopus* | *mark, aim*," an etymology he himself notes in another connection. In a letter to A. W. M. Baillie on March 10, 1887, Hopkins denied that the present English word *scope* ("freedom of action or play") is derived from the Greek-Latin *scopus* (L3, 284). The poet did not indicate, however, what word or words come from *scopus*. The change of *o* to *a* presents no problem, since Hopkins frequently grouped words and exchanged letters to explore their individual and family meanings: "flop, flap," "hold, halt," and "share, shore." The vowel shifts from old to modern English were familiar to him. He probably found "inscope" ambiguous and unattractive; "inscape" also successfully disguised its origins.

The first appearance of "inscape" in Hopkins's writings occurs, as we have seen, in his notes on Parmenides, dated February 9, 1868. About a year earlier, while still at Oxford, he had used the word *scopeless* as "not to be grasped and held together" (J, 118), a meaning hardly connected with the present use of "scope" but close to "inscape" as the coalescing action of the mind's encounter with Being. Later in his retreat notes he speaks of "instress . . . on each scape" and "instressing of the scope" in the same paragraph (S, 139). Finally, from Ireland Hopkins wrote a letter (no longer extant) to Professor W. W. Skeat, the famed etymologist and medieval scholar, questioning his "treatment of a whole class of words like *scope, cope, scoop, scape, cap*" (L3, 285). In the two letters to Baillie which deal with his questions and conjectures on the eytmology of this class of words, Hopkins seems intent on preserving the Greek-Latin *scopos-us* as virginal soil for his own development, a source in no way to be confused with current usage and other derivations. Whatever final meaning he gave the word would be distinctly his own.

What do the original definitions of *scopos* disclose of the poet's personal mythogenesis? Liddell and Scott's *Greek-English Lexicon* defines σκοπός as 1) "watcher," "one who marks," 2) "the distant mark or object on which one fixes the eye, a mark," and gives as extended meanings: "an aim, end, object." Both the one who aims and the thing he hits are defined by the same word. For Hopkins, then, the inscape of being is its perceived center or target, the vortex of isness that foredraws or instresses all things; it is the moment the beholder fixes his mark. In whirlpools of water, cloud, and grass, the orifices of reality open and reveal a collective focus where all curves tend. Their centers were "up ahead" or "yonder," a distant mark that opens an entrance and provides an exit for the beholder out of mere cyclicism and into cosmic time. Once it had been struck, he marveled "how fast the inscape holds a thing" (J, 127). Things bend in parabolas because they are held by an axis on which the eye focuses and which instress then fuses in the heart. Hence inscape is used of objects in relation to wholes or in association with other objects curving ahead in a single direction. It concerns itself with intentionality rather than particularity. The curling grass is, in Walt Whitman's words, "a uniform hieroglyphic" which spells out to all the same deathless message. Hopkins wrote: "Green-white tufts of long bleached grass like heads of hair or the crowns of heads of hair, each a whorl of slender curves, one tuft taking up another. . . . I saw the inscape . . . freshly, as if my eye were still growing, though with a companion the eye and the ear are for the most part shut and instress cannot come" (J, 228). In crown or whorl the inscape held; but, with solitude lacking, the full cycle of response could not always draw to a close and open into unifying instress. Occasionally, it seems, with distractions present, one might hit the mark without being one with the mark; Being could be struck without completely fusing with thought. These exceptions, however, only serve to emphasize the truth that nature's curves and parabolic outlines are meant to bend the mind back, and the body down, in worship and contemplation of the all-seeing eye of the Master. The perception of convergence is inscape.

In addition to the substantive, the Greek verb σκοπεῖν means "to look at," or further "to contemplate, examine, inquire or learn."[9] The English word the poet most often used as the equivalent of *inscape* is *mark* both as verb and noun—although the verb *look*, especially as a command, also frequently occurs. The mark on which one fixes the eye, the scapes of curving wave and skeining birdsong, are marked within: *in*-scaped. "Mark, the mark" (P28, 22), Hopkins insisted, which has been scored in "fire and night" throughout the world: sun, stars, and lightning are runes of its mystery and meaning. End and purpose are everywhere present already, for the world is riddled with apertures of light. The kingdom of daylight is not "out there," removed in space and time from experience; it is dynamically spun into the filaments, currents, and sunbeams of the present world. Men have but to look in order to see, since creation bears this primordial sign of inbuilt teleology on which to fasten and to strike full center. How is it defined and where is it discovered? This mark is "the species or scape of any object, as of sight, sound, taste, smell" found in the "intellectual imagination" (S, 136) not as a static image for recollection but as the object desired and already possessed in anticipation, the end for which one acts held fast within the mind. Thus Hopkins bent himself to "hit the mark"— a recurrent phrase with him—in each and all of his actions, in his study of nature, in his search for gnosis. All thought and doing had but one point of aim, bull's-eye, and rooting place: "the who and the why" of existence, I AM, Being, "*Ipse*, the only one, Christ, King, Head" (P28, 28). His humanity is the *prima species* for and after whom all scapes are made. Being is not blind mechanistic energy but inwardly set motive force toward a personal *telos*: Christ the Alpha and Omega. Nature, whether felled in Binsey poplars or flourishing in wilderness and weed, is predeterminately human because it exists *ab initio* in and for Jesus. Significantly, even the English "scope" at one time meant not only the material object or thing intended, but also the person pursued, sought for, and overtaken. Hopkins, in short, knew Christ to be the efficient ("the who") and final cause ("the why"), because Jesus is the man who is God and the head of creation.

"Mark Christ our King" (P63). Hopkins's faith revealed to him what the wise Parmenides considered "unthinkable and inexpressible": that Being should become, be visible and changeable in the world of time. For the Greek philosopher, Justice held Being in mighty bonds, contained in power, since what has no limits or is loosened is imperfect and lacking wholeness. Empedocles echoed him: "God is equal in all directions to himself and altogether eternal, a rounded Sphere enjoying a circular solitude" (*Ancilla*, p. 56). Hopkins, who remained a student and teacher of the Greek thinkers all his life, found in them, as the church fathers had before him, a prophetic delineation of the Word-to-be-made-flesh. What reason could not comprehend came to pass: the rounded sphere was opened, uncreated Being became a creature, the All made himself nothing, the One was lost in the midst of the many. "Ground of being, and granite of it: past all / Grasp God," he glided "lower than death and the dark" (P28, 32-33). "World's strand" became "sway of the sea." God, "an intelligible sphere whose center is everywhere and the circumference nowhere," had been nailed to the tree of the cross, the permanent axis on which the world turns: *Stat crux dum volvitur orbis.*

Saint Bonaventura's *Itinerarium Mentis ad Deum*, where this last definition of God as "an intelligible sphere"[10] appears (5. 8), offers a valuable instance of the Christian philosophy of Being at work. This celebrated masterpiece of medieval *scientia* may well have served as a precedent and model for Hopkins's own fusing of Greek metaphysics in the crucible of his Catholic beliefs. In chapter 5 of this opusculum, the Franciscan theologian, after citing the Mosaic name of God, instructs the reader: "If you wish then to contemplate the invisible traits of God in so far as they belong to the unity of His essence, fix your gaze upon Being itself, and see that Being is most certain in itself; for it cannot be thought not to be, since the purest Being occurs only in full flight

from Non-Being, just as nothingness is in full flight from Being."
Being is pure Being both in fact and in our thinking; it only enters the mind through its *self*: "Being then is what first enters the
intellect, and that Being is pure actuality. But this is not particular Being, which is restricted Being, since that is mixed with potentiality. Nor is this analogous Being, for such has a minimum of
actuality since it has only a minimum of being. It remains, therefore, that that Being is divine Being" (5. 3). The mind mounts in
contemplating the One:

> But you have ground for rising in wonder. For Being itself
> is first and last, is eternal and yet most present, is simplest
> and greatest, is most actual and immutable, is perfect
> and immense, is most highly one and yet all-inclusive.
> If you wonder over these things with a pure mind, while
> you look further, you will be infused with a greater light,
> until you finally see that Being is last because it is first.
> For since it is first, it produces all things for its own sake
> alone; and therefore it must be the very end, the begin-
> ning and the consummation, the alpha and the omega.
> Therefore it is most present because it is eternal. (5. 7)

The perfection of the mind's illumination is reached on the sixth
day in the one man made in the image of God: "Christ the Son
of God, . . . in one Being the first and the last, the highest and the
lowest, the circumference and the center, the alpha and the
omega, the caused and the cause, the creator and the creature,
the book written within and without" (6. 7).[11] Inscape is the
activity of inner ascent and the goal the mind attains. It is well
described by the Seraphic Doctor's words.

Within the continuum of Christian absorption of Greek
thought, Hopkins's theology took shape. It would be wrong,
however, to identify his mythogenesis with adherence to any particular school. Alan Heuser in *The Shaping Vision of Gerard
Manley Hopkins* surely has exaggerated the poet's dependence
on Platonism, although his own Jesuit contemporaries spoke of
Hopkins as a Platonist. He, on the other hand, classified himself
with the "Aristotelian Catholics" and admitted to Bridges that

he cared for Duns Scotus "more even than Aristotle" (L1, 31). In writing his notes on Parmenides he twice quotes from Aristotle, and he told Baillie at the time: "I find myself in an even prostrate admiration of Aristotle and am of the way of thinking, so far as I know him or know about him, that he is the end-all and be-all of philosophy" (L3, 231). The Stagirite's theory of knowledge, which insisted on the discovery of the universal in the particulars by intuitive reason proceeding from sensations, through memory and back to experience, suited Hopkins's quest for the kinetic and concrete unity of reality. Nature, for Aristotle, was no dead-weight, but "the genesis of growing things," their "source of movement" and "the form or essence which is the end of the process of becoming" (*Metaphysics* 5. 4).[12] Nature is end and full development in this teleological view, an end that is imma-nent from the first in the subject of movement and that deter-mines its whole growth, "for the process of evolution is for the sake of the thing finally evolved, and not this for the sake of the process" (*On the Parts of Animals* 1. 1).[13] Aristotle applies this concept to man's art-making as well as to organic nature. The impulse of an idea or form, when applied to material stone or wood, to gesture or sound in order to achieve a final form or end —the work of art—expands the world of knowing from within with fresh sensations and experiences of the real. "Each mortal thing does one thing and the same" by doing-being toward an end that is its form, "*myself* it speaks and spells" (P57). Even the State is a creation of nature, as the *Politics* demonstrates, born of man's gregariousness and his rage for social order and justice. Certainly Hopkins was indebted to each of the great Greek thinkers and drew from them according to his own designs, but his debt to Aristotle has yet to be fully assessed.

The *Nicomachean Ethics* particularly seems to have been of great importance to Hopkins. He twice filled notebooks (both unpublished) with his comments on Aristotle's text. Its examina-tion of the virtues in the light of the mean, its inquiry into inner happiness in relation to outward goods, and its stress on the place of habit in one's moral development, all come to play in Hop-kins's own thought and life. He notes that one must begin with self-knowledge: "See what your faculties are, what are the *ends* of your existence; for he [Aristotle] held the belief in a Creator, one God. If you realise what he meant for you, you realise what is best for you" (G1). Again the linchpin is teleology: "There is an end or object of every course of action. The multiplicity of ends converges in one end. Life is the sum of all actions; happiness of all ends." Hopkins goes on to develop this insight: "Besides the multiplicity and convergence, actions must not be infinite, or in other words they really must converge." He defines the Greek word "συνικνεῖσθαs, to converge so as to reach at last" (G1). The nature of the Aristotelian convergence is further explained in Hopkins's second set of notes: "There must be one end (and only one) to which all the others are subordinate. The knowledge of it will give life an aim, σκόπον" (M2). In acquiring a virtue man must "get hold of and carry out those things which tend to the mark aimed at." Here we find the fusion of knowledge (gnosis) with inscape (*scopos*). Because man is a knowing creature, his end is his own form, as Hopkins shows in one of his Oxford essays, "The Connection of Aristotle's metaphysics with his ethics" (see Appendix II). The virtuous life fully lived is beauty itself, and Hopkins in fact identifies "σκόπον" with "princely beauty" in an unpublished note on Homer's *Odyssey*, book 6, line 22 (M5), just as he has Lucifer "dwelling on his own beauty, an instressing of his own inscape" (S, 201). For the chasm between Christian and pagan virtues is humility, the opposite of pride—"humility: it is especially a Christian virtue because Christianity has God for its centre and invites the soul to refer itself in all things to Him" (D3, 3). Only the pure of heart attain to inscape.

"The way men judge in particular is determined for each by his own inscape," Hopkins wrote in his commentary on Parmenides (J, 129). Knowledge of his own soul's objective now enabled him to judge himself, his own life, and to determine its aim and direction. He must draw home to Being, to the heart of fire that burns, as Heraclitus saw, in the center of the cosmos. First a man must enter into himself, discover his own inscape, which he can do only by locating himself, fixed and focused, within the wide circumference of the whole of being. Then in this freedom of field, from "all this throng and stack of being, so rich, so distinctive, so important" (S, 122), he must choose one thing to do and be, so that he can say with each: *"What I do is me: for that I came"* (P57). "For this I came into the world: to bear witness to the truth," Christ replied when Pilate asked, "Are you a king?" The young knight went forth to answer the invitation of that "Eternal King and universal Lord" to "labor by day and watch by night" in his kingdom. The decisive meditation of the Ignatian *Spiritual Exercises*, "The Call of Christ the King," occasioned his "yes." The consent of the heart would follow the assent of the mind.

Two months after writing his notes on Parmenides, Hopkins began, during Holy Week of 1868, a retreat at the Oratory to help decide his vocation. Intellectually and spiritually, he had shaped the essential myth with which to follow gnosis; living that myth was another matter. The Easter retreat, which he made with the Oratory students, settled the question of neither the priesthood nor the religious life. He approached both callings with awe and self-distrust, for he knew the ideal to which he turned his mind was the perfect identification with Christ that Newman had once described: "Christ's priests have no priesthood but His. They are merely His shadows and organs, they are His outward signs; and what they do, He does; when they baptize, He is baptizing; when they bless, He is blessing."[14] Such was the ideal that towered before him. Would God so offer his inspiration that the questing knight could aspire to approach and enter in?

Hopkins drew back; he felt himself to be a "blackguard," one whose fallen nature aimed at sensuality and self-glory, the very opposite of his King and Lord. He wrote to Bridges: "The uncertainty I am in about the future is so very unpleasant and so breaks my power of applying to anything that I am resolved to end it, which I shall do by going into retreat at Easter at the latest and deciding whether I have a vocation to the priesthood" (L1, 22). Yet a new purpose and openness to life accompanied this struggle. He described it to Baillie: "The general result is that I am perfectly reckless about things that I shd. otherwise care about, uncertain as I am whether in a few months I may not be shut up in a cloister, and this state of mind, though it is painful coming to, when reached gives a great and real sense of freedom" (L3, 232). To determine his course, less than a month after his unsuccessful attempt at the Oratory he made a week's private retreat at Manresa House, Roehampton, from April 27 to May 7, 1868. Here at the Jesuit novitiate he was to enter five months later, he "decided to be a priest and religious" (J, 165). Seven years later he would vividly recall in verse the momentous hour of decision.

The Manresa experience changed his life. The struggle and victory are accurately described in the opening stanzas of *The Wreck of the Deutschland*:

> I did say yes
> O at lightning and lashed rod;
> Thou heardst me truer than tongue confess
> Thy terror, O Christ, O God;
> Thou knowest the walls, altar and hour and night:
> The swoon of a heart that the sweep and the hurl of
> thee trod
> Hard down with a horror of height:
> And the midriff astrain with leaning of, laced with fire
> of stress.
>
> The frown of his face
> Before me, the hurtle of hell
> Behind, where, where was a, where was a place?
> I whirled out wings that spell
> And fled with a fling of the heart to the heart of
> the Host.
> My heart, but you were dovewinged, I can tell,
> Carrier-witted, I am bold to boast,
> To flash from the flame to the flame then, tower from
> the grace to the grace.   (P28, 2, 3)

"What refers to myself in the poem is all strictly and literally true and did all occur; nothing is added for poetical padding"

(L1, 47).[15] The crisis in the poem is often taken to be one connected with Hopkins's conversion, but this opinion conflicts with his own account of that earlier decision and with the statement that "the hurtle of hell" was "behind" him. This sense of spiritual security could only be his after his conversion to Roman Catholicism. One of the chief concerns in his life and in this ode is the return of England from the Protestant heresy to the true Catholic faith. Damnation, he felt, threatened all those outside the fold, including himself. Five days before his reception into the Church, the young man wrote his father: "Only one thing remains to be done: I cannot fight against God Who calls me to His Church: if I were to delay and die in the meantime I shd. have no plea why my soul was not forfeit" (L3, 92).

The "altar and hour" of the *Deutschland* refer, I believe, to the chapel at Manresa House and the night of May 5, 1868. The question "Where, where was a, where was a place?" expresses a crisis of the dimensions involved in choosing one's way of life. The "place" of the retreat, also, was the same sanctuary where he would spend the first two years of his life as a Jesuit, as well as the future period of his tertianship. "Manresa"—the scene of St. Ignatius of Loyola's own *metanoia*—served as Hopkins's cell of prayer and of spiritual growth. Here were the "walls" of cloistral solitude that held out the world and kept his life hidden with Christ in imitation of the hidden years of Nazareth. In the poem, the question "Where?" is resolved through the imagery of a homing pigeon which "whirls out wings" at that moment of decision. The heart draws home to the heart of Christ in the Host of the altar. The use of "heart" and "Host" here is significant. For Hopkins, his vocation as a Jesuit priest would involve both. As a priest he would consecrate bread into the body of Christ and communicate the Host to others. "The Bugler's First Communion" is his most eloquent expression of this ideal, which finds its deepest functioning in his myth as the eucharistic Sacrifice, the "great purpose" of Christ's life and "his own chosen redemption" (S, 162). As a Jesuit he would also develop a special devotion to the Sacred Heart of Jesus, for to the Society this devotion had been entrusted by St. Margaret Mary Alacoque through her

Jesuit confessor, Bl. Claude de la Colombière. Devotion to the heart of Christ is connected with the Host by the Feast of the Sacred Heart which is celebrated on the Friday after the Octave of Corpus Christi and by the devotion to the eucharistic Heart of Jesus. These devotions, in their full Counter-Reformation fervor, provided more fuel for the poet's mythologizing.

"Carrier-witted" Hopkins flew straight to his mark, propelled to Christ by the Spirit of Christ. In "The Handsome Heart" the poet exclaims:

> What the heart is! which, like carriers let fly—
> Doff darkness, homing nature knows the rest—.   (P47)

Released to the light, the winged heart instinctively knew "the rest" ("roost" and "remainder") of its homeward flight. The repetition of "flame" and "grace" in the last line of stanza 3 of the *Deutschland* is also worth noting, since it bears directly on the relevance of this scene to Hopkins's vocation. We are meant to take "flame-flame" and "grace-grace" as parallels to "heart-heart" in line 5 of the same stanza. Through concentric spheres "ranging between fire and night," with uplifted heart the poet fled to the Sacred Heart and, homing there, mounts from Christ's flame of love to that flame of love in himself, from grace in Christ to that grace in himself. Towering, or circling on high like a falcon, "Being draws-home to Being." It is the movement from inspiration to aspiration described in the notes "On Personality, Grace and Free Will": "And even the sigh or aspiration itself is in answer to an inspiration of God's spirit and is followed by the continuance and expiration of that same breath which lifts it, through the gulf and void between pitch and pitch of being, to do or be what God wishes his creature to do or be" (S, 156). The statement is an accurate description of the meaning of vocation. Hopkins later defines "elevating" grace as that "which lifts the receiver from one cleave of being to another and to a vital act in Christ: this is truly God's finger touching the very vein of personality . . . , the aspiration in answer to his inspiration" (S, 158). "Saying *yes*," when "over again I feel thy finger and find thee," Hopkins mounts from the flame and grace of Christ's inspiration to the flame and grace of his own aspiration. The cycle is complete and keeps continually turning in a helix of impulse and response. When love quickens, heart answers to heart: *cor ad cor loquitur.*[16]

Flame and grace also point back to Christ's heart, the pierced wellspring of eternal life and "burning furnace of divine love." Margaret Mary Alacoque pictured Jesus appearing to her with his exposed heart surrounded by flames, like a brilliant sun radiating light and heat.[17] "Look at this heart," the Lord said to her from the altar, "which has loved men so much it spared nothing, even to exhausting and consuming itself, in order to testify its love." The Sacred Heart for Hopkins is the inscape of Christ, the focus and mark of his love for man and the fullness of being physically lodged there: "The heart, like all Christ's flesh, like Christ's whole body, like all Christ's human nature, is united with the godhead and deserves, requires, and must have paid to it, divine worship, that worship which . . . is due to God alone" (S, 101). The heart is the center and seat of selfhood: "What we call heart is not the piece of flesh so called, not the great blood-vessel only but the thoughts of the mind that vessel seems to harbour and the feelings of the soul to which it beats" (S, 103). In the heart converge the physical and spiritual energies of the incarnate Word.

In Christ's heart the probings of the pre-Socratic philosophers find fulfillment. In his notes on Parmenides, Hopkins quoted him on the principle of fire: " 'ethery flame of fire, comforting the heart (he is thinking of it perhaps as a vital principle), marvellously subtle, throughout one with itself, *not* one with the other' " (J, 130). But now "one with the other," for as Pascal reflected: "The heart has reasons the reason does not know." Rounded sphere, vortex of ethereal fire, sun from which all things draw light and heat, organ that pumps life to man, "vital principle . . . throughout one with itself," the Sacred Heart beckoned and, Hopkins asserts: "I did say yes." Being drew him home; the course of his life had once and for all been set, its inscape forever determined. In his own heart the noncanonical logion of Jesus, quoted by Origen (*In Jeremiah* 20.8), found fresh confirmation:

"Whoever is near to me is near to the fire; whoever is far from me, is far from the Kingdom."[18]

Such was the resolve Hopkins made in May of 1868, and recounted again seven years after in *The Wreck of the Deutschland*. But why did he choose the Jesuits? Less than one month before he had met Fr. Henry Coleridge whom he later called his "oldest friend in the Society" and who, ironically enough, was editor of the *Month* when it refused publication to the *Deutschland* and the *Euridyce*. Father Coleridge was the retreat master who directed him during the Holy Week exercises and probably suggested the seclusion of Roehampton as the proper place for the decision. Hopkins seriously considered the Benedictines at the time and, although the choice of the religious life already included a step toward the Society, he left Roehampton "still doubtful between St. Benedict and St. Ignatius" (J, 165). Within a week he had made up his mind, for Newman answered him on May 14: "I think it is the very thing for you. . . . Don't call 'the Jesuit discipline hard,' it will bring you to heaven. The Benedictines would not have suited you" (L3, 408). Nevertheless, Hopkins had little or no personal acquaintance with Jesuits before meeting Fr. Coleridge and might well have shared in the general suspicion against the order as typified by his friend Robert Bridges. Some deeper appeal must have attracted him to "Christ's Company."

In reading Matthew Arnold's *Essays in Criticism, First Series* (1865) he would have come upon Joubert's favorable contrasting of the Jesuits with the Jansenists who "seem to love God without affection, and solely from reason, from duty, from justice. The Jesuits, on the other hand, seem to love him from pure inclination; out of admiration, gratitude, tenderness; for the pleasure of loving him, in short. In their books of devotion you find joy, because with the Jesuits nature and religion go hand in hand."[19] This unison of religion and nature must have struck a responsive chord in the poet. Respect for learning and intellectual growth were also Jesuit hallmarks, dating from their founder's vision at the Cardoner River when "the eyes of his understanding began to open and, without seeing any vision, he understood and knew many things, as well spiritual as those appertaining to the faith and to the realm of letters, and that with such clarity that they seemed to him things completely new."[20] St. Ignatius's account of how "he seemed to himself to be another man, with another mind than that which was his before" perfectly matches Hopkins's own search for gnosis and St. Paul's call: "Let that mind be in you which was in Christ Jesus" and "Yours is the mind of Christ." From its origins and in its very title—an unheard of innovation for its day—the Society, unlike the orders of "Francis," "Dominic," and "Benedict," was that of "Jesus," not of "Ignatius" himself. On his way to Rome to seek approval for the new religious order, Loyola stopped in a chapel at La Storta and "saw clearly that the Father placed him with Christ his Son." Each of his followers was meant to receive this special favor of "placing" in Christ by answering the call of the King in the *Spiritual Exercises* to be identified with Jesus "in order to share in the victory as he has shared in the toil."

When he made his oblation on May 8 to the Eternal King and universal Lord, choosing the way of emptiness and toil, Hopkins knew the needle's eye to Being was in losing one's life, that the way up, as Heraclitus stated, was the way down. Perhaps the promise in Parmenides' poem that gnosis would open the Way of Truth also came to mind:

> You shall know the nature of the heavens, and all the
> signs in the heavens, and the resplendent works of the
> pure bright torch of the sun, and whence they came into
> being. And you shall learn of the wandering works of the
> round-faced moon, and its nature; and you shall know
> also the surrounding heaven, whence it sprang and how
> Necessity brought and constrained it to hold the limits
> of the stars.[21]

After seven years of silence—the biblical span of plenty and famine—*The Wreck of the Deutschland* testified to the Victorian poet-philosopher's fulfillment of that promise:

> I kiss my hand
> To the stars, lovely asunder

> Starlight, wafting him out of it; and
> Glow, glory in thunder;
> Kiss my hand to the dappled-with-damson west:
> Since, tho' he is under the world's splendour and
>   wonder,
> His mystery must be instressed, stressed;
> For I greet him the days I meet him, and bless when I
>   understand.   (P28, 5)

"Withindoors," the young Jesuit gathered and stored the bread of life, Christ the repository of being and heart of the universe. In a journal entry at this time, Hopkins wrote: "As we drove home the stars came out thick: I leant back to look at them and my heart opening more than usual praised our Lord to and in whom all that beauty comes home" (J, 254). In stars or in elm trees he found the same "beautiful inscape, home-coiling wiry bushes of spray, touched with bud to point them" (J, 243). The world opened a Way for the beholder to follow "yonder, yes yonder."

Reflecting on the providence that guides the evolutionary process in nature from grass to trees, from gnats to eagles, Samuel Coleridge pondered the provision being made in the universe for man "as subsumed in the divine humanity, in whom alone God loved the world." He wondered:

> If then we behold this economy everywhere in the irrational creation, shall we not hold it probable that by some analogous intervention a similar temperament will have been effected for the rational and moral? Are we not entitled to expect some appropriate agency in behalf of the presiding and alone progressive creature? To presume some especial provision for the permanent interest of the creature destined to move and grow towards that divine humanity which we have learnt to contemplate as the final cause of all creation, and the centre in which all its lines converge?[22]

To these advanced—indeed prophetic—speculations, Gerard Hopkins found his own concrete response. His lifework, both as priest and poet, manifests that mysterious providence at work, leading the rational and moral creature onward to a center of convergence. The force that whirled the oak tree on its star knot stirred his heart in hiding.

2

The Meaning
of St. Paul

IN HIS commentaries on the *Spiritual Exercises* and in his spiritual notes and writings, Hopkins relies most often on St. Paul for the development of his inquiries and ideas. One passage in particular, from the Epistle to the Philippians, 2:5-11, he twice subjects to exhaustive analysis. Many biblical scholars now consider the passage to be an early Palestinian hymn which embodies one of the first confessions of faith in Jesus as suffering servant and Lord of the universe. In present-day hermeneutics, in fact, the text is one of the most carefully examined of the Pauline writings and has become a keystone of modern christological thought.[1] Hopkins with sure and accurate insight turned to it for the formulation of his own inscape of Christ's meaning for man. In a letter to Bridges in February 1883, he set forward his interpretation of the hymn. Like St. Paul he places it in a context of moral action: "Christ's life and character are such as appeal to all the world's admiration, but there is one insight St. Paul gives us of it which is very secret and seems to me more touching and constraining than everything else is" (L1, 175). With this introduction, Hopkins then weaves translation and comment together in a masterful *explication de texte*. In the quotation that follows, to help distinguish the two, I have italicized the phrases that translate the Epistle:

> *This mind* he says, *was in Christ Jesus*—he means as man: *being in the form of God*—that is, finding, as in the first

instant of his incarnation he did, his human nature informed by the godhead—*he thought it nevertheless no snatching-matter for him to be equal with God, but annihilated himself, taking the form of servant*; that is, he could not but see what he was, God, but he would see it as if he did not see it, and be it as if he were not and instead of snatching at once at what all the time was his, or was himself, he emptied or exhausted himself so far as that was possible, of godhead and behaved only as God's slave, as his creature, as man, which also he was, *and then being in the guise of man humbled himself to death, the death of the cross*. It is this holding of himself back, and not snatching at the truest and highest good, the good that was his right, nay his possession from a past eternity in his other nature, his own being and self, which seems to me the root of all his holiness and the imitation of this the root of all moral good in other men. (L1, 175)

Hopkins's first notable inference lies in his remark that the passage from the start views Christ as man, a historical reality, whose personality, however, extends beyond time and space to a pre-existent, divine mode of being. From this point within himself, Christ moved downward, as the text indicates, by surrender and emptying of godly life to be a man, to be one of his own creatures. This "emptying" action has been known since the third century by the Greek noun *kenosis*. According to this accepted view—in its most general interpretation—Jesus puts aside the prerogatives and insignia of his equality with God (his *forma Dei*) to assume ordinary manhood (*forma servi*) and, further, accepts the sinful mortality that leads him even to die as an outcast and criminal. His whole motive is obedience to his Father's will. As in Milton's theology, the kenotic descent is thus the central act of God's plan of salvation.[2]

Neither Paul nor Hopkins implies that Jesus ceased to possess his divine nature, as some interpreters of *kenosis* have argued; nor, on the other hand, does either state that Jesus was man only in appearance, one who played the role of a divine apparition in

human disguise. In the incarnation God does not masquerade
as man: Christ is fully man and fully God. To Hopkins's mind
this is Christ's "secret" and inmost mark, to hold back, not to
snatch at his full being and self as Adam did when he aspired
to "be like God, knowing good and evil" (Gen. 3:5), or as Lucifer
did when he grasped at a rank with God by "instressing of his
own inscape," that is, by affirming himself as the end- and be-all
of creation. As in Milton's epic, both Adam and Lucifer loom
large in the poet's writings because both are antitypes of Christ's
action: they would not serve, and the Lord came as servant; they
desired to ascend through self-assertion, he descended to become
a man for others. Before asking man to lose his life, God first lost
his, putting it in the hands of his creatures: "The Word of God,
second person of the divine Trinity, our blessed Lord Jesus Christ,
came down from everlasting heaven, was made man, lived among
men, *was given into the hands of sinners*, first by his own hands
into Judas' in the Last Supper, then by Judas into those of the
priests, then by the priests into those of Pilate, then by Pilate
into those of the executioners, and accomplished his bloody sacrifice on the cross" (S, 236). The utmost gift of himself is the
Eucharist in which Christ as bread and wine becomes his members, emptying himself completely in his love.

The hymn of Philippians describes the process of redemption
by dramatizing the event of salvation history from eternity to
time. The center is the person of Christ himself, not as the lifeless puppet of an eternal plan, but as a hero and *dramatis persona*
in his decisions and actions. In a second analysis of the text which
he made in his commentary on the *Exercises*, Hopkins divides the
drama into scenes: "This process took place in its own fashion
(1) in the procession of the godhead; (2) in his entrance into
creation, his incarnation proper; (3) on earth, in the ἐνανθρώπευσιν,
the becoming man" (S, 181). To support this division, he rejected
the punctuation of the Vulgate which inserts a full stop after
verse 7 and substituted "what seems to me the true punctuation
of Phil. ii. 7, 8" (S, 170). His version then reads: "7 He emptied
himself, taking the form of a servant; and being born in the likeness of men and being found in human form 8 he humbled him-

self, becoming obedient to death, even to death on a cross." The point is an essential one in Hopkins's Christology for it allowed him to determine a human existence of Christ before he historically pitched his tent among us (John 1:14) and made visible a presence previously hidden from men's sight. Like Samuel Coleridge, who asserted that "the Divinity, the Filial Godhead, was humanized before he was incarnate—i.e. manifested himself *focally* (ut in foco) in an individual Man,"[3] Hopkins also concluded that before being man in Judea "when he was now actually man and born in poverty" (S, 181) the Word took on the *forma servi* in the genesis of the cosmos. Christ is engaged from the beginning with the world of time; his *kenosis* is the first act of creation. Before exploring Hopkins's speculation on the preexistent Lord, we must recall the Pauline foundation for the idea. For it was in the New Testament and not in Duns Scotus that he first encountered the Alpha and Omega of his myth, just as it was at Oxford, under the tutelage of Liddon and Jowett, that he first sifted these texts. Many years later, by his own admission, the Jesuit adopted Jowett's sense of a "snatching-matter" in interpreting the Philippians verse (L1, 177).

"There is only . . . one Lord, Jesus Christ, through whom are all things, and we through him" (I Cor. 8:6). All creation issues from Jesus—not only newness of his divine life, but natural reality from its origins: "All things have been created through and unto him, and he is before all creatures, and in him all things hold together" (Col. 1:16-17). Parmenidean Being foredraws in him now and from the beginning, issuing "from him" in creation and converging "to him" in atonement. The Epistle to the Hebrews, especially in its opening verses, embodies one of the most eloquent witnesses to Christ's existence as Son and heir of all things from the foundation of the world. The teaching is advanced with visionary force: "God . . . in these days has spoken to us by his Son, whom he appointed heir of all things, by whom also he made the world; who, being the brightness of his glory and the image of his substance, and upholding all things by the word of his power, has effected man's purgation from sin and taken his seat at the right hand of the Majesty on high" (Heb. 1:1-3). In

employing the theme of priesthood and sacrifice, this work seems
to have had a lasting effect on Hopkins. In coming into the world,
the Son proclaims:

> "Sacrifice and oblation thou wouldst not,
>   but a body thou hast fitted to me:
> In holocausts and sin-offerings thou hast
>   had no pleasure.
> Then said I, 'Behold, I come—
>   in the head of the book it is written of me—
>   to do thy will, O God.' "   (Heb. 10:5-7)

In each of these passages, Jesus himself is actor in his whole person, not simply in his divine nature. This is precisely the mystery
Paul announces, hidden in ages past and now revealed, "Jesus
Christ yesterday, today, and the same one forever" (Heb. 13:8;
adapted). He is the goal of creation, because he is its first impulse,
its abiding direction and its final destination. The Alpha in which
all begin and the Omega in which all meet has been totally present and everywhere engaged from Genesis until now.

Hopkins never employed the word *kenosis* but used his own
phrase for it instead: "the great sacrifice." In one of his sermons,
he echoed Hebrews: "Religion is the highest of the moral virtues
and sacrifice the highest act of religion. Also self sacrifice is the
purest charity. Christ was the most religious of men, to offer sacrifice was the chief purpose of his life and that the sacrifice of
himself" (S, 14). This kenotic offering is made before his earthly
life: "The love of the Son for the Father leads him to take a
created nature and in that to offer him sacrifice. The sacrifice
might have been unbloody; by the Fall it became a bloody one"
(S, 257). Jesus empties himself on the cross and in his eucharistic
Sacrifice, but these are willed actions and have a reality as the
first act of God outside himself:

> The first intention then of God outside himself or, as
> they say, *ad extra*, outwards, the first outstress of God's
> power, was Christ; and we must believe that the next was

the Blessed Virgin. Why did the Son of God go thus
forth from the Father not only in the eternal and intrinsic
procession of the Trinity but also by an extrinsic and
less than eternal, let us say aeonian one?—To give God
glory and that by sacrifice, sacrifice offered in the barren
wilderness outside of God, as the children of Israel were
led into the wilderness to offer sacrifice. This sacrifice
and this outward procession is a consequence and shadow
of the procession of the Trinity, from which mystery
sacrifice takes its rise. (S, 197)

What matters for Hopkins is that the sacrifice known in history,
the death of Jesus on the hill of Golgatha, is actual proof of the
"outgoingness" of God, Being's gift of himself to the point of
extinction, entering the unimaginable void, the "barren wilderness" outside himself. Only by contemplating Being as the
Greeks did, can the postclassical and Christian man guess the
terror and majesty of that act. Thus Hopkins, whose mind was
"much employed . . . on the subject of Sacrifice" (L2, 102), saw
all non-Christian sacrifice—Egyptian, Greek, Roman, or Chinese
—as rehearsals of the Word's immolation.

But *kenosis* is not the whole of the incarnation or Christ-event.
We have been concerned until now with only the first half of the
Philippians hymn, the verses dealing with the Son's divinity and
death. Although Hopkins's exegesis proceeds no further, he refers to the entire passage in his comment on the words of Christ
the King in the meditation on the Kingdom in the *Exercises*:
"Whosoever, therefore, desires to come with me must labour
with me in order that following me in suffering, he may likewise
follow me in glory." In the course of his life, Jesus willingly set
aside the power, wealth, and esteem that were his as the Jewish
Messiah and chose instead the lot of a poor carpenter and itiner-
ant teacher who is rejected and deserted even by his followers.
His was the way of loneliness and loss, not because he found any
attraction in such an existence, but that the least might find in
him a brother and companion. "You know the graciousness of

our Lord Jesus Christ," Paul reminded his listeners, "how, being rich, he became poor for your sakes, that by his poverty you might become rich" (2 Cor. 8:9).

For this obedience, the Philippians hymn concludes, "God has exalted him and given him a name above every other name, that at the name of Jesus every knee should bend of those in heaven, on earth and under the earth, and every tongue should confess that Jesus Christ is 'Lord,' to the glory of God the Father" (Phil. 2:9-11; adapted). God has raised Jesus to the heights: this is the climax toward which the drama has been leading us. The kenotic sacrifice terminates in the "superexaltation" of the servant who is now "Lord" of the universe, of all the living and the dead. The glorified, risen Jesus is then the Omega, end and inscape of man's faith and gnosis; he is the one the shipwrecked nun calls to in the *Deutschland* and whom Paul preached centuries before: "This gospel concerns the Son of God who, in his human nature, descended from David, but who, in the realm of the spirit—the Holy Spirit that was his—was marked out as the Son of God in full power by his resurrection from the dead: Jesus Christ our Lord" (Rom. 1:3-4; adapted).

According to Paul's teaching, the Son emptied himself of his divine mode of being in order to be filled in turn with all the completeness of godly and human life. The *kenosis* is fulfilled in the *pleroma* of Jesus, a term borrowed from biblical and Stoic literature to express the creative presence and power of God in the world.[4] The risen Christ fills creation with his being, energy, and stress, because the Father wills that everything (τὰ πάντα, the "all") from its beginning to end be focused and reunited in him: "For it has pleased God the Father that in him all his fullness [*pleroma*] should dwell, and that through him he should reconcile to himself all things, whether on the earth or in the heavens, making peace through the blood of his cross" (Col. 1:19-20). This was God's hidden purpose to be carried out "in the fullness of the times: to re-establish all things in Christ, both those in the heavens and those on the earth" (Eph. 1:10). All that was lost in man's fall regains its unity, timeliness, and function in him. But the way remains the same: through the death and ignominy of the cross alone are all things drawn home to Being. The great sacrifice is the route to the *pleroma*.

The regenerated body of Jesus is the living receptacle and homing point of this fullness: the *pleroma* of divine life now circulates within him "bodily." In his Bampton lecture on St. Paul, H. P. Liddon defined the *pleroma* as follows: "The entire cycle of the Divine attributes, considered as a series of powers or forces, dwells in Jesus Christ; and this, not in any merely ideal or transcendental manner, but with that actual reality which men attach to the presence of material bodies which they can feel and measure through the organs of sense."[5] The Son is the living icon or image of the Father, and the Son is man in face and limb. He is the pattern Man and, in Liddon's words, "He fulfills and exhausts that moral Ideal to which man's highest and best aspirations have ever pointed onward."[6] Christ then is not a static source or goal but the kinetic body which, materially and divinely, contains and energizes the whole. In him Aristotelian teleology is confirmed and comes alive.

For Paul, Jesus possesses this fullness which is himself, not for his own sake or self-glory, but for mankind, in order to give of himself to others. The *kenosis* and *pleroma* are two moments in the same act of love. Christ's members themselves become whole and complete through him: "God has made all things subject under his feet and appointed him head over all the Church, which is his body, the fullness of him who fills the universe in every part" (Eph. 1:22-23; adapted). Just as Christ's *pleroma* is an active force charging all things, so the Church is not an exterior and static institution over which the head exercises authority, but forms an inner reality transfiguring the heart and mind. Paul prays:

> I bend my knees to the Father of our Lord Jesus Christ,
> from whom all fatherhood in heaven and on earth receives
> its name, that he may grant you from his glorious riches
> to be strengthened with power through his Spirit unto
> the progress of the inner man; and to have Christ dwelling
> through faith in your hearts: so that, being rooted and

> grounded in love, you may be able to comprehend with
> all the saints what is the breadth and length and height
> and depth, and to know Christ's love which surpasses
> knowledge, in order that you may be filled unto all the
> fullness of God. (Eph. 3:14-19)

This passage was an important one for Hopkins; he copied most
of it out in the original Greek when writing his paper "On Personality, Grace and Free Will." He comments on the final words:
"This πλήρωμα τοῦ Θεοῦ is the burl of being in Christ, and for
every man there is his own burl of being, which are all 'by lays'
or 'byfalls' of Christ's and of one another's" (S, 156). The use
of the term "burl" for "fullness of being" first occurs in Hopkins's notes on Parmenides; he translates:

> "According to the matching of his members / with the
> thousand turns they take / so for each man is the thought
> the man will think, for the *sense* that lives in this frame
> man wears is only the seeing of one selfsame thing—
> one thing for all men and for every man: (there are ten
> thousand men to think and ten thousand things for them
> to think of but they are but names given and taken, eye
> and lip service to the truth, husks and scapes of it: the
> truth itself, the burl,) the fulness is the thought." (J, 130)

The fullness is the Logos, the Word who is Being. Later the poet
echoed these phrases on the multiplicity of men's actions and
thoughts, but fused with the One:

> . . . Christ plays in ten thousand places,
> Lovely in limbs, and lovely in eyes not his
> To the Father through the features of men's faces.
>
> (P57)

The "ten thousand men" of Parmenides are identified as the one
man who is the way, truth, and life of all. The one man who is
Being, I AM. Men are his members in body and brain.

Hopkins further relates the *pleroma* not only to the actual being foredrawn in the risen Jesus, but to all potential being as well.

The "burl of being" of each creature is its "possible world" where its fulfillment waits in Christ (S, 155). The word *burl* is associated in Hopkins's mind with *burly* and *bulky*. He noted in his journal: "I marked the bole, the burling and roundness of the world" (J, 251), and, not long after, told how he inscaped "the eye-greeting burl of the Round Tower" of Windsor Castle (J, 256). Besides referring to a round knot or lump of wool, *burl* may also echo the dialectic verb *birl*: to spin or whirl rapidly. This cycloid outcropping of being in Christ is caused by his own superabundance of energy and life. Another word often used in connection with *burl* is *cleave*, which he coined as a noun and derived from the verb *to cleave*: to cut or split open with a knife. The act of coming into existence or of choosing freely Hopkins called the "cleave" cut in the burl of possibles through which being excreted: "Therefore in that 'cleave' of being which each of his creatures shews to God's eyes alone (or in its 'burl' of being / uncloven) God can choose countless points in the strain (or countless cleaves of the 'burl') where the creature has consented, does consent to God's will" (S, 154). Inside or out, open to act in Christ or inclosed in his own potency to do so, each man as a free creature acknowledges the inner stress which is his union, in obedience, with Being.

Hopkins's meaning becomes clearer when we turn to another term he employs for the *pleroma*—quite similar to the burl, but more familiar—the pomegranate. This biblical fruit, ripe like the "lush-kept plush-capped sloe" (P28, 8), is brimful and bursting with being. Like Parmenides' "well-rounded ball" the poet's pomegranate is cosmic Being in all and in each and yet complete in itself. Hopkins writes:

> As besides the actual world there is an infinity of possible
> worlds, differing in all degrees of difference from what
> now is down to the having nothing in common with it
> but virgin matter, each of which possible worlds and
> this the actual one are like so many "cleaves" or exposed
> faces of some pomegranate (or other fruit) cut in all
> directions across,: so there is an infinity of possible strains

of action and choice for each possible self in these worlds
(or, what comes to the same thing, in virgin matter) and
the sum of these strains would be also like a pomegranate
in the round, which God sees whole but of which we see
at best only one cleave. Rather we see the world as one
cleave and the life of each person as one vein or strain
of colour in it. (S, 151)

Christ now within the godhead is enveloped in the divine sphere.
God sees the whole from within: he is the *pleroma*, pomegranate,
or burl of all being. The cleave cut on the outside surface is what
man sees, this universe, himself: the one opening of his thought
and being inscaping sharply to the center within—Christ. The
world then is open, a source from which stress springs and a
stem through which man's instress flows back to the king and
head. Through this infinitesimal fissure man glimpses and possesses the infinite I AM.

Hopkins found a parallel for his picturing of the *pleroma* in
the meditation on the incarnation as presented in the *Spiritual
Exercises*. St. Ignatius gives as the composition of place, "the
great capacity and circuit of the world." The poet commented:

"Magnam capacitatem et ambitum mundi"—This suggests
that "pomegranate," that *pomum possibilium*. The Trinity
saw it whole and in every "cleave," the actual and the
possible. We may consider that we are looking at it in
all the actual cleaves, one after another. This sphere is set
off against the sphere of the divine being, a steady "seat
or throne" of majesty. Yet that too has its cleave to us,
the entrance of Christ on the world. There is not only
the pomegranate of the whole world but of each species
in it, each race, each individual, and so on. Of human
nature the whole pomegranate fell in Adam. (S, 171)

Hopkins leaves little doubt about the kind of fruit Adam ate
from the tree of knowledge. This pomegranate is one in "a system of concentric spheres" ranging upward to "the sphere of the
divine being," an ultimate and all-inclusive ring. Set off from it,
another pomegranate with its multicelled and seeded fullness

holds all the *rationes seminales* or hidden life sources of creation.
In the *De Trinitate* St. Augustine describes these invisible seeds
as the material essences lodged in the physical elements of the
world. This possible store of "nature's germens," as Shakespeare
terms them, is not fictitious being, but the positive and real,
eager to be delivered and already revealing itself in all the reaches
of the global universe. Here too we see that the Son in whom "the
fullness of the Godhead dwells bodily" (Col. 2:9) himself becomes a cleave of creation; his life provides the sole opening for
mankind into the *pleroma*. Note, in addition, that the pomegranate has a rind of golden red and resembles the sun, as well as
the human heart. Both are realized in Jesus, the sun and Sacred
Heart who fills the world with his heat and light.

Since this fruit also splits open under the pressure of its many
seeds, "the bursting pomegranate" has been a traditional symbol
of the resurrection, an emblem of Christ's power in breaking
forth from the tomb on Easter morning to pour out his risen life
on all mankind.[7] It is a biblical symbol, too, of royalty, hope, immortality, and fertility, as well as a sign of the oneness of the
universe and of the *seminarium rerum*: the seedbed of being
which Edmund Spenser described as "the first seminary / Of all
things that are come to live and die" (*Faerie Queene* 3. 6. 30). In
Greek mythology the pomegranate supposedly sprang from the
blood of Dionysus, a god of vegetation who died and rose again.
Perhaps Hopkins connected it with his image of "the whole world
inclosed . . . in a drop of Christ's blood" (S, 194). Significantly, the
source of information on the Grecian origin of the pomegranate
myth is Clement of Alexandria, who notes it in the second chapter of his *Protrepticus*.[8] In their commentaries on the Canticle of
Canticles, the church fathers make free in their interpretations
of the pomegranate's symbolism. Gregory of Nyssa, for example,
explains the verse: "Thou sendest forth from thy mouth a paradise of pomegranates" (Cant. 4:13) as a reference to the fruit,
cultivated by the Word, which is the continence of pure souls.[9]
Typically, however, Hopkins employs this traditional material
in his own fashion and for his own ends, concentrating not on
its symbolic application but on its concrete appropriateness to

his personal mythopoeic scheme. Beyond words and imagery what mattered was the bond itself that held men fast to one another in their reborn king.

To affirm the reality of Christ's risen body, each disciple, according to St. Paul, plays his part by preaching in conformity to his individual call as a "witness of the resurrection": "And he himself made some apostles, some prophets, some evangelists, some pastors and teachers in order to perfect the saints for a work of service, for building up the body of Christ, until we all attain to the unity of the faith and of the knowledge of the Son of God, to perfect manhood, to the mature measure of the fullness of Christ" (Eph. 4:11-13; adapted). Jesus is the prototype and "arch-inscape" of the New Man who is the good news announced by St. Paul and his fellow preachers. All have been recreated in this Lord and to his full stature each believer is inwardly growing. United in Christ, men work toward a community of faith and gnosis which are both already actualized in the unity of the *pleroma* present here and now within the minds and hearts of the faithful. This unity is particularly evident in their actions which affirm the truth of the spoken message: "For the Son of God, Jesus Christ, whom we preached among you . . . was not Yes and No, but in him it is always Yes. For all the promises of God find their Yes in him" (2 Cor. 1:19-20; adapted). "I did say yes," Hopkins confessed in the opening lines of the *Deutschland*; he was consciously adding his assent to the fulfillment of God's promises in his own experience of Christ.

Unity of life is achieved through directed dedication. As the center makes the circle, so the goal shapes the whole man renewed in grace. The Christian hero, in the mind of St. Paul, is a soldier armed for victory, an athlete trained to win the crown, a husbandman intent on the fruits of his harvest (2 Tim. 2:4-6). Direction creates fulfillment. The philosopher Montaigne observed: "It is impossible for him to dispose of his particular actions, that hath not in grose directed his life unto one certain end. It is impossible for him to range all peeces in order, that hath not a plot or forme of the totall frame in his head. . . . A skilfull archer ought first to knowe the mark he aimeth at, and then ap-

ply his hand, his bow, his string, his arrow and his motion accordingly."[10] Hopkins's own notion of inscape is basically Pauline and rooted in the idea of the *pleroma* as a network of centers
which culminate in the Omega point or "mark" of the risen
Christ. "Forgetting what is behind," St. Paul declares, "I strain
forward to what is before, I press on towards the goal, [*scopos*],
to the prize of God's heavenly call in Christ Jesus" (Phil. 3:13-14).
"God gave things a forward and perpetual motion" (S, 198-99)
and that motion which propels all created reality is forward to
completion. According to Clement of Alexandria, beneath appearances unity underlies the universe and man's vision of the
real. Removing natural qualities, the beholder comes to the point
which is left, unity; then "we cast ourselves into the greatness
of Christ and thence advance into immensity through holiness"
(*Strom.* 5. 11). Man encounters Christ "as a center upon which
all lines converge," in the words of Maximus the Confessor.[11]
Pleroma is a vortex of energy at which all aim, to which "the
totall frame" aspires.

"The fulness is the thought" inwardly possessed and com-
munally shared in the Word-made-flesh. Not that man and creation can ever entirely reach or encompass the *pleroma*. The creature's achievement is its movement forward, its "perpetual
motion" toward Christ, the prize and goal who remains transcen-
dently himself, the author of all self-being: "For human nature,
being more highly pitched, selved, and distinctive than anything
in the world, can have been developed, evolved, condensed, from
the vastness of the world not anyhow or by the working of common powers but only by one of finer or higher pitch and determination than itself and certainly than any that elsewhere we
see, for this power had to force forward the starting or stubborn
elements to the one pitch required" (S, 122-23). As "the first intention of God outside Himself," Jesus is the unique man, distinctly conscious and completely self-fulfilled. Other men attain
"the whole object not in its fulness and 'splay' but in this 'neap'
and foredrawn condition" (S, 152). Hopkins's editor explains
these coinages as follows: " 'Splay' . . . is the radiation from an
interior force and the shape that the rays assume. The 'neap' is

the interior force . . . ; it is the bunching of the tide when the moon is young with the impetus of the spring-flood, as it were, coiled in it" (S, 294). The human being aims—or is pitched—at the foredrawn center where the "Holdfast" Christ keeps "in the neap" the spinning source of the *pleroma*. But only Christ contains and controls the "splay" or spreading out of being through the universe. For he not only activates and fills the cosmos, he is that which he activates and fills. "He emptied himself . . . that in him all fullness would dwell."

The last act of the great sacrifice is the return of all things, which are then, through the ultimate gesture of the Son's obedience, to be resigned to the Father. The *pleroma* itself ends in *kenosis*: "And when all things are made subject to him, then the Son himself will also be made subject to him who subjected all things to him, that God may be all in all" (1 Cor. 15:28). When the cosmos is his and in him, it will be surrendered in love by the Son's free gift to the Father. His obedience on the cross presages his submission at the Parousia: his triumph is this ever-lasting homage.

Hopkins himself connects the *pleroma* and the *kenosis* in his paper on "Creation and Redemption: the Great Sacrifice." After showing Christ to be "the first outstress of God's power," he proceeds, as we have seen in the section quoted earlier in this chapter (p. 39), to examine the nature of sacrifice: "It is as if the blissful agony or stress of selving in God had forced out drops of sweat or blood, which drops were the world, or as if the lights lit at the festival of the 'peaceful Trinity' through some little cranny striking out lit up into being one 'cleave' out of the world of possible creatures. The sacrifice would be the Eucharist, and that the victim might be truly victim like, like motionless, help-less, or lifeless, it must be in matter" (S, 197). In this passage Hopkins sees the sphere as full of light within, where the Trinity abides; then one opening is slashed on its surface and a ray of light shoots outward into the exterior darkness and void. This ray is the eucharistic Christ, the Host who focuses and centers all reality back within himself. The first moment of the sacrifice is also its last, for the end Christ proposes for himself is the giving

of his body on the cross once and for all time: "It was to offer
first this great sacrifice and to set on foot the after offering of this
sacrifice to God's glory and for man's redemption and for all
blessings on the sons of men that he came into the world" (S,
236). In Christ's beginning is his end.

The movement outward and the return complete the cycle of
the eternal plan. Hopkins was fond of imagining it as a procession, so pictured in the Apocalypse, in which all creation takes its
place behind the universal head. He defended and explained the
theory of the Corpus Christi procession to the unimpressed
Bridges who had attended the ceremony while visiting Hopkins
in 1882 at Manresa House. The procession, he states, "represents
the process of the Incarnation and the world's redemption":

> As Christ went forth from the bosom of the Father as the
> Lamb of God and eucharistic victim to die upon the
> altar of the cross for the world's ransom; then rising
> returned leading the procession of the flock redeemed /
> so in this ceremony his body *in statu victimali* is carried
> to the Altar of Repose as it is called and back to the
> tabernacle at the high altar, which will represent the
> bosom of the godhead. The procession out may represent
> the cooperation of the angels, or of the patriarchs and
> prophets, the return the Church Catholic from Christ's
> death to the end of time. (L1, 149)

It is worth comparing this description with one given in "Creation and Redemption" which Hopkins wrote in the same period
of his tertianship:

> In going forth to do sacrifice Christ went not alone but
> created angels to be his company, lambs to follow him the
> Lamb, the flower of the flock, "withersoever he went,"
> that is to say, first to the hill of sacrifice, then after that
> back to God, to beatitude. They were to take part in the
> sacrifice, and he was to redeem them all, that is to say /
> for the sake of the Lamb of God who was God himself
> God would accept the whole flock and for the sake of one
> ear or grape the whole sheaf or cluster; for redeem may be

> said not only of the recovering from sin to grace or
> perdition to salvation but also of the raising from worth-
> lessness before God (and all creation is unworthy of God)
> to worthiness of him, the meriting of God himself, or,
> so to say, godworthiness. (S, 197)

Both these passages embody the cosmic meaning of inscape.
Christ is not simply a fixed target but a flowing current, a spearhead who not only directs man to the goal and is the goal himself,
but is the direction also. He is both aim and mark, "entrance" and
"steady 'seat or throne' " (S, 171). The procession in time, as out-
lined in the letter to Bridges, reaches back and forward to include
all salvation history from the patriarchs to the Parousia, and, in
addition, extends from the aeonian descent of Christ in *forma
servi* to his death and resurrection, the process related in the
Philippians hymn. The second passage sees the action as encom-
passing mankind and creation from its first stirrings: "Christ
went not alone." The details of "sheaf" and "cluster" of grapes
suggest the bread and wine which become the body and blood of
the eucharistic victim. Not just the Corpus Christi ceremony, but
all spring and harvest processions enact man's mythic quest.

The circuit of the pilgrim's "progress" issues from the bosom
of the Father and returns to him. For man in the present the essential action here is summed up in the adverb "back." Like other
direction words in Hopkins's poetry ("up" to the risen Jesus,
"down" in the Lord's descent) "back" indicates the returning
action of man's response to God: it marks the exact point, midway in the curving orbit, at which that return begins. He defended its use in "The Leaden Echo and the Golden Echo" to
Bridges: "*Back* is not pretty, but it gives that feeling of physical
constraint which I want" (L1, 162). Man must strain and struggle
in running to his mark, just as Christ "held back" and humbled
himself by not snatching at the divine glory that was rightfully
his. For man "goes not alone," but in company with all men and
creation itself; he attains "godworthiness" only from the human
touch and leadership of the Good Shepherd, Jesus.[12]

The line from Parmenides to Paul, in Hopkins's mythopoeic

development, itself forms a circle of interacting forces: the fullness of being and thought, the ball and cosmological system of concentric spheres. The matter of the poet's myth emerges in a series of polarities: Being and Nothingness, fullness and emptiness, descent and ascent, darkness and light. All things are reconciled—fallen man with God—in the person of Jesus of Nazareth. A universe darkened and scattered by what Newman called "some terrible aboriginal calamity" took on shape and meaning for Hopkins as its "canon" gradually grew clear. The calamity was everywhere evidenced in man and in the "blackguard" poet himself and at times would nearly overwhelm him with despair; but his knowledge born of faith and perfected through virtue and study gave him the strength to push forward, until death reveal "the goal and prize of God's heavenly call in Christ Jesus" (Phil. 3:14). Meanwhile, gnosis led each day to new inscapes and instress as he glossed the text of experience, nature, and books.

The example of the scholarly Paul was always there before him, explicating the past in the light of the new knowledge:

> But to each of us grace was given according to the measure of Christ's bounty. Thus Scripture states: "He ascended to the heights, he led away captives, he gave gifts to men." Now the phrase, "he ascended," what does it imply but that he also first descended to the lowest level, down to this very earth? He who descended, he it is who ascended also above all the heavens, that he might fill all creation. (Eph. 4:7-10, quoting Ps. 67:19; adapted)

In all and in each the same mystery at work: "God *in forma servi* rests *in servo*, that is / Christ as a solid in his member as a hollow or shell, both things being the image of God; which can only be perfectly when the member is in all things conformed to Christ. This too best brings out the nature of the man himself, as the lettering on a sail or device upon a flag are best seen when it fills" (S, 195). The great sacrifice penetrates each human life "according to the measure of Christ's bounty." His *pleroma* from within fills out all creation, completing the "creature dear O where it fails" (P34).

Nowhere is this completive action more evident, Hopkins knew, than in the sacrificial death of Christ's saints, as the *Martyrdom of Polycarp* strikingly confirms: "For the fire, shaping itself into the form of an arch ('a hollow or shell'), like the sail of a ship when filled with the wind, encompassed as by a circle the body of the martyr" (*Polycarp* 15). The body achieves its "arch-inscape" of full being when it surrenders to seeming extinction, descending in order to ascend. At death the center opens and draws home: "For they [the martyrs] kept before their view escape from that fire which is eternal and never shall be quenched, and looked forward with the eyes of their heart to those good things which are laid up for such as endure; things 'which ear hath not heard, nor eye seen, neither have entered into the heart of man,' but were revealed by the Lord to them, inasmuch as they were no longer men, but had already become angels" (*Polycarp* 2). "The member is in all things conformed to Christ" when, like St. Paul and countless other "captives," he shares the Easter presence of the ascended Jesus through the dereliction of his cross. "Those holy martyrs of Christ, at the very time when they suffered such torments, were absent from the body, or rather, the Lord then stood by them, and communed with them" (*Polycarp* 2). The martyrs epitomize the whole Christian experience in re-enacting the great sacrifice; "Christ lived in Margaret Clitheroe" and in St. Winefred and the five drowned Franciscan nuns:

> Loathed for a love men knew in them,
> Banned by the land of their birth.   (P28, 21)

"Just like Jesus crucified," these women were victims willingly offered in self-immolation; in fact, their visible identity with the Lamb impelled men to refuse them and to cause the ruin which the martyr-master crowned with glory.

Descended in man through baptism and the Eucharist and already "ascended to the heights" in his own person, Christ lives men's temporal existence in the presence of his Father; they are even now hidden with him above where he fills all creation. For "above" is not spatial direction (even the medieval author of the *Cloud of Unknowing* makes this point) but intentional reality that includes the subconscious depth of man and the surface of his world. In the words of the seventeenth-century poet George Herbert, a favorite of Hopkins's:

> Musick and light attend our head,
> All things unto our flesh are kinde
> In their descent and being; to our minde
> In their ascent and cause.[13]

For "Man"—the title of the poem from which these lines are quoted—creation exists in another dimension, descending to him in physical service and in creaturely expectation of love and driving the mind forward and up to its mark in Christ. Matthew Arnold observed: "It is this which made the fortune of Christianity,—its gladness, not its sorrow; not its assigning the spiritual world to Christ, and the material world to the devil, but its drawing from the spiritual world a source of joy so abundant that it ran over upon the material world and transfigured it."[14]

And the miracle for Hopkins, as for St. Paul, was that the universe was different, transformed with new light—not by their doing: the miracle had already taken place. "The justice that is of faith says: 'Do not say in thy heart, Who shall ascend into heaven?' (as if to bring Christ down); 'or Who shall descend into the abyss?' (as if to bring back Christ from the dead). Rather Scripture tells us: 'The word is near at hand, it is on thy lips and in thy heart,' that is, the word of faith, which we preach" (Rom. 10:6-8; adapted). That faith, Paul explains, is the confession that Jesus is "Lord," voiced on the lips and the belief that God raised him from the dead, held fast in the heart (Rom. 10:9). The risen life is rooted in daily experience, in a deep-felt faith waiting to be uttered outright. "Whether at once, as once at a crash Paul, / Or as Austin, a lingering-out swéet skill" (P28, 10), the hero of Calvary makes mercy in all and will be adored as King.

Martyrs and saints, men and women of heroic faith, make up the vanguard of those who have won the trophy of Christ's eternal presence. From heaven they now watch over and rally the remaining contenders: "With such a cloud of witnesses over us," St. Paul exclaims, "let us run with endurance in the race set before us; looking with eyes fixed on the author and finisher of faith, Jesus, who, for the joy set before him, endured a cross, despising shame, and sits at the right hand of the throne of God" (Heb. 12:1-2; adapted). "Not to have faith," Hopkins told Bridges, "is worse than to have sinned deeply, for it is like not being even in the running" (L1, 69). And the poet exhorted the "Handsome Heart": "O on that path you pace / Run all your race, O brace sterner that strain!" (P47). "Running inscape" stretches toward its goal.

3

The Person of Christ
in the Synoptic Gospels

IN John Henry Newman, "the Father" who received him into the Church and with whom he stayed during the crucial seven months before deciding his vocation, the young Hopkins found a man of the kind of sanctity and scholarship he emulated. Above all he saw in Newman a deeply beautiful priest, one in whom nature and grace, culture and discipline, suffering and peace, fused in a personal, intimate union with Christ. In his later years friends and colleagues recognized this as the cardinal's most impressive endowment, the presence of intense spiritual reality fleshed in modest speech and gesture: "The Christ-ed beauty of [his] mind / [His] mould of features mated well" (P145). His sermons and patristic studies testify to his firm grasp of the Christian *kerygma* in the person of Jesus: God made manifest in the humanity of his Son. Constantly Newman stresses the oneness of the Word-made-flesh in eternity and time, and especially in his relationship to man. The Lord of the Gospels is the Son of God and Son of man: "He who spoke was one really existing Person, and He, that one living and almighty Son, both God and man, was the brightness of God's glory and His Power, and wrought what His Father willed, and was in the Father and the Father in Him, not only in heaven, but on earth."[1]

The view of Jesus presented in Newman and in Hopkins needs to be emphasized, for it is not as obvious or simple as it first seems. In defending the divinity of Christ against the reformers, the champions of the Counter-Reformation created in the popular mind and in their theological speculations a vacuum where the humanity of Jesus should have been. This humanity, of course, was not denied; it was either ignored or treated as a fixed quantity known only to men in its exterior accidents. As long as the faithful believed that Christ was God they were safe from heresy and capable of resolving any mystery or problem by the direct retort: "Because He was God." Newman diagnosed this sickness a century ago:

> It would be no very difficult matter, I suspect, to perplex
> the faith of a great many persons who believe themselves
> to be orthodox, and indeed are so, according to their
> light. They have been accustomed to call Christ God,
> but that is all,—they have not considered what is meant
> by applying that title to One who was really man, and
> from the vague way in which they use it, they would be
> in no small danger, if assailed by a subtle disputant,
> of being robbed of the sacred truth in its substance even
> if they kept it in name. In truth, until we contemplate
> our Lord and Saviour, God and man, as being as complete
> and entire in His personality as we show ourselves to be
> to each other,—as one and the same in all His various
> and contrary attributes, "the same yesterday, today,
> and for ever," we are using words which profit not.[2]

For many, even the religious quest for perfection had become a mechanical marshaling of acquired virtues only thinly attached to "the imitation of Christ." Dom Columba Marmion's works on the role of Christ in man's spiritual growth rose in the first quarter of this century as solitary witnesses to the forgotten heritage of the New Testament preaching.

Hopkins's approach to Christ in his sermons is remarkably fresh and searching. "If we learn no more from a Gospel or a sermon on the Gospel than to know our Lord Jesus Christ better, to be prouder of him, and to love him more we learn enough and we learn a precious lesson" (S, 17). Certainly he owed some of this christological sense to Newman and to his Oxford experiences, but his insights into the mystery of the humanity of

Jesus show a sensitivity unmatched in his time. Contemporary Christology is only now beginning to explore the questions of Christ's growing consciousness of himself, of the nature of his tragedy in personal failure and disappointment, and of the historic implications of his role as cosmic Lord and man for others. These three themes are all found in Hopkins's writings and he treats them with his usual love of exegetical detail and spirited lyricism. His description of the healing of Jairus's daughter, for example, employs drama, poetic style, and even a descrepancy in the synoptic accounts, to re-create the Gospel scene and to show Christ's readiness to "breed and nurse" men's faith in him.

Hopkins's sermon at Bedford Leigh (1879) on "Our Lord Jesus Christ" was also intended to lead his listeners to acknowledge Christ as their "hero, a hero all the world wants." The sermon is built on a carefully structured ascent from the Lord's humanity to his divine nature, never allowing the division, however, to intrude on or confuse the hearer's response to the historical Jesus as the object of one's faith. Christ's human nature—his body, mind, and character—composes the main subject of the sermon and leads up to the magnificent conclusion. The peroration, which repeats the phrase "Glory to" seventeen times, begins: "And this man whose picture I have tried to draw for you, brethren, is your God. He was your maker in time past; hereafter he will be your judge. Make him your hero now" (S, 38). Such rhetoric and rhythm, cadence and stress, had not been heard in English pulpits since John Donne held his congregations spellbound in St. Paul's. Beneath the baroque eloquence, the poet's sound Christology operates: Jesus, the God-Man, is maker and judge, Alpha and Omega; knowledge of him is each man's purpose in life. "Take some time to think of him; praise him in your hearts."

Despite his gifts of expression and insight, the poet met with little success in the pulpit.[3] He lacked the physical stature, voice, and presence of a great preacher; and the audience he needed to stimulate him to reach the heights was only at rare intervals to be found in the pews. On one occasion what he took for tears turned out to be his audience's sweat wiped away with a flurry of handkerchiefs (S, 81). Nor did his superiors provide him with the stability and familiarity that grow between priest and congregation; between 1877 and 1881 he served in six different parishes. Nevertheless, his short stay at Bedford Leigh from October to December of 1879 brought him happiness and resulted in some of his best sermons. Of these the sermon entitled "Our Lord Jesus Christ" is rightly considered his masterpiece; here matter and manner did suit perfectly to his audience. Unfortunately, he was to preach it again at Liverpool and be sadly disappointed when it failed to impress his listeners there (S, 5).

The person of Jesus who is drawn in this sermon is dramatically and theologically alive. From the Middle Ages onward, theologians, following the opinion of St. Thomas Aquinas, unfortunately tended to argue that Jesus already possessed the Beatific Vision in his earthly existence. His human mind gazed continually on the Triune God. No perfection, the Scholastics reasoned, could be lacking to Christ's human nature; therefore he enjoyed in his lifetime what his followers would experience in heaven. Naturally, no growth in ordinary knowledge would be possible for such a man; psychic and moral development in Jesus was out of the question for nineteenth-century dogmatists. Only recently has this long-held view been challenged openly and rejected by Catholic scholars of dogma and of the Bible. In marked contrast with thinkers of his time, Hopkins warns his listeners:

> You must not say, Christ needed no such thing as genius; his wisdom came from heaven, for he was God. To say so is to speak like the heretic Apollinaris, who said that Christ had indeed a human body but no soul, he needed no mind and soul, for his godhead, the Word of God, that stood for mind and soul in him. No, but Christ was perfect man and must have mind as well as body and that mind was, no question, of the rarest excellence and beauty; it was genius. As Christ lived and breathed and moved in a true and not a phantom human body and in that laboured, suffered, was crucified, died, and was buried; as he merited by acts of his human will; so he

reasoned and planned and invented by acts of his own human genius, genius made perfect by wisdom of its own, not the divine wisdom only. (S, 36-37)

"Genius," the capacity of the mind and heart for gnosis, original and creative energy for being-as-thought, plays an important role in the poet's mythmaking. He identifies it as a special possession of poets and with honest self-evaluation must have considered it a grace and perfection he possessed himself. This genius was a singular sharing in Christ's own human mind, for not only was Jesus "the greatest genius that ever lived," he is the model and source of each man's own intellectual growth. This distinguishing "beauty and perfection in the mind" must be "taught and trained . . . for without training genius is imperfect" (S, 36). Jesus's own advancement in learning and wisdom is the interior and secret school of every man's education in gnosis: "And Jesus advanced in wisdom and age and grace before God and men" (Luke 2:52).

Because Christ, in Hopkins's view, must choose freely and act according to his own lights and conscience, his life is tragic. All his actions are not a set piece practiced out and memorized beforehand and then played upon a stage of make-believe. The crucifixion, Hopkins saw, was not a Passover plot hatched by Jesus, his disciples, or his heavenly Father, but a calamity which the Nazarene gradually realized was inevitable because of the increasing failure of his mission. Still Jesus struggled against accepting defeat before finally yielding in resignation to the evil event. In a sermon explaining "The Two Paracletes," Hopkins observed: "Christ lived but a short time and in one place. He came as mortal man, in some seventy years therefore he must at any rate have died and in fact his enemies made an end of him long before that time" (S, 97-98). His end came suddenly, tragically cutting him off from the accomplishment he hoped for and planned. In his notes on "The Kingdom of Christ," Hopkins showed his insight into the frustrations and failure of Jesus: "And he had all his plans ready, matured during his hidden life, and adapted for every case. As it was, we see that only baptism of his sacraments was instituted at leisure before his death; the Eucharist was like hurried forward, forestalled perhaps by the suddenness of that event; the others, which he had always meant to institute, were put off till after he rose again" (S, 161-62). Christ had looked forward to success, but it was not to be achieved during his lifetime. Hopkins summed up his point of view in a moving account to Canon Dixon in 1886:

> Above all Christ our Lord: his career was cut short and, whereas he would have wished to succeed by success— for it is insane to lay yourself out for failure, prudence is the fruit of the cardinal virtues, and he was the most prudent of men—nevertheless he was doomed to succeed by failure; his plans were baffled, his hopes dashed, and his work was done by being broken off undone. However much he understood all this he found it an intolerable grief to submit to it. He left the example: it is very strengthening, but except in that sense it is not consoling. (L2, 137-38)

This beautiful passage not only offers a key to knowing the inner meaning of Jesus, but helps explain Hopkins himself in his quest to be an *alter-Christus*.

"The sower went out to sow his seed" (Luke 8:5). Speaking on this parable, the priest declared of Christ: "A few words dropped by him spread into theology, which is yet growing" (S, 34). Each event in Christ's life is a mystery, the seed containing all other mysteries, for the seed is himself. Because he is human, the events of his life, his preaching and miracles, are inherently mysterious: they reveal a man unlike all others in his claims for himself, in the death he undergoes and his return from the grave. He represents a beginning and process in time that is eternal, a presence that is visibly divine. In his notes on John Donne's sermons, Samuel Coleridge graphically describes the sacramental nature of Christ's life:

> As the sacrament of the Eucharist is the epiphany for as many as receive it in faith, so the crucifixion, resurrection, and ascension of Christ himself in the flesh, were the

epiphanies, the sacramental acts and *phaenomena* of the
Deus patiens, the visible words of the invisible Word
that was in the beginning, symbols in time and historic
fact of the redemptive functions, passions, and proce-
dures of the Lamb crucified from the foundation of the
world;—the incarnation, cross, and passion,—in short,
the whole life of Christ in the flesh, dwelling a man among
men, being essential and substantive parts of the process,
the total of which they represented.[4]

As a symbol renders the real intelligible and complete, so the
whole life of Christ in the flesh, seen as one moment and sense-
image, bodies forth the idea of God. Stripped of self, Jesus is
what God is, the Self of all selves. The events of his life manifest
definitively God's attitude toward the world and his actions in
man's behalf. The events are dramatic, articulate, and unique;
their message is love. Man now views that life retrospectively, as
the first followers of Christ had to recast it in their memories,
through the experience of his resurrection and exaltation. The
historical Jesus is forever transfigured by faith. Hopkins explained to Bridges in 1883:

> Christ is in every sense God and in every sense man,
> and the interest is in the locked and inseparable combi-
> nation, or rather it is in the person in whom the combination
> has its place. Therefore we speak of the events of Christ's
> life as the mystery of the Nativity, the mystery of the
> Crucifixion and so on of a host; the mystery being always
> the same, that the child in the manger is God, the culprit
> on the gallows God, and so on. Otherwise birth and death
> are not mysteries, nor is it any great mystery that a just
> man should be crucified, but that God should fascinates—
> with the interest of awe, of pity, of shame, of every
> harrowing feeling. (L1, 188)

In his meditations on the events of our Lord's life, his baptism,
temptation in the desert, his preaching, miracles, and death, the
Jesuit poet probed with psychological, as well as theological,
penetration to the interior and cosmic depth of Jesus of Nazareth.

In each scene he carefully reconstructs the persons and setting, as St. Ignatius had recommended in the *Spiritual Exercises*, and then goes on to interpret these in an original inscaping of the order and meaning of their history and their relevance to himself and to the universe. These events in time relate to all reality, from the fall of Satan to the Second Coming of Christ. The center and heart to which the man of prayer draws home is his eternal King and universal Lord. Consider one example, Hopkins's note on "Christ tempted in the wilderness," dated March 2, 1884:

> He was led by the spirit into the wilderness. Pray to be
> guided by the Holy Ghost in everything. Consider that
> he was now led to be tempted and the field and arena of
> the struggle was a wilderness, where the struggle would
> be intenser but not perhaps more really perilous—to a
> fallen man, as Satan might suppose him to be. Here
> admire our Lord in this struggle and his servants St.
> Anthony, St. Cuthbert, and others. (S, 255)

The meditation is made on the temptation scene that acts as prelude in the synoptic Gospels to the public ministry of Jesus. As presented by Hopkins, however, the scene also echoes "the barren wilderness outside of God" where the Son first offers himself in sacrifice to the Father (S, 197). Satan is pictured here as a true adversary; and the meeting in time recalls his aeonic fall when he refused to acknowledge the God-Man as the head of creation. The reference to the desert fathers completes the frame or circumference of Christ's action by including "lambs who followed him the Lamb" into the desert of the great sacrifice. Alpha and Omega, Jesus continues "the same forever." Finally, Christ's struggle "yesterday and today" is a real, endangering testing and trial; the hero enters the empty arena alone for an intense and perilous encounter. He is a cosmic paradigm for all men to follow, "a hero all the world wants."

The life of Jesus is most perfectly followed by those who choose to enter the religious life and take the three vows of poverty, chastity, and obedience that link them more closely to the Master. Two days after taking vows on September 8, 1870,

Hopkins wrote his mother: "I have bound myself to our Lord for ever to be poor, chaste, and obedient like Him and it delights me to think of it" (L3, 113). Jesus led a life of real, not pretended, poverty, one in which, during his period of preaching, he was absolutely dependent for food and shelter. He willingly placed himself at the mercy of others: "The Son of Man has not come to be served but to serve, and to give his life as a ransom for many" (Matt. 20:28). His followers are expected to share the same treatment: "If anyone wishes to come after me, let him deny himself, and take up his cross, and follow me. For he who would save his life will lose it; but he who loses his life for my sake will find it" (Matt. 16:24-25). The *kenosis* of the Philippians epistle, therefore, is repeated in the synoptic teachings of Jesus. Here too the motive is the same: obedience to the Father, sealed by a threefold offering in the repeated prayer at Gethsemane: "Not my will, but your will be done" (Matt. 26:39-44; Mark 14:36-41; Luke 22:42). For Hopkins, Christ learned to be obedient, and his "saying *yes*" to God was a vital union or instressing of his will with the divine will, an act that undid the cosmic *non serviam* of Lucifer and Adam. The Son was not an automaton mechanically responding to remote commands from heaven, but a man faced with the same destiny and the same hard decisions as other men.

With masterful insight, Hopkins at one point applies to Jesus the "Principle and Foundation" of the *Exercises*. This opening passage of St. Ignatius's work has too often been presented in Jesuit spirituality as an abstract philosophical consideration with little connection to revelation in Christ. The text of the *Exercises* begins: "Man was created to praise, reverence and serve God, and by so doing to save his soul. And the other things on the face of the earth were created for man's sake and to help him in the carrying out of the end for which he was created" (S, 122). Hopkins noted: "Say the man Christ was created to praise etc and so to save his soul, that is / enter into his glory. And the other things as in his train" (S, 257). The poet here sees the historical Lord as the firstborn of creation who leads the way back to God through his own praise and service. For Hopkins,

Christ stands on this side of time, with man in history, one with
the world he made and redeemed. He is "the man for others," in
Dietrich Bonhoeffer's salient phrase. The incarnation is a salvific
event: "All that happens in Christendom and so in the whole
world affected, marked, as a great seal, and like any other historical event, and in fact more than any other event, by the Incarnation; at any rate by Christ's life and death, whom we by
faith hold to be God made man" (S, 263). Human lives are
"marked, as a great seal," with the inscape of Christ. Each then is
meant to be, in George Herbert's term, a "Mark-man," whose
"words and works and fashion too" are "all of a piece, and all
are cleare and straight" ("Constancie"). Men must aim to be like
Christ because he was first like them.

Jesus in the synoptic Gospels is his disciples' servant and master, their hero and friend. Their relationship with him compresses
the history of man's encounter with Christ. Hopkins's devotion
to and interest in each of the apostles offer a remarkable example
of his concrete awareness of the literal accounts and his eager-
ness to penetrate inner character and motive. In a sermon to his
fellow seminarians at St. Beuno's in 1877, he retold with drama
and wit the dilemma confronting Andrew and "timid Philip"
when Jesus proposed to feed the multitude with five loaves and
two fishes. Unfortunately, as he noted, "people laughed at it
prodigiously, I saw some of them roll on their chairs with laugh-
ter" (S, 233). He had succeeded too well in catching the wonder-
ful absurdity of the situation and the subsequent effort of the
crowd to crown Christ king: "Much, much more might be said,
for the meaning of the Scripture, like this very bread, grows and
multiplies as you deal it out. But we will leave the multitude
there, orderly strewn on the fresh green grass, enjoying the
heavenly festival under Christ's eyes, then rising with hasty un-
taught zeal to make Him king" (S, 232). Saints Paul and Peter
were, of course, favorite subjects for preaching and meditation;
and the First Epistle of St. Peter, because of its emphasis on
Christ's preexistence, his Old Testament theophanies, and harrowing of hell, was one of the poet's chief sources. John the Evangelist, James, Thomas, Nathanael, Matthew, John the Baptist,

and Joseph, the foster father of Jesus, are each seen as individuals caught up in the human circumstances of the Lord's mysterious life in their midst. Mary, his mother, plays out her part with dignity and loving understanding of her Son.

The individual involvement of the first disciples with Jesus is the measure and meaning of each man's encounter with him before and since that time. These original followers are Christ's emissaries to men, bearing through history the reality of his personal message. On their behalf the Master raised this joyful hymn of praise and thanksgiving:

> In that very hour he rejoiced in the Holy Spirit and said,
> "I praise you, Father, Lord of heaven and earth, that
> you have hidden these things from the wise and prudent,
> and have revealed them to little ones. Yes, Father, for
> such was your good pleasure. All things have been
> delivered to me by my Father; and no one knows who the
> Son is except the Father, and who the Father is except
> the Son, and him to whom the Son chooses to reveal him."
> (Luke 10:21-22; adapted)

All gnosis of the Father comes through and from the Son; it is hidden "from the wise and prudent" and made plain to those who accept the Son in simplicity and faith, like the disciples. Jesus is the Pantocrator in whose hands all creation rests and by whom all hearts are weighed. This hymn is the synoptic equivalent of the Pauline *pleroma*: Christ, the unique revelation of the godhead, extends this knowledge, which is also himself, to the least and lowest with whom he has become one in the fellowship of poverty and suffering. This sharing union has been made possible through his death and rising again; for Christ in glory is not removed from men, but linked now more closely than was ever possible in his earthly existence. This theme is a recurring one in the Jesuit poet's writings.

In his sermons and poetry, Hopkins insisted on the intimacy of divine life, its saturation of everyday living. Through his passion and resurrection, Christ enters the whole field of man's interests and concerns. He first calls to men before they call to

him; he cuts across space and time to address each one: "Christ
called to us from his cross more than we call to him there. We
call to him for comfort, but long ago he said: Come unto me.
Long before John or Edward, Margaret or Elisabeth ever said /
I love our Lord Jesus Christ / he said / I love John, I love Edward,
I love Margaret, I love Elisabeth" (S, 49). As he called his first
followers in love, he summons each and all. Through the power
of his risen existence he is everywhere present within creation
and, most intimately, within the hearts of those who acknowledge
him as Lord. His presence is joyous and he rejoices in men: "Are
they handsome, healthy, strong, ableminded, witty, successful,
brave, truthful, pure, just? He admires them more than they can,
more than they *justly* can, themselves, for he made all these
things, beauty, health, strength, and the rest" (S, 49). This intimacy with Christ, which is "foredrawn" by his desire to be as
one with all as each will allow, is characteristic of the person of
Jesus as Hopkins envisioned him in sermon and song. "If we do
well he smiles, he claps his hands over us; he is interested in our
undertakings, he does not always grant them success, but he is
more interested in them than we are" (S, 49). Compare this sermon with his verse:

> There he bides in bliss
> Now, and séeing somewhére some mán do all that man
>   can do,
> For love he leans forth, needs his neck must fall on, kiss,
> And cry 'O Christ-done-deed! So God-made-flesh does too:
> Were I come o'er again' cries Christ 'it should be this.'
>
> (P63)

> Christ minds: Christ's interest, what to avow or amend
>   There, éyes them, heart wánts, care haúnts, foot fóllows
>   kínd,
> Their ránsom, théir rescue, ánd first, fást, last fríend.
>
> (P40)

Hopkins concluded the homily we have been quoting: "We must
then take an interest in Christ, because he first took an interest in
us; *rejoice in him because he has first rejoiced in us.*"

Christ living in a man whom he has made just and perfect transforms his every human endeavor. Nothing is merely "natural" about such a man's activities or concerns; he has become a new creature in the risen presence which he believes in and knows to be true. For the just man death itself has already begun to pass away and his life of glory is already dawning. In the spirited conclusion of his instructions on "The Principle or Foundation," Hopkins appealed to the least of his listeners to begin to live the greatness that is theirs:

> When a man is in God's grace and free from mortal sin,
> then everything that he does, so long as there is no sin
> in it, gives God glory and what does not give him glory
> has some, however little, sin in it. It is not only prayer
> that gives God glory but work. Smiting on an anvil,
> sawing a beam, whitewashing a wall, driving horses,
> sweeping, scouring, everything gives God some glory if
> being in his grace you do it as your duty. To go to com-
> munion worthily gives God great glory, but to take food
> in thankfulness and temperance gives him glory too.
> To lift up the hands in prayer gives God glory, but a man
> with a dungfork in his hand, a woman with a sloppail,
> give him glory too. He is so great that all things give him
> glory if you mean they should. So then, my brethren,
> live. (S, 240-41)

Nothing a man in grace does remains indifferent; his deeds may be still shadowed by sin, but within him shines the victory Christ has won over darkness. Not-being has no power over such a man: even his sweaty toil is one with the divine stress that created and works in the universe. If the world is charged with God's grandeur, much more is the creature for whom he died and rose again. One of the most memorable of the agrapha or noncanonical sayings of Jesus asserts: "Jesus said, 'I am the light which is over all of them; I am the All; the All has gone out from me and the All has reached me. Take up the stone and there you will find me; cleave the wood and there I am.' "[5] Nature is panchristic in its millionfold cycles and motions; material things act out their being-in-Christ. All the more are the actions of human nature, united to the All in grace, Christocentric in going out and reaching back in endless movement. In Sonship, in the place of the carpenter who fashioned the cosmos, man's strenuous day labor of rock-lifting and wood-splitting lays bare the inner zone or inscape where lies the solar heart of Being. The glory of God is a living man stooped with a dungfork or a woman bowed over a slop pail. The kingdom of heaven was meant, as Hopkins saw, for the ill-used workers of Liverpool and Glasgow, "without dignity, knowledge, comforts, delight, or hopes in the midst of plenty" (L1, 28). Christ came and comes again for the likes of these. Little wonder that "Communist" Hopkins's stay at the prestigious and wealthy Farm Street Church—a feather in any Jesuit's cap—was short-lived and unsuccessful.

Following the Ignatian ideal of humility in the image of the rejected and crucified Lord, the poet took the road from Jerusalem to Emmaus where the true and "greater glory of God" awaited him. The theme of "glory," which is an important one for Hopkins, always retains for him its biblical richness of meaning. In the Old Testament the word expressed the Shekinah, the shining presence of God seen on Sinai and over the ark.[6] In the New Testament it is the fiery light of God visible in the risen Jesus and already glimpsed in his lifetime in the incident of his transfiguration: "He led them up a high mountain by themselves, and was transfigured before them. And his face shone as the sun, and his garments became white as snow" (Matt. 17:1-2). The glorious hour that is to be his forever shines through the features of the historical God-Man. The concept is a central one as well in the Pauline and Johannine writings where it describes the bright radiance of the "Lord of glory" (1 Cor. 2:8).

One of the major trends in modern Catholic theology has been the fresh emphasis placed on Christ's resurrection, not as a stale proof or afterthought in the divine plan, but as the dynamic source of the world's rebirth in the Son's newness of life. The first disciples primarily considered themselves to be "witnesses of the resurrection" and their earliest preaching as recorded in the Acts of the Apostles centered on the risen "Lord." Hopkins's meditation on the "preciousness of our Lord's body, born of the Blessed Virgin of David's line, crucified, raised from the dead, seated in heaven; united to Christ's soul; united to the Word" indicates the integrity of his theological vision. Further, he considers "its mystery; it binds the Church into one, bodily into one. It is the pledge and means of our immortality" (S, 256). The risen body of Jesus adored among men is the continuity and contacting point of God's dealing with them in creation and atonement. This body, received in the Sacrifice of the mass, is the bridge and stem of stress between God and man, between man and his world. In his sermon on "Our Lord Jesus Christ," Hopkins bid his listeners:

> I leave it to you, brethren, then to picture him, in whom
> the fulness of the godhead dwelt bodily, in his bearing
> how majestic, how strong and yet how lovely and lissome
> in his limbs, in his look how earnest, grave but kind.
> In his Passion all this strength was spent, this lissomness
> crippled, this beauty wrecked, this majesty beaten down.
> But now it is more than all restored, and for myself I
> make no secret I look forward with eager desire to seeing
> the matchless beauty of Christ's body in the heavenly
> light. (S, 36)

Because he lives on in his glorified manhood, Jesus is worshipped as God. As H. P. Liddon said: "He reveals himself as the living centre, from which the higher life radiates throughout regenerate humanity."[7]

Christ's stress of being stored up by his death and his return to life is released or funneled to man through the historical event of Pentecost. The descent of the Holy Spirit on the apostles marked the entrance of the fullness of Being into the universe, spreading out from that upper room in Jerusalem to all directions from the beginning to the end of time. Christ sends his own Spirit to create his personal risen glory in each man; since he died for all, then all men everywhere and in every age can know his saving action and confess: "Over again I feel thy finger and find thee" (P28, 1). Now the hand remakes, and the result is more than elevation; it is translation into the kingdom of the Son. So Liddon defined it: "A resurrection is a transfer from one state to another. It is a passage from the darkness of the tomb to the sunshine of the upper air."[8]

Nowhere is Hopkins's grasp of the essential *kerygma* more apparent than in his handling of the person and role of the Holy Spirit. In his sermons and meditations the Spirit of Christ is a dynamic and transfiguring love at work in the universe and within human history. The Spirit channels out the stress and energy which have been gathered and foredrawn in Christ through his victorious cross. Hopkins always treated the two together, the Holy Spirit and Christ, and in his original manner calls them both Paracletes in several of his sermons. He promised his audience: "I shall shew why Christ as a Paraclete would not do alone, why it was better for him to go and another Paraclete to come, why Christ's struggle with the world taken by itself looked like a failure when the Holy Ghost's struggling with the world is a success" (S, 70).

The poet employed the biblical sense of the word *"spiritus"* as "breath" or life-force to explain the nature and role of the Holy Ghost: "As the breath is drawn from the boundless air into the lungs and from the lungs again is breathed out and melts into the boundless air so the Spirit of God was poured out from the infinite God upon Christ's human nature and by Christ, who said: Receive the Holy Ghost: as my Father sent me so I send you / , was breathed into his Apostles and by degrees into the millions of his Church, till the new heavens and new earth will at last be filled with it" (S, 98). The *pleroma* then is dispensed by Jesus from his risen body through the Holy Spirit; the first faithful breathed in this life and in turn dispensed it to others. Each one's faith is the faith of those who have believed before him. Every man is to be filled, none is overlooked, "for the Spirit, we read, searches all things, even the depths of God: if the Holy Spirit searches the infinite riches of the godhead it is but little for his subtlety to search every corner of the world" (S, 98). All that was asunder and isolated the multifarious Spirit unites, making the many One, turning darkness to light, raising nothingness to "godworthiness." "The Holy Ghost then is, as I may say, a spirit of multitude and can spread and scatter his being and breath and be where Christ, being but one and like but one, cannot" (S, 98). Christ is one, his Spirit one-making. The multiple tongues of fire are really one flame, lit by a single spark, the heart of Christ, "our hearts' charity's hearth's fire."

The peroration of the sermon on the Holy Ghost preached at Liverpool in 1881 is one of Hopkins's great prose passages and provides an eloquent summary of the new covenant history. I quote it in full:

> Christ came into this world to glorify God his Father; the Holy Ghost came to glorify Christ. Christ made God known by appearing in human shape, the Word took flesh and dwelt amongst us; the Holy Ghost makes Christ known by living in his Church, he makes his temple in Christian hearts and dwells within us. Christ glorified the Father by his death and resurrection, the Holy Ghost glorifies Christ by the persecutions and triumphs of the Catholic Church. Christ was himself but one and lived and died but once; but the Holy Ghost makes of every Christian another Christ, an AfterChrist; lives a million lives in every age; is the courage of the martyrs, the wisdom of the doctors, the purity of the virgins; is breathed into each at baptism, may be quenched by sin in one soul, but then is kindled in another; passes like a restless breath from heart to heart and is the spirit and the life of all the Church: what the soul is to the human body that, St. Austin says, the Holy Ghost is to the Church Catholic, Christ's body mystical. If the Holy Ghost is our spirit and our life, if he is our universal soul, no wonder, my brethren, no wonder he is our Paraclete, to lead us and to lift us and to fire us to all holiness and good, a Paraclete in a way too that Christ alone could never be. On this great mystery no time is left to dwell: I leave it for your thoughts to ponder. (S, 99-100)

In his meditation notes and commentaries on the *Exercises*, Hopkins throws further light on the place of the Pentecostal mystery in his myth. As Christ "was led by the spirit into the wilderness," the priest prayed "to be guided by the Holy Ghost in everything" (S, 255). Writing on the finale of the *Exercises*, "The Contemplation for Obtaining Love," Hopkins correctly saw it in terms of our Lord's ascension and the gift of the Holy Spirit ten days later. His interpretation has been missed, unfortunately, by many other commentators and retreat masters who tend to detach this meditation from its context in a christological, kerygmatic setting. Hopkins states that "it is the contemplation of the Holy Ghost sent to us through creatures" (S, 195). The purpose of this concluding meditation is to experience love of the Son for his Father as this love is shown in all reality: "Observe then it is on love and the Holy Ghost is called Love ('Fons vivus, ignis, *caritas*') . . . and the Holy Ghost as he is the bond and mutual love of Father and Son, so of God and man" (S, 195). The quest for unity is itself from God; the desire to seek him is the urge of his Holy Spirit in men's hearts. All men share the same Spirit and the work of the Spirit in each is the same: to raise up Jesus in glory.

The whole of salvation economy, as Newman observes, "in all its parts is ever in us all at once." God is no more dead or an abstract transcendent deity than Being was unreal to Parmenides. He is man in time, man for others, man in love. Newman goes on to say: "Christ Himself vouchsafes to repeat in each of us in figure and mystery all that he did and suffered in the flesh. He is formed in us, born in us, suffers in us, rises again in us, lives in us; and this not by a succession of events, but all at once: for He comes to us as a Spirit, all dying, all rising again, all living."[9] The world of nature is transfigured through Christ in man, just as it was ruined through man in Adam.

For the new creature the cosmos everywhere radiates Christ by means of "the living fountainhead, fire and love" of the Holy Spirit. Hopkins concludes the notes: "All things therefore are charged with love, are charged with God and if we know how to touch them give off sparks and take fire, yield drops and flow, ring and tell of him" (S, 195). "And if we know . . .": gnosis is the secret. One must read the mystery with the mind and heart and suffer its emptiness to be filled with its joy. " 'Did not the

Christ have to suffer these things before entering into his glory?' " Jesus asked of his disciples on the way to Emmaus. "And beginning then with Moses and with all the Prophets, he interpreted to them in all the Scriptures the things referring to himself" (Luke 24:26-27).

4
The Word
of St. John

READERS of *The Wreck of the Deutschland* will sympathize with Goethe's Faust when in his study he puzzled over the opening lines of St. John's Gospel, at a loss to translate *logos*: "Here I am balked at once! Who'll set me straight?" Hopkins, who was fascinated by the "Word" and by words, studied the nature of *logos* in Greek and biblical sources, noted the many derivatives of individual words, and theorized painstakingly over the nature of language itself. The poet found in St. John's prologue the focus of his search for verbal and real meaning and discovered there the solution he needed. The inquiry was philosophical and theological, but we would make the mistake Faust was guilty of if we abstract the "Word" of John, and of Hopkins after him, from the person of Jesus of Nazareth. With his passion for exegesis Hopkins must have explored every nuance of this central text of the apostolic witness to the good news. Two evident sources for study were open to him, the scriptural background and the Hellenic.

Saint John, who is the only New Testament author to use the title "Word" of Jesus, begins the first strophe of his hymn to Christ with the opening phrase of Genesis:

> In the beginning was the Word,
> and the Word was with God;
> and the Word was God.
> He was in the beginning with God.

> All things were made through him,
> and without him was made
> nothing that has been made.

The Greek *en arche* of the Septuagint here announces the new creation and dispensation which not only parallel the old but are contemporaneous with it. The Greek phrase also conveys both the beginning of time and the heart of the cosmos; in the origin and depth of the godhead and of the universe the Word already existed. Then the creating word was spoken: "God said, 'Let there be light' and there was light" (Gen. 1:3). God's Word is being: he speaks and it *is*. For God's Word is God. This same Word, according to St. John, is the man Jesus who said to his challengers: "Before Abraham came to be, I AM" (John 8:58).[1] Even before creation was summoned into being, the Lord whom men accept and acknowledge through faith had known a mysterious, divine preexistence. In the fullness of time he not only brings word of God, he is that Word himself. On earth he shows men the way back to life, by being the Way and the Life: "I am the Beginning, I who speak to you" (John 8:25).

Into the silent void outside God, the Word descends to fill it from his abundance with the horn of his plenteous being. The cycle of descent and return, a favorite of Hopkins and the Evangelist, is associated with the generating word in Isaiah 55:10-11: "And as the rain and snow come down from heaven and return no more until they soak the earth, and water it, and make it spring, and give seed to the sower and bread to the eater; so shall my word be, which shall go forth from my mouth: it shall not return to me empty, but it shall do whatever I please, and shall prosper in the things for which I sent it" (adapted). An ever-renewing spiral of stress is the inscape of the Word's presence in the world.

The primary biblical source for the Johannine *logos* is found in the Wisdom Literature of the Old Testament where the heavenly *sophos* is pictured as preexistent and creative, establishing the design and pattern of the universe and revealing to man the hidden purposes of God. Of many poetic passages, one example must suffice. The cosmic vision of Parmenides is not far from this soliloquy of wisdom from Proverbs 8:22-30:

> The Lord possessed me in the beginning of his ways,
> before he made anything from the beginning. I was set
> up from eternity, and of old before the earth was made.
> The depths were not as yet, and I was already conceived,
> neither had the fountains of waters as yet sprung out.
> The mountains with their huge bulk had not as yet been
> established: before the hills I was brought forth. He had
> not yet made the earth, nor the rivers, nor the poles of
> the world. When he prepared the heavens, I was present:
> when with a certain law and compass he enclosed the
> depths, when he established the sky above, and poised the
> fountains of waters, when he compassed the sea with its
> bounds, and set a law to the waters that they should not
> pass their limits: when he balanced the foundations of
> the earth; I was with him forming all things.

As elsewhere in scripture, the act of creation is seen here not as the conceptual *creatio ex nihilo* of the Scholastic tradition, but as a shaping of circular form out of chaos, a forging of light from darkness, a continuous energizing and ordering of the concrete universe. Like the master of cosmogonic poetry John Milton, the Jesuit poet looked at the world with biblical eyes and heart. In *Paradise Lost*, the Word is pictured as the architect who with "golden compasses" (an emblem and homomorph of Alpha) circumscribed

> This universe, and all created things:
> One foot he centered, and the other turned
> Round through the vast profundity obscure,
> And said, "Thus far extend, thus far thy bounds,
> This be thy just circumference, O World!"[2]
>
> (7. ll. 227-31)

Retracing the hand of the incarnate Logos in nature, Hopkins studied how "to turn the compass on the all-starr'd sky" (P102), in hopes of discovering its primordial design.

Finally, the scriptural Word of God has a summoning power not only in creating the world but in changing men's hearts. The word comes to individual prophets, calls them and sends them forth to deliver its message to others. It is uttered in time and works in sacred history by aiming men in a new direction and purpose or by turning them back to the promises made in past covenants between God and his people. Always the word operates through chosen representatives or prophets who sacrifice personal comfort and status to serve the community at large. Success is never their lot, and John the Baptist, the last of the heroic line, appears in St. John's prologue as the final, doomed witness to the coming Lord: "He who comes after me has been set over me, because he existed before me" (John 1:15; adapted). John testifies to the mystery of Jesus as preexistent and risen Word-made-flesh.

The Hellenic roots of the *logos* were first of all known to Hopkins from his study of the pre-Socratic philosophers. For Heraclitus the *logos* frames and orders the cosmos which is otherwise flowing and formless, a river never the same. He wrote of the *logos*: "Though men associate with it most closely, yet they are separate from it, and those things which they encounter daily seem to them strange"; and again: "Although the *logos* is universal, the majority live as if they had understanding peculiar to themselves."[3] The Word's intimacy and men's estrangement are important Johannine themes which Hopkins would have appreciated in the earlier Greek writer. "When you have listened, not to me but to the *logos*," Heraclitus wrote, "it is wise to agree that all things are one."[4] Parmenides also called his "Way of Truth" "a trustworthy *logos* and thought concerning the truth." The Stoics regarded the *logos* as the principle of reason which permeates and controls reality; they personify it to the point of making *logos* a cosmic deity. To Marcus Aurelius, for example, the *logos spermatikos* is the seminal All in whom the whole cycle of becoming is reabsorbed after once issuing through the consciousness of men. The best known enunciator of the *logos* theory, however, was the Jewish philosopher Philo who wedded both Greek and Hebrew traditions in conceiving a *logos* which is the pattern of the human soul, the instrument of creation, and the intermediary between God and man. Despite superficial similarities to the Word of St. John, Philo's *logos* seems to be an impersonal and abstract force utterly removed from the human and historic person of the prologue.

In his use of the Wisdom Literature, Hopkins emphasized the identification of the divine *sophos* with the mental activity and transtemporal role of the God-Man. In one of his meditation notes, he refers to the first antiphon before Christmas, which translated reads: "O Wisdom, you came forth from the mouth of the Most High, and reaching from beginning to end, you ordered all things mightily and sweetly. Come and teach us the way of prudence." He observes, "Personally wisdom is Christ our Lord, as applied in this antiphon" (S, 257), and then goes on to apply the prayer, the first of the so-called "Great O Antiphons," to "God the Holy Ghost as the spirit of wisdom" and to the Virgin Mary. "Christ our Lord's wisdom, the divine wisdom which dwelt in him, the human wisdom and genius which were his as man" (S, 89) forms a favorite subject for his sermons. Hopkins insisted on the human side of Christ's wisdom and genius and on both wisdoms together in the same person. From the beginning the one incarnate being has been active in the universe on its behalf, molding it in his creative mind. For him to think is to be and to cause all else to be.

The Word, for Hopkins, expresses God and the world; his face is turned to both; gazing on the Father, his look is fixed on man. Christ first inscapes mankind before they inscape him; he is their aim and mark because he already holds each one fast in his loving sight. Through the whole of reality the one Word speaks the reality that is himself: "God's utterance of himself in himself is God the Word, outside himself is this world. This world then is word, expression, news of God" (S, 129). His presence, however, is not the amorphous, pantheistic dilution imagined by the Stoics, but an immanence in which he remains always what he is now: "The *Word* but really made flesh. . . . His presence is a reality though invisible," for "though God gives us His Word and Image, the Word and Image has with it the divine substance" (S, 194). The Word of St. John is both God and man, creator and creature.

In his copy of the *Exercises*, Hopkins copied out a spurious Welsh text on "The Roll of Tradition and Chronology" which purported to be an ancient account of a pre-Christian "announcement of the Divine Name." The account begins:

> God, in vocalising his NAME said "⁊ [I AM], and with the Word, all worlds and animations sprang co-instantaneously to being and life from their non-existence: shouting in extacy [*sic*] of joy, "⁊ [I AM] and thus repeating the name of the DEITY. Still and small was that melodiously sounding voice, (i.e. the Divine utterance) which will never be equalled again until God shall renovate every pre-existence from the mortality entailed on it by sin, by re-vocalising that name, from the primary utterance of which emanated all lays and melodies, whether of the voice or of stringed instruments; and also all the joys, extacies, beings, vitalities, felicities, origins, and descents appertaining to existence and animation. (S, 354)

God first speaks his name, I AM, for he is Being, and this Being is the Word. This Word which each creature then chants is its own inner being: "Heaven and earth are word of, worded by" the Word I AM, the "Ground of being, and granite of it: past all / Grasp God" (P28, 29, 32). In addition, the inner rhythm and rhyme of words are resonances of the things themselves, heightened in the mind which, instressing Christ's own mind, returns all nature to him. Inscape in things becomes inscaped language lifted back to Christ.[5] The man in grace is the man fully in nature, who listens and speaks, and his words mark the center of the cosmos, Being himself. Just as "every word may be considered as the contraction or coinciding-point of its definitions" (J, 125), so the incarnate Logos contracts in himself all meaning and defines all other human beings as "*logoi*," derivatives of himself.

The words of the new man, then, seek fresh rhythm and "scope" in song. For Jesus himself is "the New Song, the manifestation of the Word that was in the beginning, and before the beginning," according to Clement of Alexandria. "This Word, then, the Christ, the cause of both our being at first (for He was in God) and of our well-being, this very Word has now appeared as man, He alone being both, both God and man—the Author of all blessings to us; by whom we, being taught to live well, are sent on our way to life eternal" (*Protrepticus* 1). The same scriptural note is struck by Hopkins in one of his early poems:

> He hath put a new song in my mouth,
> The words are old, the purport new,
> And taught my lips to quote this word
> That I shall live, I shall not die.   (P8)

Christ, the New Song, like Orpheus calls creation into tuneful being, harmonizes reality anew in fallen man, and sounds the deathless strain of the risen life: "Behold the might of the new song: It has made men out of stones, men out of beasts. Those, moreover, that were as dead, not being partakers of the true life, have come to life again, simply by becoming listeners to this song. It also composed the universe into melodious order, and tuned the discord of the elements to harmonious arrangement, so that the whole world might become harmony" (*Protrepticus* 1). Similarly, Thomas Carlyle, another Victorian student of the Word, wrote: "Our highest Orpheus walked in Judea, eighteen-hundred years ago: his sphere-melody, flowing in wild native tones, took captive the ravished souls of men; and, being of a truth sphere-melody, still flows and sounds, though now with thousandfold accompaniments, and rich symphonies, through all our hearts; and modulates, and divinely leads them."[6]

One begins to see why Walter Pater's observation, "All art approaches the condition of music," has such import for its age and for understanding Hopkins. Musical theory and composition, which so absorbed the poet's creative talents, lie not on the surface of his interests but spring from the recesses of his inventive Christology. Music was for him the inner ontology of the Orphic Word who tunes the universe and strings the heart of man, his instrument of praise and modulation: "I counted in a bright rainbow two, perhaps three / complete octaves, that is / three, perhaps four / strikings of the keynote or nethermost red, counting from the outermost red rim" (J, 237). Mounted in a drop of Christ's blood, new heaven hymns the new earth, "an ark for the listener" under a rainbow of concord. Through its arc of color the keynote of inscape sounds.

Sonnet 57 presents an excellent illustration of creation's harmonious unity in the *pleroma* of the Word. The octave and sestet operate not on two independent levels of reality, but fold in a "single sonnet-like inscape" of oneness:

> As kingfishers catch fire, dragonflies draw flame;
>> As tumbled over rim in roundy wells
>> Stones ring; like each tucked string tells, each hung bell's
> Bow swung finds tongue to fling out broad its name;
> Each mortal thing does one thing and the same:
>> Deals out that being indoors each one dwells;
>> Selves—goes itself; *myself* it speaks and spells,
> Crying *What I do is me: for that I came.*
>
> I say more: the just man justices;
>> Keeps gráce: thát keeps all his goings graces;
> Acts in God's eye what in God's eye he is—
>> Chríst. For Christ plays in ten thousand places,
> Lovely in limbs, and lovely in eyes not his
>> To the Father through the features of men's faces.

Here the twofold role of the Johannine Word toward his universe, as creator and as redeemer, becomes one being-thought in the mind and heart of man who is fulfilled in a perfect circle of response. The objects named, the person naming, and the word as "the expression, *uttering* of the idea in the mind," all unite, fleshed in sound, spiritualized in meaning. Poetry then is incarnational, a descent into the silence and an ascent of a living body of sound "to existence and animation." The Spirit of Christ, as at Pentecost, pours out a universal language known to all who hear it. The poet himself functions as an "AfterChrist" who words the cosmos with ever-renewing creativity. Shakespeare so describes him in *A Midsummer Night's Dream*:

> The poet's eye, in a fine frenzy rolling,
> Doth glance from heaven to earth, from earth to heaven;
> And as imagination bodies forth
> The forms of things unknown, the poet's pen
> Turns them to shapes, and gives to airy nothing
> A local habitation and a name.   (act 5, sc. 1, ll. 12-17)[7]

Each poem is a microcosm of the whole visible and invisible frame, and the more intensely unified its word texture, approximating the vast complexity of the universe, the more perfect the inscape of the one Christ in multifarious reality.

An important christological distinction was made by Hopkins in his interpretation of St. John's statement: "The Word was made flesh, and dwelt among us" (John 1:14). He found two moments of the divine design to create all things in Christ in the two phrases of the verse: The Word 1) was made flesh, and 2) dwelt among us as man. He wrote: "Incarnation then, ἐνσάρκωσις, is not the same thing as ἐνανθρώπευσις" (S, 171). The division also appears, as we saw, in his analysis of Philippians 2:7-8; Christ first "emptied himself" by assuming the *forma servi* toward creation from its initial moment of existence, and then became man born of Mary in Bethlehem. The "being-made-flesh" in the original covenant and the "becoming man" in the new both describe Christ's activities not in eternity but in time; they unify salvation history in Jesus. "In his entrance into creation, his incarnation proper" at the beginning of time (S, 181), Christ set aside the riches of godhead and made himself obedient in the service of his Father, as recorded in the verses from Proverbs quoted earlier in this chapter.

Before being focused in one man, the Word appeared in the likeness of men. According to Hopkins, the incarnation is already assumed in Genesis: "In this Christ *deambulabat ad auram post meridiem*, which seems to describe a ranging in the spirit through a world of his own. So that man lived at first rather in Christ and his mother, who came afterwards to live among men" (S, 171). When Adam and Eve "heard the voice of the Lord God walking in paradise at the afternoon air," they heard Christ the Word.

All God's dealings with man in the Old Testament are through his Son; every divine encounter is an experience of him. When Hopkins pictured himself as wrestling with God, he had in mind Jacob's struggle with Christ in the appearance of an angel. Thus he writes: "I suppose Melchisedech to be a theophany of Christ in human shape out of this pre-human being of his and to differ from other theophanies in that when Christ appeared as an angel he might be 'installed' or 'steaded' in some real and personal angel, as St Michael or St Gabriel, and this was their dignity to be vessels of Christ, but that there was no man Melchisedech, no such person but in person Christ" (S, 171). These speculations on the Christic theophanies, which have a basis in the New Testament practice of finding types of the Lord in Scripture, were developed extensively by the early fathers of the church and by traditional Christian art up through the Middle Ages. In numerous cupolas and tympanums Christ presides over a myriad of Old and New Testament scenes from Genesis to the Last Judgment. The mosaics depicting the creation of the world in St. Marks at Venice, for example, which were completed between 1100 and 1275, show a youthful Christ at work in each of the six days. In Christian poetry and art, often it is our Lord who directs Noah to build his ark, who visits Abraham, and reveals to Moses the Ten Commandments and his secret name "I AM." In the words of Samuel Coleridge: "Christ as the Logos Θεάνθρωπος was the Jehovah of the Old Testament."[8]

The prologue of St. John, together with the texts of the Pauline epistles mentioned in chapter 2, provided the reason and reality for Hopkins's view of these theophanies (Coleridge calls them "Epiphanies") of the Word-made-flesh before his birth in time. Only one way, truth, and life, exists for everyone, and as man Christ gratuitously places himself at the service of all. A favorite Johannine theme which develops this idea is the title of "light" (phos) for Jesus. The term recalls the Shekinah of the old covenant, the divine presence in the pillar of fire, and the candles of the Feast of the Tabernacles. This light shone in the features of Jesus from the beginning, and the powers of darkness have never mastered it. In his Bampton lecture on St. John, H. P. Liddon explained: "Light is not merely the sphere in which He dwells: He is His own sphere of existence; He is Himself Light, and in Him is no darkness at all."[9] Primarily, the light intended by St. John is the sun, shining on all, generating and feeding life, illuminating the eye from within and without. Jesus is the new and original sunlight risen from the grave and enlightening the mind of everyone who enters the world. This title he claims himself: " 'I am the light of the world. He who follows me does not walk in the darkness, but will have the light of life' " (John 8:12). In his First Epistle John applies this light to the inner life as the sign of the Christian: "The darkness has passed away and the true light is now shining. He who says that he is in the light, and hates his brother, is in the darkness still. He who loves his brother abides in the light, and for him there is no stumbling" (1 John 2:8-10). In the heavenly Jerusalem the source of illumination will be the Lamb himself: "And the nations shall walk by the light thereof; and the kings of the earth shall bring their glory and honor . . . for there shall be no night" (Apoc. 21:24-25).

Hopkins once admitted: "I have . . . a considerable belief in the Solar myth" (L3, 263). Christ, the sunlight of the world, is a dominant and pervasive subject of his mythmaking. Taking his writings as a whole, one would venture to say that in his viewpoint the sun is Christ univocally and is never for him a merely natural phenomenon. An important statement on the theme is found in his sermon at Bedford Leigh on "Walking in the day." He asks his congregation: "What is the sun that makes that day? —It is no other than our Lord Jesus Christ," and he then quotes John 1:4-5: " 'In him was life and the life was the light of men and the light shone in darkness and the darkness did not take it in' " (S, 40). In his frequent references to sunlight in his journal, these eventful epiphanies of each day, dawn and sunset, with the attendant clouds and earth, are biblical revelations of the Word shining on the heart of the beholder. For each object to be seen in its fullness, it must be stressed by the sun's energy and being. Following Plato, the Victorian poet pictured the sun as the cause of vision in the eye and an image of the goodness which bestows truth and reality to the soul (Republic 6. 508).

A random selection from Hopkins's journal shows how the sun acts as a focus and cleave that releases the risen "Son" to the eye and heart of the watcher: "I saw the wholeness of the sky and the sun like its ace" (J, 154); "The sun lit up the bright acres of the snows at first with pink but afterwards clear white" (J, 171); "Very beautiful sunset; first I think crisscross yellow flosses, then a graceful level shell of streamers spreading from the sundown" (J, 224); "Two beautiful sights: printed upon the sun, a glowing silver piece, came out the sharp visible leafage of invisible trees, on either side nothing whatever could be seen of them, and these leaves handful for handful, changed as I walked; the other was splays of shadow-spokes struck out from any knot of leaves or boughs where the sun was / like timbers across the thick air" (J, 239). Here nature and man, through the catalyst of language, are transfused with a light that is physical, mental, and spiritual all and at once, without, however, exteriorly drawing our attention to this union, for the inscape is the concrete Christ-event. The sun acts as a transfiguring mark from which stress flows and to which it returns. Out of the kenotic emptiness it creates a *pleroma* of new being, whole and individuating. In an unpublished passage from his "Notes on the history of Greek Philosophy" (1868), Hopkins observed:

> The figure shewing how the Idea can be one though it exists in many is that of the sun in broken water, where the sun's face being once crossed by the ripples each one carries an image down with it as its own sun; and these images are always mounting the ripples and trying to fall back into one again. We must therefore think that wherever we see many things having one idea that they all are falling back or wd. fall back but are held away by their conditions, and those philosophers have very truly said everything is becoming. (D12, 1)

The variable world, fragmented into prisms of light, strains to return to the one Light, whose face is reflected in time; "it is old earth's groping towards the steep / Heaven whom she childs us by" (P149). Everything is becoming and becoming is Christic.

Creation is a son of God, as St. Athanasius declared, made in the image of the only-begotten Son:[10]

> Wording it how but by him that present and past,
> Heaven and earth are word of, worded by?   (P28, 29)

The Word is texture and substance of the words of the diaries and journal. The fallen and transfigured world, for Hopkins, is the only nature he knows. To draw all things back to Christ, as a crossbow strains to propel its arrow, the poet inscaped and worded what he saw and understood. These personal entries on natural phenomena were for his own reading and recollection; therefore he seldom has to tell himself the method he is following. When he indicates on occasion that he knows our Lord in nature, we should not conclude that these are isolated instances. Observation is continually "flushed" with light that suffuses and renews the universe where the crucified and risen king reigns and shines in glory. All things circle, like the windhover, kingfisher, and dragonfly; like the ashboughs that "new-nestle at heaven most high," all turn around a burning center, take flame from it, and draw home there in loving surrender to the Alpha and Omega of their being. "The sun" all life "from death ha[s] won" (P23).

In addition to the Johannine teachings on Jesus as the Word, Hopkins also found in the Gospel of St. John the source for his view of the sacrifice and glory of Christ as a "lifting up" to another kind of existence. The central text here occurs in Jesus' last appeal to the Jewish people when he exclaims: " 'Now is the judgment of the world; now will the prince of the world be cast out. And I, if I be lifted up from the earth, will draw all things to myself.' Now he said this signifying by what death he was to die" (John 12:31-33). A moment before, the Father speaks from heaven for the first and only time in the fourth Gospel: " 'I have both glorified [your name] and I will glorify it again' " (John 12:28). This scene, as Rudolf Bultmann has noted, contains several parallels to the synoptic narratives of Christ's transfiguration "on a high mountain." It also echoes their account of his agony in the garden: "Now my soul is troubled. And what shall I say?" (John 12:27). Both the transfiguration and agony, missing in

John's version, are brilliantly summed up in the verb "lifted up" which describes the death Jesus is about to die and his exaltation above the earth. His "name" will then be glorified as promised by his Father, the sacred name spoken to Moses and now revealed in the flesh: "Jesus therefore said to them: 'When you have lifted up the Son of Man, then you will know that I AM, and that of myself I do nothing: but as the Father has taught me, I speak these things'" (John 8:28; adapted). As we saw in the hymn in Philippians, Christ empties himself and dies in obedience: therefore God has exalted him so that all creation will acclaim Jesus Christ as "Lord." Jesus is the foredrawn purpose of creation and the drawing energy of history; his cosmic person and role form the heart of Hopkins's myth. In John's words: " 'No one can come to me unless the Father who sent me draw him, and I will raise him up on the last day'" (John 6:44). Christ by his great sacrifice is become the crucified center at which all lives aim, knowingly or not:

> . . .—Hither then, last or first,
> To hero of Calvary, Christ's feet—
> Never ask if meaning it, wanting it, warned of it—men go.
> (P28, 8)

Through the centrifugal force of creation all reality whirls out from Christ and through the centripetal action of atonement all hurls back to him again.

The climax of the fourth Gospel occurs on the hill of Golgotha to which the whole of Jesus' being has been inexorably drawn, his hour of trial and triumph. John offers his own solemn witness to the truth of a striking aspect of that death: "One of the soldiers opened his side with a lance, and immediately there came out blood and water. And he who saw it has borne witness, and his witness is true; and he knows that he tells the truth, that you also may believe" (John 19:34-35). In the First Epistle of St. John, the incident is recalled and its meaning developed:

> This is he who came in water and in blood, Jesus Christ;
> not in the water only, but in the water and in the blood.
> And it is the Spirit that bears witness that Christ is

> the truth. For there are three that bear witness in heaven:
> the Father, the Word, and the Holy Spirit; and these three
> are one. And there are three that bear witness on earth:
> the Spirit, and the water, and the blood; and these three
> are one. (1 John 5:6-8)

Despite the Vulgate's unfounded reference to the Trinity—the reading known to Catholics in Hopkins's day—this passage clearly connects the death and resurrection of Jesus with the new life poured out in baptism and in the gift of the Holy Spirit. The water and blood were subsequently interpreted by the church fathers as signs of baptism and the Eucharist, the two sacraments which create and sustain Christ's being in man and which, as Hopkins noted (S, 161-62), were instituted by Christ himself during his lifetime.

The eschatological water streaming from the right side of the temple, described in chapter 47 of Ezechiel, was also identified by the fathers with the living water issuing from the temple of Christ's body, a theme already implied in St. John: "He who believes in me, as the Scripture says, 'From within him there shall flow rivers of living water.' He said this, however, of the Spirit whom they who believed in him were to receive; for the Spirit had not yet been given, since Jesus had not yet been glorified" (John 7:38-39). This water from within Jesus is eternal life: "And he showed me a river of the water of life, clear as crystal, coming forth from the throne of God and of the Lamb" (Apoc. 22:1). For the church fathers, the historical counterpart of the heavenly river is the Jordan, where John the Baptist pointed out the Lamb of God and knew him in the baptismal descent of the Holy Spirit. "This river runs forever," Hopkins reflected in his notes on the baptism of Jesus (S, 268); it is joined by all the rivers of the globe, reminding man of the outrushing presence of Christ's forgiving and renewing grace: "Laus Deo—the river today and yesterday" (J, 200). Of all elements, water is most clearly Christic: "The strong unfailing flow of the water," Hopkins wrote of St. Winefred's well, "took hold of my mind with wonder . . . , the sensible thing so naturally and gracefully uttering the spiritual reason of its being" (J, 261). Water, like light, becomes a new reality in his myth.

In *The Wreck of the Deutschland* the poet describes the pierced side of Christ releasing "the stress felt" throughout the cosmos and history, a stress that "rides time like riding a river." The redeeming Lord created and sustains all things with the word of his power. The poet adds, however, that in perceiving this *mysterium Christi* "the faithful waver, the faithless fable and miss." Critics and readers have themselves sometimes fabled and missed the meaning of this crucial section of the poem. Using "stress" as the governing noun in stanzas 6, 7, and 8 (the pronoun "it" appears six times in reference to "stress"), Hopkins traces the source of divine presence in creation through two stanzas that move from nature and man to Jesus' life on earth and that reach a climactic exclamation in the third: "Only the heart, being hard at bay, / Is out with it!" Christ's heart is the burl of being in which all infinite, possible pressure of love and causality is pent up and which, suddenly pierced, discharges through the cleave in his side the whole active, redeemed universe.

This redemptive act in time includes and repeats the initial fiat of Genesis. By retrieving the world from nothingness and filling it with light and life, Christ acts in his own person in the one great sacrifice. Only his heart discovers the ever-present origin and end of existence by its total corporeal *kenosis*, now reenacted in the Sacrifice of the mass. The devotion to the Sacred and eucharistic Heart of Jesus is not a periphery adjunct of the poet's growth in gnosis, but the literal heart of his myth of creation and redemption as one experiential reality for man. Through this wound, the Father's love is freely given to each and is hopefully returned by all. For, when the lance struck its mark on the Son's lifeless body, it revealed the inscape from which love and being issue and to which they both verge.

Hopkins's sermon on the Sacred Heart is pertinent in the context of John's witness to the open side of Christ. One of his most accomplished—although unfinished[11]—prose pieces, it contains a number of echoes of his poetry. The most significant of these helps clarify stanzas 7 and 8 of his ode: "The Sacred Heart is that heart which swelled when Christ rejoiced in spirit and sank when he was sad, which played its dark and sacred part in all Christ's life, in all he did and suffered, which in his Agony with frightful and unnatural straining forced its blood out on him in the shape of teeming sweat, and after it had ceased to beat was pierced and spent its contents by the opening in his side" (S, 103). The cosmic nature of this struggle may be implied from Hopkins's note on the sacrificial role of Christ as *forma servi* in creation: "It is as if the blissful agony or stress of selving in God had forced out drops of sweat or blood, which drops were the world" (S, 197). And again: "Suppose God showed us in a vision the whole world inclosed first in a drop of water, allowing everything to be seen in its native colours; then the same in a drop of Christ's blood, by which everything whatever was turned scarlet, keeping nevertheless mounted in the scarlet its own colour too" (S, 194). The sun in setting, as Hopkins often noted in his journal, transfigures earth and sky with golden, fiery, "bleeding red" (J, 240; see especially pp. 216 and 260). The solemn witness of Calvary to the blood and water that issued from the lanced heart of Jesus was heard and heeded by the Victorian poet who lashed "with the best or worst / Word last" to speak his own testimony to the truth of its inscape.

In Hopkins's mythopoesis the concentric circles of the universe and the foredrawing center of Christ's passion form a cosmic rose, its native color, "immaculate white," now turned bloodred:

> But what a wild flush on the flakes of it stood
> When the rose ran in crimsonings down the cross-wood!
>
> (P27)

Instress is defined as "the flush and foredrawn" (J, 127) in a literal way, because it is the experience of the blood from Christ's side, the cleave of being. The secret and mystery of this rose are neither shut away in the skies nor uttered in nebulous symbolism, but stand in the fields of spring, ready for sight and praise. Hopkins wrote in his journal for June 16, 1868: "The passage of the roses through the following scale of colours, perhaps from the dryness of the season, most marked—scarlet, blood-colour, crimson, purple, then the red retiring to the shaded or inner part of the petal the outer or coiled part bleaches lilac or greenish" (J, 167). The shades of Passiontide recede into the colors of Easter. From blood red and the purple of mourning the world gradually brightens with primordial white and verdant green once more. Gold, the chromatic medium of glory, already shines through in creation's sharing of the Lord's conquest over not-being and night, the winter world. The journal entry for the same day includes the following description: "Honeysuckle at the hedge on the big bank in bloom, the crests coiled back into a crown, the tongues or spurs curled at heel, the lashes (anthers) giving off all round: this is their time of greatest beauty. They look gold or honey color.— Gold too is the colour of the fringes in the middle of the syringa.—"(J, 166-67). The crown of *Christus Victor* and the tongues of his Holy Spirit are woven and wound into the fabric of reality. Inscape leaps from coiled centers marked in the farthest stars and in the nearest flowers:

> The Pansy at my feet
> Doth the same tale repeat.

Hopkins had found Wordsworth's "visionary gleam." "Where is it now, the glory and the dream?"[12] In the witness to "hero of Calvary," in the things of this world and in his own transparent heart refracting the rainbow colors of the light.

St. John ends the prologue with the firm confession that "we saw his glory—glory as of the only-begotten of the Father—full of grace and of truth" (John 1:14). The divine and human wisdom who created and redeemed mankind had walked in their midst: "I write of what was from the beginning," the Evangelist asserts in opening his First Letter, "what we have heard, what we have seen with our eyes, what we have looked upon and our hands have handled: of the Word of Life" (1 John 1:1). Jesus is not for the few but for all; the listener must in turn become propagandist and fill up his own " 'byfall' of Christ's and of one another's." The prologue concludes: "And of his fullness we have all received, grace for grace" (John 1:16). Jesus who is "full of grace and truth" lifts up man so that he can "tower from the grace to the grace" (P28, 3). The *pleroma*, which occurs only here in the Johannine writings, recalls the Pauline theme treated in chapter 2 of this study. Placed here at the close of the prologue, it sums up John's teaching on the Word-made-man and connects his view of the person of Christ with the apostolic *kerygma*.

Hopkins's analysis of grace in his paper "On Personality, Grace and Free Will" makes use of John's phrase "grace upon grace" to examine the nature of man's consent to the divine activity within him, "clothing its old self for the moment with a gracious and consenting self" (S, 154). This shift from the old self to the new being in Christ, Hopkins defines as grace:

> For grace is any action, activity, on God's part by which,
> in creating or after creating, he carries the creature to or
> towards the end of its being, which is its selfsacrifice
> to God and its salvation. It is, I say, any such activity on
> God's part; so that so far as this action or activity is God's
> it is divine stress, holy spirit, and, as all is done through
> Christ, Christ's spirit; so far as it is action, correspondence,
> on the creature's it is *actio salutaris*; so far as it is looked at
> *in esse quieto* it is Christ in his member on the one side,
> his member in Christ on the other. It is as if a man said:
> That is Christ playing at me and me playing at Christ,
> only that it is no play but truth; That is Christ *being me*
> and me being Christ. (S, 154)

Hopkins's investigation of the existential quality of grace was well ahead of the theological thinking of his time. The placing of the central action in Christ's Spirit roots his mythmaking in biblical reality. Pentecost is the afterseason of the whole Christian experience, and man lives a post-Pentecostal existence. Newman writes: "Once for all He hung upon the cross, and blood and water issued from His pierced side, but by the Spirit's ministration, the blood and water are ever flowing, as though His cross were really set up among us."[13]

Each of the divine persons is implicated in the whole economy of salvation. Hopkins distinguished three stages in God's approach to his creatures by finding three kinds of grace: 1) "creative grace, the grace which destined the victim for the sacrifice, and which belongs to God the Father"; 2) corrective or redeeming grace whose "function is always *ramener à la route*. This then is especially Christ's grace, it is a purifying and a mortifying grace, bringing the victim to the altar and sacrificing it"; and 3) elevating grace which was given at Pentecost and "which fastened men in good. This is especially the grace of the Holy Ghost and is the acceptance and assumption of the victim of the sacrifice" (S, 158). Hopkins found evidence of the three kinds of grace in the Epistle to the Romans, 8:29-30: "For those whom he has foreknown he has also predestined to become conformed to the image of his Son, that he should be the firstborn among many brethren. [1] And these whom he has predestined, them he has also called; [2] and those whom he has called, them he has also justified; [3] and those whom he has justified, them he has also glorified." Of the final Greek word for "glorified," the poet commented: "raised to the state when their deeds should be the doing of God in them" (S, 158). Two further texts from Romans completed his argument on the form of God's "grace and truth" in man: "For I am sure that neither death, nor life, nor angels, nor principalities, nor things present, nor things to come, nor powers, nor height, nor depth, nor any other creature will be able to separate us from the love of God, which is in Christ Jesus our Lord" (Rom. 8:38-39). The second passage deals with the Jewish people: "Now if their offense is the riches of the world, and their decline the riches of the Gentiles, how much more their full number" (Rom. 11:12). Hopkins underlined the final Greek word of this verse: *pleroma*.

St. John's statement "And of his fullness we have all received, grace upon grace" is supported, then, in Hopkins's interpretation, by St. Paul's Epistle to the Romans. Even the unbelieving Israelites will return to the full fold of the chosen people to form the *pleroma* of Christ all-in-all. Although "he came unto his own, and his own received him not" (John 1:11), their final conversion will be "life from the dead," an affirmation of the resurrection (Rom. 11:15). At various times in his life, Hopkins too expected large-scale conversions in England and throughout the world as

a prelude to the restoration of mankind in its maker and Lord.
Jesus is at work changing men's hearts and bringing each to full
stature, for this is the nature of his peculiar grace: "corrective,
turning the will from one direction or pitting into another, like
the needle through an arc, determining its choice (I mean / stimulating that determination, which it still leaves free): this touches
the elective will or the power of election and is especially the
grace of the mature mind" (S, 158). Christ is the magnetic pole
and axis that draws the needle of man's will toward him; he is
the inscape of the questing heart.

Marie Lataste, a French nineteenth-century mystic, is frequently and extensively cited by Hopkins in his spiritual writings. He
shared Patmore's enthusiasm for her; Patmore wrote: "Her life
was all grace and miracle, and her writings full of living sanctity
and vigorous perceptions of things hidden to the wise" (S, 325).
Her words on "Jesus, Light of soul and body" are particularly
Johannine in their moving simplicity and in their witness to the
interior presence of Christ "in spirit and truth" (see S, 335-36).
In her meditation on the annunciation to Mary and her fiat to
the Spirit, "Be it done to me according to your word," Marie
places the following words, which Hopkins underlined as he
copied them, on the lips of Jesus himself: " 'Je suis la grace de
Dieu le Père' " (S, 330). All the complex and static speculations
of last century's textbook theologians on the De Gratia tract are
swept away with this confession of faith and love. Gnosis penetrates to "things hidden to the wise" with "vigorous perception"
and telescopes vast mysteries into plain sentences. For the Word
is ultimate oneness and clarity; through the labyrinth there runs
a single thread: "From the Person of Christ gathered the doctrine
of the Trinity, of the Incarnation, of the Blessed Sacrament. A
few words dropped by him spread into theology, which is yet
growing" (S, 34). George Herbert in his poem on "Aaron," the
perfect type of priest, summed up the poet-priest's ideal:

> Christ is my onely head
> My alone-onely heart and breast,
> My onely musick, striking me ev'n dead,

> That to the old man I may rest,
> And be in him new-drest.

> So, holy in my head,
> Perfect and light in my deare breast,
> My doctrine tun'd by Christ, who is not dead,
> But lives in me while I do rest,
> Come, people; Aaron's drest.[14]

The Christian Hermetic tradition, preserved in the verses of Herbert and, more directly, in the alchemical poems of Henry Vaughan, had set the poetic standard which the orthodox Victorian poet, like Richard Crashaw before him, refined to pure gold in the flame of Christ's evangelic doctrine as taught by the apostolic see of Rome. Indirectly, Hermetism, with its Stoic insistence on the oneness of the cosmos and its Gnostic emphasis on the knowledge of God, reappears in the Platonic strain of Hopkins's mythopoeic thought. In St. John's Gospel, however, where Hermetic similarities are also traceable, Hopkins found the direct source of that truth which "became a fountain of water within, welling up to eternal life" (John 4:14; adapted). What "the bosom friend of the Sacred Heart" had heard in secret he shared freely with all: "And he who sat on the throne said, 'Behold, I make all things new!' And he said, 'Write, for these words are trustworthy and true. . . . I am Alpha and Omega, the beginning and the end. To him who thirsts I will give water without stint from the fountain of the water of life'" (Apoc. 21:5-6; adapted). Here was "the finding and sake / And cipher of suffering Christ," here the "lettering of the lamb's fleece, ruddying of the rose-flake" scored in scarlet in the open wounds "beforetime-taken, dearest prizèd and priced" (P28, 22).

The challenge to Hopkins of preserving the original *evangelion* in its cosmic wholeness had been anticipated by the religious reflections of Samuel Coleridge. With great mastery and insight he wrote:

> Yet if Christianity is to be the religion of the world, if
> Christ be that Logos or Word that *was in the beginning*,
> by whom all things *became*; if it was the same Christ

who said, *Let there be light*; who in and by the creation
commenced that great redemptive process, the history of
life which begins in its detachment from nature, and is
to end in its union with God;—if this be true, so true must
it be that the book of nature and the book of revelation,
with the whole history of man as the intermediate link,
must be the integral and coherent parts of one great work:
and the conclusion is, that a scheme of the Christian faith
which does not arise out of, and shoot its beams downward
into, the scheme of nature, but stands aloof as an insulated
afterthought, must be false or distorted in all its
particulars.[15]

A Christianity that does not make of the material universe a new
Mythus is not true to its origins nor relevant to contemporary
man. A demythologized Jesus who spoke as a wise man but was
not the eternal Wisdom is hardly worthy of allegiance or consideration. The poetry of faith, nevertheless, has become an
appendage; myth and ritual are the excess baggage of modern
man's pilgrimage. "Such a blight has certainly descended on the
Bible and on a great part of the Christian cult," writes Joseph
Campbell. "To bring the images back to life, one has to seek, not
interesting applications to modern affairs, but illuminating hints
from the inspired past. When these are found, vast areas of half-
dead iconography disclose again their permanently human meaning."[16] Like St. John, one must pick up the scroll of God's promises and swallow it whole: " 'Take the scroll and eat it up, and it
will make thy stomach bitter, but in thy mouth it will be sweet
as honey' " (Apoc. 10:9). Hopkins tasted the word's sweetness
and knew its inner bitterness as well, "the being with it, sour or
sweet." But, true to the inspired past, he composed a scheme of
Christianity that bound nature and revelation in one "scroll-
leaved" volume, "the word of it Sacrificed."

5

The Fathers
of the Church

THE renewed scholarly interest in the early fathers of the church, which Newman helped spearhead in Anglican circles over a century ago, is only now taking hold in American Catholic universities and stimulating individual research there. The young Hopkins, however, was an immediate beneficiary—but, as always, with a difference. While Newman studied and translated the ante-Nicene fathers with assiduity and detachment, Hopkins thought and wrote like one of them. His theorizing on the aeonic struggles of the angels and on the prehistoric and patriarchal activities of Christ breathe of the second and third centuries. Perhaps as research into the thought of that earlier period becomes better known through translation and commentary, affinities with our modern view of an expanding cosmos will grow more apparent and Hopkins's own reflections will become of greater value. An attempt can be made here merely to sketch his knowledge of and debt to some of the patristic writers.[1]

Of the apostolic fathers we know that Hopkins admired St. Ignatius of Antioch and held St. Clement of Rome in highest regard (L1, 195). Ignatius has always had a special claim to Jesuit interest since their founder, Inigo of Loyola, took his name as a talisman of his new kind of life after the *metanoia* at Manresa. Of the martyr's seven letters, the one to the Romans is justly the most famous. It contains a resounding statement of the Christian's reliving of the passion and resurrection of Christ. The best known passage, in which he repeats Paul's longing "to be dissolved and to be with Christ," brilliantly associates this idea with the Eucharist: "I am the wheat of God, and let me be ground by the teeth of the wild beasts, that I may be found the pure bread of Christ" (*Romans* 4). Ignatius then asks to be "made a sacrifice to God" through his martyrdom. The Victorian poet's myth of the great sacrifice also terminates in the eucharistic victim who makes himself nothing by physically being eaten. Ignatius writes: "Then shall I truly be a disciple of Christ, when the world shall not see so much as my body." According to Hopkins our Lord would have undergone an earthly *kenosis* even if he had time and opportunity to complete his life's work: "The Eucharistic Sacrifice was the great purpose of his life and his own chosen redemption: perhaps [had he not died a violent death] he would have instituted it and into it have disappeared—as at Emmaus" (S, 162). The presence of Jesus in the bread and wine is inherently ordered and intended for sacrifice. The Sacrament is not a static hiding of the godhead, but a dynamic action of self-giving, a circle and center, for Hopkins, into which all contracts and which still fills all who partake of this body and blood. The great sacrifice is the trajectory and terminus of Christ's life and of every man's, the inscape of gnosis. In the words of Thomas Aquinas's hymn to the Blessed Sacrament, which the poet translated:

> O thou our reminder of Christ crucified,
> Living Bread the life of us for whom he died,
> Lend this life to me then: feed and feast my mind,
> There be thou the sweetness man was meant to find.
>
> (P168)

The vigorous language and imagery of Ignatius's epistle, as well as its emphasis on Christ's reality and his oneness with man, assuredly held a great appeal for Hopkins. How ardent and imaginative he must have found the martyr's renowned avowal of the cross: "My love is crucified, and there is no fire in me desirous of anything; but there is in me a living water springing up and whispering in me inwardly: 'Come to the Father!' " (*Romans* 7). The stirring theme of this epistle, Ignatius's longing to die for Christ, almost certainly inspired Hopkins in his interpretation of the nun's cry in *The Wreck of the Deutschland*. Just as his heroine's confession is a "wording" and "birth of a brain," so the apostolic father had wished to be a "wording" (*logos*) of God in his martyrdom, rather than "mere sound" (*phoné*) by living (*Romans* 2). "The pangs of birth are upon me," he too exclaimed in chapter 6, "Him I seek who died for us; Him I desire who rose again for our sake." According to Hopkins, the nun's experience and shipwreck repeat, verbally and actually, the burden of the early martyr's death. For all martyrdoms are in fact recitals of the Master's.

Both authors, it should be noted, shared a fondness for coining new words. One of Ignatius's most effective is the adjective *axiotheos* (similar to his *theoprepes*), which he often employed in the inscriptions and salutations of his letters. Hopkins's term "godworthiness," which describes the effect of Christ's redemption on man (S, 197), accurately translates the Greek and may have been prompted by his reading of the original texts. Among the other letters, the opening chapter of the *Epistle to the Smyrnaeans* contains two notable images developed by Hopkins. Ignatius declares that Christ was "truly pierced by nails in His human flesh (a Fruit imparting life to us from His most blessed Passion), so that by His resurrection He might set up a beacon for all time to call together His saints and believers, whether Jews or Gentiles, in the one body of His Church."[2] The Lord's flesh is a fruit hanging from the new tree of life, and his risen body is "a beacon, an eternal beam" (P72) signaling all men. The Victorian poet's imagery has its roots in the apostolic age.[3]

Hopkins's esteem for Clement of Rome is attested by his remark to Bridges in which he ranks his writings with the Pauline and the Catholic Epistles (L1, 195). *The Epistle to the Corinthians* eloquently proclaims in its poetic verses the creative and redeeming presence of Christ in the universe:

> This is the way, beloved, in which we find our Saviour
> Jesus Christ, the High Priest of all our offerings, the
> defender and helper of our infirmity. By Him we look up
> to the heights of heaven. By Him we behold, as in a glass,

His immaculate and most excellent visage. By Him are the eyes of our hearts opened. By Him our foolish and darkened understanding blossoms up anew towards His marvelous light. By Him the Lord has willed that we should taste immortal knowledge [gnosis], "who, being the brightness of His majesty, is by so much greater than the angels, as He has by inheritance obtained a more excellent name than they." (*Corinthians* 36; quoting Heb. 1:3-4)

Recalling the Epistle to the Hebrews, Clement "fixes our eyes on Jesus," the risen Lord who acts as mediator or filter through whom all attention and knowledge ascend. The ascent is marked in four stages and a conclusion: each opens with the emphatic *dià toútou*, "He it is through whom. . . ." The four steps correspond to Hopkins's own activity of inscape ("Look" and "see") and of instress ("feel" and "understand"). The first two mark Christ in his cosmos; the second two open "our hearts" and minds. The result is the taste of immortal gnosis, knowledge of Jesus as light and king. Stanza 5 of the *Deutschland* (P28) and "The Starlight Night" (P32) both inscape the sky in this way and instress "Christ home" to the beholder.

Hopkins also would have known the so-called *Second Epistle of St. Clement* which opens with an introduction similar to the first stanza of the *Deutschland*: "We are to think, brethren, of Jesus Christ as of God, that he is the 'judge of the living and dead.' . . ." We owe him praise, "for he had mercy on us and saved us out of pity . . . with no hope of salvation except as comes from Him. For He called us when we were not, and out of nothing willed us to be" (2 *Clem.* 1). One of the most memorable expressions of apostolic Christology appears in chapter 9 of this letter: "If Christ the Lord, who saved us, being spirit at first, became flesh and so called us, so also shall we receive our reward in this flesh." Here the preexistent Christ and man's bodily resurrection, the extreme poles of salvation history and two profound concerns of Hopkins's religious thought, join in an epitome of faith and the theology of hope.

The mythic knot that ties the strands of Hopkins's thoughts

together is, as we have seen, the oneness of redemption with creation, and the resultant coupling of nature and grace. "The first intention of God outside himself" is also his final aim: Christ. The accomplishment of this design in Jesus, the *fons et clausula*, "fountainhead and ending-point" of all reality, has provided poets from Prudentius to Hopkins with a challenging heroic theme. Few writers, however, in poetry or prose have matched the apostolic author of the *Epistle to Diognetus* in wording of the mystery. This anonymous work relies on the insights of St. Paul in its delineation of the divine plan, kept secret in the Son and now made plain. Chapter 7 interprets the cosmic unity of that design:

> God Himself, who is almighty, the Creator of all things, and invisible, has sent from heaven, and placed among men, Him who is the truth, and the holy and incomprehensible Word, and has firmly established Him in their hearts. He did not, as one might have imagined, send to men any servant, or angel, or ruler, or any one of those who bear sway over earthly things, or one of those to whom the government of things in the heavens has been entrusted, but the very Creator and Fashioner of all things— by whom He made the heavens—by whom He enclosed the sea within its proper bounds—whose mystic ordinances all the elements faithfully observe—from whom the sun has received the measure of his daily course to be observed—whom the moon obeys, being commanded to shine in the night, and whom the stars also obey, following the moon in her course; by whom all things have been arranged, and placed within their proper limits, and to whom all are subject—the heavens and the things that are therein, the sea and the things that are therein—fire, air, and the abyss—the things which are in the heights, the things which are in the depths, and the things which lie between. This is the messenger He sent to them.

To redeem the world, God sent the maker of the world; to restore humanity, he gave his Son in whose image man was made. Time and the cosmos are Christic in shape and intent, marked with his character in each particle and in the total frame. Sun, stars, earth, and sea reveal in motion the inscape of their origin and end. The cycles of the seasons and the day are, for Clement of Rome also, proof that Christ the firstfruits and Orient rose to afford his resurrection to mankind.

The first lasting contribution of the postapostolic period to systematic theology was made by St. Irenaeus in his *Adversus Haereses*. His theory of the *recapitulatio* views all history and creation as capsulated in Christ who now fills the universe in turn. In the first man, Adam, all fell; now in the second man all are raised up and seated with Christ in the heights of a new heaven and earth. Irenaeus is the first Christian philosopher of history: Christ comes at the midpoint and center of time and sums up in himself the beginning and end of the world in one *oikonomia* or household of God. Reality is revealed in the incarnate Word alone; both creation and redemption are known only through him who manifests God in nature, in the law and prophets, and finally in his own flesh (4. 6. 6). Against heretical Gnosticism, he asserted that the Son is the sole source of gnosis, for he is the embodiment of knowledge of the Father (4. 6. 1-3). Irenaeus explained Christ's recapitulation in the following celebrated passage from book 3, chapter 16, section 6:

> There is one God the Father, and one Christ Jesus, who came by means of the whole dispensational arrangements connected with Him, and gathered together all things in Himself. But in every respect, too, He is man, the formation of God; and thus He took up man into Himself, the invisible becoming visible, the incomprehensible being made comprehensible, the impassible becoming capable of suffering, and the Word being made man, thus summing up all things in Himself: so that as in super-celestial, spiritual, and invisible things, the Word of God is supreme, so also in things visible and corporeal He might possess the supremacy, and, taking to Himself the pre-eminence, as well as constituting Himself Head of the Church, He might draw all things to Himself at the proper time.

Irenaeus joined the teachings of St. Paul and St. John with the best of Greek thinking to write a synthesis that contains the core of Hopkins's Christology. The Word who existed from the beginning united himself with his own workmanship, was made a man for others: "When He became man, He commenced afresh the long line of human beings, and furnished us, in a brief, comprehensive manner, with salvation; so that what we had lost in Adam —namely, to exist according to the image and likeness of God— that we might recover in Christ Jesus" (3. 18. 1).

The New Testament parables of sowing and harvesting were used by Irenaeus to delineate "the secret hidden from the foundation of the world," Christ the epitome of creation. The Word is the sower who first plowed his field and planted it with seed; he is the same Lord of the harvest who gathers into his barn the corn ripe for reaping. "Since He joined the beginning to the end," writes Irenaeus, "and is the Lord of both, He has finally shown forth the plough, in that the wood has been joined on to the iron, and has thus weeded His land; because the Word, having been firmly united to flesh, and fixed in the way it [the plough] has been, has reclaimed the savage earth" (*Adv. Haer.* 4. 34: 4). Just as wood and iron make the one plow, so the Word and man's human nature are fused in one reality. In "The Windhover" the plow cutting deep into the earth shines with the union of the creature with his maker and redeemer. In becoming man, the Son has been made one with all men; in his great sacrifice he is joined firmly and "fixed" to them in nature and grace. He who shaped man restores him at last, the fresh labor of his hands.

The principle text for Irenaeus's theory of the recapitulation is found in Ephesians 1:9-10: God "in the fullness of time has purposed to resume all things in Christ, both those in the heavens and those on the earth" (adapted). Tertullian, after quoting these verses in his *De Monogamia*, draws an analogy that plays a major part in our poet's teleological mythmaking:

So, too, the two letters of Greece, the first and the last, the Lord assumes to Himself, as figures of the beginning and end which concur in Himself: so that, just as Alpha

> rolls on till it reaches Omega, and again Omega rolls back
> till it reaches Alpha, in the same way He might show
> that in Himself is both the downward course of the begin-
> ning on to the end, and the backward course of the end
> up to the beginning; so that every economy, ending in Him
> through whom it began,—through the Word of God,
> that is, who was made flesh,—may have an end
> correspondent to its beginning. And so truly in Christ
> are all things recalled to "the beginning." (*De Monogamia* 5)

Among the things brought back into the sphere of their original
integrity—the "economy" of the primordial family—Tertullian
lists faith without circumcision, freedom from dietary laws, marriage without divorce, "and, lastly, the whole man into Paradise,
where he was 'from the beginning.' " But "the second man" bears
a new likeness, better than the first, since his are the features of
the risen firstborn, the true Adam and Messiah: "But again: if
the beginning passes on to the end (as Alpha to Omega), and as
the end passes back to the beginning (as Omega to Alpha), thus
our origin is transferred to Christ, the physical to the spiritual—
inasmuch as 'it is not the spiritual that comes first, but the physical, and then the spiritual.' " Quoting 1 Corinthians 15:46, on
the new man's identity with the risen body of his Lord, Tertullian
here graphically sums up the great cosmic procession from its
first moment in the Son's *kenosis* "downward" to the "backward
course" of creation's return through the reborn believer. The
process is epitomized in the Word-made-flesh, Alpha-Omega in
whom the whole salvific event has been consummated and
achieved in order that it be transmitted to all others, entire in
each. The alphabetic Christ-cross-row offers a hornbook summary of the Hopkins myth.

Like his contemporary Origen, Clement of Alexandria com-
bined a far-reaching concern "for the common salvation of man"
with a deep sense of personal search for truth. This way of gnosis
was an attempt, moreover, not only to learn Jesus but to align
oneself with him so that every thought and deed united the soul
in further identification with its model and maker. True Gnostics

are "those who really know." They must not be confused, according to Clement, with heterodox Gnostics, members of a sect who disputed Christ's two natures, who saw the material universe as sinful, and who secretly practiced immoral and unnatural vices. Jesus is the true gnosis, for he is the Word who enlightens those seeking perfection of mind and character, and he is the object they seek to know (*Strom.* 6. 1). This concept of gnosis is of major significance for our understanding of Hopkins. In the Victorian we find the same overwhelming ambition to choose the hidden path of inquiry and virtue in order to know the person and role of Jesus in the cosmos and in his own life. The ideal of gnosis is to say with St. Paul, "I live now, not I, but Christ lives in me"; through self-denial and study Hopkins pursued this goal as "the dominant of [his] range and state." The Christian Gnostic tradition can be traced back from Clement and Origen through St. Clement of Rome and the *Didache* to the writings of St. Paul and St. John. The Jewish Christian community in Jerusalem originally provided the seedbed for further development by its exclusive adherence to purity of doctrine and life. The Church of Alexandria, as Newman showed in his *Arians of the Fourth Century,* extended the speculative pale while preserving the apostolic teachings intact.

Hopkins would also have discovered in Clement of Alexandria's writings confirmation of his own fascination for the theophanies of Christ in the Old Testament, a topic first developed by Justin Martyr in his *Dialogue with Trypho.*[4] Clement's use of the sun as the ruling force in nature and a reflection of Christ's power over men may also be echoed by the poet, as it was by Milton in the invocation to book 3 of *Paradise Lost.* This impressive analogue is found in Clement's *Protrepticus* or *Exhortation to the Heathen,* chapter 11. The Word is the light that fills the mind, and man is exhorted to sing this hymn of praise:

Hail, O light! For in us, buried in darkness, shut up in the shadow of death, light has shone forth from heaven, purer than the sun, sweeter than life here below. That light is eternal life; and whatever partakes of it lives.

> But night fears the light, and hiding itself in terror, gives
> place to the day of the Lord. Sleepless light is now over
> all, and the west has given credence to the east. For this
> was the end [*telos*] of the new creation. For "the Sun of
> Righteousness," who drives His chariot over all, pervades
> equally all humanity, like "His Father, who makes His
> sun to rise on all men," and distils on them the dew of the
> truth. He has changed sunset into sunrise, and through
> the cross brought death to life; and having wrenched man
> from destruction, He has raised him to the skies, trans-
> planting mortality into immortality, and translating
> earth to heaven.

Here the world of nature and the mythology of the past reach
their fulfillment in the new Sun and Apollo who, risen now, no
longer sets.

The light of the Logos is reason in the mind, directing every
man most intimately to his end and meaning, the *telos* or Omega
of existence. Further, the mind enlightened by Christ's more profound presence through the gift of his own Spirit searches into
mysteries "hidden from the wise and prudent." Hopkins was
well aware, in the path of gnosis he was following, of the dangers
of self-deception which he risked. In his sole mention of Gnosticism, he connects it with ever-zealous inquiry into angelic pedi-
grees or genealogies about which "St Paul discouraged St Timo-
thy from enquiring; St Ignatius the Martyr says that he could if
he chose explain them, and out of them sprang the Gnostic
heresies (in which the place of Sige, silence[,] should be remarked)" (S, 200). Sige, whose name means "Silence," is reported
by Irenaeus to have been a female aeon who, impregnated by
Bythus (Profundity), "gave birth to Nous, who was both similar
and equal to him who had produced him, and was alone capable
of comprehending his father's greatness" (*Adv. Haer.* 1. 1). Later
Irenaeus refutes the existence of such an aeon in the same *pleroma*
with Logos, for silence and speech cannot, any more than darkness and light, exist in the same presence (2. 12. 5). Hopkins perhaps remarked the place of Sige because she is the Gnostic equiv-

alent of Mary, the preexistent virgin mother and instructress in secrets for the spiritually elite. He shunned, of course, any cabalistic recasting of her role. On the other hand, he may be only contrasting occult silence with Christian use of music to proclaim "what ear has not heard."

Origen was Hopkins's chief enthusiasm at Oxford.[5] This prolific and neglected genius was the first to attempt a theological *summa* and the first Christian exegete and commentator to create a method of studying revelation, which he rigorously followed. The Jesuit's retreat notes in Ireland in 1889 when he "had ever so much light on the feast [Epiphany] and the historical interpretation of the gospel," show a speculative and yet detailed approach to prayer that is more typical of Origen than of St. Ignatius of Loyola. The fundamental illumination he records receiving deals not with an affective response to grace, but with the harmony of the gospel accounts and the spiritual truths deduced from this discovery.

The threefold method, developed by Origen from Philo and offered as the key to reading the true depth of Scripture, is Origen's best-known legacy to Western theology and literature. He found three levels of meaning coexisting at once in the inspired text: 1) the historical or literal, 2) the moral or interior, and 3) the anagogical or universal. Each of these levels corresponds to parts of man: his body, soul, and spirit (*De Principiis* 4. 1. 11). The "key to gnosis" is exegesis of the whole divine word. Its literal or bodily sense and its spiritual or divine mystery unite in the body-spirit of the reader who thereby becomes one with the Word-made-man. Only the perfect achieve this high aim; they are the true Gnostics who, guided by the inspiring Spirit, penetrate the inner secrets of the Logos's purposes and his inner meaning for man. Then, in turn, the instructed disciple goes forth to be a teacher of others, beginning with the "body" of Scripture and ascending to the knowledge of the Spirit (4. 1. 14).

Hopkins's pervading concern in both his sermons and personal meditations on the one hand for the exact wording of the biblical text, for the correct punctuation, and for literal agreement between differing versions, and on the other for personal applica-

tion and cosmic understanding, springs from his knowledge of
the method presented in the *De Principiis* rather than from the
allegorical treatment later elaborated in the Middle Ages. This
concern also led the Jesuit poet to plan commentaries on the
works of other authors—the *Spiritual Exercises* (partly completed), Newman's *Grammar of Assent*, St. Patrick's *Confession*
—and to embark on numerous projects on Greek drama and
metrics, Homer and Greek lyric art, all in the nature of scholarly
critique and explication. These ambitious schemes are another
side of the same quest for gnosis:

> Where lies your landmark, seamark, or soul's star?
> There's none but truth can stead you. Christ is truth.
>
> (P157)

Christ was the pilot and polestar of inscape; his truth is to be
found wherever man's reason, *logos*, has followed its natural
course. What Hopkins might have accomplished had he carried
out even some of these proposed interpretations may be measured
by his genius and gift for perceptive expression; certainly, the
exegetic form itself was well suited to his temperament and mind.
The genre also has given Western man some of his most significant books: Origen's *Commentary on the Gospel of St. John* and
On the Canticle of Canticles are two of this author's masterpieces.
And his *Commentary on the Epistle to the Romans* began a tradition that continues to the present day in the works of Karl Barth,
C. H. Dodd, and Stanislas Lyonnet.

Origen is the theologian par excellence of the Logos. His most
important study *On First Principles* (*De Principiis*) opens with a
christological manifesto:

> All who believe and are assured that grace and truth were
> obtained through Jesus Christ, and who know Christ
> to be the truth, according to His own declaration, "I am the
> truth," derive the knowledge [gnosis] which incites men
> to a good and happy life from no other source than from
> the very words and teaching of Christ. And by the words
> of Christ we do not mean those only which He spoke
> when He became man and tabernacled in the flesh; for

before that time, Christ, the Word of God, was in Moses
and the prophets. For without the Word of God, how
could they have been able to prophesy of Christ?

The Logos is the medium through whom God speaks to man
and man answers God. "Christ lived in Margaret Clitheroe,"
wrote the poet of the martyr who was pressed to death in Queen
Elizabeth's reign. How did Christ assert his presence in her? The
poet explains:

> She caught the crying of those Three,
> The Immortals of the eternal ring,
> The Utterer, Utterèd, Uttering,
> And witness in her place would she.   (P145)

Man acknowledges the oneness of the Trinity by a multiplicity of
words and deeds. His Being and man's nothingness are bridged
by special titles given to Christ who, one in himself, is reached
only through a multiple, ordered ascent from within creation's
center, in the human heart and mind. These titles or *epinoiai*
Origen defines as words which are realities of Jesus, who is
"Wisdom," "Power," "Truth," "Shepherd," and a multitude of
other names which are properly his as Son, Man, and Savior. By
acquiring knowledge of these *epinoiai*, Christians climb step by
step toward him who is fullness of being, the Word. The ascent
to truth, one of the great themes of Western literature, is movingly described in the preface to the *Commentary on the Canticle
of Canticles*:

> The soul is moved by heavenly love and longing when,
> having clearly beheld the beauty and fairness of the Word
> of God, it falls deeply in love with His loveliness and receives
> from the Word Himself a certain wound of love. For this
> Word is the image and splendour of the invisible God,
> the First born of all creation, in whom were all things
> created that are in heaven and on earth, seen and unseen
> alike. If, then, a man can so extend his thinking as to ponder
> and consider the beauty and the grace of all the things
> that have been created in the Word, the very charm of

> them will so smite, the grandeur of their brightness will
> so pierce him—that he will suffer from the Word a saving
> wound and will be kindled with the blessed fire of His love.

The terms *inscape* and *instress* breathe through this forceful witness to the grace and beauty of all things created in the Word
who then wounds the beholder's heart "when they once meet."

Origen extended Irenaeus's theory of the *recapitulatio* to embrace a cosmic restoration of all present and possible worlds and
ages in the Word incarnate. The term he employed to describe
this event, *apocatastasis* or "reestablishment," is a technical word
used by Aristotle to define a return to a previous state or condition. Through gnosis men will be led out of the nonbeing of evil
to their predestined goal: fulfillment of the human spirit in holiness and truth. The process stretches across vast areas of space
and time and involves the education of all mankind in the dignity
of their true selves, once theirs, forefeited in Adam, now restored
in the perfected humanity of Jesus. The time will come when
Christ will be all in all and the original man will return the whole
of being to his Father. Ignorance and the corruptible flesh will
reach their final sublimation by slowly dropping away, and the
integrity of creation will turn back to the purity and simplicity
of the divine Logos, all contrasts between good and evil dissolved,
all complexity and contradictions fled: "The mind will no longer
be conscious of anything besides or other than God, but will
think God and see God and hold God and God will be the mode
and measure of its every movement; and in this way God will be
all to it" (*First Prin.* 3. 6. 3).[6] This process is already at work in
individual souls as they grow through successive stages to perfect knowledge and continues after death, "developing in intellectual power, ever approaching the pure and gazing 'face to
face,' if I may so speak, on the causes of things" (2. 11. 7).[7] One
day, the final one, all men will share that vision. The theory of
apocatastasis seems to have acted like a magnet on Hopkins's
imagination; some familiarity with it is essential for understanding the meaning of several of his major poems.

In Origen's writings Hopkins also found the seed or nutriment for another essential notion of his: the nature of the self. This philosophy is most elaborately set out in his notes on the "First Principle and Foundation." The priest observed: "Nothing else in nature comes near this unspeakable stress of pitch, distinctiveness, and selving, this selfbeing of my own" (S, 123). Certainly Scotus's theory of *haecceitas* contributed to the elucidation of his concept, but from his journal entries and essays it is clear that Hopkins had already framed the main points of reference while still a student at Oxford. Origen frequently mentions "the inner man" (*éso ánthropos*), a phrase found in St. Paul and in Clement of Alexandria, but first developed as a theory by the indefatigable exegete. He used the words to describe the deepest recesses of the mind and heart which may be penetrated and transformed by the Spirit of Christ. Hopkins also noted the phrase when quoting Ephesians 3:16-17. Exhorting his listeners, St. Paul prays that the Father may "grant you to be strengthened with might through his Spirit in the inner man, and that Christ may dwell in your hearts through faith." In a gloss, Hopkins explains *éso ánthropos* as "known to God, the man created in Christ as ii 10" (S, 156). Ephesians 2:10, reads: "For his workmanship we are, created in Christ Jesus in good works, which God has made ready beforehand that we may walk in them." This inner man is a hollow or shell in which Christ "as a solid in his member" comes and dwells, a presence "which can only be perfectly when the member is in all things conformed to Christ" (S, 195). Both in his human nature and in his life in Christ man is "the image of God," so that his new existence is not a destruction of the old but a rejuvenation of it. For Origen also the inner man is the image of the Logos stamped there in mind and will by creation and then actualized by the atonement. He states in his *Homily on Genesis* 1. 13: "The man who was made in God's image is the inner man, the incorporeal, incorruptible, immortal one."[8]

For both Origen and Hopkins the first step toward gnosis of God in Christ is knowledge of one's own self-being. The poet's commentary on the "Foundation" is the cornerstone of his Christology. The Delphic axiom "Know thyself" (*gnothe seauton*) becomes the biblical source of the inner man's return to his creator. Among his notes on this first section of the *Exercises* are clear indications that the faculty of individual *logos* or reason, which "takes the measure of things, brings word of them" (S, 174), partakes of the divine Word's own probing of the universe and of man. The descent into the inner self is *kenosis*, the great sacrifice, in accordance to nature itself as "word, expression, news of God" experienced within. Hopkins wrote: "Searching nature I taste *self* but at one tankard, that of my own being" (S, 123). Once a man has thus descended into himself, he finds the secret to be surrendered, losing his life to gain all: "The world, man, should after its own manner give God being in return for the being he has given it or should give him back that being he has given. This is done by the great sacrifice. To contribute then to that sacrifice is the end for which man was made" (S, 129). Of its essence, self-knowledge is a kenotic activity.

Before turning to St. Augustine, two Greek fathers whose ideas are pertinent to the evolution of Hopkins's myth remain to be treated. The work of St. Athanasius would have been known to the poet, if in no other way, through the research and writings of Newman for whom the champion of orthodoxy against the Arians was an epic maker and mentor. Among his studies on the Arian controversies, the cardinal's monograph on the *Causes of the Rise and Successes of Arianism* (1872) presents an analysis of ideas similar to those cherished by the younger scholar. In his chapter on "The Doctrine of the Primogenitus," Newman argues that word and deed with God, according to St. Athanasius, are one act: "When, then, it is said, 'He spoke the Word,' what is meant, is 'He uttered the Logos,' as elsewhere, 'By the Word of the Lord were the heavens made.' "[9] The Son is therefore called the "Hand of God." The Word is "Himself the Divine *Fiat*, the Hypostatic Will and Operation, the Counsel, Idea, Design, Purpose, and Effective Force, the Wisdom and Power, which called up the universe out of nothing" (*Tracts*, p. 201). Here are also reviewed the theophanies of our Lord, "the Divine Presence . . . or Angel who visited Abraham in his tent, or who spoke to Jacob from the heavenly ladder, or who called to Moses from the Burning Bush" (*Tracts*, p. 195). In his own person, the Son not only fashioned man but conducted him through sacred history.

Most of Newman's presentation centers on St. Athanasius's theory of the *syncatabasis* which resembles the Pauline *kenosis* as interpreted by Hopkins. This is the Son's descent to the creature, first made in Genesis: "The co-eternal Word became in the beginning the ministrative Word, who created and upholds all things . . . the First-born in creation, or, to use the Platonic term, the Prophoric Word, giving existence, life, light, order, and permanence to the whole world" (*Tracts*, p. 198). Newman quotes Athanasius: " 'The Word, when in the beginning He framed the creatures, condescended (συνκαταβέβηκε) to them, that it might be possible for them to come into being' " (p. 202). The first gift of grace was the elevation of the universe from the first moment of coming into being to divine sonship and familyhood: " 'By this condescension of the Word, the creation also is made a son through Him' " (p. 203). "The Son of God . . . was born into the universe, as afterwards He was born in Mary, though not by any hypostatic union with it" (p. 203). Although Athanasius does not use the word "incarnation" of Christ's *syncatabasis*, he does see it as a figure of that event, "a sort of prelude and augury of it." This ministration of the Word is identical with Hopkins's picture of him in *forma servi* pouring out his being and grace as God's first outstressing of himself. Historically, according to Athanasius, nature and grace have never been separated, for the Son applied to the cosmos his own impress, " 'so that the whole world, as being in one body, might be, not at variance, but in accord with itself' " (p. 205). Newman sums up the teaching: "It follows that, while the creation was exalted into sonship, the Son, in exalting it, was lowered. His condescension seemed to make Him one of His own works, though of course the first of them; for the greatest and highest glory of creation was not what it had by nature, but what it had by grace, and this was the reflection and image of Him who created it" (p. 205). Grace has been at work from the beginning, raising the world in Christ.

Hopkins's translation of St. John Chrysostom's "Sermon on Eutropius" (S, 222-24) displays the poet's prose style at its best. The Greek orator's rhythms and repetitions, his direct and impassioned appeals, embodied "the belonging technic, the belonging rhetoric, the own proper eloquence of written prose" which

Hopkins admired and strove for (L3, 380). Of special interest here is Chrysostom's impressive insight into the Eucharist which he saw as the ultimate immolation of Christ through the sacrifice of his body and blood. This sacrament is the perfect mark of his love, for Jesus was not satisfied at being a man rejected, scourged, and crucified for others, but must " 'commingle' Himself with us; not by faith only, but in all reality he makes us his body" (*In Matt.* hom. 82).[10] The Eucharist not only acts as visible sign of Christian unity, but causes the unity. Through communion in his sacrifice Christ makes the partakers one: "For as the bread consisting of many grains is made one, so that the grains nowhere appear; they exist indeed, but their difference is not seen by reason of their conjunction; so are we conjoined both with each other and with Christ" (*In 1 Cor.* hom. 24). The Word-made-flesh is the high priest who feeds the faithful with the sacrifice he has prepared on the altar of his body, with the divine manna of the new people of God.

The homely practicality of Chrysostom's sermons led him to speak frequently of the results of the faithful's oneness in the eucharistic Christ. Family charity, patience, chastity and, among his favored topics, almsgiving are subjects on which he preaches most often. Hopkins's abrupt—but well-intentioned—instructions to Bridges that he should with urgency begin to give alms "up to the point of sensible inconvenience," originated very probably from reading these stirring homilies. The idea that an apparent nonbeliever may be saved by almsgiving underlines the primacy of loving actions over empty promises and prayers; its basis is found in the parable of the goats and sheep when all will be judged not by their calling on Christ but by their having lived for others. For, in George Herbert's words:

> Man is God's image; but a poore man is
> Christ's stamp to boot: both images regard.
> ("The Church-Porch")[11]

Those who give to the poor will be saved because, although they did not recognize him, the object of their charity was Jesus himself. The offended Bridges, of course, had no way of knowing the motives of his priest-friend and the deep roots into his myth from which his advice grew. In his homily on Matthew 25:40, "Whatever you did to one of these least, you did it to me," Chrysostom vividly pictures the despised poor of Antioch as the hungry, naked beggar Christ who goes from door to door and stands at the street corner with outstretched hand. Hopkins also explained the hymn in Philippians as the surrender by Christ of the riches of the godhead so as to make himself poor and contemptible in his *kenosis*, "and then all over again, when he was now actually man and born in poverty" (S, 181). It is the indigent and downtrodden Christ with whom Christians must identify themselves by emptying self of "love of our goods, which are wholly outside ourselves; love of our good name . . . , which is ourself indeed, but in others' minds; love of our own excellence, of our very selves, pride" (S, 180). Almsgiving is dramatic proof of man's seeking Christ and the living answer to his question, *"What good have you done?"* as Hopkins phrased his "pure christianity" (L1, 61). For "to give alms . . . changes the whole man, if anything can; not his mind only but the will and everything" (L1, 60-61).

The final index of the poet's admiration for Chrysostom is the conscious imitation of his pulpit style, especially evident in his translation of the Eutropius sermon and in his own "Dominical" delivered while he was studying theology at St. Beuno's. The Greek father's celebrated homilies on the Gospel of St. John best exemplify the effect Hopkins was striving for in addressing his congregations: an enlightening and attractive style which led to knowledge and the promise of a virtuous life. Homily 14 on the text: "Of his fullness we have all received" (John 1:16) is especially pertinent, as is the homily on Philippians 2:5-11, cited in the introduction of this study, which Hopkins referred to in explaining the Pauline hymn to Bridges (L1, 177).[12]

The last father to be examined here, and the greatest representative of the Latin patristic period, is St. Augustine, the most frequently mentioned of the church fathers in Hopkins's writings. His conversion is contrasted with that of St. Paul's in *The Wreck of the Deutschland*; its "lingering out sweet skill" as narrated in his *Confessions* made this one of the poet's favorite books (L1, 195). He knew it well enough to quote—if with slight inaccuracy —sentences by heart when he needed to explain God's relationship to his creature (see p. 128, below). He also made use of the *De Musica* in describing his theory of rhythm (J, 273) and the nature of the sonnet (L2, 72). In this work he found developed the idea of the *carmen universitatis* (the world as song). The *De Magistro*, which Hopkins seems to have used in arriving at his own theory of language, treats of the connection between words, signs, and things, and, like the poet in his own search for meaning and myth, calls on Christ in the inner man to be teacher and oracle of truth.

But the primary source of Hopkins's Augustinianism remains the *Confessions*. The employment of the theme of ascent as a biographical structure gives Augustine's work its shape and direction and additionally underlines the value Hopkins always stressed and found in experience. For gnosis is the activity of living men and the events of their own lives are the cleaves of their returning to God through Christ. A major point of the *Confessions* is that man does not ascend directly through exterior creation to the Father, but turns within and discovers him in the inner self; then man mounts back through creatures to the creator, or, rather, all reality becomes his potential field of knowledge of the One. Both the turning to God in conversion and the rising to him in responsive love take place through "that Mediator between God and man, the Man Christ Jesus" who "was showed forth to the holy men of old; that they, through faith in His passion to come, as we through faith of it passed, might be saved. For as Man, He was Mediator; but as the Word, not in the middle between God and man, because He was equal to God, and God with God, and together one God" (bk. 10. 43).[13] Christ is not midway between God and man, but wholly on both sides at once; not half man and half God, but fully both. "The only Son, in whom are hid all the treasures of wisdom and knowledge, has redeemed me with His blood. . . . And they shall praise the Lord who seek Him" (10. 43). He saves all men before and after his time "through faith in His passion to come" or in his passion past.

St. Augustine's speculations on time were the first of their kind in the development of Western philosophical thought. The *Confessions* itself is cast in a time mold of past (bks. 1-9), present (10) and future (11-13), the last books including a reflection on the beginnings of creation in Genesis as the direction personal faith must take in confessing the Triune God. One of the most significant sections of this classic autobiography is the meditation on time itself in book 11. 14-30. According to Augustine, it is in the mind that man measures the sequence of events, now distractedly, but the impress is definite and constant (11. 27). The fixed point or inscape of time is Christ within us:

> But because Thy loving-kindness is better than all lives, behold, my life is but a distraction, and Thy right hand upheld me, in my Lord the Son of man, the Mediator between Thee, the One, and us many, many also through our manifold distractions amid many things, that by Him I may apprehend in whom I have been apprehended, and may be re-collected from my old ways of acting, to follow the One, forgetting what is behind, and not distended but extended, not to things which shall be and shall pass away, but to those things which are before, not distractedly but intently, as I follow on for the prize of my heavenly calling, where I may hear the voice of Thy praise, and contemplate Thy delights, neither to come, nor to pass away. (11. 29)[14]

The extended dimension of man's experience and the intentional direction of consciousness cross in the foredrawing center of Christ the Lord who first took hold of man, as St. Paul pointed out in Philippians 3:12, before he took hold of Christ. On the road to Damascus he is seized all at once, "at a crash," and his task ever after is to master the height of that mercy and mastery. The first encounter—"sudden in a shaft of sunlight"—unfolds in fresh sensations of what Eliot calls "the intersection of the timeless moment."[15]

In addition to time as a personal object of reflection, St. Augustine also developed a theory of cosmic time in history. His considerations of the Greek and Roman past in the *City of God* (bk. 5. 11-21) led him to see pagan history as submitting to the purposes and providence of God. Hopkins's writings about time, like those of many of his contemporaries, show a similar concern for personal and cosmic realities in their temporal perspective.[16] "The telling time our task is," he wrote in his unfinished sonnet "To his Watch," for "to tell time" is to read its meaning correctly. His most elaborate statement on the subject opens "Creation and Redemption":

> Time has 3 dimensions and one positive pitch or direction.
> It is therefore not so much like any river or any sea as
> like the Sea of Galilee, which has the Jordan running through
> it and giving a current to the whole.
>
> Though this one direction of time if prolonged for ever
> might be considered to be parallel to or included in the
> duration of God, the same might be said of any other
> direction in time artificially taken. But it is truer to say
> that there is no relation between any duration of time
> and the duration of God. And in no case is it to be supposed
> that God creates time and the things of time, that is to
> say / this world, in that duration of himself which is
> parallel with the duration of time and was before time.
> But rather as the light falls from heaven upon the Sea
> of Galilee not only from the north, from which quarter
> the Jordan comes, but from everywhere / so God from
> every point, so to say, of his being creates all things.
> But in so far as the creation of one thing depends on that
> of another, as suppose trees were created *for* man and
> *before* man, so far does God create in time or in the
> direction or duration of time. (S, 196)

Parmenides' words come to mind: "Being never was nor will be, because it *is* now, a whole all together, one, continuous. . . ." Little could the Greek philosopher imagine that the eternal entered time, descended into the Heraclitean river of past, present, and future, as Christ did in his baptism, submerging himself in the current so that the river now moves in him. His presence "rides time like riding a river" (P28, 6). He who issues from the Father now pours through the temporal world, "yesterday, today, *ipse et in saecula*" (Heb. 13:8). One of the Son's titles, according to St. Athanasius, is "Stream from the Fountain."[17]

Through his corporeal existence in time Jesus gives direction to the whole of human history, just as the Jordan creates a current in the Sea of Galilee, the river of his baptism and the sea of his public ministry. In his "Dominical" the poet demonstrates the importance to him of the biblical locale as the physical and literal shell in which the spiritual mystery lies hidden. In that sermon he also notes that "the Jordan runs from north to south," a fact he stresses because for him the "North" signifies "the culmination of the firmament towards the pole" (S, 198). Christ descended from the *pleroma* of godhead to lead men back to their end, *telos*, and mark; all were created *for* him who is before all. In the passing sequence of three dimensional time, therefore, there is a countermovement within the mind and heart toward the source and goal, the Alpha and Omega who "from every point of his being creates all things."

The just man's inner life is like one of the poet's most significant sources of inspiration, St. Winefred's well. While at St. Beuno's he wrote: "The strong unfailing flow of the water and the chain of cures from year to year all these centuries took hold of my mind with wonder at the bounty of God in one of His saints, the sensible thing so naturally and gracefully uttering the spiritual reason of its being" (J, 261). Nature and grace are renewed in the miraculous resurrection of St. Winefred, which the waters, springing up with her, still memorialize (see L1, 40). The sacred well visibly embodies the fullness of Christ's "gospel proffer" in history and in man's consciousness, "the spring in place leading back the thoughts by its spring in time to its spring in eternity: even now the stress and buoyancy and abundance of the water is before my eyes" (J, 261). "Roundy wells," a rich and suggestive object for Hopkins, thus incorporated the depth and height, flow and stillness of the Lord's inner existence, the river and its goal in man: "I steady as a water in a well, to a poise, to a pane" (P28, 4). In Palestine or in Wales, the love of Jesus takes hold in time, physically and spiritually transforming nature and men's lives by "giving a current to the whole."

In his analysis of time Hopkins made use of St. Augustine's distinction between the *extensio* (or horizontal) and the *intensio* (or vertical) directions of temporality, verified by man's impression of fleeting words and events. Man is stretched back and forward, yet remains fixed and open to the moment. Past and future, for the poet, flow from and into the Word-made-man and are summed up in his present, for in his risen person the fullness of time and eternity now forever exist. The presence of Christ is precisely that: a being-in-the-present in him, the "prize of man's heavenly calling." Achieving this gnosis, the mind blesses all reality:

> Thee, God, I come from, to thee go,
> All dáy long I like fountain flow
> From thy hand out, swayed about
> Mote-like in thy mighty glow.
>
> What I know of thee I bless,
> As acknowledging thy stress
> On my being and as seeing
> Something of thy holiness. (P155)

Hopkins, like T. S. Eliot after him, discovered in Augustine an extract of his own personal probing for God and response to him. For history is not an endless cycle, but a biblical procession as Israel experienced it, looking back to God's purposes planted in the beginning, striven for in the present, longed for in the coming deliverer. Time is directed toward an end which is always present; it is an arrow shooting at its mark, the inscape of Christ. "Did one come to show you the way?" Augustine asked in a sermon on Psalm 70. He replied: "It was the Way itself that came to you." "With regard to the Idea before hand and after —" Hopkins reflected, "we may say the Idea asks us a riddle of which the question is more beautiful than the answer" (D12, 1). To seek him is to find him, to aim is to hit the mark.

6

Scotus and the
Scholastic Tradition

THE LAST important contribution to Christology in the Catholic West was made by the British Franciscan and favorite of Hopkins, John Duns Scotus. The thirteenth-century theologian's teachings on the incarnate Word show greater affinity to the thought of the fathers of the church than to that of the Scholastics who immediately preceded him. For, unfortunately, the rich christological heritage of the patristic period passed from sight during the Middle Ages, although vividly alive on a popular, devotional level—and few insights or intellectual investigations into the nature and role of Christ were forthcoming. Instead, a juridical approach to the Lord's universal preeminence as creator and redeemer replaced the earlier, vigorous, mental research into the *mysterium Christi*.[1] The clarifying formulation of the Council of Chalcedon in 451, which declared that "Our Lord Jesus Christ is one and the same Son, the Same perfect in Godhead, the Same perfect in manhood, truly God and truly man, the Same consisting of a rational soul and a body; *homoousios* with the Father as to his Godhead, and the Same *homoousios* with us as to his manhood"[2]—this very formula helped close the door for many future Schoolmen whose intellectual encounter with the divine carpenter of Nazareth became a fixed "truth" no longer in need of reexamination. Until this century, the study of Jesus as the cosmic center of God's dealings with man made no further strides after Scotus; his own ideas were ignored or refuted by the schools. "He saw too far, he knew too much" was Hopkins's conclusion (L3, 349).

The originality of Hopkins's development of a Christocentric myth through scriptural, patristic, and Scotist studies cannot be exaggerated. Between himself and Scotus there stretches an unbroken plain of repeated questions and familiar answers based on the Chalcedon definition. Ironically, Scotus himself contributed to the theoretical monotony by the method and expression of his own Christology. The Subtle Doctor's celebrated question: Is the redemption the primary reason for the Son of God becoming man? he answered with a resounding "No!" The Word would have become incarnate even without man's fall (*Oxoniense*, 3 sent. d. 20. q. 1). Unfortunately, in the controversy that followed with the Thomists, who held that the creative and redemptive orders must be clearly separated, the original question and response became a purely abstract debate about possible acts of God if human history had not taken the course it did. Would the Son have been made man if Adam had not fallen? is in reality unanswerable; and the effect of such a conundrum was to remove the mystery of Christ's exaltation from the realm of biblical event to a theological disaster area that quickly became a speculative no-man's-land. Attempts to reconcile the two positions, by the Jesuit Suarez for example, never moved off the theoretical course on which the problem first had been launched.

Scotus's intention, indeed, was far otherwise. He hoped, by establishing the purpose of God's creative act as genesis in Christ, to show the unity and perfection of the divine concern for creatures. This unity is the Father's love for man made manifest in the likeness of his Son. The natural order is existentially oriented toward Christ who is its masterpiece and culmination. Christ's priority of nature, as Hopkins examined it in his "Creation and Redemption," places him first in the order of causality which is counterpointed to the order of time: "And as for the prophecies of his death, these are like histories written beforehand and are in nature after the event they tell of" (S, 162). The Lamb is slain from the beginning. The act by which the Father sums up all the *pleroma* in his crucified Son, this is the one creative act of love from and to which all being flows. Creation and atonement, two decrees from man's temporal point of view, are actually simultaneous in God; both offer different ways and degrees of sharing in the one Word of life. They are, in Karl Barth's words, "the outer and inner sides" of God's decision to form a covenant with man. The only reason for the first is to act as a moment or springboard to carry the creature over into the fullness of Being, the godhead itself. Nature exists from the start in a supernatural order, creation in Christ, and waits patiently for the deliverance of man and his passing over into completion in his Lord. Nature has never lost this marking and glory; Adam and his descendants have fallen, but the trees and hills still stand erect. Only the redeemed man is one with the cosmos, for he has answered the call that brought him into existence. Only he is truly one with nature.

Such in summary was the sublime myth Hopkins saw as the integrating force of his life and which he found confirmed and profoundly interpreted in Scotus. The Spirit of Christ, who is Love, releases and reveals the stress that created and controls the universe. Man, brought into being out of nothingness and falling back into nothingness through sin is lifted to a higher level of being in a single act of divine love. Christ, the head and king, as Scotus frequently titled him, is "predestined to be the Son of God in power" (Rom. 1:4); he returns mankind to his Father through his death on the cross. The approach of Scotus, so frequently misunderstood, is thus a realistic, rather than abstracted, assertion of the primacy of Christ as firstborn and end, Alpha and Omega, of the present world. The human nature of Jesus is the aim and final cause God had in mind when creating. The Word-made-flesh is also the image or exemplary cause in which men and, in lesser gradations, other creatures were fashioned. The mind and heart of man is the crown and zenith of the work of Genesis since he most authentically embodies the Son who was to be, is now, and ever shall exist.

The universe is inherently and originally Christic and bears the mark of its creator-redeemer; as Hopkins in his notes on the "Contemplation for Obtaining Love" graphically pictured it, the whole world appears suffused in Christ's luminous blood (S, 194). This blood, which "streams in the firmament," is real and not fanciful, ingrained in stars and sky. Notice how Hopkins ascends in the following passage to the same vision of the cosmic sacrifice while employing metaphors that express biblical realities and not clever rephrasings of conventional Christian verities. In his "Instructions on the Principle or Foundation," he asks: "Why did God create?" and answers with a tapestry of images rich in New Testament and liturgical associations:

> He meant the world to give him praise, reverence, and
> service; *to give him glory*. It is like a garden, a field he sows:
> what should it bear him? praise, reverence, and service;
> it should yield him glory. It is an estate he farms: what
> should it bring him in? Praise, reverence, and service;
> it should repay him glory. It is a leasehold he lets out:
> what should its rent be? Praise, reverence, and service;
> its rent is his glory. It is a bird he teaches to sing, a pipe,
> a harp he plays on: what should it sing to him? etc.
> It is a glass he looks in : what should it shew him? With
> praise, reverence, and service it should shew him his own
> glory. It is a book he has written, of the riches of his
> knowledge, teaching endless truths, full lessons of wisdom,
> a poem of beauty: what is it about? His praise, the reverence
> due to him, the way to serve him; it tells him of his glory.
> It is a censer fuming: what is the sweet incense? His praise,
> his reverence, his service; it rises to his glory. It is an altar
> and a victim on it lying in his sight: why is it offered?
> To his praise, honour, and service: it is a sacrifice to his
> glory. (S, 238-39)

The world is Word in which man reads to achieve gnosis, for which man listens to hear its poetry, and on which God looks to see the crucified imprint of his Son: "the word of it Sacrificed" (P28, 22). Things are sacraments of grace to give him glory.

Adam's sin, according to Scotus, has changed the nature of the Son's coming, but it did not oblige him to be made flesh and dwell among men. Hopkins noted: "The love of the Son for the Father leads him to take a created nature and in that to offer him sacrifice. The sacrifice may have been unbloody; by the Fall it became a bloody one" (S, 257). Such is his love that the Word would have shared most intimately in his creation no matter what man's response to his love might be. He does not wait on his creature's return but anticipates and foredraws all reality to himself. Christ chose to descend in the beginning, in the heart of creation, as a ministering servant in order to mount with a multitude of followers in procession after him. "Man must have had a Christ, even if Adam had continued in Paradise," Coleridge asserted.[3]

The difference between the Jesus who might have lived in a paradisal universe and the servant who actually suffered is the gift of man's freedom. This freedom is an essential note in both Scotus and Hopkins because it changed the whole course of the incarnation and resulted in the atonement. The Word serves man: he "bodes but abides" in attending him, ministers in creation as he ministered in his lifetime: "He encouraged men, stirred them up, and led them on to good in every way by his words and works, by sermons, by miracles, and most of all by his example" (S, 97). This providence and waiting-on-man Hopkins called "forestalling," the gift and governance of that "pitch" which each self exercises before becoming an actualized being in the world. The noun "pitch," derived from the verb "to pitch, throw, hurl," denotes the dynamic motion and course of each prebeing as it is propelled and propels itself into its niche in time and space. Hopkins wrote: "So also *pitch* is ultimately simple positiveness, that by which being differs from and is more than nothing and not-being" (S, 151). Connecting pitch with its meaning in music, the poet observed that this hurling toward is not arbitrary motion but exists in a scale or tonal series, and that "God then can shift the self that lies in one to a higher, that is / better, pitch of itself; that is / to a pitch or determination of itself on the side of good" (S, 148). Alone of all creatures man can determine, every moment of his existence, the direction his life will take. The highest identity with Christ, however, remains the pitch God wills for him as an individual. For man is free insofar as he has Christ for his goal.

Hopkins reflected: "Is not this pitch or whatever we call it then the same as Scotus's *ecceitas*?" (S, 151). This key—and much discussed—Scotist concept of *haecceitas* defines the thisness that constitutes an existent, that makes this being *be*. Here Hopkins associates it not with inscape, as has been often done by critics, but with pitch. For Scotus, as for Parmenides, being is univocal, unique, not a sharing in other being or an analogous reflection, but its self, one in the One, word of the Word. Inscape, as the directing energy of pitch and its mark or target, is the dynamic vortex in which all things are scaled and which foredraws or instresses each with active and meaningful sway. This center is found in the core of all reality and in each particularity as a point of outward pressure and inward suction. The self, however, "is not a mere centre or point of reference for consciousness or action attributed to it, everything else, all that it is conscious of or acts on [,] being its object only and outside it" (S, 127). The center is not a vacuum or pigeonhole in which objects are deposited; rather, being and thought are the same:

> Part of this world of objects, this object-world, is also
> part of the very self in question, as in man's case his own
> body, which each man not only feels in and acts with
> but also feels and acts on. If the centre of reference spoken
> of has concentric circles round it, one of these, the inmost,
> say, is its own, is óf it, the rest are tó it only. Within a
> certain bounding line all will be self, outside of it nothing:
> with it self begins from one side and ends from the other.
> I look through my eye and the window and the air; the
> eye is my eye and of me and me, the windowpane is my
> windowpane but not of me nor me. A self then will consist
> of a centre *and* a surrounding area or circumference, of
> a point of reference *and* a belonging field, the latter set out,
> as surveyors etc say, from the former; of two elements,
> which we may call the inset and the outsetting or the
> display. (S, 127)

This passage from Hopkins's notes on the "Foundation" supplies an indispensable link in our analysis of his mythopoeic development. The text connects Parmenides' system of limits and spheres, Origen's concept of the "inner man," and Scotus's theory of the self. While demonstrating the oneness of being, Hopkins still preserves the independence of individuality, the basic problem a metaphysics of freedom must solve. The inner circle of self is not a hollow shell alone unto itself but a microcosm of the whole. And freedom is man's openness, his capacity and need, for fullness and completion.

Hopkins continues his analysis in the passages that follow and, without explicit mention by name of the Word-made-man, works forward to an explanation of man's free acknowledgment of him:

> Now this applies to the universal mind or being too; it will have its inset and its outsetting; only that the outsetting includes all things, with all of which it is in some way, by turns, in a series, or however it is, identified. But then this is an altogether different outsetting from what each of those very things to its own particular self has. And since self consists in the relation the inset and the outsetting bear to one another, the universal has a relation different from everything else and everything else from everything else, including the universal, so that the self of the universal is not the self of anything else. In other words the universal is not really identified with everything else nor with anything else, which was supposed; that is / there is no such universal. (S, 127)

There is no such essentialistic universal or *intellectus agens* of the Averrhoists (S, 125); nor, by extension, is there a pantheistic Christ whose only identity is his otherness, or an amorphous self in man so identified with the Logos that man loses his own freedom. "The Eternal King and universal Lord" is no vacuum needing creation to fill and replenish him; rather, when an individual reads himself and the cosmos aright, a wonderous selfhood of the One opens in the mind of the seeker, self answering to self. Hopkins explains: "In shewing there is no universal a true self which is 'fetched' or 'pitched' or 'selved' in every other self, I do not deny that there is a universal really, and not only logically, thus fetched" in the individuals (S, 128). The "universal really" is knowable being in things, reached through abstraction, and

the intuition of being as the first natural object of the mind knowing individual objects; these ideas Hopkins had already developed
in his notes on Parmenides. Man experiences being as one because concretely and objectively "is" as a whole can be thought
and said of each and every entity. This all-embracing concept of
being, arrived at through abstraction and intuition, is what makes
different things intelligible. Hopkins found these notions further
expounded in Scotus.[4] "But these universals are finite only," the
poet adds, while being as such is applied in an unlimited way and
is unconnected with anything material. Only under the aspect
of being as being, therefore, can reason prove that God exists.[5]

The poet now reaches the goal of his inquiry:

> Neither do I deny that God is so deeply present to every-
> thing ("Tu autem, O bone omnipotens, eras superior summo
> meo et interior intimo meo") that it would be impossible
> for him but for his infinity not to be identified with them,
> or, from the other side, impossible but for his infinity
> so to be present to them. This is oddly expressed, I see;
> I mean / a being so intimately present as God is to other
> things would be identified with them were it not for God's
> infinity or were it not for God's infinity he would not be
> so intimately present to things. (S, 128)

The slightly inaccurate quotation from the *Confessions* (3. 6)
sums up man's response to the *mysterium Christi*: the immanent
presence in the world of transcendent Being who is farther than
any reach outside and nearer than any drawing home within.
His infinity is not only his height but his closeness as well, and
because he has sounded the depths of self even before man begins his exploration within, he already awaits the free man there.
St. Augustine expressed the truth in his moving admission: "Late
have I loved Thee, O Beauty ever ancient, ever new! Late have
I loved Thee! And look, Thou wert within and I was without, and
there I searched for Thee; a deformed self, plunging amid those
fair forms which Thou hadst made. Thou wert with me, but I
was not with Thee' (*Conf.* 10. 27).[6] All creation witnesses to his
nature and speaks its secret to the listening heart: "These things

did my inner man know by the ministry of the outer: I the inner knew them; I, the mind, through the senses of my body. I asked the whole frame of the world about my God; and it answered me, 'I am not He, but He made me' " (*Conf.* 10. 6).[7]

Men's reason, following the operation of the divine Reason within, knows God as Being, naturally but circuitously and dimly. He is only to be fully possessed through the Word's free gift of himself to the atoned intelligence; then is he acknowledged in the freedom of the inner man. In returning through the great sacrifice, man reciprocates the outstressing of the eternal action in time and attains the purpose of creation in experiencing the truth of his inner release from bondage and nothingness. Having searched in vain outside and within himself, he discovers cosmic meaning, purpose or inscape, in the Lord who searches hearts and penetrates the cosmos. Being makes him know and makes him free; I AM is uttered "in ten thousand places." Man lives his true existence: "That is Christ *being me* and me being Christ" (S, 154). One with Christ, he is at last free to be himself. "Love and do what you will," said St. Augustine.

In these considerations, as Christopher Devlin argues in his notes (S, 284-86), Hopkins followed the reasoning of Scotus in proving the existence of God from an interior, psychological starting point. But the line of thought is the traditional one of the Greek philosophers and St. Augustine which Duns Scotus and the other Schoolmen mastered and made their own. This synthesizing is exactly what Hopkins himself has done as he worked toward the gnosis that is in the mind of Christ. For the Logos, whom St. John calls "I AM," is existentially present as reason and uncreated being in the inner self and as created nature in the outer world, not as a deity exhausted in visible forces and laws, but as "*Ipse*, the only one" who is healer and shepherd. His self-being, whose circumference extends to the whole cosmos and to possible worlds beyond, is found in each man who accepts him; he lifts each rational creature from the pit of nothingness to his own fullness of being. Each pitch of being is foredrawn even before it is fixed in space and time and, once so fixed, is drawn to return to Omega. Inscape defines this unity of tension between the creature's holding back in nothingness and multiplicity, and its flight toward the center: Being, the One. For man to see and know Christ existing in himself and in the universe is inscape: "The fulness is the thought."

Only Christ then, whose limits are the *pleroma*, enjoys full freedom of pitch, play, and field. These Hopkins described in his "On Personality, Grace and Free Will": "Freedom of pitch, that is / self determination, is in the chooser himself and his choosing faculty; freedom of play is in the execution; freedom of field is in the object, the field of choice" (S, 149). An illustration is then given: "It is freedom of pitch to be able to choose for yourself which of several doors you will go in by; it is freedom of play to go unhindered to it and through the one you choose; but suppose all were false doors or locked but the very one you happened to choose and you do not know it, there is here wanting freedom of field" (S, 149). Man's personal freedom is nothing else than his conformity, "*the doing* be," with the servant who was obedient to the Father even to death on a cross. Man's purpose is to allow Christ to be obedient in his own heart and mind: "God *in forma servi* rests *in servo*" (S, 195). All that is expected by God from his human loved one is the desire to be united with him:

> For there must be something which shall be truly the creature's in the work of corresponding with grace: this is the *arbitrium*, the verdict on God's side, the saying Yes, the "doing-agree" (to speak barbarously), and looked at in itself, such a nothing is the creature before its creator, it is found to be no more than the mere wish, discernible by God's eyes, that it might do as he wishes, might correspond, might say Yes to him; correspondence itself is on man's side not so much corresponding as the wish to correspond, and this least sigh of desire, this one aspiration, is the life and spirit of man. (S, 154-55)

Hopkins says that "this sigh or aspiration or stirring of the spirit towards God is a *forestall* of the thing to be done. . . . And by this infinitesimal act the creature does what in it lies to bridge the gulf fixed between its present actual and worser pitch of will and its future better one" (S, 155). Christ therefore enjoys full freedom of play in the heart as the Spirit of counsel and understanding who opens the fields of possible being and guides men to choose, as he chose, a life of unselfish love. As Wisdom in the Old Testament he testifies to this role which he plays in every man from the beginning: "I was with him forming all things: and was delighted every day, playing before him at all times; playing in the world: and my delights *were* to be with the children of men" (Prov. 8:30-31).

The place of Christ's Mother in that preexistent universe may strike some readers as incongruent and pious daydreaming. The concept is particularly identified with Scotist theology, although a disciple and not Scotus himself originated it. The passage from Proverbs just quoted in part and cited at greater length in chapter 4 of this study (p. 76), supplies the epistle reading for the mass of the Feast of the Immaculate Conception. The idea then, although never officially defined as a dogma of the Catholic faith, has at least won liturgical approval. Hopkins often turned to the Scotist teaching in writing of Mary: "The first intention then of God outside himself or, as they say, *ad extra*, outwards, the first outstress of God's power, was Christ; and we must believe that the next was the Blessed Virgin" (S, 197). He also referred to her as Wisdom, "the Blessed Virgin in that being which she had from the beginning, as expressed in the Book of Wisdom" (S, 257). Hopkins's Latin poem "May Lines" (P179) develops this theme of her predestination as Mother of God "a saeculorum saeculis"; before the ages she is predestined through "the merits of the Innocent One" to be identified with him in creating, as she is in saving, the world. The poem's opening apostrophe, "O praedestinata bis," praises this double role in creation and redemption as Mary's greatest privilege, uniquely and initially prepared for her alone. The epigraph of "May Lines" also repeats the Wisdom motif: "*Ab initio et ante saecula creata sum et usque ad futurum saeculum non desinam*" (Eccles. 24:14).

The idea of Mary's preexistence must be seen as part of the development of the dogma of the Immaculate Conception, defined on December 8, 1854. As a convert to the Roman Church,

Hopkins embraced this doctrine and the devotion derived from it with fervor and enthusiasm, even to the point of offering "the Mother of sorrows" as an example for his father to follow in accepting his son's conversion. The Victorian poet's attraction to the "Marian Doctor" received much of its impetus from the heroic defense offered by Scotus against strong opponents to the teaching. Not only St. Thomas Aquinas and the Thomists, but St. Bernard, Peter Lombard, and his fellow Franciscan, St. Bonaventure, took up the opposing position. Single-handedly, Scotus turned the tide by lecturing on the Immaculate Conception at Oxford and carrying the day at a previously hostile Paris. "It is a comfort to think," Hopkins once told his Bedford Leigh parishioners, "that the greatest of the divines and doctors of the Church who have spoken and written in favour of this truth came from England: between 500 and 600 years ago he was sent for to go to Paris to dispute in its favour. The disputation or debate was held in public and someone who was there says that this wise and happy man by his answers broke the objections brought against him" (S, 45). For Hopkins, John Duns Scotus was eminently the shining knight "Who fired France for Mary without spot" (P44).

Hopkins himself preached on the Immaculate Conception and explained it in his best pulpit manner. He followed Scotus in insisting on the role of Christ in bestowing this honor on his Mother: "The Blessed Virgin was saved and redeemed by Christ her son not less than others but more, for she was saved from even falling but they were let fall and then recovered (that is / redeemed): now, as the proverb says, prevention is better than cure" (S, 43). Scotus also presented his argument in favor of the future doctrine by stressing the power and dignity of the Son of God, who could accomplish this miracle in his creature and did in fact perform it (see his *Oxoniense* 3. d. 3, q. 1). The atonement Christ accomplished for others and offers in baptism, this he gave to Mary in its fullness from the beginning. She is living witness of the "breadth and length and height and depth of Christ's love which surpasses knowledge," for she is "filled with all the *pleroma* of God" (Eph. 3:18-19). Mary then is the firstfruits of her Son's "lifting up," his death and resurrection, and partakes completely by her total human life in the power of his Spirit released in her presence at Pentecost. She is the concrete sign of the reality of his risen life and of the fidelity of his promises to men. All Christ can do for others is made plain and visible in this woman.

The Mother too descended by the kenotic way of poverty and emptiness. She was not born, Scotus held, in original justice, with the innocence of nature left intact; she was not privileged above her Son, but shared the same human nature with other men, a fallen one, subject to the mortal strains of suffering and death. Her nature, however, was immediately and initially redeemed and exalted in Christ's. Hopkins wrote: "For redeem may be said not only of the recovering from sin to grace or perdition to salvation but also of the raising from worthlessness before God (and all creation is unworthy of God) to worthiness of him, the meriting of God himself, or, so to say, godworthiness. In this sense the Blessed Virgin was beyond all others redeemed, because it was her more than all other creatures that Christ meant to win from nothingness and it was her that he meant to raise the highest" (S, 197). In the cosmic procession of all men from the Father and back through the cleave of the Son's heart, she took her stand closest to him in his agonizing death and now follows next to him in glory. She embodies the meaning of the great sacrifice, its purpose and aim; she is Christ's most perfect inscape.

In his notes on the incarnation, Hopkins summarized his view of the atonement and gave to Mary a central place:

> Christ then is the redeemer in three or four senses: of his own created being, which he retrieves from nothingness, when it becomes divine and of infinite worth; of the Blessed Virgin not only from nothingness but also from the worthlessness towards God or unworthiness of God which is in every pure creature, and this he retrieves to divine motherhood, a status in kind and not in degree higher than what is attainable by any other creature's correspondence with grace; of the angels not only from

nothingness and from worthlessness but also from that
shortcoming which all creatures but the Blessed Virgin
would seem to have from their want of correspondence
with grace, and these, as the *Redemptor Saeculorum*,
he relieves from imperfection; of fallen man, whom he
reprieves from original and actual sin. (S, 170)

Through his emphasis on the poles of being and nothingness in
terms of man's redemption, Hopkins placed Christ the Savior at
the source of creation. These two orders of reality are not located
side by side in history or on two separate planes; the order of
redemption exists within that of creation but penetrates it, colors
it and transfuses it with Christ's victorious love.[8] The world is
incorporated in all its naturality into the *mysterium Christi*, as
Mary in her stainless body proves. She is the unique physical
vessel (the Litany's *vas insigne devotionis*) in which his incorruptible life is still being sustained.

Mary is also living proof that Jesus is really man; his body
was conceived in her womb, "she gave him birth and suckled him
at her breast" (S, 34). So intimately was she united with him in
the mysteries of her Son's life that, Hopkins conjectured, even
if men had not sinned, "Christ would have been in some *specie
Mariana* and this would then have been his *forma servi*" (S, 170).
"Christ would have been Son of Mary but not 'Son of Man.'"
She would still have been "mother of all men in the spirit, but
without sorrow" (S, 170). The point of these speculations for
Hopkins as for Scotists generally is that they establish the historical and literal truth of God's mysterious workings in creation.
To become man, he must possess a body. The poet's meditation
on "How Christ said Goodbye to His Blessed Mother and came
from Nazareth to the River Jordan" (S, 177) is not an exercise of
devotional fancy, but an Origenic effort to achieve gnosis of
"Christ's descent into human nature" in eternity, in the "aeon
of Mary," in the past theophanies and in the events of his birth
and hidden life. For Hopkins, everything in God's design in
Christ connects in visible and invisible reticulations, and the inner circle of the pattern is Mary. The Father intends each man to

be another Son; he "means us to copy His nature and character as well as we can and put on His mind according to our measure" (S, 134). She not only fulfilled this mark most perfectly in herself, but she now embodies him as man's Omega:

> Jesu that dost in Mary dwell,
> Be in thy servants' hearts as well,
> In the spirit of thy holiness,
> In the fullness of thy force and stress.   (P169)

Finally, Mary's fiat, her "saying *yes*" to the descent of the Spirit at the annunciation, initiated salvation history even as her presence with the apostles in the upper room climaxed the Pentecostal dispatching of that Spirit. The beginning and the end of man's redemption meet in her. Just as she is the first to follow the Lamb in his descent, through the centering of her will in obedience—even to the death of her Son on the cross—she completes the full cycle of ascent to the Father in Christ. The hymn in Philippians is therefore the song of her story, since it resonates of the Word who was made her flesh. For if, as Newman stated, the whole economy of salvation in Christ exists in each Christian entire and all at once, the *pleroma* of the Christ-event, already attained in her, now becomes available through her mediation. Because her freedom of pitch was higher and more intense than any other creature's, her play or scope of action, and her field of possible influence and choice extend to the whole universe and to all men.

What she was for her Son, "a nursing element," Mary becomes for her adopted children:

> She holds high motherhood
> Towards all our ghostly good
> And plays in grace her part
> About man's beating heart.   (P60)

In all truth, as the title of the poem from which these lines are taken declares, the Blessed Virgin may be compared to the air we breathe, but not by any ordinary simile; for Mary is the blue cosmic air of Spirit that the just man inhales in the risen being of her Son. Scotus's univocity of being as a christological concept has nowhere been more clearly or eloquently framed than in the couplets of this poem:

> Men here may draw like breath
> More Christ and baffle death;
> Who, born so, comes to be
> New self and nobler me
> In each one and each one
> More makes, when all is done,
> Both God's and Mary's Son.

The sky is the literal sky, now heightened by spiritual inscape:

> Yet such a sapphire-shot,
> Charged, steepèd sky will not
> Stain light. Yea, mark you this:
> It does no prejudice.
> The glass-blue days are those
> When every colour glows,
> Each shape and shadow shows.

This blue heaven transmits the sunbeam perfectly, it does not alter it. Now Christ the sun no longer punishes as he did Sodom and Gomorrah with "quartz-fret, or sparks of salt," but his light is "sifted to suit our sight" through his Mother (see S, 29).

In this passage of the poem occurs the only explicit reference in Hopkins's poetry to the "angry God of wrath" supposedly pictured in the Old Testament. Hopkins employs the idea: "So God was god of old," to heighten the role of Mary's motherhood as it affected men's attitude toward their creator. Critics who find the revenging godhead, especially in the *Deutschland*, everywhere present with his dark threats of thunder and fierce lightning, mistake the poet's mystical reading of storms. The cosmos and Christ have been *in forma Mariae* from the beginning, if man but knew how to greet them:

> World-mothering air, air wild,
> Wound with thee, in thee isled,
> Fold home, fast fold thy child.

Love is the element in which the human creature lives and dies; even storms impart this message. All the more clearly do "the glass-blue days." Scotus's contemporary, Dante Alighieri (they were both born in the year 1265), voiced the same vision of Mary's cosmic place in God's design. In canto 32 of the *Paradiso*, St. Bernard commands the poet to look on her face in order to prepare his sight for the beatific inscaping of the divine essence:

> "Riguarda omai nella faccia che a Cristo
> più si somiglia, chè la sua chiarezza
> sola ti può disporre a veder Cristo."[9]

Her features most closely resemble Christ's, and the light that shines from them fortifies men's gaze for beholding his holy face. Just as the Veronica, the *vera icon* of his image imprinted on the sudarium at St. Peter's in Rome, elicits from the humble peasant the most profound act of faith: "*Signor mio Gesù Cristo, Dio verace, / or fu si fatta la sembianza vostra?*" (*Paradiso* 31. 107-08)[10]—so the "Virgin Mother, daughter of her son," is the truest image, "the O-seal-that-so-feature," physically and spiritually, of the Word-made-flesh. "Self flashes off frame and face" (P62) in no one more brilliantly than in Mary, her body assumed into heaven and living in the risen Christ.

What important insights Hopkins gained from other major Schoolmen, especially from St. Thomas Aquinas, cannot easily be measured. Even though Suarezianism was followed in most of the tracts that he studied at St. Beuno's, Hopkins probably read some of the Angelic Doctor's works directly. Neither Aquinas or Suarez, however, seems to have exerted much influence on the growth of his myth. Of the Jesuit theologian the poet expressed a sober opinion in a letter to Dixon: "Suarez is our most famous theologian: he is a man of vast volume of mind, but without originality or brilliancy; he treats everything satisfactorily, but you never remember a phrase of his, the manner is nothing" (L2, 95). He refers to Suarez's *De Mysteriis Vitae Christi* and an "article of St. Thomas embodied there" in the first paragraph of his essay "On Personality, Grace and Free Will," and his opinion on the nature of Lucifer's revolt in heaven may be derived from

Suarez's *De Angelis* (8. 13). But Hopkins's need for "bidding" in the style and manner of his authors would exclude the Spanish theologian as a significant magister of gnosis. Hopkins held a higher opinion of Luis de Molina, another Spanish Jesuit, whose celebrated *Concordia* (1588) dealt with the problems of free will, providence, and predestination. His solutions started a controversial theological movement, mostly made up of other Jesuits, called Molinism. Hopkins wrote of him: "Molina is the man who *made* our theology: he was a genius and even in his driest dialectic I have remarked a certain fervour like a poet's. But in the greatest controversy on the Aids of Grace, the most dangerous crisis, as I suppose, which our Society ever went through till its suppression, though it was from his book that it had arisen, he took, I think, little part" (L2, 95). The controversy mentioned here revolved around the relative influence of God's grace, insisted on by the Dominicans, and of man's free will, emphasized by the Jesuits, in the creature's response to the divine impulse toward its goal. Hopkins's essay "On Personality" skirts many of the issues, but his treatment is an original blending of Parmenides, St. Paul, and Scotus.

The poet's greatest gain in reading in the Scholastic sources was more than any one new insight or the sum of one author's ideas. These writings instructed him in more than precept and method; they initiated him to the more arduous turns of the uphill way of truth. For the vision of the Schoolmen extended far beyond the limits too often ascribed to them; the stereotype of clerical pedants intent on the number of angels perched on a pinhead is both unfounded and unfair. Ralph Waldo Emerson was closer to the truth when he observed: "The difference between the actual and the ideal force of man is happily figured by the schoolmen, in saying, that the knowledge of man is an evening knowledge, *vespertina cognitio*, but that of God is a morning knowledge, *matutina cognitio*."[11] This was the essential lesson Hopkins and others have gained from direct contact with the doctors of the past rather than with the manuals later amassed to inculcate their teachings. The power of negative knowledge of God and of his presence in the world as a positive line of inquiry

—that is, the pursuit of gnosis in the midst of mystery—this, the *via negativa*, proved to be the cornerstone of medieval thought and has become the foundation of the neo-Scholastic renewal. Before this recent development, however, the truth of man's rational dependency on Christ's revelation—*ex umbris et imaginibus in veritatem*—had long since floundered in the tides of distinctions and counterdistinctions that ebbed and flowed with the grating roar of the schools.

The Scholastic tradition as preserved in nineteenth-century seminary training had little intellectual life left in its sclerotic system. Some of Hopkins's teachers may have been learned men —although they failed him in the crucial examination that would have allowed further study in the field of theology and thereby closed that career for him—but the method of instruction was one of standardized handbooks, lecture notes, set disputations, and reviews. A system that radically separated philosophy from theology, that built a conceptual wall between nature and the supernatural, and that fragmented the study of revelation into a dozen disciplines with no connecting force, this was the sad heritage of the Council of Trent's efforts to impose its remedies and reforms. Scholasticism decayed in the late Middle Ages and nowhere was the sickness more apparent than in the preparation of future priests. The doctrinally pure textbooks, which attempted a cure for ignorance, actually deprived the patient of healthy mental growth through meaningful study. For Hopkins, the intellectual freedom of Oxford must have contrasted painfully with the rigors of rote imposed by Rome. To his everlasting credit, the poet pursued the way of truth he had entered on before coming to the Society; he explored and scaled the heights of gnosis, experiencing its rhythms and its silences; he shaped his myth and, after seven years of secrecy, expressed it in verse.

Poetry

How teach again, however, what has been taught correctly and incorrectly learned a thousand thousand times, throughout the millenniums of mankind's prudent folly? That is the hero's ultimate difficult task. How render back into light-world language the speech-defying pronouncements of the dark? How represent on a two-dimensional surface a three-dimensional form, or in a three-dimensional image a multi-dimensional meaning? How translate into terms of "yes" and "no" revelations that shatter into meaninglessness every attempt to define the pairs of opposites? How communicate to people who insist on the exclusive evidence of their senses the message of the all-generating void?

Joseph Campbell
The Hero with a Thousand Faces

7

Inscaping

The Wreck of the Deutschland

GERARD HOPKINS found inscape in every facet of created reality, whether the creator be God or man, the object an ash tree or a poem.[1] Both artifact and nature embody the uncreated and creating Word-made-flesh at work in the universe. At the apex and center of that universe emerges the mind of man, the *imago Dei* and microcosm of creation. In all things made, the poet sought union with the divine maker's mind, for man's intelligence itself reflects and even contains—and more perfectly—the same Christ within as shone without. Hopkins would have dismissed—kindly, but firmly—Joyce Kilmer's "Trees" as heretical nonsense. No reflective Christian would prefer a tree to a poem, for poetry produces inscape of a higher order and intensity. He informed Bridges: "But as air, melody, is what strikes me most of all in music and design in painting, so design, pattern or what I am in the habit of calling 'inscape' is what I above all aim at in poetry" (L1, 66).

Inscape, as we have seen, is not static pattern or particular design, but dynamic and unifying force; it is what causes the design, the "aim . . . in poetry." A year or two before the composition of the *Deutschland*, Hopkins elaborated on his use of the word in his lecture notes on "Poetry and Verse":

> Poetry is speech framed for contemplation of the mind by the way of hearing or speech framed to be heard for its own sake and interest even over and above its interest

of meaning. Some matter and meaning is essential to it
but only as an element necessary to support and employ
the shape which is contemplated for its own sake. (Poetry
is in fact speech only employed to carry the inscape of
speech for the inscape's sake—and therefore the inscape
must be dwelt on. Now if this can be done without repeating
it *once* of the inscape will be enough for art and beauty
and poetry but then at least the inscape must be understood
as so standing by itself that it could be copied and
repeated. If not / repetition, *oftening, over-and-overing,*
aftering of the inscape must take place in order to detach
it to the mind and in this light poetry is speech which
afters and oftens its inscape, speech couched in a repeating
figure and verse is spoken sound having a repeated
figure.) (J, 289)

Hopkins is here distinguishing between poetry and verse which
he then defines as "inscape of spoken sound, not spoken words,
or speech employed to carry the inscape of spoken sound." Poetry
may be couched in the figures and metrics of verse, but it is distinct from verse. Critics have sometimes confused the two; W. H.
Gardner, for example, examines inscape as a poetic term only
in the sense of "inscape of verse."[2]

Poetry then deals not with the inscape of sound, but with inscape itself. While it may be multiplied many times in a poem,
inscape is single, the musical key in which the whole is written.
It rests on the surface and yet underlies everything, giving the
poem coherence and control. Inscape is form as well as content,
structure as well as tone. It is all these, because inscape is poetical
intention, the aim and purpose of the poet in his poem. Poetry
not only is its vehicle, it *is* inscape expressed and revealed. Its
counterpart, "instress," is the effect felt and understood by the
reader once he has grasped, and been grasped by, the inscape or
selfhood of a poem.[3]

In the *Deutschland*, Hopkins makes use of repetition, "*often-*
ing, over-and-overing, aftering of the inscape," in order to shape

it for contemplation in the mind. Once its elements have been perceived by the reader, a unity of purpose will emerge and detach itself, to be dwelt on for its own sake. Since the inscape of each poem is its mark of identity, it can only be defined and described poetically within the context of the poem itself. What then is the inscape of *The Wreck of the Deutschland*?

In the first part of this study the answer to this question has already been implied; for, often, reference to this poem was the only way of illustrating or confirming some thread of the poet's myth. Of all his writings, the *Deutschland* contains the most complete statement of that gnosis or living knowledge of the Lord Jesus which was his constant aim of perfection. What Hopkins said of Wordsworth in his writing of the *Intimations of Immortality* may be justly applied to him and to this ode:

> There have been in all history a few, a very few men, whom common repute, even where it did not trust them, has treated as having had something happen to them that does not happen to other men, as having *seen something*, whatever that really was. Plato is the most famous of these. Or to put is as it seems to me I must somewhere have written to you or to somebody, human nature in these men saw something, got a shock; wavers in opinion, looking back, whether there was anything in it or no; but is in a tremble ever since. Now what Wordsworthians mean is, what would seem to be the growing mind of the English speaking world and may perhaps come to be that of the world at large / is that in Wordsworth when he wrote that ode human nature got another of those shocks, and the tremble from it is spreading. This opinion I do strongly share; I am, ever since I knew the ode, in that tremble. (L2, 147-48)

What was the something Hopkins saw in his ode of shipwreck "to the happy memory of five Franciscan nuns"? How did he "read the unshapeable shock night" so that "the tremble from it is spreading"? Did he, like those who attained to the highest

grade of perfection in the Greek rites of Eleusis, the *epoptai*
("those who saw something"), also see into "the mystery of
things"?

Despite close critical attention to the vocabulary, syntax, imagery, and rhythm of this celebrated poem, basic problems of comprehension and response still remain. Its inscape eludes even the
most attentive reader. Hopkins, who intended that his poems
should explode in the mind and emotions, succeeds in his sonnets; but the length and complexity of the *Deutschland* seemingly fail to produce the desired explosion, or inscape of the whole.
The occasion and background of its writing are more easily summarized than the events as the poet interprets them in the poem.
Synopses, such as the familiar one Gardner provides in his editions of the poems, are helpful in explicating parts of the ode,
but fail to illuminate the central crisis and conclusion. Where is
the "happening" Hopkins obviously wished to make us *see*?
Ninety years after, his words to Bridges remind us that we may
yet stand at the threshold: "When a new thing, such as my ven-
tures in the Deutschland are, is presented us our first criticisms
are not our truest, best, most homefelt, or most lasting but what
come easiest on the instant" (L1, 50). Hopkins himself wrote that
he "was not over-desirous that the meaning of all should be quite
clear, at least unmistakeable" (L1, 50). In addition to what has
been written in part 1 of this book, a fresh look at the poem is
worth attempting here.

The *Deutschland* is divided in two unequal parts, each marked
by a climax in which the poet's expression threatens to collapse,
but, recovering, reaches the pitch of thought and emotion required of it. These two climaxes balance one another, each oc-
curring four-fifths of the way through the two sections: the eighth
stanza out of ten and the twenty-eighth out of the total thirty-
five.[4] In each case the utterance that breaks through is a confession of faith in Christ as God and Man. In stanza 8, lines 6–8:

> . . .—Hither then, last or first,
>   To hero of Calvary, Christ's feet—
> Never ask if meaning it, wanting it, warned of it—men go.

And in stanza 28, lines 4–6:

> . . . There then! the Master,
> *Ipse*, the only one, Christ, King, Head:
> He was to cure the extremity where he had cast her.

This second confession, foreshadowed by the first, is the dramatic point for which the entire poem has prepared us. In stanza 24, the poet presents his nun-heroine in the midst of shipwreck, her voice rising above the turmoil as she calls: "O Christ, Christ, come quickly," her actual cry as reported in the London *Times*. The prayer repeats the liturgical refrain of the apostolic witnesses, *Marana tha*, "Lord, come!"[5] The poet asks himself and his listeners: "The majesty! What did she mean?" Tentative answers are offered: "Is it love in her of the being as her lover had been?" Is she remembering the historical Jesus on the cross as an object of imitation and inspiration? "Or is it that she cried for the crown then?" Did she long to be with the risen Jesus in heaven? Hopkins answers for us: "No, but it was not these." The nun did not seek deliverance from either danger or routine in the crucified and glorious Christ as a model and recompenser of merit: "Other, I gather, in measure her mind's / Burden." In the midst of "electrical horror," neither past nor future spiritual realities concern her; she is wholly swept up in the tragic moment: her own imminent death and that of the other nuns and their "comfortless unconfessed" companions.

The confession of Christ, the climax of the poem, is then made. Not the Christ of the past or the future, but the Lord of the present, now within the heart and in the universe he made, rises from the ruins of the storm to ride here "in his triumph." The nun professes her belief in him by an intuition of his being. She is called "The Simon Peter of a soul," because she acknowledges him as God, I AM. Hopkins later noted in his meditation points on St. Peter's confession: "Thou art the Christ the son of the living God —Praise our Lord in the words of this confession.—There are two acknowledgments, that our Lord was the Christ and that he was son of God. The Christ is the chosen and anointed man, the Son of God is God" (S, 254). For it is precisely in his manhood alive and victorious over chaos and death that he is Being. His body is the *pleroma* for all men in time. Thus he walked upon the waters of the Sea of Galilee and "drawing near to the boat, . . . said to them, 'I AM, do not be afraid' " (John 6:19-20). "But they who were in the boat came and worshipped him, saying 'Truly you are the Son of God' " (Matt. 14:33).

Christ is present in the crisis of the *Deutschland* through an act of loving faith in his real and personal existence. Must we suppose that this appearance is in fact miraculous? Elisabeth Schneider has recently proposed that the context requires a miracle.[6] Hopkins accepted miracles, but he would hardly invent one where eyewitness reports gave no grounds for its occurrence. He was, in addition, a respecter of accuracy, as he informed Bridges: "What refers to myself in the poem is all strictly and literally true and did all occur; nothing is added for poetical padding" (L1, 47). The actual details of the shipwreck as given in contemporary accounts are otherwise exactly reproduced in the poem. A miracle, therefore, is not a likely hypothesis on which to justify the poem's intensity and conviction.

The heightened language and imagery of these stanzas are justified alone by the poet's sense of the power of man's confession of Christ in an act of faith and gnosis: the nun "knew the who and the why." The conversion of the others is shown to be the result of the one sister's awareness of Jesus, the author and finisher of faith, not the effect of a miracle they have all witnessed. What Hopkins dramatizes here is the moment of inscape, made more profound in that it occurs in the act of dying, the last instant before the divine design of the Son's role in the universe will be revealed to her and the other dead passengers. "So death doth touch the resurrection," John Donne exclaimed. The new life already bursts through to take hold of the last heartbeat and breath of man's body. Christ comes at the last, desperate summons to make man's final moment of life the first moment of resurrection. As pictured in the early martyrologies, the believer's risen *soma* stands forth on this side of death, already marked for glory.[7]

The *Deutschland* actually is a dramatic bodying forth of the theology of death that has preoccupied recent Catholic thinkers like Karl Rahner and Roger Troisfontaines. In the moment of departure from this life, the whole man, present to himself, reaches the height of his encounter with the servant who emptied himself even to death on a cross and is lifted up with him in suffering and the promise of his risen life. The entire experience of man's existential being is recapitulated in this action. For death is not a passive stupor or aggressive rage, but the choice that answers *yes* in obedience with Christ's great sacrifice or *no* with the demonic overreaching of those who refuse to lose their life for another, their brother, the slain Lamb of God. For the man in grace this hour is the climax of his union and identity with the Lord who descended into the depths of man's loneliness, "who loved me," in the words of St. Paul, "and gave himself up for me" (Gal. 2:20). The openness of the world, its cleave to meaning and integrity, reveals itself in the dying Christian who "gives up his spirit" in Jesus. With his Spirit, love is then released to share in the dynamic *pleroma* of cosmic union one with the other and all with Christ. The shipwreck is then a harvest and the tempest carries the grain for him in the hands of the tall nun.

Her utterance of Christ, moreover, is itself an act of creation as well as an act of saving efficacy for others.[8] Just as Jesus creates and redeems, so the sister becomes the maker and savior, the "AfterChrist," of that stormy winter night. Without her, by implication, the electrifying presence of the God-Man would not have been felt, no opening for his stress would have been found, and the doomed men would have perished "in unchrist." Such is the precarious fate of the men on the Eurydice who have none to call out for their salvation at the actual critical moment of their destruction. The nun remakes the physical disaster into a cause for celebration: "to bathe in his fall-gold mercies, to breathe in his all-fire glances." The storm becomes what Christ intended it to be: a glorious return through an innocent act of nature, since "in thy sight / Storm flakes were scroll-leaved flowers, lily showers—sweet heaven was astrew in them." The "martyr-master" is always ready to welcome his creature home, but someone must "fetch" him to creation's door for it to open and reveal him there. Death is meant to be a homecoming not an upheaval.

Just as Hopkins in his journals inscaped Christ's presence in stars and bluebells, and in his poems in sunlight and fields, so the nun inscapes the risen Jesus in the storm. Her unerring aim is here the fulfillment of her whole life of dedicated service through poverty, chastity, and obedience, which in her death is focused and summed up in her fetching of the master. The nun's inscape then is the inscape of the poem:

> Ah! there was a heart right!
> There was single eye!
> Read the unshapeable shock night
> And knew the who and the why;
> Wording it how but by him that present and past,
> Heaven and earth are word of, worded by?

The initiate's "single eye" saw something, not a miraculous appearance of Jesus, but the Christ of living faith, man's sole real contact with the Father. For the nature of faith, as Hopkins noted, "is God / in man / knowing his own truth" (S, 157). The Word-made-flesh sounds his worship within creation and within himself so that the one cry, the nun's call to him, becomes a cosmic echo, a verbal "burl" of the "miracle-in-Mary-of-flame." By naming him, she brings the *pleroma* to being and Jesus to the world. Through her, Hopkins claims, a new consciousness enters history.

The same confession of Christ is to be found in the climax of part 1. "The faithful waver, the faithless fable and miss" when faced with the mystery of God present in the world and in man, in suffering and repentance. God is known only through the human heart responding to Christ's humanity as a revelation of the divine. This revelation is made through his crucifixion and resurrection:

> The dense and the driven Passion, and frightful sweat:
> Thence the discharge of it, there its swelling to be,
> Though felt before, though in high flood yet—

> What none would have known of it, only the heart,
> being hard at bay,
>
> Is out with it!

The important "it" which runs through three stanzas is, as previously noted (p. 89), the "stress" of divine presence experienced by man in "stars and storms," in joy and sorrow, in the calm of contemplation and in sudden calamity. What is the nature of this presence? Christic being, energizing and filling man through his Spirit. What is its source and how is it known and acknowledged? From and through the heart. First of all, Christ's heart "is out with it" when it "was pierced and spent its contents by the opening in his side" (S, 103). Hopkins reflected in his meditation points: "The piercing of Christ's side. The sacred body and the sacred heart seemed waiting for an opportunity of discharging themselves and testifying their total devotion of themselves to the cause of man" (S, 255). From the wounded rib of Christ the Second Adam, out of which flowed water and blood, the Christian, a new creature through baptism, is traditionally described as being born anew like another Eve. The only way to the Father is this passageway or cleave opened in Christ's side; his death frees his risen life and in his risen body he still bears the open wound in which St. Thomas plunged his hand.

Through the union of hearts man encounters the hidden godhead. The "heart" that "is out with it" is also the heart of each man: the nun's "heart right" which when "hard at bay" utters its confession of faith; and Hopkins's own "mother of being in me, heart," who in an earlier spiritual crisis "fled with a fling of the heart to the heart of the Host." The heart "expresses in itself what goes on within the soul" (S, 103).[9] It is the power of intuition by which we inscape Christ in the present and receive his instress within. "Heart" is repeated eighteen times in the poem, most frequently in the reflective and climatic stanzas (2, 3, 6, 7, 9, 17, 18, 26, 27, 29, 30, 31, 34, and 35). For Hopkins, the act of faith is a recognition of the heart and mind, revealing the presence of Christ and his "double-naturèd name."

Since the nun's inscape of Christ in the storm governs the entire poem, her experience in the narrative is the reader's inscape of the *Deutschland* from the opening lines to the last. Hopkins wrote of the poem that "it is an ode and not primarily a narrative" (L1, 49). But the two are interrelated. The narrative dramatizes the ode's intent as a hymn of praise to Christ, the God-Man, shaper and rescuer of the world. The *Deutschland* is a Pindaric song of triumph in Christ's victory over chaos and death. The historical Jesus is now the Lord of glory, reigning in the universe and in the hearts of men. The purpose of the ode is that expressed in the conclusion of Hopkins's sermon on "Our Lord Jesus Christ": "And this man whose picture I have tried to draw for you, brethren, is your God. He was your maker in time past; hereafter he will be your judge. Make him your hero now. Take some time to think of him; praise him in your hearts. . . . Glory in all things to Jesus Christ God and man" (S, 38).

The whole poem is a confession of "Jesus Christ God and man" and is addressed to him: he is its inscape. Christ is invoked in the opening lines as a hero, the poet's maker and judge:

> Thou mastering me
> God! giver of breath and bread;
> World's strand, sway of the sea;
> Lord of living and dead;
> Thou hast bound bones and veins in me, fastened
> me flesh,
> And after it almost unmade, what with dread,
> Thy doing: and dost thou touch me afresh?
> Over again I feel thy finger and find thee.

Christ is praised as the speaker's most intimate molder and renewer of self. As he once fashioned Adam and probed the naked flesh of Job, the human Word touches the just man's body with the finger of his Spirit. That "God" here is an epithet of Christ's becomes explicit in the second stanza: "Thou heardst me truer than tongue confess / Thy terror, O Christ, O God" where "God" is clearly an appositive. When, in stanza 9, Hopkins shifts to address the Trinity as God, he carefully indicates the fact: "Be adored among men, / God, three numberèd form." Christ as mediator leads men to the adoration of the triune godhead, and he again becomes the subject of the following stanza. The conversions of Paul ("I am Jesus whom you persecute") and Austin ("Put on the Lord Jesus Christ"), which conclude part 1, were both acts of Christ's mediating "mastery." And "Be adored King" is more appropriately applied to Christ the King.

"Lord of living and dead" is another of the *epinoiai* which compose this hymn to the Word of life.[10] The title is echoed in stanza 28 where Christ is called on: "Do, deal, lord it with living and dead." The ode ends with a crescendo of seven epithets of Christ, of which the final and most emphatic is "our thoughts' chivalry's throng's Lord." *The Loss of the Eurydice* also opens with an invocation to the "Lord" and ends with a closing prayer to "Christ lord of thunder." In all his writings Hopkins, following the practice of the New Testament in which this name expresses the special character won by Jesus in his death and resurrection, employs "Lord" as an exclusive title of Christ. The adjective, "mastering me," is the form of another title, "Master," also applied to Jesus: "A master, her master and mine!" (19), "Thou martyr-master" (20), and "the Master" (28). In stanza 10 the poet bids his Lord: "Make mercy in all of us, out of us all / Mastery"; by "stealing as Spring" through man, "melt him but master him still." Thus, through an *overing* of *epinoiai*, as Origen prescribed, the one Word-made-man is known in his multiple roles from the first line of the poem to the last. The one Christ is the aim and mark of the entire ode. Gnosis of his nature and of his heroic deeds is the reason of its being. His is the mystery—as the Greek mysteries had foreshadowed—into which his adherents are initiated and through which, after mystic knowledge is revealed, the garland of victorious new life is bestowed. "The Lord is the hierophant," writes Clement of Alexandria, "and seals while illuminating him who is initiated, and presents to the Father him who believes, to be kept safe for ever" (*Protrepticus* 12).

A sermon or "Dominical," preached at St. Beuno's two years after the composition of the *Deutschland*, contains a number of parallels to the opening lines of the poem. One passage seems almost a paraphrase and confirms our reading of this stanza as a confession of Christ. Hopkins is addressing his fellow Jesuits:

> But we, brethren, *we will*, if you please, crown Christ king; He is and shall be king, lord, and master of my mind, heart, and will. . . . This man whom just now we seemed to see dealing out the barley bread, this man, Jesus of Nazareth by name, at this moment while I speak seated at the right hand of the Father is dealing me out my life, my voice, my breath, my being: let Him withdraw it if it is His will, if not let me employ it much better than heretofore to His glory. . . . His hand created you once, now it deals out to you your being and the bread and all things that keep you alive; in the end it will either crown you or it will cast you away. Crown Him now who can crown you then, kiss the hand that holds the dreadful rod. (S, 232)

The words "Lord," "master," "bread," "life," "breath," "hand," and "dreadful" echo stanza 1 of the *Deutschland*. Even "rod" occurs in stanza 2, line 2, as "lashed rod." "This man . . . is dealing me out my life, my voice, my breath, my being": here is the epitome of the poet's Christology. The sermon and ode, beyond these verbal similarities, also share the same purpose and theme. Both affirm the intervention of divine life in the cosmos, in history, and in personal existence. In both Jesus of Nazareth is hailed as "Eternal King and universal Lord" to whom the Jesuit poet made his oblation in the meditation of the Kingdom (S, 160-61). In both "this man," maker and judge, Alpha and Omega, creates, heals, punishes, and rewards.

The first stanza is balanced by stanza 32 in part 2:

> I admire thee, master of the tides,
> Of the Yore-flood, of the year's fall;
> The recurb and the recovery of the gulf's sides,
> The girth of it and the wharf of it and the
> wall;
> Stanching, quenching ocean of a motionable mind;

> Ground of being, and granite of it; past all
> Grasp God, throned behind
> Death with a sovereignty that heeds but hides, bodes
> but abides;

The sentence continues into the next stanza where it is clear that Christ is addressed, since his harrowing of hell is described. The previous two stanzas and the three that follow and end the poem form a six-stanza finale in praise of "Jesu, heart's light" and creation's King. Stanza 32 belongs in that movement and does not break it. The inscape of "The Christ of the Father compassionate, fetched in the storm of his strides" concludes, in stanza 33, the narrative material of the ode. Christ is here the Being of Parmenides, "held in mighty bonds," "quenching becoming," "Ground of being, and granite of it," just as he was the "World's strand, sway of the sea," in the opening stanza. He is the cause of the world, as well as the archetype and image in which it was made. All things were created through him and in him, as St. John wrote in his prologue. In stanza 32, then, Hopkins makes his confession of faith and achieves the perfection of gnosis in acknowledging—that is, he owns the knowledge of—the man Jesus as God, I AM: he is the creator as, in stanza 33, he is the redeemer of mankind. From the heights of godhead he empties himself "with a love glides / Lower than death and the dark." In these two stanzas the whole drama of the great sacrifice, as sung in the Philippians hymn for example, is brilliantly summarized. Like Pindar, Hopkins hails his champion in his struggle against "death and the dark" and in his race for being and light.

The concreteness of the language and imagery by which Christ is made existentially present testifies to Hopkins's intense identification of the world with the incarnate Word. He avoids pantheism because his faith asserts Jesus as a person, the God-Man, creator and judge of the human race. "Past all / Grasp" he is God, "throned behind / Death" in the glory of his risen body. Hopkins never conceptualized a Word apart from the man he became. The humanity of Christ is the primal, innermost fact of creation. For him Jesus of Nazareth is the Pantocrator: "Mid-numberèd he in three of the thunder throne!" Like Prudentius before him, he sang the whole Christ of creation, the Alpha and Omega of historic revelation. The early Christian Spanish poet in his *Liber Cathemerinon* or *Poems of the Daily Round* thus describes the Son in his "Hymn for Every Hour":

Corde natus ex parentis ante mundi exordium,
alpha et omega cognominatus, ipse fons et clausula
omnium quae sunt, fuerunt, quaeque post futura sunt.
　Ipse iussit, et creata, dixit ipse, et facta sunt
terra, caelum, fossa ponti, trina rerum machina,
quaeque in his vigent sub alto solis et lunae globo.
　Corporis formam caduci, membra morti obnoxia
induit, ne gens periret primoplasti ex germine,
merserat quen lex profundo noxialis Tartaro.
　O beatus ortus ille, virgo cum puerpera
edidit nostram salutem feta Sancto Spiritu,
et puer redemptor orbis os sacratum protulit.[11]

This ninth hymn treats of subjects central to the *Deutschland*: praise of the creating and historic Jesus, the virgin birth, the harrowing of hell, the storm at sea, and the walk upon the waters; it too concludes in an apotheosis of the king's triumphant cross and a choral salute to his eternal glory: "*Macte iudex mortuorum, macte rex viventium, / dexter in parentis arce.*" On the right hand of his Father, the Son receives the singing procession of old and young, mothers and maidens, their paean released through the poet's "tuneful heart" and "nimble tongue." "Let the gliding waters of the rivers, the shores of the seas, rain, heat, snow, frost, woodland and wind, night and day unite to extol Thee for ever and ever."

The theological implications of Christ's role in creation have previously been examined in this book. To formulize the mystery, Hopkins adapted from the fathers and Duns Scotus the theory of the preexistence of Christ's created nature. The basis for the belief is found in the New Testament itself, especially in the writings of St. John and St. Paul. Traditionally, Christ is often pictured in Byzantine and medieval art as calling the world into being, walking in the Garden of Eden, directing Noah to build his ark. He is master of the "Yore-flood" and of all human history since he predates it and since it leads up to and follows from his place in time. Hopkins's use of these theophanies is nowhere more graphic than in this section (stanzas 32 and 33) of the *Deutschland*. Christ's presence in the midst of the disaster of December 7, 1875, is but one facet of his ubiquity and penetration in space and time, of which the Bible offers a full and compendious account.

The poem is in fact rich in references to the Old and New Testaments, from "the Spirit of God moved over the waters" in Genesis 1:2, to the promise: "Surely I come quickly," and the cry: "Come, Lord Jesus" of Apocalypse 22:20. These allusions form an important part of the *oftening* and *aftering* of the inscape of Christ, Lord of history and nature. One reference concerns us here for its particular relevance to the meaning and purpose of the poem. It is perhaps typical and worthy of Hopkins that the interpretation that follows hinges on one word; he was fond of the microcosm that inscaped the whole.

In his writings and letters, Hopkins showed a marked talent for scriptural exegesis. His reading of Philippians 2:5-11, anticipated, as we have seen, the modern critical attention to Christ's *kenosis* in his incarnation. Another key passage from St. Paul, although nowhere explicitly examined in Hopkins's extant writings, assuredly was known and studied by him: Colossians 1:15-20. Reference to it occurs in the inscape of the nun's dramatic confession: "*Ipse*, the only one, Christ, King, Head." Hopkins avoided foreign words in his poetry: the *ipse* is an unusual choice for him. Beyond the force of selfhood and identity denoted by the Latin word, it receives special connotation in the Vulgate version of St. Paul's famous passage.[12] God has transferred us, he writes, "into the kingdom of his beloved Son, in whom we have our redemption, the remission of our sins":

> who is the image of the invisible God, the firstborn of
> every creature, for in him were created all things in the
> heavens and on earth, things visible and things invisible,

whether Thrones, or Dominations, or Principalities, or
Powers; all things have been created through him and
in him, and he is before all creatures, and in him all things
hold together. And he [*ipse*] is the head of his body, the
Church; he, who is the beginning, the firstborn from the
dead, that in all things he may have the first place; for it
has pleased God the Father that in him all his fullness
should dwell, and that through him he should reconcile to
himself all things, whether on the earth or in the heavens,
making peace through the blood of his cross.

In the Greek original this poetic passage is one grammatical entity, a relative clause divided in two parts which closely parallel
one another: image = head; firstborn of every creature = firstborn from the dead; all things created = all things reconciled;
all things hold together = all his fullness should dwell. The poem
completes the circle by returning, in the final reference to the
cross, to the introductory "remission of our sins." The phrases
and clauses all depend on the initial reference to "the Son," who
is described by repeated use of relative and personal pronouns.
In the Latin translation, the pronoun *"ipse"* in one case or another
appears nine times in the six verses; the pivotal *"ipse"* occurs in
the middle verse between the two parts of the poem where St.
Paul states that Christ who is firstborn of creation, creator of the
world, is the very same one who is head of the Church, the first
to rise from the dead, and the redeemer through his reconciling
death. *Ipse* also identifies selfhood, the Self of all selves, the individual and focal Man.

Hopkins's use of "the only one" is an echo of the twice repeated *"primogenitus"* of the Colossians poem; in the authorized
Douay translation (Dublin, 1846), the word is annotated: "The
first born. That is, first begotten; as the Evangelist declares, *the
only begotten* of his Father." In his commentary, "Creation and
Redemption," the poet himself employed the word in the same
sense in which St. Paul develops it:

Man himself was created for Christ as Christ's created
nature for God (cf. "omnia enim vestra sunt, vos autem

Christi, Christus autem Dei" I Cor. iii 22, 23.). And in this way Christ is the firstborn among creatures. The elect then were created in Christ some before his birth, as Abraham, some before their own, as St. Ignatius; that so their correspondence with grace and seconding of God's designs is like a taking part in their own creation, the creation of their best selves. And again the wicked and the lost are like halfcreations and have but a halfbeing.

The first intention then of God outside himself or, as they say, *ad extra*, outwards, the first outstress of God's power, was Christ. (S, 196-97)

Christ is the first and only begotten because all men are created *to be* Christ; the present order of existence is life in Christ. The choice for man is between being and not-being, not between a natural and supernatural life. For Hopkins and St. Paul the world of "the merely natural" does not exist, for the cosmos and mankind within it have but one head, the risen Lord Jesus. As the opening stanza of the *Deutschland* declares, man is made in Christ and goes on being made in him. Here and now, the orders of creation and redemption are the same and have the same source, Christ, in whom the whole *pleroma* "foredraws," "draws-home to Being" as its dwelling place. The bond of being now is the body of Jesus. His "finger" creates and re-creates in each fresh instant of existence, for he is the extended "Hand of God" in human history.[13]

The epithet "Head," which Hopkins applies to Christ in this culminating line of *epinoiai* ("*Ipse*, the only one, Christ, King, Head"), also appears in the dramatic turning point of the Colossians passage: "And he is the head of his body, the Church." J. B. Lightfoot, in his classic commentary on this Epistle—which first was published in May of the year the *Deutschland* was written—comments on this verse: " 'And He', [is] repeated from the preceding verse, to emphasise the identity of the person who unites in Himself these prerogatives. . . . The Creator of the World is also the Head of the Church."[14] St. Paul originated the analogy of head and body to Christ and the Church in order to explain the existential relationship between the faithful and the risen Lord Jesus (see Eph. 4:7-16).[15] "Christ in his member on the one side," Hopkins noted, "his member in Christ on the other. It is as if a man said: That is Christ playing at me and me playing at Christ, only that is no play but truth; That is Christ *being me* and me being Christ" (S, 154). The same "super-exalted" Jesus then who is head of original creation is himself head of the new creation. He is reality revealed, "the image of the unseen God," and inscape of all that exists. Man must glorify him by aiming at gnosis, by initiation into the *mysterium Christi* that is the Omega of existence:

> Since, tho' he is under the world's splendour and
>   wonder,
>   His mystery must be instressed, stressed;
> For I greet him the days I meet him, and bless when I
>   understand.

Christ's presence must be felt within ("instressed") and acknowledged without ("stressed"), for he is ruler of hearts and maker of the world. Since Bridges's adverse initial commentary on the use of these two verbs, their meaning here has been subject to close critical scrutiny, to be defended or to be dismissed. The two verbs are defined by the twofold role of the Lord as redeemer and creator at work in man and in the universe. The poet rightly places "instressed" first, because it is only by accepting the reconciling activity of the Son within him that a man recognizes Jesus as Pantocrator. The source of the "stress that stars and storms deliver" is found at "hero of Calvary, Christ's feet." For Hopkins and St. Paul, man discovers creation through atonement. "Now, as heretofore," in Cardinal Newman's words, "a secret supernatural system is going on *under* this visible scene. And therefore he [the true Christian] looks out for Christ, for His present providences, and for His coming."[16]

The Pauline description of Jesus as head of all creation develops within the context of "the kingdom of his beloved son" which the faithful occupy as their promised land. In fact, when the Feast of Christ the King was promulgated in 1925, the text of the Colossians hymn was chosen as the epistle of the mass. In this climatic line of the *Deutschland* Christ is also greeted as "King." The Jesuit poet had often meditated on Christ's Kingship in the *Spiritual Exercises* and later frequently used the theme in his sermons. The *Deutschland* concludes with the prayer: "Our King back, Oh, upon English souls!" The same hope is found in his Dublin notes: "Wish to crown him King of England, of English hearts and of Ireland and all Christendom and all the world" (S, 255). May not the German nun's prayer open a new age of faith in modern-day Europe?

Hopkins shared with many of his contemporaries, especially Roman Catholics, a nostalgia for the Middle Ages, for "the Thirteenth: the Greatest of Centuries," when England and all Europe worshipped Christ in the one true Church and found him in each other and in the world. Saint Francis of Assisi best embodied this ideal, bearing the wounds of Christ in his body and welcoming the birds and beasts as his sisters and brothers. He was Christ's "Lovescape crucified," his inscape mark, with the marks of the nails and the lance stigmatized in his flesh by the six-winged seraph in the likeness of the crucified. Hopkins also was attracted to John Duns as much by the man and his period as by his ideas. His poem, "Duns Scotus's Oxford," beautifully evokes that imagined golden age. The Victorian priest longed for its return, as he notes in an entry to his journal: "I thought how sadly beauty of inscape was unknown and buried away from simple people and yet how near at hand it was if they had eyes to see it and it could be called out everywhere again" (J, 221). The inscape involved here is not one of nature, but of an artifact, the beams of a barn which looked "like bold big *A*'s with the crossbar high up." Looking upward, Hopkins saw there the Alpha and *arche* of reality and knew the words of the Lamb in the Apocalypse: "I am the Alpha and the Omega, the first and the last, the beginning and the end" (Apoc. 22:13). Men, returned to Christ, would again know him in their work and in the world around them. The secret of gnosis would again be revealed to "little ones," the simple people for whom Christ died. For even in their worst crime—deicide—mankind struck the inscape that is Word of Life and of Love:

> Five! the finding and sake
> And cipher of suffering Christ.
> Mark, the mark is of man's make
> And the word of it Sacrificed.

The great sacrifice was the Son's special aim and is the mark by which all are to be saved. Joy and adoration stand revealed in his unselfish love. "All the Law and the Prophets," wrote the Franciscan *doctor seraphicus*, St. Bonaventure, "depend upon these two Commandments: the love of God and of one's neighbor, which two are united in the one spouse of the Church, Jesus Christ, who is at once neighbor and God, at once brother and Lord, at once king and friend, at once Word uncreated and incarnate, our maker and remaker, the alpha and omega."[17]

The final stanzas of the ode, which build to a crescendo of rhetoric, music, and religious enthusiasm, are justly triumphant and theologically sound, since death—both moral and physical—has been defeated. The shipwreck and loss of lives are not a disaster but a harvest for Jesus, the Good Shepherd, who welcomes the dead, led by the nun his alter ego, into newness of life. Through her obedience, "the breast of the / Maiden could obey so," the kenotic offering leads to the *pleroma*; her cry of *Marana tha* could "startle the poor sheep back." The theme here is that of the *apocatastasis* developed by Origen and adapted by St. Gregory of Nanzianzen and St. Gregory of Nyssa, that all creation will eventually, after a series of aeons or cyclic ages, share in the total victory of the Word-made-man.[18] The whole *pleroma* will reach its potentiality of being as promised in Ephesians 1:9-10: "He has made known to us the mystery of his purpose, the hidden plan of his good pleasure prepared in Christ from the beginning and dispensed in the fullness of time: to re-establish all things in Christ, both those in the heavens and those on the earth" (adapted). This *recapitulatio* will see all things restored to unity with the godhead, when souls, plunging into nothingness, turn back to receive their full eternal being in the Lord. Christ's atonement will be completed and the Father will hand over the perfected cosmos to his Son. The text of 1 Peter 3:18-22, which Origen used as a basis for his idea of *apocatastasis* is paraphrased in stanza 33 of the poem. Christ is "an ark / For the listener . . . A vein for the visiting of the past-prayer, pent in prison, / The-last-breath penitent spirits," just as he is declared to be in the Epistle: "Put to death indeed in the flesh, he was brought to life in the spirit, in which also he went and preached to those spirits that were in prison. These in times past had been disobedient when the patience of God waited in the days of Noah while the ark was building." In the new ark of Christ's risen body a multitude is saved in the waters of baptism. The "comfortless unconfessed" shipwrecked souls of the Deutschland are rescued by the "all of water" that becomes their baptismal font through the nun's blessing and call. The wreck is therefore a prefigurement of the final recapitulation: then even the "uttermost" lost spirits, most remote and removed from him by sin, will "mark" or inscape "the Christ of the Father compassionate," when they are "fetched in the storm of his strides." This last picture of Jesus walking on the water is also reminiscent of the vision of the Good Shepherd in the closing lines of Milton's *Lycidas*:

> So Lycidas sunk low, but mounted high,
> Through the dear might of him that walked the waves.[19]

The spectacle of the *pleroma's* actuation in the final "lifting-up" of Jesus sums up the whole dramatic movement of the ode, which as the epigraph informs us takes place "between midnight and morning of Dec. 7th, 1875," the eve of the Immaculate Conception. A remarkable feature of the poem is the absence of any mention of sunlight until the second last stanza. Stars, lightning, flares, and beacons are the only sources of light to illumine the night of suffering and drowning. "When daylight dawned," the London *Times* later reported, a scene of carnage and horror was visible. Christ the sunlight of the world and its new dawn rises from the waves in stanza 33, transforming the storm's havoc and radiating his peace through Mary, the blue sky. The phrase

"our passion plungèd giant risen" announces the Lord's emergence into the poem's narrative. The finale of the ode is bathed
in his light: "Now burn, new born to the world." In the words of
the Eighteenth Psalm, Jesus is "the sun, which comes out like a
bridegroom from his chamber, it rejoices like a giant hurrying on
his way. From the end of heaven is its starting point, and its circuit extends unto the end of heaven, and nothing escapes its
flaming heat"[20] The circuit of descent in the darkening sky and
storm of his passion to the rising new day of his ascension completes the perfect framing of the myth. "The sun is new each
day," wrote Heraclitus, ". . . an intelligent burning mass, which
has arisen (and daily renews itself) from the sea."[21] What the
nun sees is Christ the light, aurora, the miracle of day.

Our reading of the *Deutschland* is strikingly paralleled by a
passage from Clement of Alexandria, which will serve here as a
summary of the poem's mythopoeic structure:

> Assuming the character of man and fashioning Himself
> in flesh, He [the Son] enacted the drama of human salvation:
> for He was a true champion and a fellow-champion with
> His creatures. And being communicated most speedily
> to men, having dawned from His Father's counsel quicker
> than the sun, with the most perfect ease He made God
> shine on us. Whence He was and what He was, He showed
> by what He taught and exhibited, manifesting Himself
> as the Herald of the Covenant, the Reconciler, our Saviour,
> the Word, the Fount of life, the Giver of peace, diffused
> over the whole face of the earth; by whom, so to speak,
> the universe has already become an ocean of blessings.
> (*Protrepticus* 10)

Even "the dark side of the bay of thy blessing" vaults seafaring
man and becomes "a crimson-cresseted east" in the person of
Christ, the champion who reaches out to rescue and holds fast
the drowning "Simon Peter of a soul." His question to man is
put directly: "Where is your faith?" And man responds, marvel-
ling the more, with his own deeply felt inquiry: "Who, then, is
this, that he commands even the winds and the sea, and they obey

him?" (Luke 8:25). The answer comes to each as it came to St. John when he saw Christ standing by the Sea of Tiberias after his resurrection: "It is the Lord!" (John 21:7). "*Ipse*," the same one whom David acclaimed:

> The Lord reigns, he is clothed with beauty: the Lord is clothed with strength, and has girded himself.
> For he has established the world which shall not be moved.
> Thy throne is prepared from of old; thou art from everlasting.
> The floods have lifted up, O Lord: the floods have lifted up their voice. The floods have lifted up their waves, with the noise of many waters.
> Wonderful are the surges of the sea: wonderful is the Lord on high.
> Thy testimonies are most worthy of belief. Holiness becomes thy house, O Lord, unto length of days.   (Ps. 92)

The singer's and maker's art reveals the dynamic order and direction that underlie existence. In the *Deutschland* Hopkins worked to shape in words the meaning of the "unshapeable shock night" of his own and others' lives in relationship to the God-Man's life. The mystery of his person and of his dealings with men defies expression, but Hopkins's experience of "the Master" in his vocation made him bold to attempt a ritual—yet deeply personal—proclamation of faith and love. The nun's call, "O Christ, come quickly!" resounded in his own heart, and from her inscape the whole poem grew. He began by writing the narrative sections of the verse with "the *Bremen* stanza" (12) and probably worked toward her confession first, before reconstructing his own in part 1. As she summoned Jesus and christened "her wild-worst Best," so the poet rang her Word-made-word through the inscape and body of the poem, "*over-and-overing, aftering* of the inscape . . . to detach it to the mind," for "the inscape must be dwelt on" (J, 289). Everywhere present, gnosis of the hidden spiritual sense must still be earned. The poet's labor of creation and the reader's effort in re-creating that inscape are summed up in the poet's comment on his heroine:

But here was heart-throe, birth of a brain,
Word, that heard and kept thee and uttered thee outright.

The tone of joy that is the ode's "air and melody" is a result of Hopkins's new confidence in himself as poet, after years of self-imposed silence, and of his assurance in the good tidings he believed in, handed down from St. John in the prologue of his Gospel: "We saw his glory—glory as of the only-begotten of the Father" (John 1:14). He was never again, at such length, to repeat his success; years later Patmore could still call it "your favorite Poem" (L3, 353). No other English poet has more tellingly conceived and proclaimed the height, depth, and breadth of the "master of the tides" and "an ark / For the listener," Christ the maker and remaker of mankind. Few Christian poets, in any language, have been so inventive in their mythmaking and so urgently eloquent in venturing "a new thing."

8

"Let him easter in us": Sonnets of 1877

FOURTEEN MONTHS after completing *The Wreck of the Deutschland*, Hopkins wrote his mother on March 1, 1877: "I think I must send you two sonnets I wrote in a freak the other day; they will make a little gift" (L3. 144). The two poems, long cherished and displayed by the family, were "God's Grandeur," dated February 23, and "The Starlight Night," dated the next day. Although he felt himself free to write poetry after composing his great ode, he had done nothing more than a few occasional pieces in the year 1876. In the following seven months of 1877 he wrote ten sonnets, several of which are among his best-known poems and one of them, "The Windhover," the single most scrutinized sonnet of modern literary criticism. Much of his poetry was written in such parcels of released energy, of which the *Deutschland* itself is an excellent example; but the periods between these poetic outbursts were often unproductive. The poet himself seems at times to have been all too willing to acquiesce in his aridity: "I have done little and shall do less" he declared to Canon Dixon (L2, 15). He did, however, dedicate long hours to the painful task of correction and rewriting.

Nature and man in their relation to God form the theme of this group of sonnets. They follow the seasons from spring to fall in this his ordination year at St. Beuno's in Wales. The period ended in disappointment—even tragedy, if we look at the effect on his whole career—when he failed to pass an examination in theology that would have allowed him another year of studies in

167

the field.[1] Abruptly in October he left Wales, "always to me a mother of Muses," as he later wrote Bridges (L1, 227). The sonnets trace a unifying growth in phrasing the promise and prayer that concludes the *Deutschland*: "Let him easter in us, be a dayspring to the dimness of us, be a crimson-cresseted east." Through the lines of these poems, the risen Jesus shines from within the poet's heart and in the innocent cosmos. His myth becomes the subject matter of sonnets unequaled in their fusion of intense sensibility and religious conviction.

Critics have sometimes viewed nature and grace as conflicting one with the other in Hopkins's response to the real; but the poems not only join the two, they are the unity they express. They announce the oneness-in-duality that Christ himself embodied as man and God and that the sonnet structure of two unequal parts also attains. The world of nature is reached through the mind of redeemed man, for in acknowledging atonement he penetrates creation. Grace does not oppose nature but fulfills and upholds it. In the achievement of gnosis one reality and presence is apprehended, one man is known in all his genius and godhead. Throughout the cylindrical cosmos all things are directed toward his glorified body. Existence itself is the *pleroma* in whose atmosphere or environment man becomes totally immersed in Christ, the firstborn of creation and firstborn from the dead.

The opening quatrain of "God's Grandeur" (P31) declares the myth in all its secrecy and beauty; it also signals the difficulties readers encounter in Hopkins's poetry:

> The world is charged with the grandeur of God.
>   It will flame out, like shining from shook foil;
>   It gathers to a greatness, like the ooze of oil
> Crushed. Why do men then now not reck his rod?

"God" here is not a philosophical concept nor a remote Christian deity; he is in this and the sonnets that follow the Father of Jesus in whose Sonship men and even the universe share. The flames that flash out like light off gold foil in the world of creation are the tongues of flame that prefigure the conclusion of the poem. The fire is the Holy Spirit's action of communicating Christ to the world. The olives also are a biblical image of abundance. The squeezing action by which a drop of oil is released recalls the "burl" or *pleroma* from one cleave of which being issues forth. The shape of the earth also suggests the "mass of the well-rounded sphere" Parmenides pictured. "All things therefore are charged with love, are charged with God"; they "give off sparks and take fire, yield drops and flow" (S, 195). All things are full of the Triune Being.

The theme of the sonnet then is that of the liturgical prayer to the Son of God: "Send forth thy Spirit and they shall be created and thou shalt renew the face of the earth." The source and setting of this appeal are particularly relevant to the poem; they are set forth in a passage on the messianic day of the Lord from the second chapter of the Prophecy of Joel:

> Fear not, O land, be glad and rejoice, for the Lord hath done great things. Fear not, beasts of the fields, for the beautiful places of the wilderness are sprung, for the tree hath brought forth its fruit, the fig tree and the vine have yielded their strength. And you, O children of Sion, rejoice, and be joyful in the Lord your God, because he hath given you a teacher of justice, and he will make the early and the latter rain to come down to you as in the beginning. And the floors shall be filled with wheat, and the presses shall overflow with wine and oil. . . . And you shall know that I am in the midst of Israel, and I *am* the Lord your God, and there is none besides; and my people shall not be confounded forever. And it shall come to pass after this, that I will pour out my spirit upon all flesh; and your sons and your daughters shall prophesy; your old men shall dream dreams, and your young men shall see visions. Moreover upon my servants and handmaids in those days I will pour forth my spirit. (Joel 2:21-24, 27-29)

Here the land—the Hebrew word means "soil"—will no longer be barren, but trees and vines, beasts and men will grow fertile physically and spiritually when the spirit of the Messiah-Teacher is poured out on all. This text is used by St. Peter in his discourse on the day of Pentecost, as reported in Acts 2:17-21. The promised gift of renewal has actually been fulfilled through the death and resurrection of Jesus of Nazareth. Hopkins's sonnet is indebted to the prophecy in details, such as "oil," "soil," and "spirit," and in its eschatological intention. With Joel and St. Peter, the poet views the world as already sharing the day of fulfillment; man, however, sadly fails to realize the kind of world he lives in.

Nature, anointed with an "oil of gladness" and radiant with sunlight, is risen with Christ in his Easter exaltation which affirms, rather than destroys, the original freshness of "the beginning / In Eden garden" (P33). Hopkins does not picture nature as wounded or groaning in itself for an unreceived redemption. He apparently followed the tradition that interprets St. Paul's famous verses in Romans 8:18-23, which state that "all creation groans and travails in pain until now" while it awaits its deliverance, as a reference either to human nature or to the expectation of the Son who has come and already renewed the natural world. True, Hopkins shows nature as subject to decay and submitting to man's abuse; but the basic position assumed in his poetry is that earth and sky are avenues through which man may inscape Christ if he but choose to correspond with the Holy Spirit who "helps our weakness." "Nature is never spent" because she has remained true to herself and to her maker. Sharing in the fall only because men refuse redemption, she is everywhere ready to refresh and renew.

The second quatrain of "God's Grandeur" has led to some misunderstanding. It reads:

> Generations have trod, have trod, have trod;
> And all is seared with trade; bleared, smeared with toil;
> And wears man's smudge and shares man's smell: the soil
> Is bare now, nor can foot feel, being shod.

These lines are not intended as a romantic diatribe against the industrial revolution. Hopkins nowhere shows himself an enemy to social progress; quite the contrary, he shocked Bridges by calling himself a Communist, since their ideals, if not their means, were just: "It is a dreadful thing for the greatest and most necessary part of a very rich nation to live a hard life without dignity, knowledge, comforts, delight, or hopes in the midst of plenty—which plenty they make" (L1, 27-28). The object of the poet's indignation is man himself, abusing others, refusing them the "plenty" that the Father lavishes on all. Man turns his back on "the dearest"—most cherished and costly—"freshness deep down things" by wearing the earth bare but never probing the inner knowledge of the Word who made and redeemed the universe. The light shines but man fails to master it; the soil blossoms but hearts will not read the Easter message.

For, had they but the faith to see it, men would find in the earth a tabernacle of the divine dwelling. The soil on which they tread is sanctified: "Take off your shoes," the Lord commanded Moses as he approached the burning bush, "for the place on which you stand is holy ground" (Exod. 3:5; adapted). The God of Abraham, Isaac, and Jacob reveals himself in the flames that blaze out but do not consume. But no one bares his feet now to worship at his sanctuary "in spirit and in truth." The earth, however, is "bare" and, since God turns even man's abuse to good purpose, offers its inexhaustable witness to his immanence everywhere in action. The *pleroma* is never spent. Even the punishment of Adam and his sons: "Cursed is the earth in her work; with labor and toil shall you eat of it all the days of your life" (Gen. 3:17; adapted), has been made a blessing through the "labor and toil" of the lowly Son of God. The interstices of physical and human nature are filled with his presence through the *kenosis*. The very rod of chastisement has been turned against himself and is now a staff of leadership held in the hand of the Good Shepherd.

Although the creature will not "reck" the rod of the Father's authority, the sestet of the sonnet describes the Son's appeal to man through his presence in nature as the sun born new each day:

> And though the last lights off the black West went
> Oh, morning at the brown brink eastward, springs—.

"The Sun of Justice shall arise," Malachi prophesied, "with healing in his wings" (4:2; adapted). The risen Lord renews the face

of the earth, because he has sent his Spirit of love to "brood"—
hatch and hover—over the world until he returns:

> Because the Holy Ghost over the bent
> World broods with warm breast and with ah! bright
>   wings.

These final lines make explicit the Pentecostal underthought of
the poem by showing the Spirit at rest and re-creating the earth:
the day of the Lord is the present morning. The sonnet, employing circular shapes like "world," "olive," sun, and nest, forms a
semantic and structural circle, scaled down in the octave to the
"bare now" of man's emptiness and upward in the sestet to the
breast and wings of love's fulfillment. The dove is not only the
usual image of the Spirit, but the peace of reconcilement and understanding which he brings. Because of his activity and watch-
fulness over the earth, Christ the sun is present in the power of
his risen life.

A command and invitation to see the heavens in imagination
opens Hopkins's next sonnet, "The Starlight Night" (P32):

> Look at the stars! look, look up at the skies!
> O look at all the fire-folk sitting in the air!
> The bright boroughs, the circle-citadels there!
> Down in the dim woods the diamond delves! the elves'-
>   eyes!

The reader is told to inscape (the Greek *scope* for "look") the
stars as distant marks shaped like circular medieval castles and
townships. Hopkins presents a world of fairyland as a mythological system through which man views the universe. The pre-
Christian folk myth of elves and fairies is further fortified by
references to the ordinary world of farmyard and "flake-doves
sent floating forth." The two worlds, however, do not fuse; the
mythological "fire-folk" and the "farmyard scare" do not form
one vision of the real. The elves, like the doves, are easily fright-
ened away. Make-believe and everyday living look forward to
completion in the transmuting realism of the revealed Word.
He makes all myths true and life itself mythical in his person,

human and divine. For he alone knows the alchemist's secret of "where gold, where quickgold lies!"

How is Christ inscaped? How do mind and imagination find their treasure and light? The sestet answers: "Buy then! bid then! —What?—Prayer, patience, alms, vows." The way to ascend to gnosis is to lower oneself and follow the path of sacrifice expressed in deeds of love and giving; the line ends with the culminating gift of religious imitation of the servant Jesus through the three vows of poverty, chastity, and obedience. Paradoxically, this descent moves man toward fullness of being; it is not a falling away into nothingness: one wins the world by losing it. Christ's bidding and pledge are thereby substantiated: "Lay up for yourselves treasures in heaven, where neither rust nor moth consumes, nor thieves break in and steal. For where your treasure is, there will your heart be also. The light of the body is the eye; if your eye be single, your whole body will be full of light" (Matt. 6:20-22; adapted).

Thus the second command:

> Look, look: a May-mess, like on orchard boughs!
> Look! March-bloom, like on mealed-with-yellow sallows!

not only parallels the first call to inscape, but transmutes and completes it. The stars are a springtime of renewal, the risen world made real; they are the harvest world of Christ's victory and "the bonds of that bound that guards it [Being] all about" (J, 128):

> These are indeed the barn; withindoors house
> The shocks. This piece-bright paling shuts the spouse
> Christ home, Christ and his mother and all his hallows.

The stars are the surface of the burl of Christ-being, the cleaves through which the watcher glimpses the round light of the godhead housing within. The heavens are a tabernacle of gold reserving the "leaf-light housel" or communion of the risen body of Jesus; they are the harvest of the Gospel promise, the myth of fairyland and farmyard come true in the heavenly city. "The bright boroughs" of the octave become "the barn," and the "fire-

folk" are Christ and his saints. The purchase and prize offered
for kenotic self-emptying is fullness of existence, where "Being
draws-home to Being."

A Latin poem, which Hopkins may have written in this same
period, throws light on the inscape, or potential intention, of
these two sonnets and of those which follow. The poet first describes the hunter constellation Orion rising in the sky at the turn
of the new year; then he addresses Christ:

> O Jesu qui nos homines caelestis et alta haec
>   Contrahis astra manu,
> Omnia sunt in te: nostrum vivat genus in te,
>   Quod tua membra sumus,
> Omnes concessas inquam quot carpimus auras
>   Suspicimusque polum.
> Gratia deest sed enim multis: ut gratia desit,
>   Omnibus alma tamen,
> Alma etiam natura subest, cui tenditur ista
>   Provida cunque manus.[2]

Christ creates and sustains nature: all things are from him and
in him, stars, wind, and sky "to which we look up." The poet
prays that man, our "genus," may live in him because we are
members of his risen body; but many, unfortunately, are without
"gratia," grace and the spirit of grateful recognition of Jesus
which is its outward sign and inscape. The hand, however, that
draws men and stars into being is stretched out everywhere in
gracious nature to aim the graceless heart providentially back to
its temporal and eternal beginning. Jesus is the "Orion of light"
—harbinger of spring's "scroll-leaved flowers, lily showers" (P28,
21)—that mildly and steadily pursues men and directs them to
their mark. He rises, a transfigured hero, over a world no longer
bound by winter and night since they too proclaim his glory as
Pantocrator: "Ice and snow, stars and moon, praise the Lord."

Four of Hopkins's poems are dated for May of 1877: "Spring,"
"In the Valley of the Elwy," "The Sea and the Skylark," and "The
Windhover" (P33–36). With the simple exclamation, "Nothing

is so beautiful as Spring," the poet introduces one of his richest
evocations of the fullness of eastering earth. Heaven appears in
earth and earth in heaven, both translated by the poet's vision:
"Thrush's eggs look little low heavens" and:

> The glassy peartree leaves and blooms, they brush
> The descending blue; that blue is all in a rush
> With richness; the racing lambs too have fair their fling.

Here the "lambs" are both their literal selves and at the same time
"clouds" racing across the blue sky. The absence of "like" after
"look" identifies the eggs with the heavens, the natural with the
godly, the visible with the invisible, in Christ. In Hopkins's
poetry conventional metaphors and comparisons are rarely employed because being is univocal, things are similar by being
known for what they are: Christlike. Natural objects are fused
in man's unifying encounter of thought with things; fullness is
what we know. "What is all this juice and all this joy?" the poet
asks, and answers: this "sweet being" of creation and "innocent
mind and Mayday in girl and boy" issue from the incarnate
Word, born of Mary, who as creator and redeemer returns all
reality to himself: "Most, O maid's child, thy choice and worthy
the winning." The Alpha "in the beginning / In Eden garden"
is Omega, the end and plenitude of men's illumined minds.

    "In the Valley of the Elwy" takes the theme of "a house where
all were good / To me" and extends it to "this world of Wales."
The sonnet continues the themes of the previous sonnets, the
house itself becoming a microcosm of the burl of being in Christ
actualized in the risen world of his members unified with him.
The "kind people" are "a hood / All over" and the "cordial air"
of their home makes of them "a bevy of eggs" protected by "the
mothering wing" as "mild nights the new morsels of Spring."
The poem thus employs the objects established previously—
eggs, wings, air, and spring—in a fresh context of the familiar
and the mysterious, the literal world and the mystical reality. But
where the family treated Hopkins with warmth and renewing
kindness and, much more, where the Father pours all his hospital-

ity and warmth on his guests, men will not turn in love to him by simply recognizing the beauty and cordiality of their dwelling place:

> Lovely the woods, waters, meadows, combes, vales,
> All the air things wear that build this world of Wales;
>   Only the inmate does not correspond:

> God, lover of souls, swaying considerate scales,
> Complete thy creature dear O where it fails,
>   Being mighty a master, being a father and fond.

The final prayer is again biblical in intent, asking that the *pleroma* be made real in the creature who has cost the Father so dearly, the price of his Son. God can bring the world of man to completeness because he is almighty, and he will do so because he is all-loving.

The poet shifts his "composition of place" in "The Sea and the Skylark," although the seacoast is that of Wales, and the theme of nature's innocence and man's lack of response—for the Welsh were fallen in heresy—continues. The fluctuating, horizontal activity of the ocean is contrasted with the lark's vertical flight, singing as it ascends. The geometric pattern of both is circular and perfect; both word their being in self-spending amid a world of change, "till none's to spill nor spend" of all their roar and music. Their doing is directed toward the one Word who made them; but man, in almost hopeless contrast, slips back to dust without aiming at Christ and fulfilling himself:

> How these two shame this shallow and frail town!
>   How ring right out our sordid turbid time,
> Being pure! We, life's pride and cared-for crown,

>   Have lost that cheer and charm of earth's past prime:
> Our make and making break, are breaking, down
>   To man's last dust, drain fast towards man's first slime.

This moving statement of man's tragedy, unrelieved by any explicit reference to his possible risen state, sets forth a theme important to Hopkins: man's fatal depravity when, called to ascend, "life's pride" chooses to remain in his falling away condition. Without direction forward, man's sphere becomes a coil of diminishing motion. His final dust joins his initial clay in a cycle that satanically mocks his true destination. And God's curse is fulfilled as the inscapeless mold returns to its primal nonbeing. Life's coronal lies shapeless in the mud.

Circular motion and form dominate "The Windhover": the kestrel moves in slow, wide, sharp, and gliding circles which the rhythm and language perfectly mimic. Christ is present here as throughout the other sonnets, in the sun illuminating the scene; he is the dawn drawing the bird to a brilliant expression of itself and hence of its Lord. The poet inscapes its flight as a "coinciding-point" in relation to the morning light:

> I caught this morning morning's minion, king-
> dom of daylight's dauphin, dapple-dawn-drawn Falcon.

The chivalric underthought already implied in the epithets for the kestrel becomes part of the drama in the identity of horse and bird turning round on a rein: "How he rung upon the rein of a wimpling wing / In his ecstasy!" The imagery is reminiscent of the opening lines of Clement of Alexandria's "Hymn to Christ the Savior" at the conclusion of his *Paedagogus* or *Christ the Teacher*.[3] Christ the King is evoked through his *epinoiai*:

> Bridle of colts untamed,
>   Over our wills presiding;
> Wing of unwandering birds,
>   Our flight securely guiding.
> Rudder of youth unbending,
>   Firm against adverse shock;
> Shepherd, with wisdom tending
>   Lambs of the royal flock.

This section of Clement's poem repeats and recapitulates poetically a just-previous prose paragraph:

> A horse is guided by a bit, and a bull is guided by a yoke, and a wild beast is caught in a noose. But man is transformed by the Word, by whom wild beasts are tamed, and fishes

> caught, and birds drawn down. He it is, in truth, who
> fashions the bit for the horse, the yoke for the bull, the
> noose for the wild beast, the rod for the fish, the snare
> for the bird. He both manages the state and tills the ground;
> commands, and helps, and creates the universe.
> (*Paed.* 3. 12)

"The Windhover" employs some of the same details as are found in Clement: the bird is caught and drawn by the poet's inscape; the horse is guided by its bit; the ground is ploughed down. The theme is also the same: the incarnate Word creates and controls reality by reining all being to himself, its center. In this activity man's transformation takes place as his will submits and his mind heeds Christ "The Teacher, the Creator of the world and of man ... by whose command we and the universe subsist" (*Paed.* 3. 12). Thus Hopkins's "heart in hiding / Stirred for a bird,—the achieve of, the mastery of the thing." The falcon and the gentle heart— identified with one another in the sestet—are tamed by submission to their king. The poem invokes the hidden way of seeking God through gnosis: knowledge of the Word in his cosmos experienced in the penitential, disciplined heart and sounded in turn in "*awe*" (the dominant assonance of the poem) back to Christ the Lord.

Another analogue confirms the theme which Hopkins intended to develop in his most famous sonnet. Shakespeare's tragedy *Macbeth* presents the opposite vision of "The Windhover," a chimera of unrestrained ambition. Cosmic obediential power, shown in nature's bending to the creator's will, projects man's submission and depends on it. When man rules himself with reason, he moves with and acts on the forces that harmonize the universe. When, on the contrary, a hero like Macbeth breaks faith with himself and his society, he brings down chaos on the macrocosm and the little world of man. After the night of Duncan's murder and its discovery, the day following is enveloped in darkness and marked by internecine disorders. Two minor characters act as a chorus which interprets the cataclysm. Part of their discussion throws light on Hopkins's poem:

Old Man	'Tis unnatural, Even like the deed that's done. On Tuesday last, A falcon, towering in her pride of place, Was by a mousing owl hawk'd at, and kill'd.
Ross	And Duncan's horses (a thing most strange and certain) Beauteous and swift, the minions of their race, Turn'd wild in nature, broke their stalls, flung out, Contending 'gainst obedience, as they would make War with mankind. (act 2, sc. 4, ll. 10-20)[4]

The juxtaposing of falcon and horse again recalls "The Wind-hover," as the repetition of "pride," "beauty," and "minion" echo Shakespeare's text. Like "rung upon the rein," "pride" is a term from falconry which describes the highest pitch or point the bird attains in its flight. Hopkins also pictures the falcon "towering" or soaring upward in wider gyrations. Not darkness but sunlight and not "war with mankind" but oneness of hearts here govern the Victorian poet's vision of the "great chain of being" forged by obedience.

Throughout the octave the kestrel is seen not in isolation but in "ecstasy," straining outside itself and locked in a relationship to the whole valley, hills, and sky which its flight in the direction of the sun concentrates and configures. Flying with perfect control, the bird first moves with the wind currents, turns, hovers, and, mounting ever higher on rapid wingbeats, momentarily counterbalances the wind; then it sweeps off, like a projectile or a shot from a bow, almost out of range of the poet's awestruck gaze, its activity fixed in an immensity of space. The falcon seems to soar with ease, in sharply defined circles, as if around some distant invisible point. The statement, "The hurl and gliding / Rebuffed the big wind" accurately sums up the two maneuvers of the bird's flight, the two arcs—with and against the wind—that compose its circling pattern. When the distance between observer and object grows great enough that visual contact is lost, or when the kestrel itself swoops out of sight, the poet, reluctantly taking his eyes away, comes home to himself, not in solitude or quiet reflection but with excited wonder at the cosmic relevance of what he has witnessed. The morning ambience, with its resonances of beginning, turns in the sonnet's *volta* toward the final consummation of the ash embers that are exhausted in their acting out of Christ's light in the world. The poem is itself a circle, Alpha ending in Omega, the alchemy of art producing at last the "gold of philosophy," *aurum volatile* shining "gold-vermilion."

The windhover itself is not a religious nonce symbol of Christ, but, acting on a literal level, performs its creaturely wording of its maker and guide, the Word and universal Lord. As we saw, Christ appears as the sun, the "king of daylight" of an earlier manuscript version, who enlightens and penetrates everything in the poem: bird, air, soil, embers, and heart. As in Homer, whom Hopkins studied assiduously, the falcon here is the messenger of Phoebus Apollo, the new Helios-Lord of early Christian art. Perhaps the poet further saw Christ prefigured in the Egyptian sun-god Ra, usually depicted with a falcon's head and a solar-disk crown. In any case, the Lord illumines the landscape and the inward sight. Hopkins also follows Plato's description of the sun in the sixth book of the *Republic* (sec. 508) in which the Greek philosopher claims that the sight is the most sunlike of man's senses and mirrors the activity of the soul: "And the soul is like the eye: when resting upon that on which truth and being shine, the soul perceives and understands and is radiant with intelligence; but when turned towards the twilight of becoming and perishing, then she has opinions only, and goes blinking about."[5] The contrast between the way of truth and the way of opinion is important to Hopkins who once noted: "Our souls alternate between a transcendental and a phenomenal, a γνῶσις—and δόξα —, life" (D8). The "evening of becoming" will grow longer in his poetry to be finally "spelt from Sibyl's leaves" with overwhelming definitude. Like the ideal philosopher the Jesuit priest would later return to his cave of shadows. In "The Windhover," meantime, light radiates the outer and inner worlds of being and intelligence.

The opening lines of the sestet are the most problematic of this esoteric sonnet. In tone and intent they mark an entirely new movement:

> Brute beauty and valour and act, oh, air, pride, plume, here
>   Buckle! AND the fire that breaks from thee then, a billion
> Times told lovelier, more dangerous, O my chevalier!

The slow, heavy cadence of the first half of line 9, accentuated by the repetition of "and," contrasts with the accelerated, compressive, and intensifying effect which climaxes in "Buckle!" perhaps the most discussed word in English literature. Question first arises, however, on the literal level: Does the sestet continue the description of the kestrel's flight and, if so, does it picture the bird swooping down from the sky? Or is the action here entirely interior, in the poet's imagination as he reacts to the "achieve of, the mastery of the thing"? Another alternative exists and would embrace both exterior and inner experience, the fusion of being and thought in the moment of instress; this solution I believe to have been the poet's intention. The sestet is addressed to the "chevalier" heart which, inspired by the bird's spiraling aspiration, "whirled out wings that spell." Whether the windhover plunges earthward or not—I believe that Hopkins imagines the act of a kestrel contracting its wings to its sides and then diving[6]— its wheeling climb of pursuit breaks off visually, suddenly transfixed and translated to a new realm of existence, drawn home within the immolating mental snare of its ascetic admirer. The bird's arc bends inward "here" in the watcher's heart in contrast to the "striding / High there" of the octave. "Buckle" then defines the coalescing action of inscape and instress: as a kestrel pulls in its wings before falling, so the poet's heart draws home to itself. A more detailed analysis of the verb's meaning will be made in the final chapter of this study (p. 278).

Hopkins targets the motion of the falcon's "hurl and gliding" and interiorizes its buckling action. Inscape again leads him to instress, intuition to union. The poet sees this surrender of flight as the emptying of self in *kenosis*, the sacrifice of "pride" and "plume" of station in the hidden way of gnosis. The fire of Christ-being that bursts from this redemptive activity within the heart of the Christian knight is infinitely more beautiful and precariously ablaze than the light of Christ the creator shining in the calm and dappled dawn. Phoenixlike, the falcon is reborn from flames "a billion / Times told lovelier" in the poet's "heart in hiding." So much greater is the uncreated presence of Christ in grace than the gift of himself as creating Word. For as Word-made-flesh he transforms man into himself, the servant whose obedience, humility, and suffering now bring him eternal glory. Even in nature man discovers kenotic action as the secret of exaltation, for the inscape of Christ, the true finding of love, is the fire that burns at the heart of reality, his pierced heart. Man may read the meaning in the world, once it has been revealed to him through Jesus:

> No wonder of it: shéer plód makes plough down sillion
> Shine, and blue-bleak embers, ah my dear,
>   Fall, gall themselves, and gash gold-vermilion.

Redemption is at work in nature, in the inner law of diminishing that governs beauty. The breaking of the circle can be more lovely than the original form.

The poet, reflecting within himself in the second part of the sonnet, finds evidence for the great sacrifice of "putting one's hand to the plough" and of submitting to the penance of sackcloth and ashes in the objective proofs of creation's own epiphanies of loss and gain: the shining plowshare and flashing embers. The light of Christ, the crucified and risen Lord, unifies the sestet: the sun reflected from the blue and russet falcon, the gleaming plow—and, by extension, the glow of the newly turned furrows—and the sparks of the smoldering ashes leaping back into life. This light in its concrete manifestations lives on in the mind. But it reveals itself to the pure of heart in the simple things of this world grandly conceived and expressed. Hopkins once exclaimed in one of his sermons: "Poor was his station, laborious his life, bitter his ending: through poverty, through labour, through crucifixion his majesty of nature more shines" (S, 37). Now over and within the just his sun shines, never to set.

Poetry itself thus becomes, in Philip Sidney's phrase, a "Glasse of reason" in response to the interior light of reason, as the two are described by Francis Bacon in his *Advancement of Learning*: "Poesy was ever thought to have some participation of divineness, because it doth raise and erect the mind, by submitting the shows of things to the desires of the mind; whereas reason doth buckle and bow the mind unto the nature of things" (2. 4. 2).[7] Even poetic inspiration yields to the inner Logos who subjects all things to himself because previously he was made subject to all (see Heb. 2:7-10). In "The Windhover," the poet's heart first stretches out to the bird and seizes its upward flight as a spherical imaging forth of the universal Logos; then the Logos within, "the Word and sovereign Reason now made flesh" (S, 261), bends the mind to "the nature of things," the dynamic process of self-emptying at work in reality, "the word of it Sacrificed."

"The Windhover" is dedicated "To Christ our Lord" in the same way as the poet himself is consecrated, through the gift of one's self in utter emptiness to be filled with the fullness of the Word of life, "grace after grace." The kestrel, lowest in degree of the falcon pedigree and identified as the heraldic emblem of the servant,[8] shows the way to the hidden heart. Its soaring flight embodies the ideal of gnosis, controlled action and concentration which opens to inscape of the sacrificial aim and mark of Jesus: his lifting up above the earth in pain and glory. One early morning in May, Hopkins caught forever the transforming life of the God-Man at work in the world and in the inner man. The creator of the octave is the same Lord and savior of the sestet: "*Ipse*, the only one, Christ, King, Head." At the sight of that falcon circling toward the sun the poet's heart reared wings and flew to the Heart and light of the world.

The world already transfigured through the creating action of the Son becomes the manifest subject matter of Hopkins's curtal sonnet, "Pied Beauty" (P37). Nature's variety and man's diverse tasks issue from the one Word in whose Sonship all reality shares:

Glory be to God for dappled things—
  For skies of couple-colour as a brinded cow;
    For rose-moles all in stipple upon trout that swim;

> Fresh-firecoal chestnut-falls; finches' wings;
> > Landscape plotted and pieced—fold, fallow, and plough;
> > And áll trádes, their gear and tackle and trim.
>
> All things counter, original, spare, strange;
> > Whatever is fickle, freckled (who knows how?)
> > With swift, slow; sweet, sour; adazzle, dim;
> He fathers-forth whose beauty is past change:
> > > Praise him.

God, "lover of souls," is a "father and fond" toward his universe. Thus the world is his son, as St. Athanasius declares in Newman's summary of his teachings: "He who was the Son of God became in a certain sense Son towards the creation for the sake of it and in it."[9] Through the Word's *syncatabasis* or "lowering ministration," says Athanasius, "the creation also is made a son through Him." He continues: "The Word of God is in the world, which is a body, and has taken possession of the whole and all its parts . . . for it becomes Him to enter into the world and to be manifested in the whole of it."[10] In "Pied Beauty" God is in every sense "the Father of our Lord Jesus Christ, from whom all fatherhood in heaven and on earth receives its name" (Eph. 3:14-15). The incarnate Word is the firstborn of primal creation as he is the firstborn of the new creation, since from the beginning he adopts the world, elevating it, as through grace he elevates mankind, and stamps on each creature an "impress, so that the whole world, as being in one body, might be, not at variance, but in concord with itself."[11]

Natural objects and human artifacts appear in a contrasting and prismatic kaleidoscope, assuming ever new shapes and patterns. The purpose of man's existence is to inscape reality, to unify it through his encounter with Christ the Son of God and the Son of man. Through his condescension, the One is made visible in the many, that man may ascend through the many to the One. The invisible Father "is past change," greater than all. By means of multiple experiences in seeing and doing, the one Lord is known, as the "Great Amen" of the mass confesses: "Through him you give us all these things. You fill them with life and goodness, you bless them and make them holy. Through him, in him, with him, in the unity of the Holy Spirit, all glory and honor is yours, almighty Father, for ever and ever, Amen." The final "Praise him" of the sonnet counterpoints and climaxes the whole descending movement of the poem from the "skies of couple-colour," down to the landscapes and mundane trades. All things opposite and individual at last coalesce in an abrupt command to ascend to the Father in gnosis, the praise of the Son in man and in the world, who alone reveals things hidden "from the wise and prudent," for "all things have been delivered" to him by the Father; "and no one knows the Son except the Father; nor does anyone know the Father except the Son, and him to whom the Son chooses to reveal him" (Matt. 11:27). Praise is offered only in and through the Son.

The theme of an ascending return of being is given dramatic and personal expression, hardly matched even in Hopkins's poetry, in the sonnet "Hurrahing in Harvest" (P38). Dated shortly before his ordination and the impending separation from St. Beuno's that he knew would follow, the poem proclaims the majesty of finality: "Summer ends now; now, barbarous in beauty, the stooks rise / Around." Death and all departures, even in the lowliest and most inarticulate of creatures, announce the risen presence of the Lord Jesus:

> . . . up above, what wind-walks! what lovely behaviour
> Of silk-sack clouds! has wilder, wilful-wavier
> Meal-drift moulded ever and melted across skies?

Transformation in Christ is worded in the "doing-be" of all reality, dissolving and being born again, freely ranging and reshaping in new diaphanies of the Word in glory. "The Hurrahing Sonnet," Hopkins later told Bridges, "was the outcome of half an hour of extreme enthusiasm as I walked home alone one day from fishing in the Elwy" (L1, 56). Nowhere does he more graphically describe the act of inscape:

> I walk, I lift up, I lift up heart, eyes,
> Down all that glory in the heavens to glean our Saviour.

Christ the sunlight and Shekinah manifests the divine presence in the skies as he did in his transfiguration, and man's encounter with being-in-Christ is active energy of recognition in which "the fulness is the thought." Ascended into heaven, departed from this life, he shines in the world and in the heart, for he responds sensually and spiritually to the poet's whole physical and psychic awareness:

> And, éyes, heárt, what looks, what lips yet gave you a
> Rapturous love's greeting of realer, of rounder replies?

The sounds and semantics of language itself enter into the transforming action of nature in the poet, the poet in Christ, and all three in the poem as one wording of the real, the *pleroma* of person and being summed up in the name I AM. The repetition of "I lift up" reminds the reader that sacrifice and glory are identified here as they were in the "lifting up" of Jesus expressed in the phrase of St. John for the redemptive moment when men will know that name (John 8:28) and all things will draw home to him (John 12:32). The experience of Christ is more actual and full than any acquaintance with another person: gnosis is thus best defined solely in terms of "knowing" Jesus not merely as "friend and acquaintance" but as "loved one" embraced in rapture and intimately possessed. He is the bridegroom of the soul and body, so loved that all things remind of him:

> And the azurous hung hills are his world-wielding shoulder
> Majestic—as a stallion stalwart, very-violet-sweet!

Even the hills, suffused with light, resemble him; in their rotundity and softness they become the burl of being bound within him. Christ is thus revealed in inanimate ("hills") and animal ("stallion") nature, both in turn metamorphosed in his humandivine natures united in his one selfhood.

The sestet of the sonnet closes with a description of instress, the response of the whole man in confession of faith and in perfected knowledge which returns the cosmos to its source and end, Alpha and Omega:

> These things, these things were here and but the beholder
> Wanting; which two when they once meet,

The heart rears wings bold and bolder
And hurls for him, O half hurls earth for him off under
   his feet.

The "totus Christus" of St. Augustine fills the universe and penetrates the heart of gnostic man, obedient with the servant and
transfigured with him already in glory. With the wings of his
Holy Spirit, man flies to the mark of inner and cosmic love. Love
half lifts him off his feet as he runs his race toward Jesus.

In "The Caged Skylark" (P39) Hopkins makes man's resurrection itself the subject of a poem. The skylark, bringing to mind
the ascending lark of the previous sonnet (P35), is here pictured
as "scanted in a dull cage" and is compared to man's earthly condition: "Man's mounting spirit in his bone-house, mean house,
dwells." The spirit or *pneuma* is not intended by Hopkins as an
equivalent of the Greek concept of "soul" contrasted with "body"
but is employed in its Hebraic and biblical usage, as the "breath"
that vitalizes man's entire being, somatic and ghostly. Lark and
spirit are not simply compared, however, but are also identified
in activity:

    Both sing sometímes the sweetest, sweetest spells,
    Yet both droop deadly sómetimes in their cells
      Or wring their barriers in bursts of fear or rage.

Rhythm and syntax imitate, and operate as, inhalation and ex-
halation; the beat of man's body-soul is echoed in nature. Yet
the song-fowl is at home in his melodious, regulated world; he
drops down to "his own nest, wild nest, no prison." So will the
pneuma draw home at last to Being when released from captivity
in the moment of the resurrection of the body:

    Man's spirit will be flesh-bound when found at best,
    But uncumberèd: meadow-down is not distressed
      For a rainbow footing it nor he for his bónes rísen.

In their spiritualized *soma*, already realized in "the matchless
beauty of Christ's body in the heavenly light" (S, 36), human
beings will be limited by matter; but not weighed down or destroyed by it. They will no longer "droop deadly . . . in their

cells," but "drop down" to their nest, their origin and Omega, the contraction of all things in Jesus. Man's last inscape will be an eternal domiciling, and the whole of himself and his universe will share in it. For the rainbow is a pledge of the Word's covenant with Noah: "Never again shall all flesh be destroyed by the waters of the flood; never again shall there be a flood to destroy the earth" (Gen. 9:11). The land is "meadow-down" where the waters of death have receded; it forms the floor, just as the rainbow shapes the frame, of man's transfigured "cage."

"The Caged Skylark" exemplifies once again the threefold levels of meaning offered by Origen, for whom Scripture spoke to man's body through its literal meaning, his soul through its moral lesson, and his spirit through its mystical sense. The sonnet conveys the three levels in the caged lark and "bone-house" of man, the captive spirit "in drudgery, day-labouring-out life's age," and the risen man "found at best" in his new body and setting. The last reading preserves the first, literal one, just as man's final state does not "distress" or undo to the point of nonbeing the flesh-bound human condition. Being, as Parmenides saw, is forever held in bonds. At death and rebirth in Christ, the spirit retains—or gains in new dimensions—its relationship with the whole play and field of existence. In losing his life, the Christian wins the world back "a billion / Times told lovelier." He finds the green world underfoot and a rainbow above confining him home.

In affirming the goal, the final lines of "The Caged Skylark" light the way. Earth and heaven are even now circumscribed and illuminated by the act of being known in true gnostic contemplation. The new man in Christ, alive with fresh perception and desires, recasts his world in his own image, the *imago Dei*. Clement of Alexandria describes this activity by quoting its scriptural basis: " 'I make new things,' says the Word, 'which eye has not seen, nor ear heard, nor has the heart of man conceived.' With a new eye, a new ear, a new heart, whatever can be seen and heard is to be apprehended, by the faith and understanding of the disciples of the Lord, who speak, hear, and act spiritually" (*Strom.* 2. 4). These poems express the sense perception of the afterlife in Christ already present. What was from the beginning "in Eden garden" is now and ever shall be, no matter how men fail or how changeably "times go by turns." Literally, as St. Bonaventure asserts in his classic treatise, *The Mind's Road to God* (4. 3), in accepting Jesus, the Christian recovers his senses.

The theme of finality developed in the harvest sonnet and in this poem on eschatological release is given conclusive expression in the last poem Hopkins may have written at St. Beuno's, "The Lantern out of Doors" (P40). Watching a lantern move along the night, the poet wonders whence the light has come and where it goes. The "wading light" reminds him:

> Men go by me whom either beauty bright
> In mould or mind or what not else makes rare:
> They rain against our much-thick and marsh air
> Rich beams, till death or distance buys them quite.

The individual appears helpless to resist the current and flow that carries all before it. Even the just man, anxious to draw all things back to Christ, must wait in "all down darkness wide," watching helplessly in spite of his concern and care:

> Death or distance soon consumes them: wind
> What most I may eye after, be in at the end
> I cannot, and out of sight is out of mind.

The proverbial observation takes on new truth and meaning in Hopkins's context. In spite of the inscapes of seeing and eyeing after his friends and marking there the "Christ-ed features" of their character, the poet cannot "be in at the end," because each man's inscape of the Son is his own identity with him and never can belong to anybody else. Only Christ, the light of the world and dayspring of the heart, knows how to draw men home within:

> Christ minds: Christ's interest, what to avow or amend
> There, éyes them, heart wánts, care haúnts, foot fóllows kínd,
> Their ránsom, théir rescue, ánd first, fást, last friénd.

Only Christ, who is first and last, can follow each lantern out of doors to its destination, for he not only leads them as teacher and redeemer, he is the end they seek. Logos is the light of reason within and the burning fire of love.

Hopkins's sonnet recalls Clement of Alexandria's words in a similar vein: "For, just as the sun not only illumines heaven and the whole world, shining over land and sea, but also through windows and small chinks sends his beams into the innermost recesses of houses, so the Word diffused everywhere casts His eye-glance on the minutest circumstances of the actions of life" (*Strom.* 7. 3). Gnosis only exists in its fullness in the mind and heart of Christ; he alone sees the whole and all its facets; he alone completely inscapes reality. To him then the poet commends his friends, his fellow priests and seminarians and the Welsh people whom he had met and grown to love, whose language he had learned, and whose conversion he longed for. In this poem he bid them not "farewell," but "fair fall"—fair fortune befall them in their "first, fást, last friénd," Alpha and Omega. Before the poet himself lay darkness and new challenges, like those pictured in the closing lines of *Lycidas*:

> And now the sun had stretch'd out all the hills,
> And now was dropt into the western bay.
> At last he rose, and twitch'd his mantle blew:
> To morrow to fresh woods, and pastures new.[12]

Now he must be the "pastor," the good shepherd to Christ's flock; to them he turned as priest and as poet.

9

Poems of the
Apostolate

THE LOSS OF THE EURYDICE (P41) is Hopkins's most neglected major poem. Written in April 1878, while he was stationed at Mount St. Mary's College in Derbyshire, the poem is transitional in development, looking back to the *Deutschland* in its theme of shipwreck and steering forward to the poems of the apostolate where care of souls and individuals become the poet's chief concern and subject matter. Often compared with the *Deutschland*, the poem has only its theme in common; the two differ in form, for the *Eurydice* is a literary ballad and the other an ode in which narrative is subsumed in a hymn of praise to Christ. The two forms therefore impose different intensities of inscape in purpose and content, and the result is one of differing excellencies in both. The ballad meter, for example, was well suited for Hopkins's experiments in sprung rhythm and produced some of his most striking effects in "inscape of verse":

And you were a liar, O blue March day.
Bright sun lanced fire in the heavenly bay;
    But what black Boreas wrecked her? he
Came equipped, deadly-electric,

A beetling baldbright cloud thorough England
Riding: there did storms not mingle? and
    Hailropes hustle and grind their
Heavengravel? wolfsnow, worlds of it, wind there?

The calm rhythm of the first two lines belies the complex, almost jarring, crowding of stresses that accumulate in the later lines. Syntax also becomes more dense; and the rhetorical devices, such as the use of questions, pile up in planned confusion. Style, in short, mimics the action. The sun seemed to promise a safe course for the training ship homeward bound, but black snow clouds blow off from the land and capsize the frigate.

The literal reading is complemented by an anagogical meaning: Christ the light of the world is opposed in his efforts on men's behalf by the powers of darkness, here pictured as Boreas, the pagan god of the north wind. England, fallen away from the true faith found only in Rome, is locked in a northern heresy and even harbors the enveloping and increasing evil. From north to south, shire after shire, down finally and across the Isle of Wight: Carisbrook, Appledurcombe, Ventnor, and Boniface Down— places whose medieval names hint of an age of faith now past— all England is hurled under the freezing snow and gloom. Sunk close off shore, the ship and its fate are a microcosm of the country's dilemma and of the root of its troubles:

> Too proud, too proud, what a press she bore!
> Royal, and all her royals wore.
> Sharp with her, shorten sail!
> Too late; lost; gone with the gale.

Three centuries after the Reformation, Hopkins sees the realm foundering in pride and apostasy. Will Christ-Orpheus come to her rescue once again?

The main section of the *Eurydice* describes the wreck through accounts of the destiny of certain of her crew members who act as types of modern man. The first of these is the captain, Marcus Hare. Faced with death, he chooses heroism by going down with his ship and thereby wins Christ. Although in life he shirked his duties, he carries them out finally to full measure. His ultimate "Yes!" is an instress of the Savior.

> It is even seen, time's something server,
> In mankind's medley a duty-swerver,

> At downright 'No or Yes?'
> Doffs all, drives full for righteousness.

The poet's use of "righteousness" is significant, for it expresses in the King James Version the Pauline idea of justification through Christ's cross and resurrection which remained a Christian ideal in the mainstream of Protestant reform. Given the choice of affirming or denying Jesus in the moment of death, Marcus "drives full" to the *pleroma* of life by complete fidelity to the duties of his calling.

One crewman manages to free himself of the wreckage and "takes to the seas and snows." "Sidney Fletcher, Bristol-bred" all but drowns as "he wrings for breath with the deathgush brown"

> Till a lifebelt and God's will
> Lend him a lift from the sea-swill.

Having escaped one disaster he seeks for rescue or refuge on land:

> But his eye no cliff, no coast or
> Mark makes in the rivelling snowstorm.

The key word here is "Mark," for the young sailor, his face wrinkled in the blinding snow, can see no aim or destination, no fixed and distant point by which to set his course to safety. A spiritual exegesis of the passage shows the wreck to be the foundering of faith among the English people; individuals, however, may avoid the general ruin and yet find no immediate way to inscape Christ in confession of true faith and in knowledge of him. Man is helpless to attain the Father's favor, unless, like the Father of the prodigal son, God first run out to fetch and welcome the wayward home. Fletcher, "after an hour of wintry waves, / A schooner sights . . . and saves." Rescue comes in the form of the familiar bark of Peter, the fisher of souls who founded the Church of Rome:

> And he boards her in Oh! such joy
> He has lost count what came next, poor boy.

In contrast with Hare and Fletcher, both of whom are saved
spiritually either through death or rescue, a nameless "sea-corpse
cold" is next described in the waters of seeming destruction:

> He was all of lovely manly mould,
>   Every inch a tar,
> Of the best we boast our sailors are.

The reader is asked to inscape his body in a brilliant example of
decorum which places these stanzas among Hopkins's most
memorable:

> Look, foot to forelock, how all things suit! he
> Is strung by duty, is strained to beauty,
>   And brown-as-dawning-skinned
> With brine and shine and whirling wind.
>
> O his nimble finger, his gnarled grip!
> Leagues, leagues of seamanship
>   Slumber in these forsaken
> Bones, this sinew, and will not waken.

In his notes on Parmenides, Hopkins observed that the Greek
philosopher believed "the corpse which can no longer feel heat,
because the fire has left it, feels cold, silence, etc." (J, 130). The
corpse remains beautiful and suitable for spirit and life, ready
to perform its duties, but lacks the pneumatic fire which would
revive its "leagues of seamanship." On the mystical level, the
dead body signifies England and functions as a microcosm of the
coldness and indifference of a nation in which the love of Christ
once burned. Just as the sailor's corpse lies ready for life and duty,
so England, although dead to the true faith, retains a sense of its
former, pre-Reformation belief and awaits rebirth.[1]

Hopkins draws the lesson clearly:

> He was but one like thousands more.
> Day and night I deplore
>   My people and born own nation,
> Fast foundering own generation.

The poet then remonstrates with himself that he "might let by-gones be" and overlook the shrines, desecrated by "robbery's hand," which are now left neglected and unvisited. He could forget the past but that the living who now die outside the faith force him to speak out:

> Only the breathing temple and fleet
> Life, this wildworth blown so sweet,
> These daredeaths, ay this crew, in
> Unchrist, all rolled in ruin—
>
> Deeply surely I need to deplore it,
> Wondering why my master bore it,
> The riving off that race
> So at home, time was, to his truth and grace
>
> That a starlight-wender of ours would say
> The marvellous Milk was Walsingham Way
> And one—but let be, let be:
> More, more than was will yet be.

Thinking of the present loss and the wider disaster from which it grew, Hopkins slips back to remembering and regretting the age when earth and heaven were inscaped together *in forma Mariana*: the Milky Way led to the Virgin's shrine at Walsingham. And Duns Scotus . . . but the narrator breaks off in an effective aposiopesis and abruptly looks to the future with hope of a greater period of love in English hearts for Christ and Mary.

In his conclusion, the poet directly addresses the mothers, wives, and sweethearts of the perished men, a gesture traditional with the ballad. Natural grief, he implies, may yet win divine compassion. Better still, let them turn to "Christ lord of thunder" and pray:

> 'Holiest, loveliest, bravest,
> Save my hero, O Hero savest.
>
> And the prayer thou hearst me making
> Have, at the awful overtaking,
> Heard; have heard and granted
> Grace that day grace was wanted.'

This prayer expresses the hope that, as Jesus saved men before his time, so prayers after the event may be efficacious through him (see L1, 174). The women's heroes may have been saved in anticipation of their loved ones' sacrificial offering of widowhood and bereavement to the hero who died and was placed in his mother's arms. The pietà is recalled in "mother have lost son" and the "tears sad truelove" shed. As in the finale of the *Deutschland*, Origen's *apocatastasis* is introduced, here with the orthodox clarification that hell itself will not be abolished:

> Not that hell knows redeeming,
> But for souls sunk in seeming
> Fresh, till doomfire burn all
> Prayer shall fetch pity eternal.

Until the Last Judgment, all men, past, present, and to come, may share in the grace of the church universal; even those apparently lost may be potentially saved, awaiting their deliverance in a purgative state after death.

The inscape of the *Eurydice* can be put in the following summary form: just as three men, a hero, a convert, and an unknown corpse, may be breathed upon by the Spirit of Jesus and rise again in him, the first by his free choice, the second by his symbolic delivery, the third by his body's capacity for resurrection-life; so an unchristian nation may draw home to God by the power of petition to the risen savior. Mankind and nature do not perish utterly, but retain an openness, and in man an existential longing, for the reception of new being in Christ.

The spring and summer of 1879—one year after the composition of the *Eurydice*—resulted in an unexpected poetic flourish of nine poems written in six months. During this period Hopkins was assigned to do parish work at St. Aloysius' Church in Oxford, and the atmosphere of his first growth in gnosis seems to have offered him fresh outlets for his myth. "Duns Scotus's Oxford" (P44) evokes the thirteenth-century town with its "poisèd powers" of town and gown, church and state, nature and man, dedicated to Christ and Mary. Circular and "river-rounded," it enclosed the fullness of a unifying way of life and belief, a place "that country and town did / Once encounter in." Here the practical and intellectual pursuits of men fused in a harmonious worship and sharing of gnosis, still imaged in the contrasting setting of towers and trees, the frail balance of natural and architectural beauties. But now the center no longer holds, the city sprawls into ugly suburbs and confounds "rural rural keeping—folk, flocks, and flowers." The result is "graceless growth," lacking aim, purpose, or structure in both natural and spiritual orders. In the past, inscape could be found, and the sestet turns back to discover a man who best embodied the true mark:

> Yet ah! this air I gather and I release
> He lived on; these weeds and waters, these walls are what
> He haunted who of all men most sways my spirits to peace;
>
> Of realty the rarest-veinèd unraveller; a not
> Rivalled insight, be rival Italy or Greece;
> Who fired France for Mary without spot.

Duns Scotus, whose mind probed the inner recesses of knowledge and who lived the truth he contemplated, especially in his defense of Mary's Immaculate Conception, lives on in the meadows and buildings of Oxford and in the poet's mind and heart. In him also learning and doing were wedded in perfect imitation of Christ. He who inscaped reality becomes himself an inscape for others.

Hopkins carefully explained his next sonnet, "Henry Purcell" (P45), in several letters to Robert Bridges (L1, 83, 170-74). In his preamble to the poem, the poet praises the seventeenth-century musician because, beyond giving utterance "to the moods of man's mind," he has "uttered in notes the very make and species of man as created both in him and in all men generally." The sonnet's moment of inscape is clearly marked in the "colossal smile" flashed off the great stormfowl, when "meaning motion fans fresh our wits with wonder." Hopkins explained: "It is as when a bird thinking only of soaring spreads its wings: a beholder may happen then to have his attention drawn by the act to the plumage displayed" (L1, 170). Through such seemingly chance encounters, the watcher and the object fuse in a union of being and thought; the mind is drawn to its mark from the motion to its source, and the splendor of the outer and inner Word is revealed in the act of knowing. The result is the wonder of instress, the experience of oneness within. The poem is remarkable in that nature is used to inscape the genius of man and music. The microcosm is thus complete from the lowest to the highest scale, and from the many to the one.

The opening stanza of "Henry Purcell" repeats the prayer that concluded the *Eurydice*:

> Have fair fallen, O fair, fair have fallen, so dear
> To me, so arch-especial a spirit as heaves in Henry Purcell,
> An age is now since passed, since parted; with the reversal
> Of the outward sentence low lays him, listed to a heresy,
>   here.

Hopkins paraphrased: "May Purcell, O may he have died a good death and that soul which I love so much and which breathes or stirs so unmistakeably in his works have parted from the body and passed away, centuries since though I frame the wish, in peace with God! so that the heavy condemnation under which he outwardly or nominally lay for being out of the true Church may in consequence of his good intentions have been reversed" (L1, 170-71). He later noted that "one can say in the third person not only 'Fair fall' of what is present or future but also 'Have fair fallen' of what is past. The same thought (which plays a great part in my own mind and action) is more clearly expressed in the last stanza but one of the *Eurydice*" (L1, 174). Great men of the past have contact with the present in their living works as words of the one genius who recapitulated all human gnosis. The redeeming Christ, as St. Augustine observed in his *Confessions* (10. 43), reaches back and forth through time, a Mediator radiating in all directions to all men with the intense and ever-present stress of his Being. Prayers uttered through him are truly timeless.

"It is the rehearsal / Of own, of abrupt self there," Hopkins reasons, that "so thrusts on, so throngs the ear." The mysterious nature of music as spiritual reality echoes the inscapes of nature below man and the angelic orders above him:

> Let him oh! with his air of angels then lift me, lay me!
>   only I'll
> Have an eye to the sakes of him, quaint moonmarks, to
>   his pelted plumage under
> Wings.

The striking inscape of the stormfowl's "colossal smile" immediately follows, but has been prepared for in the "quaint moonmarks" or "crescent shaped markings on the quill-feathers" of the bird (L1, 83). Hopkins admitted that " 'sakes' is hazardous: about that point I was more bent on saying my say than on being understood in it" (L1, 171). Yet in an earlier letter to Bridges he gave a valuable analysis of this key concept of his myth and in the context of this poem:

> *Sake* is a word I find it convenient to use: I did not know
> when I did so first that it is common in German, in the
> form *sach*[e]. It is the *sake* of "for the sake of," *forsake,*
> *namesake, keepsake.* I mean by it the being a thing has
> outside itself, as a voice by its echo, a face by its reflection,
> a body by its shadow, a man by his name, fame, or memory,
> *and also* that in the thing by virtue of which especially it
> has this being abroad, and that is something distinctive,
> marked, specifically or individually speaking, as for a voice
> and echo clearness; for a reflected image light, brightness;
> for a shadow-casting body bulk; for a man of genius,
> great achievements, amiability, and so on. In this case it
> is, as the sonnet says, distinctive quality in genius. (L1, 83)

Hopkins thus possessed a word for the precise inscape of the poem, a word that telescopes its meaning—as did *"ipse"* in the *Deutschland*—and that opens up the theme and intention of the poems of the apostolate that follow: the "being abroad" of Christic presence in man. Defining the *pleroma* as "the burl of being in Christ," Hopkins observed, "and for every man there is his own burl of being, which are all 'by lays' or 'byfalls' of Christ's and of one another's" (S, 156). This "being" is not a superreality removed from experience or found only in Roman Catholics; for Hopkins the Word-made-man assimilates all human achievements in arts, trades, soldiery, or statesmanship to himself. Therefore, *anima naturaliter Christiana*, in Tertullian's celebrated adage, and each can say with Terence: "I am a man, and one that thinks he has everything to do with what has anything to do with man." So Hopkins translated the Roman playwright, insisting on identification through action (L1, 262). Christ alone is able to speak the full truth of these words, because only he as man can have "everything to do with" all other men: "I am the man" for and after whom all others are made. He exists for their *sake*.

In Duns Scotus and Henry Purcell the Victorian poet found the embodiment of the cultured humility and earnestness he admired. Both men were true Gnostics in their dedication to the mind and their insight into "the very make and species of man." In "The Candle Indoors" (P46) the scene turns to the world of everyday people, the present working-class English among whom the poet-priest labored and served. Unlike the "house where all were good / To me" (P34), these doors are closed to him, the passerby:

> Some candle clear burns somewhere I come by.
> I muse at how its being puts blissful back
> With yellowy moisture mild night's blear-all black,
> Or to-fro tender trambeams truckle at the eye.

Hopkins told Bridges that the poem was "a companion to the Lantern, not at first meant to be though, but it fell in" (L1, 84). As the "lantern moves along the night," so the candle radiates lines of light in all directions. In both sonnets the light in "night's blear-all black" "interests our eyes" as the object of inscape. Like delicate antennae of Christ, the Word whose beams penetrate "into the innermost recesses of houses" (*Strom.* 7. 3), the candle of the title and the theme of this poem recall the image used by Hopkins to describe the great sacrifice and *pleroma*: "It is as if the lights lit at the festival of the 'peaceful Trinity' through some little cranny striking out lit up into being one 'cleave' out of the world of possible creatures" (S, 197). Thus Being, even in its most ordinary epiphanies, is a stirring calling forth of the inner godhead. As in Prudentius's "Hymn for the

Lighting of the Lamp," the household flame reflects the light of Christ's glorious body in heaven.

Called out of the wide expanse of possible existence, the "Jessy or Jack" withindoors still is free to choose each task and ultimately to accept or reject God himself. The poet wonders how these people inside act "There / God to aggrandise, God to glorify." But he immediately turns back into himself and calls for inscape "there":

> Come you indoors, come home; your fading fire
> Mend first and vital candle in close heart's vault:
> You there are master, do your own desire.

The heart must first answer to the heart of Jesus burning with love for his priest and people. Possibly the lines intend a reference here to the consecration of the home to the Sacred Heart, an aspect of the devotion well known to Hopkins in his parish work. Before preaching and admonishing others, the inner man must be first renewed:

> What hinders? Are you beam-blind, yet to a fault
> In a neighbour deft-handed? are you that liar
> And, cast by conscience out, spendsavour salt?

Through an ingenious intervolving of familiar Gospel sayings: the beam in the eye (Matt. 7:3-5), the salt of the earth and the lamp set in the window (Matt. 5:13-16), the false swearer (Matt. 5:33-37), and the sound eye (Matt. 6:22-23), and finally the parable of the wedding guest "cast into exterior darkness" (Matt. 22:1-14), the poet-priest manages to draw the lesson home to himself in terms of Christ's own teaching.[2] The commonplace scene and familiar message become a dramatic, personal statement of his convolute myth. Just as the new law does not destroy the old but rather fulfills it, the fresh inscape of the poem pours new wine of imagery and language into ancient sayings and household conventions. As a result, the "economy" of salvation regains its original sense, and half-dead iconography again discloses its permanently human meaning, as Joseph Campbell envisions (see above, p. 96).

"The Handsome Heart" (P47) and "The Bugler's First Communion" (P48) both deal with "innocent Mayday" in young men as yet uncorrupted by sinful contact with the world. The boy who leaves to Father Hopkins the choice of reward for a favor done evokes the poet's twin admiration and analysis:

> What the heart is! which, like carriers let fly—
> Doff darkness, homing nature knows the rest—
> To its own fine function, wild and self-instressed,
> Falls light as ten years long taught how to and why.

The heart instinctively knows its aim and hits its mark, the heart of Christ spent in loving generosity for man. The sacristy drama here between priest and altar boy reenacts the drama of man's relationship with the Father; each is called to be his child and the brother of his Son. Grace creates in a moment what years of schooling attempt to inculcate and allows the will's natural bent full power and play. Nothing the priest can offer will match the child's mannerly heart, "more than handsome face," "all, in this case, bathed in high hallowing grace." His best return is a prayer which becomes part of the reward given in the form of the sonnet itself:

> Of heaven what boon to buy you, boy, or gain
> Not granted!—Only . . . O on that path you pace
> Run all your race, O brace sterner that strain!

Hopkins's advice is reminiscent of Erasmus's instructions to the young Christian soldier in the *Enchiridion Militis Christiani*: "That thou mayst haste and make speed unto felicity with a more sure course, let this be unto thee the fourth rule, that thou have Christ alway in thy sight as the only mark of all thy living and conversation, unto whom only thou shouldst direct all thine enforcements, all thy pastimes and purposes, all thy rest and quietness, and also thy business."[3]

The command to "brace sterner that strain" is also significant. Gregory of Nyssa made a virtue of "strain," which he called *epectasis* or "straining-out-towards" and which he based on the Pauline text (Philip. 3:13–14): "I strain forward to what is be-

fore, I press on towards the goal."[4] Hopkins speaks of God's pre-
venient grace as a "continued strain and breathing on" man's
actions, and man's response as a "drawing in of breath" (S, 157).
From "an infinity of possible strains of action and choice," each
person receives and finds his own strain of life, his own inherited
tendency toward Christ, and "the sum of these strains" of possible and real being is the burl or *pleroma* (S, 151). By keeping
on the strain inbred in him by grace, the disciple runs the good
race and reaches his goal, union with the crucified Lord of glory.
Because he is both physically and spiritually "strained to beauty,"
each man, like the "sea-corpse cold" of the *Eurydice*, yearns for
the renewal of his body. Christians would be better described as
those whose hope it is not simply to save their souls, but, most
profoundly, to save their bodies: "All . . . bathed in high hallowing grace."

The bugler boy of the next poem (P48) is pictured as a direct
and forward character. He comes to the priest with one aim and
purpose, to receive Christ. "A bugler boy from barrack . . ."

> This very very day came down to us after a boon he on
> My late being there begged of me, overflowing
> Boon in my bestowing,
> Came, I say, this day to it—to a First Communion.

The narrative style attempts to re-create this frank and intimate
tone by "bidding," which Hopkins described as "the art or virtue
of saying everything right *to* or *at* the hearer, interesting him,
holding him in the attitude of correspondent or addressed or at
least concerned, making it everywhere an act of intercourse—
and of discarding everything that does not bid, does not tell" (L1,
160). The reader is meant to partake of the sacramental experience of this poem, to communicate and become one with the
young hero and narrator in sharing the Word's body and blood.

The poet continues:

> Here he knelt then ín regimental red.
> Forth Christ from cupboard fetched, how fain I of feet
> To his youngster take his treat!
> Low-latched in leaf-light housel his too huge godhead.

Then communion:

> There! and your sweetest sendings, ah divine,
> By it, heavens, befall him! as a heart Christ's darling,
>   dauntless;
>   Tongue true, vaunt- and tauntless;
> Breathing bloom of a chastity in mansex fine.

With dispatch and élan, the narrator has introduced his actors and the main action: set for the mark and go. After asking the boy's guardian angel to "dress his days to a dexterous and starlight order," the priest reflects on the consolations of his calling and particularly of his service as an assisting military chaplain for the barracks "over the hill":

> How it dóes my heart good, visiting at that bleak hill,
> When limber liquid youth, that to all I teach
>   Yields tender as a pushed peach,
> Hies headstrong to its wellbeing of a self-wise self-will!

Hopkins again employs a fruit to represent the fullness of being in Christ; here the youthful burl is pliable and ready to accept the shape and substance of the eucharistic Lord. The natural bent for "wellbeing" is ever self-instressed in aiming at the person of Jesus who fulfills individual personality without undoing it. The bugler boy is his best and true self in his response to Christ's grace. And Christ himself deserves the best:

> Nothing élse is like it, no, not all so strains
> Us: fresh youth fretted in a bloomfall all portending
>   That sweet's sweeter ending;
> Realm both Christ is heir to and thére réigns.

The underthought of military imagery thus culminates in the role of Christ the king and heir to all that is spiritually fresh and young. For as Lord of the new creation, he has a particular claim to the "innocent mind" and "bloomfall" of mankind: was he not cut down in the prime of youth in order to renew that life in others by giving of his own? The theme here and in the previous poems about innocence is based on the belief that in the risen state everyone enjoys the full bloom of beauty, health, and strength of body: "Man's spirit will be flesh-bound when found at best" (P39).

Doubts concerning the young convert's perseverance in grace next beset the poet and he wishes to "see no more of him," lest he be disappointed. He does not cry disaster; he does ask: "But may he not rankle and roam / In backwheels though bound home?" Again the poet answers that salvation is Christ's doing: "That left to the Lord of the Eucharist, I here lie by." The task and duty of the poet-priest is discharged by writing the poem:

> Recorded only, I have put my lips on pleas
> Would brandle adamantine heaven with ride and jar, did
>   Prayer go disregarded:
> Forward-like, but however, and like favourable heaven
>   heard these.

So perseveringly has the poet knocked that "it shall be opened" and in all likelihood the words of the poem-prayer have been heard and stored for future need.

"Morning, Midday, and Evening Sacrifice" (P49) takes up the theme of sacrificing sensual pleasure and dedicating "thought and thew" to "Christ's employment." Man and woman's offering of "beauty blooming" and "freshness fuming" in the body-soul can escape the hand of death and the snatch of hell, by the gift freely offered now:

> What death half lifts the latch of,
> What hell hopes soon the snatch of,
> Your offering, with despatch, of!

By making one's own great sacrifice here and now, one already shares the there-and-then of the heavenly reward.

The subject of a human springtime, inscaped in the eastering of Christ's present risen life already begun in his faithful, attains its grandest expression in "The Leaden Echo and the Golden Echo" (P59), the Maidens' choral song from Hopkins's projected play, *St. Winefred's Well.* Here the choir of varied voices hymns the manifold ritual of change in a seemingly endless and contrasting profusion of words:

> How to kéep—is there ány any, is there none such, nowhere
> known some, bow or brooch or braid or brace, láce, latch
> or catch or key to keep
> Back beauty, keep it, beauty, beauty, beauty, . . . from
> vanishing away?

The "Leaden Echo" is answered by the "Golden" one: the way to keep back bodily beauty is to give it back to God. Here is the alchemical secret that changes lead to gold and bestows immortal youth. Place this "enumeration of parts," the poet states, at Christ's disposal, for he is the one Word who expresses and preserves the physical reality of man. In "the matchless beauty of Christ's body in the heavenly light" (S, 36), God's promise to creation is fulfilled: "Never again shall all flesh be destroyed" (Gen. 9:11). "For in him dwells all the fullness of the Godhead bodily" (Col. 2:9). Fleeting objects and life itself find their meaning and completion when directed toward their Omega. Beauty does not falter or tarnish with Christ's transmuting touch:

> The flower of beauty, fleece of beauty, too too apt to, ah!
> to fleet,
> Never fleets móre, fastened with the tenderest truth
> To its own best being and its loveliness of youth: it is an
> everlastingness of, O it is an all youth!

The multiple threads of the poem gather at the climax in one inscape, the thrust of being's trajectory toward the distant mark "Yonder," the divine *locus* or Omega by and in whom all things are delivered to the Father through the ministry of the Spirit. The Paraclete is at work within, helping man's weakness and transforming him even while man remains at rest. The chorus of maidens sums up the mystery:

> Nay, what we had lighthanded left in surly the mere mould
> Will have waked and have waxed and have walked with the
> wind what while we slept,

This side, that side hurling a heavyheaded hundredfold
What while we, while we slumbered.

Hopkins explained in a paraphrase for Bridges: " 'Nay more: the seed that we so carelessly and freely flung into the dull furrow, and then forgot it, will have come to ear meantime' etc." (L1, 159). The phrase "hurling a . . . hundredfold" not only echoes the hundredfold that sprang up from good ground in the parable of the sower, but also recalls the last line of "Hurrahing in Harvest": "And hurls for him, O half hurls earth for him off under his feet." In both the case of the crops and of the beholder, an upward motion against gravity is depicted. Perhaps borrowing an image from the game of hurling, Hopkins employs the verb in the sense of aiming and striking vigorously at a goal, an extreme physical exertion that results in an overpoweringly weightless action. The word then is another equivalent of inscape, the creature's forward sweep in its own field of play toward Christ the solar force and drawing power "yonder."

The Holy Spirit prepares the harvest, which "waxed and walked with the wind," but the cosmic procession back to the Father is led by the Son who now reaps what he once sowed. As in Egyptian and Eleusinian eschatology, the ears of corn are themselves symbolic of man's resurrection. His task completed, Christ has reached his goal and has become the harvest home where he keeps the offerings made to him by young men and women as a pledge of their share in his risen glory. "Lift up your eyes," Jesus commanded, "and behold that the fields are already white for the harvest" (John 4:35). From man's point of view the gifts are surrendered and kept "yonder," with someone distant and yet within touch, for of his fullness even now man is receiving "grace after grace." The reverse side to the great sacrifice, whose obverse is etched with the sign of condemnation and defeat, is the *pleroma* immediately known and felt in the initiated mind and heart. For without the resurrection-life already evidenced in experience, the cross is mere masochistic folly. "The thing we freely forfeit is kept with fonder a care, / Fonder a care kept than we could have kept it." "When we love God he first loved us," Hopkins reflected in his last sermon at Bedford Leigh, "first loved us as a ruler his subjects before we loved him as subjects their ruler; so when we love Christ with a fonder love than that / he with a fonder love than that first loved us" (S, 48).

"Beauty's self and beauty's giver" are found in the one perfect man who is God; bodily comeliness and "beauty-in-the-ghost" meet in him. Therefore the question: "To what serves Mortal Beauty?" (P62) may be readily answered without supposed tensions between the artist's sensibility and the disciple's sacrifice: "Merely meet it." For beauty "keeps warm / Men's wits to the things that are; what good means." The poet's judgment on physical and sensual charm in face and form is one with its being, a being that is open to a higher pitch of perfection through charity: "Yea, wish that though, wish all, God's better beauty, grace." The Greek ideal of beauty and "the good," immortalized in Plato's *Symposium*, becomes the Christian's springboard to the "everlasting loveliness which neither comes nor goes, which neither flowers nor fades, for such beauty is the same on every hand, the same then as now, here as there, this way as that way, the same to every worshiper as it is to every other."[5] The Jesuit's aestheticism was spiritually abetted by his classical study of the One, "*ipse*" ever the Same, whose archetypal beauty draws to him every man, present and past. Hence Hopkins defined beauty as "the virtue of inscape" (J, 288) and, in his own heart, "praised our Lord to and in whom all that beauty comes home" (J, 254).

"Felix Randal" (P53) is Hopkins's most rewarding sonnet on the apostolic theme we have been considering. Here concern for the body in its handsomeness and health and care for "beauty-in-the-ghost" come together in a masterly insight that is both highly personal in expression and yet universal in its emotion. Repeated readings of the poem yield fresh perceptions into the characters of the two protagonists, one of whom is presented entirely through the experience of the other: the priest-narrator and the young blacksmith whom he grew to respect and love during his parish work in Liverpool in 1880. The surprised expression of the opening line catches the dramatic moment of attention: "Felix

Randal the farrier, O is he dead then?" and the reflection that follows: "my duty all ended." Between the question and the response, the hearer pauses, reflecting on the severance the news has brought. The relationship between priest and penitent is thus immediately and effectively established; then the nature of the bond is examined: that of suffering hero and sympathetic observer:

> Who have watched his mould of man, big-boned and
>   hardy-handsome
> Pining, pining, till time when reason rambled in it and some
> Fatal four disorders, fleshed there, all contended.

The effects of disease on body and mind are described with accuracy, tenderness, and horror. Why must the body die, wearing away to disorder? The simple statement that opens the second quatrain, "Sickness broke him," is more than a grammatic contrast with the first one-sentence stanza. Before the mystery of suffering, man is forced to the literal meaning in the terrible fact of another's incommunicable pain. The directness of subject-verb-object is precise and declaratory, but avoids all element of the inexpressible.

The poet next attempts to evaluate the course of the spiritual experience of pain:

> . . . Impatient, he cursed at first, but mended
> Being anointed and all; though a heavenlier heart began
>   some
> Months earlier, since I had our sweet reprieve and ransom
> Tendered to him. Ah well, God rest him all road ever he
>   offended!

The spirit, reluctant to change at first, mounts at last while the flesh declines. The destructive encroachment of death, cursed and struggled against, makes way for the growing transformation in Christ present in his sacraments: extreme unction and, a few months previously (Felix had become lax as a Catholic), confession and communion. The verb "tendered" wittily sums up the priest's relations with the Lancashire blacksmith: he tenders his sacerdotal duties and feels tenderness as well in the man-to-man encounter. This reciprocity reaches across both lives, for the priest now ministers to the sick human spirit just as the farrier as a veterinary once treated animal ills.

The nature of this encounter is developed in the first stanza of the sestet:

> This seeing the sick endears them to us, us too it endears.
> My tongue had taught thee comfort, touch had quenched thy tears,
> Thy tears that touched my heart, child, Felix, poor Felix Randal.

The farrier is here the poet-priest's spiritual child, the order of grace complementing the natural affinity of the two men.[6] The resulting bond between them, the real matter of the poem, is seen in all its firm and human existentiality. The observer-speaker expresses actual grief in the other man's anguish and, without calling attention to his own tears, creates the experience of weeping in the words of the poem by the simplest and truest inscape of sorrow: a man's name remembered and mourned for. The same effect is achieved in the closing line of "Spring and Fall," one of Hopkins's deservedly most popular poems precisely because it fashions the emotions of the situation by reproducing them again within the reader. One cannot communicate suffering, but the poet can make the mind feel the *lacrimae rerum*, the tears in things themselves.

The full reality of this untimely death is thus drawn home to the speaker and to his readers. But the priestly voice does not turn down the path of despair; as in "The Golden Echo," he "welcomes destiny" with Thomas Nashe and bids: "Mount we unto the sky" in the confident knowledge faith brings in the face of death. Hopkins expresses this hope, however, not by referring the reader to a heavenly vision, but to a concrete human experience, the memory of a man:

> How far from then forethought of, all thy more boisterous years,

When thou at the random grim forge, powerful amidst
  peers,
Didst fettle for the great grey drayhorse his bright and
  battering sandal!

The picture evoked here is appropriate to the blacksmith's character and role and yet quite startling and unexpected. The vigorous phrasing creates a powerful impression that goes beyond the
recollected scene of a young man at work before the fiery stone
forge and suggests an element of mystery. The literal level yields
to the spiritual one in the final unifying object of the poem. The
inscape comes in the semicircular sandal, the mark of Christ—
capital Omega—held and glowing with fire. The horseshoe focuses on the fidelity to duty that marked the farrier's life. Felix
now lives with Christ because in his labor he gave God glory, as
Hopkins had observed: "Smiting on an anvil, sawing a beam,
whitewashing a wall, driving horses, sweeping, scouring, everything gives God some glory if being in his grace you do it as your
duty" (S, 240).[7]

The sonnet's final epiphany of the blacksmith, "powerful
amidst peers" and "smiting on an anvil," is a flashback to the
past when no forethought of the future was present. At that
moment this picture dramatically holds, foredraws, in a framed
instant of time but now made eternal. For we see Felix Randal
risen, his body in glory, "an everlastingness of, O . . . an all
youth!" His end glows in this timeless, luminous moment—his
kenosis fulfilled. The poem itself lends its meaning and immortality of poetic form to the sacred and secret inscape of a man's
life. The labor of art attains a unity beyond itself in the Word
who is light of the world, whose heart is a furnace of love, and
who was once himself a carpenter "sawing a beam."

"The heart," Hopkins wrote in "The Soldier" (P63), a sonnet
written in his Dublin years, "fancies, feigns, deems, dears the
artist after his art." People judge by the heart and rely on appearances to attain the real; a soldier's eye-catching red coat, for
example, leads the onlooker to think of courage there and "the
spirit of war." So each "hopes that, makesbelieve, the men must

be no less." Thinking must be being for the mind and heart of man; no other way is open to the fullness he knows himself lacking. Yet there is one historical surety, one man who can truly guarantee to be what he seems. Hopkins turns in the sestet of his poem to the meditation on the call of Christ the King:

> Mark Christ our King. He knows war, served this
>   soldiering through;
> He of all can reeve a rope best. There he bides in bliss
> Now.

Christ best knows the details of human duty; he is a hero who first served before calling others to his service after him. He best can pass a rope through a ring, can find the opening "near at hand" where "simple people . . . if they had eyes to see it" could call out inscape everywhere again (J, 221). Let men then set their sights on Jesus who teaches the lowly way to glory: "Learn from me, for I am meek and humble of heart; and you will find rest for your souls" (Matt. 11:29).

This sonnet comes between "Spelt from Sibyl's Leaves" and "Carrion Comfort" in the standard edition of Hopkins's poetry; its position is noteworthy. In the suffering and loneliness of the Dublin exile, Hopkins not only never doubted his faith in Christ "in bliss" and the gnosis of his own service to the eternal king, but he even deepened both faith and gnosis in the purifying crucible of suffering. His imitation of Jesus would be such that " 'Were I come o'er again,' cries Christ, 'it should be this.' " Hopkins wrote in his retreat notes: "In meditating on the Crucifixion I saw how my asking to be raised to a higher degree of grace was asking also to be lifted on a higher cross" (S, 254). No matter what the cost, the poet, in Walter Pater's words, had "apprehended the *Great Ideal,* so palpably that it defined personal gratitude and the sense of a friendly hand laid upon him amid the shadows of the world."[8] The ideal is Christ himself who "seeing somewhere some man do all that man can do, / For love he leans forth, needs his neck must fall on, kiss." Hopkins remained the good soldier throughout his ordeals. Although he could not feel it, he knew the friendly arm around him would never be withdrawn.

In an essay written in his Oxford days, the future Jesuit clearly defined in outline what living one's ideals involved: "Ideal answers to idea: an idea is our thought of a thing as substantive, as one, as holding together its own parts and conditions; an ideal is the thing thought of when it is most substantive and succeeds in being distinctive and one and holding its parts or conditions together in its own way" (J, 124). Unity defines and sets its own terms on the mind; inscape itself is an epiphany of the Ideal to which the mind gives what Newman would call "real assent." Later Hopkins found these insights verified in Scotus's concept of the *species specialissima* which, as Father Devlin describes it, "does not represent any particular individual, a woman, a horse, or a mulberry tree, as it is afterwards known by abstraction and secondary images; no more does inscape. It represents the Ideal Person to whom universal nature tends."[9] Christ the Ideal would work in his own way within the poet; the myth would reach its most distinctive expression; and the great sacrifice would now be known and lived. How and where was this mastery to take place? Again, Duns Scotus gives the answer: "God's knowing is life, creative life. The creature as He knows it here and now, *is* the Ideal."[10] Not as the priest knew but as God knows, and not in the bluebells whose inscape is "made to every sense" but in the subconscious self, Hopkins became the Ideal he had sought for, until, "*centre-hung*" or "sprung from the hood or arch itself" of inscape, out of suffering and the grace of a happy death, his last words, thrice repeated, "I am so happy!" showed that then he knew even as he had been known, and no longer "as through a glass darkly" but "face to face" with arch-Omega.

10

"In a Whirlwind":
Last Poems

TWO sonnets, unparalleled in English for their length and density, stand as the final grand formulation of Hopkins's myth: "Spelt from Sibyl's Leaves" and "That Nature is a Heraclitean Fire and of the comfort of the Resurrection." Clustered between these two poems are the sonnets of desolation, also unequaled in the language for their personal expression of spiritual distress. This entire group of sonnets written in the period between 1885 and 1889 when Hopkins served as a professor of Greek at the Royal University in Dublin presents a final challenge to the reader who has traced out the labyrinthine evolution of the poet's thought. Amid the paradoxes and tensions of these lines, emerges a unity of myth and gnosis not achieved before.

What Hopkins wrote in 1868 in his "Notes on Greek Philosophy" is particularly relevant to the composition and reading of these last poems:

> The more intellectual, less physical, the spell of contemplation the more complex must be the object, the more close and elaborate must be the comparison the mind has to keep making between the whole and the parts, the parts and the whole. For this reference or comparison is what the sense of unity means; mere sense that such a thing is one and not two has no interest or value except accidentally.
>
> Works of art of course like words utter the idea and in

representing real things convey the prepossession with more or less success.

The further in anything, as a work of art, the organisation is carried out, the deeper the form penetrates, the prepossession flushes the matter, the more effort will be required in apprehension, the more power of comparison, the more capacity for receiving that synthesis of (either successive or spatially distinct) impressions which gives us the unity with the prepossession conveyed by it. (J, 126)

The poet creates out of unity to a diversity of techniques, images, words. The reader works back from surface complexity to the unity which carries the original passion or enthusiasm ("prepossession") of inspiration. This resulting contemplation "in which the mind is absorbed (as far as that may be), taken up by, dwells upon, enjoys, a single thought" is gnosis, "the contemplative enjoyment of the unity of the whole" (J, 126).

"Of this long sonnet," Hopkins wrote of "Spelt from Sibyl's Leaves" (P61), "above all remember what applies to all my verse, that it is, as living art should be, made for performance and that its performance is not reading with the eye but loud, leisurely, poetical (not rhetorical) recitation, with long rests, long dwells on the rhyme and other marked syllables, and so on. This sonnet shd. be almost sung: it is most carefully timed in *tempo rubato*" (L1, 246). The unity will emanate finally in the dramatic recitation; but this is performance of a high order possible only after exhaustive study of parts in their relation to the whole and the whole to the parts. The reader is re-creator of the prepossession of the poem, and the song he at last hears himself singing is said by heart and known in the mind. The first and final fact about this sonnet of Hopkins's is to recognize its form: it is a dirge in "stolen time," hastened or slackened as expression requires. It echoes and resembles in theme and imagery the medieval chant from the Mass of the Dead:

> Dies irae, dies illa
> Solvet saeclum in favilla:
> Teste David cum Sibylla.

Quantus tremor est futurus,
Quando judex est venturus,
Cuncta stricte discussurus![1]

The title of the sonnet recalls the sequence in its reference to the Sibyl, Greek prophetess of doom, as a witness to the Second Coming of Christ to probe the inner motives of all men's lives. Justin Martyr, for example, quotes the Sibyl's prediction that all things corruptible will then be dissolved by God (1 Apology 20). Hopkins told Patmore: "So far as I understand, our Lord says that his second coming shall be sudden, surprising, and unforseen, but when it comes utterly unmistakeable; in that differing from his first coming and all other tokens of himself" (L3, 346).

The present tokens of Christ in time form the main part of this apocalyptic poem which opens with seven adjectives that build to a climax in "evening" which in turn is climaxed by "night":

> Earnest, earthless, equal, attuneable, | vaulty, voluminous,
> . . . stupendous
> Evening strains to be tíme's vást, | womb-of-all, home-of-
> all, hearse-of-all night.

The very first word offers a cryptic clue to the meaning of the whole: "earnest" means both "ardor" (a quality Hopkins admired) and "assurance of something to come." The crescendo of adjectives creates a sense both of fullness and of a vast and empty scene. In a spacial moment of change, the world hangs in the balance between day and night; but its direction is clear as it heaves steadily toward the sphere of darkness, the past enclosure ("womb"), present dwelling ("home"), and future resting place ("hearse") of all finite creation. Becoming "strains to be" and at the same time is moved relentlessly to nonbeing.

In the next sentence the poet continues his description of evening:

> Her fond yellow hornlight wound to the west, | her wild
> hollow hoarlight hung to the height
> Waste; her earliest stars, earlstars, | stárs principal,
> overbend us,
> Fíre-féaturing heaven.

Like the haunting twilight of a Rouault biblical landscape, Hopkins's scene shines with penumbral beauty. The yellow glow spun on the western horizon, the fading light straight above at the zenith, and the first stars appearing in the east complete the briefly harmonious panorama. Looking from one horizon upward to the other, our vaulting gaze returns to the earth; there objects now mass in dark confusion:

> . . . For earth ǀ her being has unbound; her dapple is at
>   an end, as-
> tray or aswarm, all throughther, in throngs; ǀ self ín self
>   steepèd and páshed—quíte
> Disremembering, dísmémbering ǀ áll now.

Darkness is pictured as a storm submerging and tossing objects one through the other; they lie soaked and shattered, without distinctiveness or character, all unity between them dissipated and spent. Earth is in the process of forgetting and undoing her self and selves; her being seems no longer held in any Parmenidean bond.

Such is the literal meaning of the octave which ends with the reminder from the poet's heart that there is another level yet to be sounded:

> Heart, you round me right
> With: Our évening is over us; óur night ǀ whélms, whélms,
>   ánd will end us.

An individual moral reading ("me") and a universal spiritual one ("us") must next be made. The verb "round" is well chosen: a fullness remains within to instruct and charge the listening watcher with the truth to come:

> Only the beakleaved boughs dragonish ǀ damask the tool-
>   smooth bleak light; black,
> Ever so black on it.

The black leaves incised against the flat pale sky are the only permanent and proximate objects in the poem. They are both the actual leaves of a nearby tree and the parchment leaves of the title ready to be interpreted: "Our tale, O óur oracle!" The underthought, "conveyed chiefly in the choice of metaphors" (see

L3, 252-53), is that of a script to be read and studied, already
present in the sonnet in a series of puns: "voluminous" as a volume to be read, "hornlight" as a hornbook to instill one's alphabet from Alpha to Omega, "unbound" like a book, and "pen,"
in the following line, an instrument for writing. Dante, in his
Paradiso, also speaks of the universe strewn with pages that are
bound up in the Eternal Light.[2] Thomas Carlyle lamented, however, that men hardly knew the Alphabet of the Volume of Nature "spread out through Solar Systems" and "written in celestial
hieroglyphs, in the true Sacred-writing" of its divine Author.[3]
Hopkins would have us read and learn by heart the unsealed
book with eyes fastened on the prophetic page.

The reference to the Sibylline Oracle, as has been often pointed
out, indicates the sixth book of the *Aeneid* as an analogue for
Hopkins's sonnet.[4] Virgil's hero requests the Cumaean Sibyl who
presided at the entrance to the underworld of the dead to guide
him in his excursion. She attempts, in vain, to dissuade him; then
tells him of the means to secure the golden bough. She warns
him that the return from hell will be more difficult than the descent. Virgil's myth includes reflections on death, the necessity
of purification, and the judgment at death on the basis of right
and wrong done in one's lifetime. From early Christian tradition
the Sibyls and Virgil himself, on the basis of his *Fourth Eclogue*,
were regarded as forerunners and prophets of Christ, almost on
an equal footing with the Old Testament seers. Pagan and Jew
bore witness to the world deliverer to come. In Plato's shadowy
cave the prisoners awaited the arrival of their risen hero and king
to release them.

In the sestet the narrator and his readers explore "óur tale"
and "óur oracle" as we descend to view purgatorial punishments
and the Day of Judgment:

> Lét life, wáned, ah lét life wind
> Off hér once skéined stained véined varíety | upon, áll
>   on twó spools; párt, pen, páck
> Now her áll in twó flocks, twó folds—black, white; | right,
>   wrong; reckon but, reck but, mind

But thése two; wáre of a wórld where bút these | twó tell,
  each off the óther; of a rack
Where, selfwrung, selfstrung, sheathe- and shelterless, |
  thóughts agaínst thoughts ín groans grínd.

The cylindrical forms of "skeined" and "spools" echo "womb"
and "wound" in line three; here life's threads are unraveled and
rewound on two separate spools. The theme of separation now
introduces the Gospel parable of the last day when the Son of
man comes in glory and places the sheep on his right and the
goats on his left (Matt. 24:31-33). The reader is instructed by
the poet, who is of course primarily addressing himself, to focus
on "but these two," forgetting the maze he has been through and
the shades of light and dark encountered. Simplify and clarify;
reduce issues to their essential truth and falsehood; judge and
act accordingly: *yes* and *no*. Every thought, word, and deed bear
an indelible character and must one day be accounted for.[5] The
verb "ware" does not mean "beware" but is a command to "be
aware" and take heed in the present of that world to come where
moral choices are clearly defined, where right and wrong are
marked off one from the other, not "throughther" or all mixed
together. The same verb "ware" governs the grammatical structure of the final lines: "Be aware" and take heed of that rack of
tortuous thought where, stripped to bare self, you know the
choice of right that must be painfully made. The scene is one
familiar to English Jesuits whose followers, among them Saints
Edmund Campion and Robert Southwell, were stretched on the
rack, interrogated, and tortured in order to force them to reject
their faith. Martyrdom, Hopkins states, awaits each dedicated
man in the cross he takes up when following Jesus. Whether the
persecutor be one's enemy or one's self, faith in Christ and knowledge of his truth must be tested and not found wanting. The
theme then is universal and spiritual in scope and application;
critics who find here the private, interior anguish of the poet
without reference to all other men have missed the threefold
reading that operates within the poem from its first word.
Origen's ascent to gnosis governs its total development.

The inscape of the sonnet is the suffering servant himself, the hero who "descended into hell" as the Creed declares, and underwent all the mental and spiritual disruption of fallen man. Death is punishment for sin, and the consequent sense of abandonment, fear, and moral responsibility were all experienced existentially and completely by Jesus of Nazereth. "Spelt from Sibyl's Leaves" then is a dramatic realization of the *kenosis* or great sacrifice. On the "dragonish" or Satanic boughs, the black leaves open a cleave to the waste of night, death, judgment, and hell. The oracle is *pleroma* in reverse, the vacuum of Parmenides' Not-Being, which cannot be thought or spoken of, but which in the Christian myth becomes the desert outside God where the Son entered to create and redeem mankind. The Lord descends and empties himself, his "being has unbound" and the night of the grave awaits him. As Isaiah predicted, he "bore the sins of many" (53:12), and St. Paul affirmed: "He was made sin for our sake, who knew nothing of sin" (2 Cor. 5:21). *Ipse et in saecula,* he will return to judge the living and the dead. In one of his most beautiful sentences, Newman wrote: "Earth and sky are ever failing; Christ is ever coming; Christians are ever lifting up their heads and looking out, and therefore it is the evening."[6] One watches and waits, not knowing the day or the hour.

Christ himself is the tale and oracle of mankind. He teaches men how to meet the hour of death and judgment, and it is his heart that "rounds" men right. His "mind" is to be theirs: "mind / But these two," for his mind was to put aside all else and obey the Father's will (Phil. 2:5-8). The kenotic activity involved is gnosis, "the being *ware,*" which Hopkins defined as the "faculty of attention, advertence, heed" (S, 174). Know the tale and oracle of Christ who became obedient—chose "white" and "right"—even to death on the cross, his "rack" of martyrdom. If you are "ware," the poet implies, then you will acquire through repeated acts of "wareness" "its habit, knowledge, the being *aware*" (S, 174). You will achieve gnosis, "Identification" with Christ, the "martyr-master" whose *agon* or struggle in the garden of Gethsemane drove out drops of blood: "sheathe- and shelterless, thóughts agaínst thoughts ín groans grínd." There

Jesus had no "sheath" to protect him: "Put back your sword into its sheath" (Matt. 26:52) and no "shelter": "And going forward a little, he fell upon the ground, and began to pray that, if it were possible, the hour might pass from him" (Mark 14:35). The hour did not pass: "Jesus will be in agony until the end of the world," wrote Pascal.

The Word of life is the secret to be spelt from the page and sung with "loud, leisurely, poetical recitation." This sonnet then is his majestic dirge, and in and through him, the poet's and Everyman's. Its literal and moral meanings yield a scripturally spiritual sense: Christ's "blissful agony or stress of selving" that "forced out drops of sweat or blood" (S, 197) created and redeemed the world. He is Being in becoming, reality's *yes* and *is*. His consent to the Father's will is the reason for the universe.

The sonnets of desolation that follow "Sibyl's Leaves" enact the same cosmic drama and remain, at the same time, intensely personal in their anguish and dread. Six of the seven poems were written in one critical year, 1885, and four "came like inspirations unbidden" (L1, 221). Hopkins is "exceedingly troubled," in the words Mark uses to describe Jesus in the garden. So the poet himself depicts his master: "However much he understood all this he found it an intolerable grief to submit to it. He left the example: it is very strengthening, but except in that sense it is not consoling" (L2, 138). However much Hopkins understood, the grief was real; for faith and gnosis are not an antidote for suffering nor a panacea Christ miraculously dispenses to those who receive him. Critics who have been scandalized by the authenticity of Hopkins's grief and anxiety or who have sought ready remedies in St. John of the Cross and "the dark night of the soul" are simply evading the mystery of the real nature of suffering. Neither ignorance nor mysticism can answer the Grand Inquisitor. The desolation sonnets frame a profound and moving response to man's agonizing probings, and they deserve to take their place, as such, with the great literature of lamentation.

Significantly, the first of this group of poems, "Carrion Comfort" (P64), opens with a bold refusal to despair:

> Not, I'll not, carrion comfort, Despair, not feast on thee;
> Not untwist—slack they may be—these last strands of man
> In me ór, most weary, cry *I can no more.* I can;
> Can something, hope, wish day come, not choose not to be.

The choice "not to be" is, like Hamlet's, a spiritual option, not simply involving suicide but damnation as well. An everlasting falling into nothingness is Hopkins's picture of hell: "The wicked and the lost are like halfcreations and have but a halfbeing" (S, 197). "This throwing back or confinement of their energy is a dreadful constraint or imprisonment and, as intellectual action is spoken of under the figure of sight, it will in this case be an imprisonment in darkness, a being in the dark; for darkness is the phenomenon of foiled action in the sense of sight" (S, 137). The poet continues to *see*, no matter how dense the night spelt in Sibyl's leaves. But the experience is like that of the damned, since each man is a potential candidate for hell, and in Hopkins's view a "blackguard" runs a greater risk. For even in the lost there lives on the "strain or tendency towards being, towards good, towards God—being, that is / their own more or continued being, good / their own good, their natural felicity, and God / the God at least of nature, not to speak of grace" (S, 137).

The powers of nothingness and darkness are aligned against the Christian adventurer. Yet one struggles on, not only against Lucifer, but with the angel that wrestled Jacob, with the Lord who oppressed Job, his faithful servant and "the work of thy own hands" (Job 10:3):

> But ah, but O thou terrible, why wouldst thou rude on me
> Thy wring-world right foot rock? lay a lionlimb against me?
>   scan
> With darksome devouring eyes my bruisèd bones? and fan,
> O in turns of tempest, me heaped there; me frantic to avoid
>   thee and flee?

The giant adversary, the Lion of Judah, is shown to be powerful and persistent; he watches, grapples, and holds fast. "Thou huntest me as a fierce lion: and again thou shewest thyself marvellous upon me" (Job 10:16, King James Version). In the Genesis account, Jacob, although physically injured, is the victor in the nightlong contest: he proves himself and wins God's favor. In the sestet of the sonnet, the poet too enjoys victory: "My heart lo! lapped strength, stole joy, would laugh, chéer." But his confidence is short-lived:

> Cheer whom though? The hero whose heaven-handling
>   flung me, foót tród
> Me? or me that fought him? O which one? is it each one?

In that struggle and triumph did Hopkins merely seek self after all or were his intentions purely for Christ? As Thomas à Becket discovers in T. S. Eliot's *Murder in the Cathedral*, no ultimately safe answer is possible in this life; one can only point to the event and hope. Hopkins recalls the moment of crisis: "That night, that year / Of now done darkness I wretch lay wrestling with (my God!) my God." In this conclusion the poet puts in the past tense what was described in the present tense in the octave. The occasion of the struggle is "now done," completed and yet still present in its effects; he refers most likely to the choice of his vocation, made seventeen years previously and already recalled in the opening stanzas of the *Deutschland*: "Thou knowest the walls, altar and hour and night." Thus Jacob's life was changed in his struggle with the angel "until the break of dawn," because he challenged the Lord: " 'I will not let you go until you bless me.' " For reward he is answered: " 'You shall no longer be called Jacob, but Israel, because you have contended with God and men, and have triumphed.' Jacob asked, 'What is your name?' He answered, 'Why do you ask my name?' But he blessed him there. Jacob named the place Phanuel, saying 'I have seen a heavenly being face to face, yet my life has been spared' " (Gen. 32:27-31). Like Jacob, Hopkins knew himself to be a new man, set on a lonely and honorable path, but living the original inscape of the theophany of "the knowledge of the glory of God, shining on the face of Christ Jesus" (2 Cor. 4:6).[7]

In sonnet 65, "No worst, there is none," the poet employs the myth of a Greek hero, Prometheus, the bestower of fire on mankind, who was nailed to a cliff in symbolic punishment: "The mind, mind has mountains; cliffs of fall / Frightful, sheer, no-man-fathomed." He acts as another epic underthought, like that of Aeneas and Jacob, to elevate the theme of personal suffering to a universal idea expressive of the "Great Ideal." The introductory quatrain, for example, is "selfwrung" and yet contains no personal reference. Christ and his Spirit are invoked as "Comforter," and "Mary, mother of us," is asked: "Where is your relief?" The poet's own cries open the second quatrain; they "huddle in a main, a chief- / woe, world-sorrow; on an age-old anvil wince and sing." His grief is that of mankind everywhere and for ages past; but nonetheless his own, packed "herds-long" within his troubled heart. Even these cries, however, "lull, then leave off," since respite is a part of human misery. Fury, a deity sent to punish crimes, has little time to waste on each and every individual: "Fury had shrieked 'No ling- / ering! Let me be fell; force I must be brief.'" The punishment must be terrible, but mercifully swift.

The figure of Prometheus, a pre-Christian type of Christ the Savior, dominates the sestet; his suffering is that of the one man who brought down the true divine fire, his love, to other men.[8] The last lines, however, return to the ordinary sufferer whose "small durance" cannot long "deal with that steep or deep." All that is left for the unheroic, among whom the poet classes himself, is a shelter apparently away from the main action and passion of redeeming pain. But like King Lear's hovel, it offers more than a roof against the storm:

> Here! creep,
> Wretch, under a comfort serves in a whirlwind: all
> Life death does end and each day dies with sleep.

The final line marks the beginning of wisdom; it returns us to the prosaic cycle of everyday living, so orchestrally treated in "Spelt from Sibyl's Leaves." Yet the trivial too is charged with Christ's presence, as Hopkins observed twenty years earlier: "It is one adorable point of the incredible condescension of the Incarnation (the greatness of which no saint can have ever hoped to realise) that our Lord submitted not only to the pains of life, the fasting, scourging, crucifixion etc. or the insults, as the mocking, blindfolding, spitting etc, but also to the mean and trivial accidents of humanity" (L3, 19). Hence the "comfort" which serves him is an inscape of the "Comforter" (line 3) who took the *forma servi* and sent his Spirit to support man's weakness. "It seems therefore that if the Incarnation cd. *versari inter* trivial men and trivial things it is not surprising that our reception or non-reception of its benefits shd. be also amidst trivialities" (L3, 20). Hoping for a magnanimous, undaunted response to his trials, Hopkins had to settle for less in himself. These poems are the honest admission of failure and in this the greatness of their humanity lies.

The most personal and yet calm statement of grief among the desolation sonnets is found in sonnet 66, "To seem the stranger." The poet lists the causes of his sorrowing: separation from parents and homeland, and acute spiritual loneliness. Here again there is frank self-evaluation that leads to some form of consolation: "Not but in all removes I can / Kind love both give and get." His affliction, he tells us, is his continued inability to create, to respond with words to the Word of life, for "dark heaven's baffling ban / Bars or hell's spell thwarts" all efforts to express "what word / Wisest my heart breeds" either in prayer or the writing projects he felt to be part of his vocation. He lacks all means of communicating the "word / Wisest," Christ the Logos and Wisdom whom he loves. The poem concludes with a familiar Shakespearian device: "This to hoard unheard, / Heard unheeded, leaves me a lonely began." The demonstrative pronoun "this" refers to and incorporates the sonnet itself as its own poetic material. The poem then is the poet's prayer, falling on deaf ears on earth and in heaven. Both the poet and his poem find themselves, finally, back where they began: "among strangers."

"I wake and feel the fell of dark, not day" (P67) announces the poet-priest's *de profundis*. Waking from nightmarish sleep to dark hours of lying awake in conscious self-loathing, Hopkins experiences the night within, the edge of breakdown and the absence of any awareness of God's presence. The modern association of personal guilt with mental illness parallels the older superstition of physical suffering as a consequence of sin. No moral evil, as Job protested of himself, need be involved in Hopkins's anguished isolation and melancholia. St. Thérèse of Lisieux, for example, achieved holiness in and through her neuroses; such sickness can be the instrument of personal salvation or eternal loss. Whatever the nature of the "nervous prostration" and near madness that the priest complained of in his later years, the sense of being utterly forsaken by God is a spiritual experience witnessed for by the Old Testament writers and by Christ himself on his cross. Had not the founder of the Jesuits been brought to the brink of suicide at Manresa and written discerningly of desolation in his *Exercises*?

Profoundly personal as this sonnet remains, it is more than a *cri du coeur*; it dramatizes the depravity and heartache of man's sinful state inherited from Adam. The key word is "fell" which expresses in the past tense of the verb "fall"—like "began" in the previous sonnet—the action of the fall of night, on the literal level, and, on the spiritual, the fall of man.[9] The preterit fixes the action in history and existence; the deed of wickedness is done and never as such can be undone: all men are sinners now. "With witness I speak this," the poet exclaims, echoing Christ's words: "It is I who bear witness to myself, and he who sent me, the Father, bears witness to me" (John 8:18). Hopkins's witness is his master who became a child of Adam, who "was made sin" and tasted the full horror of its fruit. But even Christ's witness is no immediate comfort to the poet:

> And my lament
> Is cries countless, cries like dead letters sent
> To dearest him that lives alas! away.

The simile of his cries to "dead letters" recalls the theme of the impotent words of the previous poem; his use of an unassuming image underlines the poet's plight. No answers come to him, his pleas are left forgotten in some obscure corner. Christ is a distant mark, and distant indeed.

In the sestet, the poet, to all appearance thrown back on himself with the common lot of fallen mankind, gives full outlet to his Job-like distress and, at the same time, manages to fuse both personal and universal meanings in one bold, direct statement:

> I am gall, I am heartburn. God's most deep decree
> Bitter would have me taste: my taste was me;
> Bones built in me, flesh filled, blood brimmed the curse.
>
> Selfyeast of spirit a dull dough sours. I see
> The lost are like this, and their scourge to be
> As I am mine, their sweating selves; but worse.

"Purge out the old leaven, that you may be a new dough," St. Paul commands (1 Cor. 5:7). But the old Adam remains within and will not allow the new man, "Christ our pasch," to rise. Both "decree" and "curse" refer to the punishment inflicted on man through Original Sin. "In the sweat of your brow you shall eat bread till you return to the ground, since out of it you were taken" (Gen. 3:19). Hopkins's own flesh is a vessel in which the curse brims over; he becomes "gall," a poisonous herb of the Bible, fulfilling the curse: "You shall eat the herbs of the earth" (3:18). This gall, mixed in wine, was given Jesus on the cross "that the Scripture might be fulfilled": "And they gave me gall for food, and in my thirst, they gave me vinegar to drink" (John 19:28 and Psalm 68:22). "Their sweating selves" in the closing line indicates the rigorous prosecution of the decree: the unredeemed sweat unproductively and without hope of relief. "The lost are like this": what distinguishes them from living fallen men is not the curse, which is the same for both, but the irrevocable execution of the sentence. Their lot is "worse," because the damned cannot escape their selfishness and turn to God; it is too late. The terrible plight of Satan in book 4 of *Paradise Lost* is probably intended to be echoed here in the emphatic "worse" that ends this sonnet:

> Now conscience wakes despair
> That slumber'd, wakes the bitter memory
> Of what he was, what is, and what must be
> Worse; of worse deeds worse sufferings must ensue.
>
> (*PL* 4. ll. 23-26)[10]

The Prince of Darkness embodies the complete contradiction of Christ's great sacrifice. "But Satan, who had fallen through pride and selflove, resolved that through pride and selflove man should be brought to fall" (S, 63). In these poems Hopkins answers pride with his own emptiness, despair with his own groping toward the Lord who he knows "lives" and who yet remains "alas! away." In this confession he believes he is not among the lost for whom "the strain or tendency towards God through Christ and the great sacrifice had by their own act been broken, refracted, and turned aside, and it is only through Christ and the great sacrifice that God had meant any being to come to him at all" (S, 137-38). Through scriptural, doctrinal, and literary echoes, Hopkins has created in this poem a new witness in the tradition of man's expression of private moral grief.

The sonnet that follows, "Patience, hard thing" (68), omits all first-person-singular pronouns and deals with an objective remedy for failure and disappointment. Hopkins's whole attitude toward suffering is totally free from the clichés of consolation, classically etched forever in the words of Job's self-righteous friends, the self-appointed counselors and consolers. The effect of earnestness and honesty that transfigures the sonnet on "Patience," for example, is accomplished through concrete, original definition: "Natural heart's ivy, Patience masks / Our ruins of wrecked past purpose." The picture is personally observed and graphically universal: "There she basks / Purple eyes and seas of liquid leaves all day." In warmth and rain the ivy flourishes on the ancient walls of abandoned abbeys and churches. The berries ("eyes") of ivy watch and grow in a world of ruin and renewal, the forsaken land and the regenerating waters. England's "bare ruined choirs," Hopkins implies, await through the seasons the return of God's people to true faith and worship.

The final definition of Patience is the Lord Jesus himself, the *apis aetherea*:

> And where is he who more and more distills
> Delicious kindness?—He is patient. Patience fills
> His crisp combs, and that comes those ways we know.

Christ who "lives alas! away" and "bides in bliss" is seen here working everywhere in the cosmos to bring creation to fulfillment. And "we know" through gnosis the ways he comes, from all directions of the sky and earth to the honeycomb centers of men's hearts. Patience is his inscape who makes all men his mark, filling them with the immortal nectar of his love.

Not since the fading "hoarlight" of "Spelt from Sibyl's Leaves" has the poet allowed the presence of sunlight to reappear in the sonnets of desolation. The Lord of light has left his priest to loneliness and night, without vision or fervor. Six months before his death, Hopkins observed: "There is a happiness, hope, the anticipation of happiness hereafter: it is better than happiness, but it is not happiness now. It is as if one were dazzled by a spark or star in the dark, seeing it but not seeing by it: we want a light shed on our way and a happiness spread over our life" (S, 262). Now in the next poem, sonnet 69, the poet turns to himself, hopefully, for some relief:

> My own heart let me more have pity on; let
> Me live to my sad self hereafter kind,
> Charitable; not live this tormented mind
> With this tormented mind tormenting yet.

He recalls the agonizing "thoughts against thoughts" of the earlier "song," and asks himself to be "kind"—considerate and natural—to his own heart from this point on. He next reviews his own state of soul, only to conclude that he turns to himself in vain:

> I cast for comfort I can no more get
> By groping round my comfortless, than blind
> Eyes in their dark can day or thirst can find
> Thirst's all-in-all in all a world of wet.

The use again of "comfort" recalls "carrion comfort, Despair" in sonnet 64 and the Spirit of Jesus, the "Comforter," of sonnet 65, as well as the twofold Paraclete of the sermons. Here the noun "my comfortless" acts as a dramatic coinage to define the absence of any consoling presence of Jesus within his soul: the

"my" acting as both adjective and implied substantive "me."
The poet may direct his eyes ("cast"), but he can find no inscape. "By groping round" in self nothing "round" or full is discovered; hence the quite sound advice to look outside and employ the "natural heart's ivy" of patient acceptance of natural
joy. Christ fills the heart from within creation. Thus Hopkins
begins the slow ascent upward from his *Inferno* to the dawn of
Easter Day. He is "blind eyes" in the midst of that day and
"thirst" in a *pleroma* of redeeming baptismal waters. Christ's
universe has not changed; but the speaker is incapable of losing
himself to the extent of experientially sharing in the risen Lord,
who remains as he was in the beginning: the light of the world
and the water of life.

In his retreat at Beaumont in 1883, Hopkins wrote:

> Sept. 10. The walk to Emmaus. This morning in Thanks-
> giving after mass much bitter thought but also insight in
> things. And the above meditation was made in a desolate
> frame of mind; but towards the end I was able to rejoice
> in the comfort our Lord gave those two men, taking that
> for a sample of his comfort and them for representatives
> of all men comforted, and that it was meant to be of
> universal comfort to men and therefore to me and that
> this was all I really needed; also that it was better for
> me to be accompanying our Lord in his comfort of them
> than to want him to come my way to comfort me. (S, 254)

Man needs the "comforter" to, etymologically, "be strong-with,"
to thoroughly strengthen him for making progress on his road.
For the comforter acts precisely in terms of the goal ahead; he is
the batsman in cricket who cries: "Come on, come on!—a Paraclete is just that, something that cheers the spirit of man, with
signals and with cries, all zealous that he should do something
and full of assurance that if he will he can, calling him on, springing to meet him half way, crying to his ears or to his heart: This
way to do God's will, this way to save your soul, come on, come
on!" (S, 70). Comfort then is action and a call; it is not a passive
sense of well-being. Comfort means Christ's company, known

and affirmed in his risen reality, stirring the soul to possess him forever.

In the absence of all sensible spiritual comfort, the poet addresses himself in the sestet:

> Soul, self; come, poor Jackself, I do advise
> You, jaded, let be; call off thoughts awhile
> Elsewhere; leave comfort root-room; let joy size
>
> At God knows when to God knows what; whose smile
> 's not wrung, see you; unforseen times rather—as skies
> Betweenpie mountains—lights a lovely mile.

The noun "joy" governs the final tercet:[11] allow joy to mount or grow to the proper time and to the objects of comfort sent by God whose gnosis is infinitely wiser than your own. The inscape of the sonnet, like that of the "colossal smile" in "Henry Purcell," occurs in the spontaneous "smile" that breaks from joy; this smile is not forced, rather it illumines the way, just as skies interdapple ("betweenpie") two dark, deep-cut mountainsides with a long vista of further light. Thus, at last, the sun of the creator and savior returns and opens a way ahead. "See you," the poet tells himself, "the direction to be taken." A luminous curve unexpectedly beckons from the distance, showing the route and a passageway beyond to Omega. "I lift up my eyes to the mountains, whence shall help come to me? My help is from the Lord, who made heaven and earth" (Ps. 120:1-2). Then joy deeper than sorrow—sudden and uncoerced—beams within the self from off the mountains of the mind. Such joy none can lay claim to; the Lord alone provides it. "Now you are sad, but I will see you again, and your heart shall rejoice, and your joy no one shall take from you" (John 16:22). Hopkins has glimpsed "a light shed on" his way and felt "a happiness spread over" his life.

"That Nature is a Heraclitean Fire and of the comfort of the Resurrection" (P72) may be justly regarded as Hopkins's *summa*, the culmination of years of studying nature and mankind in his own search for inner gnosis. W. H. Gardner has drawn attention to the number of parallels in the octave to the poet's journal entries, some written down almost twenty years before.[12] Such an integrating vision shows no diminution of his poetic powers, rather it testifies to the memory and imagination that continued to shape new forms of knowing even in the hardest hours of loneliness. In framing this new mythogenetic expression, the sonnet, written in July 1888, employs traditional subject matter: the consuming elemental cycle of fire, air, water, and earth. The spiral turns downward, the wind drying up the drenched ground after a summer rainstorm. The octave is crowded with inscapes of nature in motion and itself moves in a descending cyclic order from clouds to elm trees to earth. This first act or musical introduction is then summed up in a Heraclitean-like fragment: "Million-fuelèd, ' nature's bonfire burns on." The second movement begins with man, already foreshadowed in the first by his muddy footprints, "manmarks ' treadmire toil there / Footfretted in it." His inscapes appear in the ooze that turns to dust, but only momentarily; they are quickly "stanched" and "starched" or flattened out by the wind. Man's fate is annihilation:

> But quench her bonniest, dearest ' to her, her clearest-selvèd
> spark
> Man, how fast his firedint, ' his mark on mind, is gone!
> Both are in an unfathomable, all is in an enormous dark
> Drowned. O pity and indig ' nation! Manshape, that shone
> Sheer off, disseveral, a star, ' death blots black out; nor mark
> Is any of him at all so stark
> But vastness blurs and time ' beats level.

All man's inscapes as Christ's created image, his own "mark," time and space overwhelm: "manmarks," "clearest-selvèd spark," "firedint," "manshape," and saddest of all, "his mark on mind," the achievement of gnosis; no matter what the mark or how fixed and bold his aims, they are obliterated by death.

For the last time, the image of a storm at night on "the widow-making unchilding unfathering deeps" (P28, 13) recurs in Hopkins's poetry. As in the two shipwreck poems and in "Sibyl's Leaves," the storm drowns all "in an enormous dark," in immense and monstrous night. Here the reference gains from past poetic connotation as a recapitulatory statement of the myth, for the waters of the sea are both those in which the Christ-hero met destruction as he "descended into hell" and those he redeemed with his blood, the water issuing from his side as a baptismal flood. "Do you not know," St. Paul asked the Romans, "that all we who have been baptized into Christ Jesus have been baptized into his death?" And then, alluding to baptism by immersion: "For we were buried with him by means of Baptism into death, in order that, just as Christ has arisen from the dead through the glory of the Father, so we also may walk in newness of life" (Rom. 6:3-4). The implications of this Pauline teaching become explicit in the third movement of the sonnet:

> Enough! the Resurrection,
> A heart's-clarion! Away grief's gasping, | joyless days, dejection.
> Across my foundering deck shone
> A beacon, an eternal beam.

As the tall nun inscaped Christ in her confession of faith and recognition of him as "Lord," his response in her—"a blown beacon of light" (28, 29)—is repeated here: "A beacon, an eternal beam." The "beacon," as the *Deutschland* makes clear, is "Jesu, heart's light," shining within in timeless, godly splendor. The *OED* gives as one meaning of *beam*: "the roodtree or cross." There may even be here, as Justus Lawler notes of "beam-blind" (P46), a pun on "be-am," the name and isness of God.[13] This light and being are called forth from the chaos and darkness of the passion. Note, in addition, that the Greek noun σκοπή, a sourceword for Hopkins's "inscape," also denotes a "watchtower," one of the meanings of "beacon." From the lighthouse of Christ's risen body there flashes the signal of rescue across the sinking deck of man's corruptible flesh. On the "beam" of the cross ("Across") man reaches a safe haven.[14]

In the midst of the resurrection-event, nature's bonfire, like a witness to its reality, continues to burn on: "Flesh fade, and mortal trash / Fall to the residuary worm; | world's wildfire, leave but ash." Here the poet actually commands the process of decomposition to take place as a counterpart to personal renewal ("ash" is followed by a colon in the text). The first part of the poem's title, therefore, does not negate the second, but conditions and prepares it. As Hopkins confided to Bridges: "A great deal of early Greek philosophical thought was distilled" in this sonnet (L1, 291). Although "the liquor of the distillation did not taste very Greek," the insights of the pre-Socratic philosophers remain true and valid, at this point in the poem, before the presence of the new world and the life promised by Christian revelation. The Sibyl's augury of the final dissolution is being fulfilled in Christ's triumph over death.

The whole growth of gnosis, nurtured through study, reflection, and prayer, the sum of Hopkins's life and vision, exists intact as the fourth movement begins:

> In a flash, at a trumpet crash,
> I am all at once what Christ is, | since he was what I am, and
> This Jack, joke, poor potsherd, | patch, matchwood, immortal diamond,
> Is immortal diamond.

Within the self's multiplicity of matter and psychic complexity, here and now in the justified man there shines the uncreated being of the God-Man. This same frail, ridiculous creature in the moment of his rising after death *is* what he has been all along: an "AfterChrist"—"that is Christ *being me* and me being Christ." The insight of Parmenides is verified at last: "Being is and Not-being is not," for "I AM then what Christ IS, since his I AM was what I am now." The simple statement which begins and ends with "I am" and centers on the words "Christ is" synthesizes personal and cosmic atonement, the transformation of being when *I am all* instantaneously and completely will be said by each and every redeemed creature because of the historical *was* of Being. God became man (I AM was) that man might become God (I am IS). The *mot de l'enigme*, therefore, must be the simple copulative "Is" in the final line. Gnosis attains its definitive statement: "To be and to know or Being and thought are the same. The truth in thought is Being, stress, and each word is one way of acknowledging Being and each sentence by its copula *is* (or its equivalent) the utterance and assertion of it" (J, 129). In Christ man speaks and knows and has his being. This core of being is diamondlike in its purity, light, durability, and beauty. For the "inner man," the "immortal diamond," does not cease to be himself in living this life or dying his death: he becomes that true self in Jesus. This identity is his definition. The entire poem with all its rich reality of nature and of man, with its universal and remarkably distinctive *persona*, equals, balances with, and is defined by the last two words. In this "poor potsherd," "God in *forma servi* rests *in servo*, that is / Christ as a solid in his member as a hollow or shell" (S, 195). "Our outer man is decaying," St. Paul declared, "yet our inner man is being renewed day by day" (2 Cor. 4:16). Christ the potter (the *figulus* of patristic writers) first moulds his creature and then fires him for eternal life.

"Poor potsherd" man, fashioned from clay and doomed to the "last dust" which is also his "first slime," is yet destined to physical revival by the promise that "he who believes in me shall never die" (John 11:26). The light of the world will glow on within him. "They are not dead who die, they are but lost who live," Hopkins once reflected (J, 141). Gregory of Nyssa observed: "Man, like some earthen potsherd, is resolved again into the dust of the ground, in order to secure that he may part with the soul which he has now contracted, and that he may, through the resurrection, be reformed anew after the original pattern; at least if in this life he has preserved what belongs to that image" (*De Oratione Catech. Magna* 8).[15] Created in the image of Christ and wonderfully new created through his death, human nature returns in the end to its "original pattern" preserved hidden and untarnished and ready for the light in this "matchwood" existence as a crystalline allotrope of carbon.

This immortal diamond here is that immortal diamond then. Light answers to light: time joins eternity, and immanence meets transcendence. Christ, the everlasting man (*homo philosophicus*) and Second Adam, is the philosophers' stone that transmutes the four elements into one pure, circular, and incorruptible essence, Himself.[16] *Per ipsum et in ipso*, the end reveals its origin: man's

Alpha becomes Omega, the aim of the eucharistic transubstanti-
ation finds fulfillment in the one Body of Christ. The long-sought-
for unity is attained in the closing lines of this sonnet: the "new
self and nobler me" discovers the words and imagery of man
made fully human through the humanity of Jesus who descended
even unto death on a cross in order to bring permanence and
meaning into ordinary life. Heraclitus's idea of the soul's immortality, as well as the "downward road" from fire to stone, which
advances the movement of the poem, achieves an unforeseen
depth of realization in the fiery brilliance of the hardest substance known, cut round and tapering, the irradiant diamond.[17]
In this focal point of prismatic light, the poet with magisterial
artistry sets forth man's final inscape: Omega. Translucent and
changeless, the just shine like terrestrial stars: *lumen de lumine*,
light of that light.

The following two sonnets do not come as an anticlimax to
the mythmaking of "Heraclitean Fire"; rather, they resume the
dialogue with Christ that Hopkins has continuously tried to maintain. The forthrightness of "Thou art indeed just, Lord, if I con-
tend / With thee" (P74), finds its basis in familiarity with his
king, whom he addresses as "Sir," and in the scriptural tradition
of *interrogatio* with God, like that of Jeremiah whose remon-
strance supplies this sonnet with its epigraph and opening statement. The enigma of Christ's treatment of his servants, a theme
well established in the Church and found in St. Theresa of Avila's
autobiography, for example, is here set forth in a semiarchaic,
biblical style unusual for Hopkins. The poet deliberately avoided
such practice as an abuse he would not generally allow. The style,
however, is suitable to the poem as a vehicle of man's age-old
dilemma in dealing with the mystery of the suffering servant
marked out for opprobrium and rejection:

> Wert thou my enemy, O thou my friend,
> How wouldst thou worse, I wonder, than thou dost
> Defeat, thwart me?

Although he spends "life upon thy cause," he remains "time's
eunuch" and does not "breed one work that wakes." "Nothing

comes: I am a eunuch—but it is for the kingdom of heaven's sake," he complained to Bridges (L1, 270). The reference, startling as it is, derives from Christ's own description of a special call to certain disciples who, in imitation of him, are never to marry (Matt. 19:12). The sonnet ends with a moving request for some kind of fertility of spirit: "Mine, O thou lord of life, send my roots rain." Christ, the maker of the universe, is asked to bring the inner man renewal.

"The shepherd's brow" (P75), long exiled to the "Unfinished Poems" section of the collected poetry, now has found its rightful place among the major poems of the fourth edition. The tone of self-mocking and the "cold eye" the poet casts on life and death keep a perfect decorum of vision and style. Sentimentally, some readers would have had a more profound and ambitious rounding of the myth; but the sonnet exactly summarizes the themes of the previous sonnets of desolation. Here the Carlylean hero worship and the epic matter, already established in the figures of Aeneas, Jacob, and Prometheus, are presented in the person of Moses "fronting forked lightning" in his brow as he descended from Sinai's great theophany. He is, of course, a type of Jesus the Good Shepherd with whom he appeared on the mount of transfiguration. Even the pride of Lucifer and the rebellious angels has grandeur and scale, "Angels fall, they are towers, from heaven —a story / Of just, majestical, and giant groans." The "story" for Hopkins is not only the Old Testament version of the angelic fall with the further hint that these angels later begat "giants" from the daughters of men (Gen. 6:1-4), but also Milton's epic account in *Paradise Lost*. For Milton, too, Moses was "That Shepherd, who first taught the chosen Seed" (*PL* 1, l. 8).[18]

In contrast with these heroic actors of good and evil, the ordinary man—"we," both the poet and his readers—is capable of neither glory nor tragedy:

> But man—we, scaffold of score brittle bones;
> Who breathe, from groundlong babyhood to hoary
> Age gasp; whose breath is our *memento mori*—
> What bass is *our* viol for tragic tones?

Man's twenty pounds ("score") of bones supports, like an execu-
tioner's scaffold, the power of life, his "breath" in the biblical
sense (Gen. 2:7) which is also his "reminder of death"; a "death's
head" is his skull. Shakespeare's celebrated description of the
seven ages of man in *As You Like It*, act 2, scene 7, offers another
echo to these lines. Further, as Gardner points out in his note to
this poem (P, p. 296), the use of "viol" recalls the King James Version of Isaiah 14:11-12: "Thy pomp is brought down to the grave,
and the noise of thy viols: the worm is spread under thee, and the
worms cover thee. How art thou fallen from heaven, O Lucifer,
son of the morning!" The figure of Lucifer thus reappears as the
unifying inscape of the octave. In Christ's words: "I saw Satan
falling like lightning from heaven" (Luke 10:18), the "forked
lightning" of Moses, the fall of the angels, and the pomp of
Satan's viol in "instressing his own inscape," all are put into focus
and "brought down." How much more then is modern man
without cause for boasting, since he degrades himself and follows
a mediocre path which chooses neither right nor wrong. How
can the poet translate for him in terms of *yes* and *no* the shatter-
ing revelation?

> He! Hand to mouth he lives, and voids with shame;
> And, blazoned in however bold the name,
> Man Jack the man is, just; his mate a hussy.

"But because thou art lukewarm, and neither cold nor hot, I am
about to vomit thee out of my mouth" (Apoc. 3:16). Scripture's
rebuke of man's mediocrity expresses an even stronger revulsion
than the poet's satiric reproach. "I know thy works," says the
Son of Man; "thou hast the name of being alive, and art dead."

Hopkins next reverts to his theme of self-justication, comparing his lot, as in the previous poems, with others; but midpoint
he abruptly breaks off with a magnificent stroke of humble self-
disclosure:

> And I that die these deaths, that feed this flame,
> That . . . in smooth spoons spy life's masque mirrored: tame
> My tempests there, my fire and fever fussy.

Himself "hand to mouth," the poet contemplates life's little woe-ful pageant in a spoon, its polished surface mirroring a distorted, humorous miniature of the face. One recalls the droll self-portrait of "Gerard Hopkins, reflected in a lake," sketched in a diary many years before (August 14, 1864; see J, fig. 27 in Appendix i). Hopkins also may be suggesting George Eliot's words in her novel, *Middlemarch*, 1. 10: "Even Milton, looking for his portrait in a spoon, must submit to have the facial angle of a bumpkin."[19] The inscape provided in the spoon reduces everything to the trivial, because it is among trivialities that the incarnation took place and is received or refused by men (L3, 19-20). The poet's "fire and fever fussy" is a tempest in a teapot to be poured out into a cup and stirred by a common spoon.

Far from being the cynical piece it is often made out to be, this sonnet is disarmingly honest and even comic in its devices and contrasts. The very excesses are deliberately employed for the exaggeration and self-caricature that Hopkins worked hard to achieve; he left an unprecedented five drafts of the poem among his working papers. It would be a mistake, perhaps, to confuse the poet's deprecatory "spying" at the world and at himself in this sonnet with the patient shaper, in the bulk of his major poetry, of a Christian *weltanschauung* unique in its time. But even here the spoon's conic mirror becomes a kind of anamorpho-scope in which the insignificant, fragmentary features of the poet's *persona* miraculously take shape and show forth with classic grace an image of contemporary heroism: a man of in-tegrity making his own myth.[20] "For the image of God," wrote Clement of Alexandria, "is His Word, the genuine Son of Mind, the Divine Word, the archetypal light of light; and the image of the Word is the true man, the mind which is in man, who is therefore said to have been made 'in the image and likeness of God,' assimilated to the Divine Word in the affections of the soul, and therefore rational" (*Protrepticus* 10). Upside down in the concave mirror of a polished spoon, Hopkins catches the inscape of modern man whose *imago Christi* shines out of emptiness in the reflected light of reason, a microcosm of its place and time.

Gnosis

Christ would not be the God of St Paul, nor the God
of my heart, if, looking at the lowliest, most material,
created being, I were unable to say, "I cannot understand this thing, I cannot grasp it, I cannot be
fully in contact with it, except as a function of
him who gives to the natural whole of which it is
a part its full reality and its final determined form."
Since Christ is omega, the universe is physically
impregnated to the very core of its matter by the
influence of his super-human nature. The presence
of the Incarnate Word penetrates everything, as a
universal element. It shines at the common heart
of things, as a centre that is infinitely intimate to
them and at the same time (since it coincides with
universal fulfilment) infinitely distant.

Pierre Teilhard de Chardin
Science and Christ

11

Poetry and Gnosis

THE task of formulating a "unifying unity" remains. The numerous strands we have traced all meet in a man, enigmatic and complex, yet singularly simple in his aim and character. How do we reconcile the mythmaker with the man himself? Eager for myriad tasks—poetry, music, metrics, numerology, history, physics, philosophy, theology—why did he leave so much undone? Why are even the basic outlines of his myth buried under layers of magical words and mysterious images, for which the poet himself offers to the reader no crib, no hornbook of basic principles for knowledge? Gerard Manley Hopkins, priest and poet, ultimately seems to defy any clear or coherent analysis of his life and work.

"I was not over-desirous," the poet once confessed to Bridges regarding *The Wreck of the Deutschland*, "that the meaning of all should be quite clear, at least unmistakeable" (L1, 50). If the amount of explication his poetry has elicited be taken as a measure, he managed to achieve "excellences higher than clearness." In aspiring to the mysterious, Hopkins cultivated concealment not only in style but in living, in his profession as well as in his writing. Even if it had been published, the *Deutschland* was to have been printed anonymously: "You must never say that the poem is mine," he warned his mother when there was still hope of the *Month*'s publishing it. In later years he resisted Canon Dixon's every effort to slip a few of his poems into print. By sending his poems to Bridges and overseeing the collection, he guaranteed their being known to another generation, but only after his death. Hopkins wished to be, and succeeded in being, a man unknown.

solution to the enigma, which is presented in this chapter, been before the reader since he read the introduction of this book. Baldly stated, I believe Hopkins to have been a Christian Gnostic as that ideal has been defined by Clement of Alexandria and Origen and to have sought a "new Mythus," in Carlyle's phrase, for his Christian beliefs. I believe that he consciously developed a system of ideas, images, and coinages, which he then deliberately kept secret—at least in their essential design—by avoiding any formal presentation of the views and conclusions drawn from his wide, introspective reading. The author and book which he particularly studied and used as a model of his thought and as a source of fresh poetic inspiration, I believe to have been Clement of Alexandria and his *Stromata* or *Miscellanies*, a literary collection in eight books on topics of poetry, philosophy, and religion.[1] The purpose and theme of Clement's work is the development of gnosis as the exploration of faith and the key to full Christian service of God and neighbor. "In his most considerable work," H. P. Liddon said of the *Stromata*, Clement "labors to impart the higher knowledge to which the Christian is entitled, and so render him 'the perfect Gnostic.' "[2] Newman, who quotes at length from the *Stromata* in his study of Arianism, observes that it "well illustrates the Primitive Church's method of instruction, as far as regards the educated portion of the community."[3] Here was the program Hopkins required: the ideal of his mind, the moral catalyst of his everyday decisions and the guiding beacon of his course of life. Preeminently, gnosis was the aim and justification of his poetry, the point of convergence where his energies focused.

This thesis has been left to be treated here because many of the conclusions already reached are valid as they stand. A reader need not take the final secret passageway to gnosis in order to benefit from knowledge of Hopkins's myth. The thesis promises, however, to help the reader to emerge with a deeper knowledge of Hopkins's poetry and of the man himself. The evidence is necessarily conjectural, for he never in his extant writings explicitly mentions either Clement of Alexandria or any of his works. (For that matter, he never cites Origen, although at Oxford he admits to "a real feeling" for him.)[4] The method followed in this chapter is a digest of that used in the entire book: beginning with the commentary on Parmenides, proceeding through the New Testament and church fathers, and ending with a study of the prose and poetry.

At the conclusion of his notes on Parmenides, Hopkins quotes Theophrastus's attribution to the earlier philosopher of the idea that "everything that exists possesses gnosis" (J, 130).[5] The concept of thinking creation was offered as an explanation of man's own thought, for he could not know the other unless it possessed a capacity to be known. The universality of knowledge is an important element in the philosophical development of gnosis. Man, particularly for Scotus, is not apart from being in his intellectual and moral pursuits; rather, being is never more itself, individually and plurally, than when it is known by man. All things have "sake . . . a being abroad" (L1, 83) by which they are identified with the mind in the act of shared gnosis. At the apex and cynosure of reality, man the microcosm rises, the creature whose capacity it is to know everything and be everything: *anima est quodammodo omnia*. Or as Plato expressed the Aristotelian aphorism: "The true lover of knowledge is always striving after being—that is his nature; he will not rest until . . . , becoming incorporate with very being, having begotten mind and truth, he will have knowledge and will truly live and grow" (*Republic* 6. 490 a-b).[6]

Of the New Testament writings, one of the most important texts for the theory of gnosis is found in the almost Johannine verses of St. Luke 10:21-22, on the Son's revelation of the Father who has "hidden these things from the wise and prudent and revealed them to little ones." Knowledge is first of the Son both from the Father's point of view and from man's, for men know the Son before they know the Father. The only historical person with knowledge of God is Jesus who elects others with whom he shares his gnosis. Among "these things" which the Father has hidden and which the Son now reveals, Jesus mentions Satan's fall from heaven, the power to subject spirits, and the inscription of his disciples' names in heaven—three topics dear to Hopkins.

For St. Paul, gnosis is first of all the knowledge God possesses of himself and of his creation: "Any man who loves God is known by him" (1 Cor. 8:3). This knowledge on man's side is only complete in heaven: "We see now through a mirror in an obscure manner, but then face to face. Now I know in part, but then I shall know even as I have been known" (1 Cor. 13:12). There is a false gnosis based on pride and not on love: "If anyone thinks that he knows anything, he has not yet known as he ought to know" (1 Cor. 8:2). For man gnosis means knowledge of Jesus, "to know the mystery of God, Christ, in whom are hidden all the treasures of wisdom and knowledge" (Col. 2:3; adapted). The term "mystery" is here identified with Christ himself. In the Pauline Epistles it specifically refers to the presence of the risen Christ in his members. Man's relationship with God has long been hidden away in the divine mind and now is shown to be the crucified Messiah, Jesus, raised on high. This *kerygma* is folly to the Gentiles and a scandal to the Jews, but to those who are called by the Lord of creation, it is the manifestation of his wisdom and his living power in man (1 Cor. 1:17-25). Gnosis then is the recognition and experience of this new life within and shows itself in acceptance of God's word and in obedience to his will.[7] Liddon wrote: "To know God truly, to have a full sight of God before the soul, is something more than mere head-knowledge, it is knowledge in act."[8]

An essential Pauline text for our purposes, in that it connects gnosis with inscape, is Philippians 3:8-14, apparently a vital letter in the formation of Hopkins's myth. Paul writes: "I count everything loss because of the excelling knowledge of Jesus Christ, my Lord. For his sake I have suffered the loss of all things . . . so that I may know him and the power of his resurrection and the fellowship of his sufferings: become like to him in death, in the hope that somehow I may attain to the resurrection from the dead." All else is "waste and garbage," in Paul's vivid phrasing, compared to gnosis, experiential knowledge, of Jesus dead and living, with whom he longs to be identified. He continues: "Not that I have already obtained this, or already have been made perfect, but I press on hoping that I may lay hold of that for which Christ Jesus has laid hold of me. Brethren, I do not consider that I have laid hold of it already. But one thing I do: forgetting what is behind, I strain forward to what is before, I press on towards the goal, to the prize of God's heavenly call in Christ Jesus." Not only are the ideas of *kenosis* in suffering and loss and of the resurrection from the dead vividly recorded here, but the noun "goal" or "mark" is the root word of Hopkins's "inscape": σκοπός. The sense of "straining forward," "pressing on," and flying to the target, the center which foredraws creation, is both an accurate summary and incisive imaging forth or "conceit" of Hopkins's basic idea. This passage perhaps provided the source of this elusive gnostic word. Clearly it identifies *scopos* as "the excelling gnosis of Christ Jesus my Lord."

Saint Paul also associated gnosis with interior light: "For God who commanded: 'Let the light shine out of the darkness,' has shone in our minds to radiate the light of the knowledge of God's glory shining on the face of Christ Jesus" (2 Cor. 4:6; adapted). Here the light of nature and the interior light of gnosis are fused in the identity of that knowledge as the sight of divine radiance in the face of the transfigured and exalted Jesus, the new Moses who brings the covenant down from the mountain heights to deliver it to his people. Moses had to veil his face, but the new glory of Christ's presence shines out for all to see: "Now the Lord is the Spirit; and where the Spirit of the Lord is, there is freedom. But we all, with faces unveiled, reflecting as in a mirror the glory of the Lord, are being transformed into his very image from glory to glory, as through the Spirit of the Lord" (2 Cor. 3:17-18).

The verb "to know" is used repeatedly in St. John's writings, but the noun "gnosis"—which appears twenty-three times in St. Paul's letters—is never used. The Johannine text insists on the action of revelation in Jesus and the reciprocal act of illumination in the mind of the believer for whom each event of the Gospel history is visible manifestation of the invisible power and presence of God. To know Jesus is to live and abide in him, to possess him in love and to spend one's self in service for others; to know him is to share in his indwelling and participate in his mission:

"Now this is everlasting life, that they may know you, the only true God, and Jesus Christ whom you have sent" (John 17:3; adapted).[9] At the Last Supper, St. John, in the exchange of Christ with his mystified disciple Philip, explicitly identifies knowledge of the Father with the acquaintance—or personal familiarity leading to recognition and acceptance—of the man Jesus as the sole way and truth of God for men: "No one comes to the Father but through me. If you had known me, you would also have known my Father. And henceforth you do know him, and you have seen him. . . . Philip, he who sees me sees also the Father" (John 14: 6-9). Christ's words, "When you have lifted up the Son of Man, you will know that I AM" (John 8:28), dramatically defines the nature and occasion of man's gnosis of God. It will be communicated through the Paraclete, "the Spirit of truth whom the world cannot receive, because it neither sees him nor knows him. But you shall know him, because he will dwell with you, and be in you" (John 14:17).

The Catholic Epistles, as Liddon shows in his Bampton lectures, are dominated by the ideal of a pure and truthful knowledge-in-action. False teachers and those they mislead are upbraided by these writers as ignoramuses. The Epistle of St. Jude, for example, says of them: "But these men deride whatever they do not know; and the things they know by instinct like the dumb beasts, become for them a source of destruction" (Jude 1:10). The brethren, on the other hand, are meant to "grow in grace and knowledge of our Lord and Savior, Jesus Christ." This knowledge has him as its object and proves itself in patience, piety, and love. The Second Epistle of St. Peter, which is the most eloquent in treating the theme, explains the result of such Christian striving: "For if you possess these virtues and they abound in you, they will render you neither inactive nor unfruitful in the knowledge of our Lord Jesus Christ" (2 Pet. 1:8). The Greek word used here, ἐπίγνωσις, is defined by Liddon as the "higher practical knowledge of Jesus Christ."[10] Here, in summary, is the New Testament moral ideal placed in its true perspective: the remembrance of Jesus, as he was and as he taught others, made alive in memory and presented in acts of intelligent love. Recalling the transfiguration, one author proclaimed: "We were not following fictitious tales when we brought you the knowledge of the power and coming of our Lord Jesus Christ, but we had been eyewitnesses of his grandeur" (2 Pet. 1:16).

In recent archaeological and biblical studies, a growing awareness of the movement in Christian and pre-Christian spheres toward integration of Judaic and pagan eschatalogical ideas has solidly established the original and bold course followed by the first disciples of Jesus.[11] This syncretism was indeed so precarious that one of the immediate results of the influx of fresh converts was the proliferation of unorthodox and confused preconceptions of who Christ was and what his revelation involved. Gnosticism apparently was not a Christian heresy in its original form, but an autonomous system of beliefs which borrowed from numerous, unconnected sources. Independent of this religion, some converts to Christianity wanted to develop a more profound knowledge of the historical mystery of the Christ-event; these were for the most part men educated in Greek and Roman literature and philosophy who saw the Nazarene as the culmination not only of Hebraic knowledge but of their own culture as well. Irenaeus championed the right course in the midst of foundering speculations and absurd persuasions by setting down in detail the abuses of Christ's revelation contrived by Gnosticism. Origen offered a cautious and reasoned theory of gnosis which he used rather to discredit false Gnostic opinions than to advance his own ideas. At the heart of his threefold reading of Scriptures, however, this special knowledge held sway as the goal of man's relentless inquiry into the secrets of the divine mind and will. But the chief fashioner of an integrated avowal of Christian gnosis was Clement of Alexandria.

Clement's definition of gnosis was quoted in the introduction of this study; his careful explication of the relationship of faith and knowledge is the cornerstone of his position. Gnosis has its source, foundation, justification, and *raison d'etre* in the acceptance of Jesus and his teachings. Yet faith also stands in need of knowledge: "In order to believe truly in the Son, we must believe He is the Son, and that He came, and how, and for what, and that

He suffered; and we must know who is the Son of God. Now neither is knowledge without faith, nor faith without knowledge" (*Strom.* 5. 1). Truth has but one origin in man; therefore, the study of Greek philosophy prepares the mind beforehand for the recognition of faith as the groundwork on which truth then constructs the edifice of knowledge (*Strom.* 7. 3). Clement, through numerous quotations and comment, carefully shows how the Greeks shared in Israel's revelation by their borrowings from Old Testament books (*Strom.* 5. 14). As God prepared man in history for the coming of his Son through a series of human teachers—to some of whom he spoke directly, like Moses and the prophets, and to others indirectly, like Plato and the Stoics—so each individual grows in gnosis and receives Christ more plentifully by study and insight into the past.

Faith then is a kind of comprehensive knowledge of the essential *kerygma*, and gnosis is the slow and steady growth in learning that builds on faith and that terminates in love. Clement thus describes the experience of interior transformation:

> Christ is both the foundation and the superstructure, by whom are both the beginning and the ends. And the extreme points, the beginning and the end—I mean faith and love—are not taught. But knowledge, conveyed from communication through the grace of God as a deposit, is entrusted to those who show themselves worthy of it; and from it the worth of love beams forth from light to light. For it is said, "To him that hath shall be given:" to faith, knowledge; and to knowledge, love; and to love, the inheritance.
>
> And this takes place, whenever one hangs on the Lord by faith, by knowledge, by love, and ascends along with Him to where the God and guard of our faith and love is. (*Strom.* 7. 10)

Gnosis is a Jacob's ladder that leads to the purchase and prize of "The Starlight Night": the spouse Christ housed cosmically and personally "withindoors"; it is the tree of knowledge that Adam lost through overreaching and Jesus restored to man by

his self-lowering love. The pledge of man's ascent with him is
the light of knowledge that guides the pilgrim here and now:

> Hope holds to Christ the mind's own mirror out
> To take His lovely likeness more and more. (P151)

"Faith, hope and love endure," notes St. Paul in 1 Corinthians
13:13, "but the greatest of them all is love," which is born of
knowledge and which will reach perfection "when we know him
even as he knows us."

The gnosis that one seeks in everything, according to Clement,
is Christ himself: "Our knowledge, and our spiritual garden, is
the Saviour Himself, into whom we are planted, being transferred
and transplanted from our old life into the good land. And trans-
planting contributes to fruitfulness. The Lord, then, into whom
we have been transplanted, is the Light and the true Knowledge"
(*Strom.* 6. 1). This true gnosis, the Lord, shines out from the
deepest recesses of the mind and heart: "Let the light then shine
in the hidden part of man, that is, the heart; and let the beams
of knowledge arise to reveal and irradiate the hidden inner man,
the disciple of the Light, the familiar friend and fellow-heir of
Christ" (*Protrepticus* 11). Like Hopkins's "eternal beam" that
signals the risen Christ, Clement's gnosis is an inner reality transforming and immortalizing the Christian follower. Gnosis, in
short, is more than mere imitation of Jesus; it is a higher identity
with him as Word-made-man, in thought and action. Its possession allows—rather, urges—each believer "to receive knowledge,
not desiring its results, but embracing itself for the sake of knowing" (*Strom.* 7. 12). "The Gnostic, then, is impressed with the
closest likeness, that is, with the mind of the Master, which He
being possessed of, commended and recommended to His disciples
and to the prudent" (6. 15). The idea is similar to that found in
Paul's text: "The spiritual man judges all things, and he himself
is judged by no man. For 'who has known the mind of the Lord,
that he might instruct Him?' But we have the mind of Christ"
(1 Cor. 2:15-16). The Son of God is himself the teacher, the truth
taught, and the means of acquiring that truth. With "that mind
which was in Christ Jesus," gnosis leads to service of God and

man, rejecting falsehood in others and hypocrisy in oneself. Its aim is to boast with St. Paul: "For to me to live is Christ and to die is gain" (Phil. 1:21).

Three qualities of gnosis presented in the *Stromata* are important in the light of Hopkins's own mythopoeic search. Clement sees knowledge as "the beginning and author of all rational action," preceding like a training period man's impulses and assent, for it is, first of all, the apprehension of particular concrete realities (6. 8). Gnosis is "excited by existing objects" and grows toward fulfillment until—its second quality—"one knows all things, and comprehends all things in the exercise of sure apprehension." Clement then offers a definition: "Knowledge (*gnosis*) is essentially a contemplation of existences on the part of the soul, either of a certain thing or of certain things, and when perfected, of all together" (6. 8). It apprehends not only species and genus but totality of being. Everything is knowable because nothing is incomprehensible to the Son of God, the Teacher: "For He who suffered out of His love for us would have suppressed no element of knowledge requisite for our instruction" (6. 8). An important corollary follows: no field of learning is closed to the dedicated Gnostic, "for to him knowledge (*gnosis*) is the principal thing. Consequently, therefore, he applies to the subjects that are a training for knowledge, taking from each branch of study its contribution to the truth" (6. 10). Clement next examines each subject area: the proportion of harmonies in music, increasing and decreasing numbers in arithmetic and their relationships, geometry, astronomy, and, lastly, dialectics—the inquirer "fixing on the distinction of existences, till he come to what are primary and single."

Knowledge comes from two sources, one through the senses and the other, the only proper gnosis, from "judgement and reason, in the exercise of which there will be rational cognitions alone, applying purely to objects of thought and resulting from the bare energy of the soul" (6. 1). Through multiplicity the mind mounts to oneness in itself as image of the divine Logos or Reason. This "bare energy of the soul" is exercised through one's study, moral life, moderation, almsgiving, and prayer. Discipline, then, is the third quality that determines gnosis. With universality and concreteness it governs all man's energies and gives value to all his judgments. Newman cites the *Stromata* to this effect: "Everything which excels the Gnostic (or Christian philosopher) accounts precious according to its worth, and estimable."[12]

Few writers, in fact, have explained the nature of this knowledge as well as Newman does in his *Idea of a University*. "In the mind of the Philosopher," he writes, "the elements of the physical and moral world, sciences, arts, pursuits, ranks, offices, events, opinions, individualities, are all viewed as one, with correlative functions, and as gradually by successive combinations converging, one and all, to the true centre." Through "this illuminative reason," he adds, "the intellect which has been disciplined to the perfection of its powers, which knows, and thinks while it knows, . . . discerns the end in every beginning, the origin in every end, the law in every interruption, the limit in each delay; . . . it ever knows where it stands, and how its path lies from one point to another."[13] Little wonder that one critic, Erich Pryzywara, S.J., has traced the origin of Newman's theory of "Wisdom or Enlargement" to Clement of Alexandria's gnosis, since Newman himself admits in his *Apologia Pro Vita Sua* that "the broad philosophy of Clement and Origen carried me away; the philosophy, not the theological doctrine. . . . Some portions of their teaching, magnificent in themselves, came like music to my inward ear, as if the response to ideas, which, with little external to encourage them, I had cherished so long."[14]

Turning to Hopkins, we find these same three qualities of knowledge to be stressed in his poetry and prose. From "The Habit of Perfection" to his sonnet on St. Alphonsus Rodriguez, "the war within" and the "world without event" (P73) are an inner drama of "prayer, patience, alms, vows" which aim at closer identification with the mind and heart of the master. Contemplation engendered by mortification provides the interior means by which exterior nature—its seasons and landscapes, its falcons and stars—is known fully and in a way sense perception alone could never approximate. The redeemed inner man, in other words, instructs the created outer man in the perception of reality. Thus, in spite of his inscaping nature in order to mark Christ's presence there, Hopkins on several occasions notes that he is "resolved to give up all beauty" until he had "His leave for it" (J, 71). One penance "prevented my seeing much that half-year" (J, 190); this was in 1869 during his Jesuit novitiate. The "bare energy of the soul" in contact with the Lord who dispossessed himself for man activates a higher gnosis of the *mysterium Christi* in the world he made and in the atoned heart.

Hopkins's fondness for particularity has been extensively examined by scholars; it is also an aspect of gnosis which concerns itself with apprehending existing objects. The poet's curiosity about all areas of human inquiry, especially his fascination with musical theory, similarly finds vindication in Clement's theory. Many hours were spent composing melodies in canon and fugue and developing a new style of music (L1, 103). He planned "a sort of popular account of Light and the Ether" (L2, 139), a work on Greek metrics, a paper on "the Argei and the Pontifices"; he delved into the field of Egyptology with his friend Baillie; he wrote an article on "Statistics and Free Will," which was not published (it has disappeared), and he contributed to his father's book, *The Cardinal Numbers* (L1, 294). These various interests —carried on almost simultaneously—were ordered to the total comprehension of Being, knowledge of the Word whose human genius "reasoned and planned and invented" (S, 37). "Being the eternal Reason," Christ was yet "catechised in the theology of the Rabbins" (L3, 20).

Two references in Hopkins would also indicate familiarity with the *Stromata*. He twice quotes a nonscriptural saying of Jesus: "My mystery is for me and for the children of my house," which is to be found in the *Stromata* (5. 10). Both the quotation and its context are significant, for Clement believed that the apostles veiled the truth in secrecy or mystery "for the instruction of the perfect." He wrote: "And the *gnosis* itself is that which has descended by transmission to a few, having been imparted unwritten by the apostles. Hence, then, knowledge or wisdom ought to be exercised up to the eternal and unchangeable habit of contemplation" (*Strom.* 6. 7). Hidden readings of Scripture are open only to those who receive the grace of gnosis, the secret transmission passed on by the Spirit either through direct inspiration or the oral teaching of those instructed by the apostles. This *disciplina arcani* is a special gift not only to be jealously guarded but to be handed on to other seekers of perfection, as the "three effacts of gnostic power" indicate: gnosis causes first, "the knowledge of things; second, the performance of whatever the Word suggests; and third, the capability of delivering, in a way suitable to God, the secrets veiled in the truth" (7. 1).

The ordinary faithful are also meant to share in the economy and benefits of this dedicated service to holy knowledge. Hopkins's sermons are unusual for this very reason: they are an effort to lift the veil and reveal the true meaning of the inspired words. "I have said nothing by way of exhortation to you," he concludes in one typical sermon, "I could not both do that and explain the Gospel, and I wanted to explain the Gospel" (S, 89). He remarks on the text: " 'Rejoice in the Lord always; again I say, rejoice'— and how?—The secret is soon out: *by dearly loving the Lord himself, our Lord Jesus Christ*" (S, 48). His most ambitious preaching effort, the four sermons at Liverpool on "The First Kingdom of God" are a recherché disquisition which attempts to explore God's original plans in creation. They embody a conscious *praxis* of the ideal transmission, "in a way suitable to God," of mysteries hidden in the original divine plan. "That's telling secrets," the poet admonished Patmore after reading his *Sponsa Dei*. His remark was not proof of his prudery, but of his unwillingness to sell in the marketplace the fruits of "high contemplation" (L3, 365).

Every effort must be made, however, to make available to the many the humanly valuable discoveries of the few, so as "to educate, to be standards" for public use: "To produce then is of little use unless what we produce is known, if known widely known, the wider known the better, for it is by being known it works, it influences, it does its duty, it does good. We must then try to be known, aim at it, take means to it" (L1, 231). The gifted few must "aim at" being Gnostics for the good of others; they must place the products of their inner struggles and victories over the inarticulate void at the service of mankind. "To be known," as to be Gnostic, is the truest inscape or purpose of their being, the highest imitation of the Word made known to men. Hopkins consciously tried to instruct his friends in this ideal, to prod them on to further creativity and to widen their audience of readers by his own personal efforts. By doing so, he knew he would "help on the knowledge of the Incarnation" (S, 263). For each man must play his part, adding his fragmentary gnosis to the building of the *pleroma* "till the whole earth is hereafter to be covered, if only for a time, still to be covered with the knowledge of the Lord" (S, 75).

The second reference made by Hopkins to the *Stromata* like the first is found in the celebrated sermon on "Our Lord Jesus Christ," which further mentions Plato's supposed prophecy of Christ's passion: "Plato the heathen, the greatest of the Greek philosophers, foretold of him: he drew by his wisdom a picture of the just man in his justice crucified and it was fulfilled in Christ" (S, 37). Clement recorded the passage: "Plato, all but predicting the economy of salvation, says in the second book of the *Republic*: 'Thus he who is constituted just shall be scourged, shall be stretched on the rack, shall be bound, have his eyes put out, and, at last, having suffered all evils, shall be crucified'" (*Strom.* 5. 14). The whole of chapter 14, which reviews Greek philosophy and poetry: Empedocles, Heraclitus, Parmenides, Homer, Pindar, and others, is a unique example of Christian recapitualation and rejuvenation of tradition; it follows the same line of thought employed by Hopkins in his treatment of the Greek spoils in the service of God's new people.

The most striking analogue remains to be studied in establishing the Victorian poet's debt to the second-century church father. Hopkins at one point examines and defines gnosis and epignosis (an intensified form) in his *Exercise* notes "On the contemplating Persons, Words and Actions." He wrote: "Memory is the name for that faculty which towards present things is Simple Apprehension and, when it is question of the concrete only, γνῶσις, ἐπίγνωσις, the faculty of Identification; towards past things is Memory proper; and towards things future or things unknown or imaginary is Imagination. When continued or kept on the strain the act of this faculty is attention, advertence, heed, the being *ware*, and its habit, knowledge, the being *aware*. Towards God it gives rise to *reverence*, it is the sense of the *presence* of God" (S, 174). Memory here is threefold: simple apprehension, memory proper, and imagination. These three levels are defined and function in three dimensions: present, past, and future, respectively. Gnostic memory, in the conscious present, is the knowledge that identifies with concrete being, and it also operates in all reality and time. Being and thought are made one in the moment of meeting. Attention leads to intention, and apprehension to inner possession. Gnosis, as Clement defines it, is likewise essentially contemplation of concrete existences in one or more or in all things together (*Strom.* 6. 8). Christopher Devlin in his note to this passage from Hopkins's meditation points (S, 298) finds here Scotus's triple distinction of the kinds of memory; but the parallel is less remarkable than Clement's description of gnosis, not only as a faculty and habit (*Strom.* 4. 22), but as concrete knowledge of things in time: "If, then, we assert that Christ Himself is Wisdom, and that it was His working which showed itself in the prophets, by which the gnostic tradition may be learned, as He Himself taught the apostles during His presence; then it follows that the *gnosis*, which is the knowledge and apprehension of things present, future, and past, which is sure and reliable, as being imparted and revealed by the Son of God, is wisdom" (*Strom.* 6. 7). Knowledge—the awareness of God's presence—originates in the historical incarnation of him who is the beginning and the end.

Gnosis then is "the faculty of Identification" of and with Christ, as human and divine Wisdom, a sharing in his species of genius. None can match his gifts of mind, but all can partake of them. He is the greatest poet who ever lived: "No stories or parables are like Christ's, so bright, so pithy, so touching; no proverbs or sayings are such jewellery: they stand off from other men's thoughts like stars, like lilies in the sun; nowhere in literature is there anything to match the Sermon on the Mount" (S, 37). Poetry expresses his genius, employing memory proper, imagination, and awareness by the re-creation and representation of the Word through the words of the poem.

Poetry as gnosis is also prophecy, a moment that looks forward from a present and past perspective, spelt from Sibyl's and David's leaves, the Hebraic-Hellenic tradition made alive in a new specific, original utterance of genius. For each poet is a species to himself and in precisely this charisma is more of an After-Christ, the unique and universal species of mankind, than other human beings. The creative artist then is a unique whole "and can never recur" (L3, 370); he is an exhaustive entity whose inscape, univocally, is the oneness of Christ's. When Hopkins sent his sonnet on the "Heraclitean Fire" to Bridges, he observed: "The effect of studying masterpieces is to make me admire and do otherwise. So it must be on every original artist to some degree, on me to a marked degree" (L1, 291). Each poet, drawing from within St. Augustine's rich "treasure-house of memory," aims straight for the mark through his imagination, strikes inscape, "the very soul of art," and then in the poem itself, "continued, kept on the strain," heeds the Spirit of Christ in time rhythmically breathing and wording reality within him until the finished and concrete "burl of being" of the completed poem stands forth: "The fulness is the thought." Locked in the present, poetry becomes transcendent expression of the past tradition and the future event; as such it is gnosis as explained by Clement: "And if, too, the end of the wise man is contemplation, that of those who are still philosophers aims at it, but never attains it, unless by the process of learning it receives the prophetic utterance which has been made known, by which it grasps both the present, the future, and the past—how they are, were, and shall be" (*Strom.* 6. 7). The theory of gnosis, therefore, harmonizes with Hopkins's ideas of both poetry and time in the "one positive pitch or direction" toward Omega, Christ all and in all. Perfection of the work and of the life "is what the sense of unity means" (J, 126).

Ill and troubled at the beginning of his last retreat in 1889, Hopkins reasoned with himself and lamented: "What is my wretched life? Five wasted years almost have passed in Ireland.

I am ashamed of the little I have done, of my waste of time, although my helplessness and weakness is such that I could scarcely do otherwise" (S, 262). He had just reflected that "philosophy is not religion" and that Marcus Aurelius's system had not brought him any closer to the truth of Christ. Rather, "the Word and sovereign Reason was then made flesh and he persecuted it" (S, 261). The myth one fashions is not the love one gives, as St. Paul told the Corinthians and as Clement of Alexandria, that optimist of gnosis, recognized and repeated. What consummation then could Hopkins devoutly wish for? To die, to be dissolved, and to be with Christ: "I wish then for death: yet if I died now I should die imperfect, no master of myself, and that is the worst failure of all" (S, 262). His Jesuit editor points out that the religious life is a state of striving for perfection, not its attainment (S, 319). Surely Hopkins was aware of this basic principle taught to every novice who aspires to that state. What the poet-priest intended by his self-denunciation was his failure to reach the perfection of gnosis, "a perfecting of man as man" in the attainment of full stature in Christ through all one's doings. For the Gnostic achieves that knowledge which always judges right and waits with equanimity to carry out the Father's will. His is the peace not given by the world because he is in earnest about the things of God.

The Christian Gnostic is every inch a gentleman; nature and grace, breeding and education meet in a harmonious self-mastery that flows not from one's own efforts but from Christ's presence within. Hopkins's description of a gentleman, in fact, may derive from Clement's picture of the Gnostic, who is "decorous in character, composed in mien" and who strives to mount to the summit of knowledge and love (*Strom.* 7. 11). Writing to Bridges on the subject of the true gentleman—which prompted him to set forth his interpretation of the *kenosis* of Philippians 2:5-11—Hopkins explained: "It is true there is nothing like the truth, and 'the good that does itself not *know* scarcely is'; so the perfect gentleman will *know* that he is the perfect gentleman" (L1, 176–77; italics added). The same idea is often stated by Clement: the Gnostic alone attains to perfection, embracing knowledge for the sake of knowing: "Therefore, regarding life in this world as necessary for the increase of science (ἐπιστήμη) and the acquisition of knowledge (γνῶσις), the Gnostic will value highest, not living, but living well. He will therefore prefer neither children, nor marriage, nor parents, to love for God, and righteousness in life" (*Strom.* 6. 12).

The failure that grated on Hopkins's heart was the deep-felt realization that the Gnostic ideal had not been given shape, expression, and actuality in his life and plans. Why did he not regard his poetry as the final achievement of his mythmaking? First, its fragmentary nature told against it. He once wrote Patmore: "It was by providence designed for the education of the human race that great artists should leave works not only of great excellence but also in very considerable bulk" (L3, 359). Each poem is a "by lay" or "byfall" of the burl of being that is the poet's myth. In addition, poetry for a man with his vocation must be counterbalanced by spiritual achievement in heroic imitation of the great sacrifice. Robert Southwell, for example, the Jesuit poet, "wrote amidst a terrible persecution and died a martyr, with circumstances of horrible barbarity: this is the counterpoise in his career" (L2, 94). Hopkins argued: "There have been very few Jesuit poets and, where they have been, I believe it would be found on examination that there was something exceptional in their circumstances or, so to say, counterbalancing in their career" (L2, 93). The poet lacked the evidence of any "counterpoise" in his work as a priest and religious which would signify God's purpose and guidance in leading him to a literary career.[15] Quite the contrary, everything from his friends' mixed reception of his poetry to the Society's indifference to it, impressed on him the futility of his poetic endeavors.

Hopkins also seems to have shared Maurice de Guérin's view of the literary career as an unreal one both in essence and in its rewards. Matthew Arnold's essay on the French poet had led Hopkins while at Oxford to read Guérin's journal, and he "admired it," as he told Dixon many years later (L2, 16). Arnold's remarks and quotations are strangely prophetic: "He published nothing: 'There is more power and beauty,' he [Guérin] writes, 'in the well-kept secret of one's self and one's thoughts, than in the display of a whole heaven that one may have inside one.' "[16] These words crystallize Hopkins's own attitude toward the sacred incommunicability of "this selfbeing of my own."

Poetry offered neither the final synthesis nor mastery of myth-making, for the myth was the whole man, his genius and achievement, and not the prophecy only. Returning to the heart of its mystery, Hopkins in his last retreat notes begins to grow again in hope as he reviews the roots of faith and gnosis in inscape: "But our lives and in particular those of religious, as mine, are in their whole direction, not only inwardly but most visibly and outwardly, shaped by Christ's" (S, 263). Not only the inner man but the outer shell are the inscape of the Word in man, his active image concretely fulfilling itself. One of the few consolations for the poet in his Dublin years was the discovery of an ancient Irish hymn entitled "St. Patrick's Breast-plate." He sent a copy of it to Bridges in 1884 with the comment that he found it "very beautiful and almost unique" (L1, 195). The hymn graphically calls on "Christ on the poop deck" and in the cosmos to shield and guide the singer who exclaims in his refrain: "I arise today / Through the strength of heaven." The incantation reads in part in Kuno Meyer's translation:

> Christ with me, Christ before me, Christ behind me,
> Christ in me, Christ beneath me, Christ above me,
> Christ on my right, Christ on my left,
> Christ when I lie down, Christ when I sit down, Christ
>   when I arise,
> Christ in the heart of every man who thinks of me,
> Christ in the mouth of every one who speaks of me,
> Christ in every eye that sees me,
> Christ in every ear that hears me.[17]

"Consider his hymn," the priest once admonished himself, "it breathes an enthusiasm which as far as feeling goes I feel but my action does not answer to this" (S, 260). One of the most regrettably unfinished—and apparently unbegun—tasks of his life must remain the projected critical text of St. Patrick's *Confession.* "The Cry of the Deer," as his hymn is also called, epitomizes the spirit and wording of inscape, "the whole direction . . . shaped by Christ."

Hopkins's enthusiasm for his myth was retained to the end; he felt and expressed it with conviction and imagination in the poems of his last period. He also lived the great sacrifice, even if he was denied the consolation of knowing that this was so; but to have had the "comfort" of such knowledge would have meant less of an identification with the "martyr-master." For *kenosis*, the action of self-emptying and its consequent experience of suffering the cross, ultimately defies all analysis and exegesis. Gnosis ends in mystery beyond the grasp of the human mind and heart, since *kenosis* is the parting of the ways between being and thought. One lives the myth without knowing it, as Hopkins lived it, dying before death, "living to live in a world of time" beyond himself. "Desire not the night," Job mourned, "when people are cut off"—not only from others, but cut off from themselves.

Before tracing gnosis in Hopkins's writings, one last quotation from Clement's *Stromata* is in order, for it dramatically illustrates the relationship of poetry and myth which is a concern of this book. "In a whirlwind" of loneliness and depression, Hopkins may have remembered the passage and understood the voice that spoke to Job out of the whirlwind of the Word's inner and cosmic stress. It still speaks with calm logic and beauty to the mind and heart:

> God, then, being not a subject for demonstration, cannot
> be the object of science. But the Son is wisdom, and knowl-
> edge, and truth, and all else that has affinity thereto. He
> is also susceptible of demonstration and of description.
> And all the powers of the Spirit, becoming collectively one
> thing, terminate in the same point—that is, in the Son.
> But He is incapable of being declared, in respect to the
> idea of each one of His powers. And the Son is neither
> simply one thing as one thing, nor many things as parts,
> but one thing as all things; whence also He is all things.
> For He is the circle of all powers rolled and united into
> one unity. Wherefore the Word is called Alpha and Omega,

> of whom alone the end becomes the beginning, and ends
> again at the original beginning without any break.
> Wherefore also to believe in Him, and by Him, is to become
> a unit, being indissolubly united in Him; and to disbelieve
> is to be separated, disjoined, divided. (*Strom.* 4. 25)

Such were the scope and scale of the myth which I believe the Victorian poet found in this second-century witness of Christ and in his theory of knowledge. Again, there is no final proof he found it there; but the goal he was striving for, Clement perfectly expressed. "What is the kernel of all these mythes?" Hopkins once asked. "Our souls alternate between a transcendental and a phenomenal, a γνῶσις—and δόξα—, life" (D8).

What then does gnosis reveal of Hopkins's particular poetic intention and its execution in his poems? In order to offer a full answer we must first establish the term's signification in his prose. The verb *to know* is inconspicuous in English and any special meaning given to it by an author might be easily overlooked. For example, an entry in his journal makes this observation: "I do not think I have ever seen anything more beautiful than the bluebell I have been looking at. I know the beauty of our Lord by it. Its inscape is mixed of strength and grace, like an ash tree" (J, 199). The technical meaning of "I know" as gnosis of Christ reveals the nature of the inscape. By seeing and looking, the poet knows his Lord as maker and redeemer; he hits the mark. This gnosis, now "unknown," may again be available to all men if they accept Christ in spirit and truth: "I thought how sadly beauty of inscape was unknown and buried away from simple people and yet how near at hand it was if they had eyes to see it and it could be called out everywhere again" (J, 221). He reminded himself: "Unless you refresh the mind from time to time you cannot always remember or believe how deep the inscape in things is" (J, 205). Of Holman Hunt's painting *The Shadow of the Cross*, Hopkins complained—on artistic grounds that are in fact christological—"No inscape of composition whatever—not known and if it had been known it could scarcely bear up against such realism" of detail (J, 248).[18] His first use of the words "inscape"

and "instress" in the notes on Parmenides link them with the
Eleatic philosopher's statement: " 'Thou couldst never either
know or say / what was not, there would be no coming at it' "
(J, 127). Inscape then is the act of gnosis, "the faculty of Identification" and the mind's contact with Being; it identifies the object of the quest. "To know" is "the being *ware*, and its habit,
knowledge, the being *aware*." Of what? "The *presence* of God"
(S, 174).

In Hopkins's poetry, "to know" is one of his most frequently
used verbs, appearing in one form or another more than eighty
times.[19] In both the early and mature verse it signifies a special-
ized, ascetical knowledge. As early as 1862, he had written in
Il Mystico:

> Touch me and purify, and shew
> Some of the secrets I would know.
>
> . . . .
>
> Grant that close-folded peace that clad
> The seraph brows of Galahad,
> Who knew the inner spirit that fills
> Questioning winds around the hills.
>
> (P77, ll. 39-44)

At the climax of the *Deutschland*, the poet exclaims:

> Ah! there was a heart right!
> There was single eye!
> Read the unshapeable shock night
> And knew the who and the why.   (P28, 29)

The nun's inscape is precisely an exercise of gnosis: she *knew*
Christ, possessed him, and uttered him into reality: "Wording
it how but by him that present and past / Heaven and earth are
word of, worded by?" Hers is an act of concrete identification of
and with Christ; she grasps "the present, future and past" in
the instant of gnosis which is, through faith, that identification;
hers is the mind of Christ. First man is known by his Lord:
"Thou knowest the walls, altar and hour and night," the poet
confesses in the opening of the *Deutschland*. For the nature of

faith "is God / in man / knowing his own truth" (S, 157). Men, however, have not learned how to reach him through gnosis:

> Not out of his bliss
> Springs the stress felt
> Nor first from heaven (and few know this)
> Swings the stroke dealt. (P28, 6)

The nun, on the other hand, "read the unshapeable shock night" with the storm for text, because gnosis is also "the meaning of a piece of writing, the Scriptures."[20] Origen's spiritual sense, developed from the literal reality, thus becomes unified knowledge. The activity of exegesis is related to the burden and the glory of living, the one Word giving integrity to all of man's acts. In his great ode, Hopkins shaped a gnostic poem that actuates its subject matter, that not only narrates an act of knowing but is that knowledge made known. Its inscape is to do and to be what it hymns and tells. Its "doing-be" is Christ.

Even a cliché may be given a new hidden meaning—as "In the Valley of the Elwy" demonstrates—if correctly understood. The tone is conversational in these opening lines, which say more than their seeming plainness implies:

> I remember a house where all were good
> To me, God knows, deserving no such thing. (P34)

The act of remembering is the second and proper function of memory, while immediate memory "of the concrete only" is gnosis. The poet remembers the house, but only God's gnosis is complete: he knows how unworthy the poet himself was of this identification with "these kind people." An opposite connotation is given to "knowing" in the last stanza of the Eurydice: "Not that hell knows redeeming." The pain of hell, it is implied, means the deprivation of the knowledge of God and his Son. "What the heart is!" Hopkins exclaimed in "The Handsome Heart," ". . . like carriers let fly— / Doff darkness, homing nature knows the rest." Guided by the sun's arc, the winged heart, intuitively "self-instressed" by its own nature, follows a direct course to its roost. In "Spring and Fall" the young girl is told that she will one day grow indifferent though "worlds of wanwood leafmeal lie; / And yet you *will* weep and know why." Man's ultimate gnosis is the cross and the sense of emptiness and loss it makes known. This suffering, Christ did not bring into the world; he inherited it from Adam and shared it—with greater feeling and compassion —with all other men. Gnosis, therefore, as human wisdom embodied in the mind and heart of Jesus, for Hopkins meant not only the insight acquired from learning, but the understanding born of experience as well.

"The Leaden Echo and the Golden Echo" employs two references to gnosis, each at the beginning of the two sections. The first part begins with the question: "Is there . . . nowhere known some, bow or brooch or braid or brace, láce, latch or catch or key to keep / Back beauty?" The Golden Echo answers: "Yes I cán tell such a key, I dó know such a place," and purposefully calls attention to the first "known" by the emphatic "dó know," which expresses the "positive pitch" of the action as being (S, 151). By the use of the simple auxiliary "do," Hopkins "the more states" his latent meaning of the true nature of the "key" and "place" where Beauty keeps its youth and being. A sonnet on a similar theme, "To what serves Mortal Beauty?" contains the lines:

> Our law says: Love what are ǀ love's worthiest, were all
> known;
> World's loveliest—men's selves. Self ǀ flashes off frame
> and face.
> (P62)

The rhyme draws attention to the technical use of "known": were full gnosis achieved, men would inscape "self" and thus love others, as Christ commanded, with the same love bestowed upon ourselves.

The device of rhyme to bring out the emphatic meaning of gnosis is also used in "Patience, hard thing!" as a concluding inscape of the whole sonnet: "Patience fills / His crisp combs, and that comes those ways we know." The verb "know," with its final positioning, focuses the poet's secret intent. The enigmatic ending, simple yet evasive, is typical of Hopkins's poetry; even after difficulties of verbal meaning and syntax have been solved, an element of aloofness remains, embedded in the hard mass of the poem itself. Here the key is again the gnostic reading of "we know": gnosis is Christ's way of filling men's minds and is drawn from the heart of reality, especially—as "honeycombs" implies—from the eucharistic Sacrifice, "the great purpose of his life and his own chosen redemption" (S, 162). The bread and wine are the products of a fertile world molded by man and transformed by the godhead who waits in patience to be recognized in order to be devoured: "Taste and see that the Lord is sweet." Mysterious are the ways he comes; man can only feebly approximate God's patient knowledge. Another of the sonnets of desolation, "My own heart let me more have pity on," ends with the wish: "Let joy size / At God knows when to God knows what." The time and occasion of gnosis rest in his hands.

"The Soldier," as has been already noted, abounds in verbs of appearances which describe the actions of the heart: "It fancies, feigns, deems . . . and fain will find." The sestet begins: "Mark Christ our King. He knows war, served this soldiering through." The stressing of "knows" in its special sense of Christic identity and knowledge of the concrete, heightens and foredraws the meaning of the *volta*: verbs of appearance give way to the one verb of existential encounter. True gnosis is Christ—this is the inscape which the poet, in the form of a military command, tells the reader to make.

In the last poem he wrote, the sonnet "To R. B.," Hopkins described the process of personal creative writing. He begins with "the one rapture of an inspiration," the original insight that brings a poem to pitch of being. This act he pictures in frank sexual imagery: "the strong / Spur, live and lancing like the blowpipe flame," for "knowing" in its Hebraic sense is carnal love, the full possession of another person in intimate identity. After the poem's conception, the poet proceeds to nurture and develop the embryonic song. The womb is the mind, "a mother of immortal song":

> Nine months she then, nay years, nine years she long
> Within her wears, bears, cares and combs the same:

> The widow of an insight lost she lives, with aim
> Now known and hand at work now never wrong. (P76)

Slowly, even over years of rewriting, the mind brings the poem
to perfection, the "aim / Now known," for gnosis attains its
ideal; it knows its goal and the work to be done. The surety and
care with which Hopkins "combed" or matured his own poetry
were born of his patient pursuit of mythmaking and the knowledge of what he was about. The myth found its final "heart-
throe, birth of a brain," in that process of a lifetime's evolving
growth in thought and being.

For gnosis itself, in the last analysis, is the faculty of psychic
and artistic birth: "When the first faculty [gnosis] just does its
office and falls back, barely naming what it apprehends, it scarcely gives birth to the second but when it keeps on the strain ('at-
tendere, advertere, et contemplari') it cannot but continuously
beget it. This faculty [the second] not identifies but verifies; takes
the measure of things, brings word of them; it is called λόγος and
reason" (S, 174). The faculty of identification, when "it keeps on
the strain" by pursuing the inscapes of existence, continuously
begets reason and expression. Gnosis produces *logos*; inscape
begets Christ. The "highest point of man's wit," as Sir Philip
Sidney argued, is reached in the knowledge achieved in poetry,
for it is fresh creation, a new birth of the Word. The Renaissance
poet wrote in his *Apology for Poetry*: "Only the poet, . . . lifted
up with the vigour of his own invention, doth grow in effect into
another nature, in making things either better than Nature bring-
eth forth, or quite anew, forms such as never were in Nature . . .
so as he goeth hand in hand with Nature, not enclosed within the
narrow warrant of her gifts, but freely ranging only within the
zodiac of his own wit."[21] For Hopkins, the poet grows into Christ's
created nature, what Scotus called his *"natura atoma,"* the one
uniting humanity of Jesus (S, 350). His mind is the zodiac which
encompasses all creation and which the poet's mind encompasses
in turn, as his gift to man. "Men of genius are said to create, a
painting, a poem, a tale, a tune," Hopkins reflected, "from themselves, from their own minds. And they themselves, their minds

and all, are creatures of God: if the tree created much more the flower and the fruit" (S, 238).

At the beginning of the first chapter, Hopkins's essay on "The Origin of our Moral Ideas" was quoted in part: "All thought is of course in a sense an effort at unity." He continued: "In art it is essential to recognise and strive to realise on a more or less wide basis this unity in some shape or other. . . . In art we strive to realise not only unity, permanence of law, likeness, but also, with it, difference, variety, contrast: it is rhyme we like, not echo, and not unison but harmony" (J, 83). How then does one bring art in line with morality where "the highest consistency is the highest excellence"? Through a poetry of gnosis. "But why do we desire unity? The first answer would be that the ideal, the one, is our only means of recognising successfully our being to ourselves, it unifies us, while vice destroys the sense of being by dissipating thought" (J, 83). In Clement's words: "To believe in Him, and by Him, is to become a unit, being indissolubly united in Him; and to disbelieve is to be separated, disjoined, divided." The one, the ideal Christ, "is the circle of all powers rolled and united into one unity," for which reason he "is called Alpha and Omega" (*Strom*. 4. 25). The Lord of time summons men, as he summons all his handiwork, to self-being. "Hearken to me, O Jacob and Israel, whom I call: I AM, I am the First and I am the Last. My hand founded the earth, and my right hand measured the heavens; I call them, and they stand forward together" (Isa. 48:12–13; adapted).

12
Inscape and Omega

DANTE, at the climax of the *Divine Comedy,* gazes up in paradise into the center of the multifoliate rose of heaven, the heart of light, and inscapes the humanity of Jesus:

> O luce etterna che sola in te sidi,
> sola t'intendi, e da te intelletta
> e intendente te ami e arridi!
> Quella circulazion che sì concetta
> pareva in te come lume reflesso,
> dalli occhi miei alquanto circunspetta,
> dentro da sè, del suo colore stesso,
> mi parve pinta della nostra effige;
> per che'l mio viso in lei tutto era messo.[1]

The Eternal Light alone understands and smiles upon itself. The second circle, that of the Son, bears the image of a human being within, and there Dante's sight is foredrawn, his desire and will revolving like a turning balanced wheel. Then "in a flash" he inscapes the man in the circle and experiences the instress of *"l' amor che move il sole e l' altre stelle."*

The mythic system that brought the Italian poet to this zenith spiraled vast and myriad below him, circle within circle downward through the winding hill of purgatory and the inversed cone of hell. No author before or since has conceived so intricate and impressive a route for himself to follow and for his readers to retrace stanza by stanza, canto by canto, through landscapes more vividly etched than any earthly terrain. The perfect formal structure of the *Comedia* acts as a frail shadowing forth of the profound organism within. The myth which Hopkins fashioned was of another kind, neither medieval or Scholastic in origin, but a synthesis of pre-Socratic, Pauline, and patristic strains. His myth is also of its place and time, late Victorian in its light and shades, innately British in its deliberate and eccentric secrecy. But its soul is beautiful and expansive once the beholder who was wanting takes the time and energy to greet it mind and heart, "which two when they once meet, / The heart rears wings bold and bolder." Formed in his psyche, born of its ultramontane setting and the emergence of modernism, Hopkins's mythogenetic zone was of necessity a private affair, ensconced in notes, personal letters, and unpublished poetry; but for modern readers freed from prejudice or fear, the bold flight "fans fresh our wits with wonder."

The task remains of further defining and identifying the heart of the mazy structure, the architectonical center of the myth. Etymologically, *inscape* is the "inward and distant mark," "the object on which one fixes the eye," and as a verb, the command to "mark," "look and see." Specifically, St. Paul's statement in Philippians 3:13-14, seems to have provided the texual source or impetus to Hopkins's use of the word for Christic activity: "Forgetting what is behind," the past in memory; "I strain forward to what is before," the future in imagination; "I press on towards the goal," the present concrete gnosis, the faculty of identification; "in Christ Jesus." Inscape then is gnosis, the act of being-one, where "the fulness is the thought" (J, 130). The union of love that follows is "instress," the "saying *yes*" to Being's I AM.

The mythic system, as we saw, begins with a Pythagorean-like search for the underlying principle of unity through the study of geometric patterns in nature; one pattern gradually emerges, the circle—not perfectly shaped, but irregular in its symmetry and beauty of form in action. We watched Hopkins carefully note the organization of the oak tree, return to it again until every detail conformed to its oneness, its "system of radiating spokes," a totality in which "the star knot is the chief thing: it is whorled, worked round, a little and this is what keeps up the illusion of the tree" (J, 144-45). This oneness was the secret:

"There is one notable dead tree in the N. W. corner of the nave, the inscape markedly holding its most simple and beautiful one-ness up from the ground through a graceful swerve below (I think) the spring of branches up to the tops of the timber" (J, 215). Notice how Hopkins almost unconsciously associates *in-scape* with its root *markedly* in this entry. Again: "In watching the sea one should be alive to the oneness which all its motion and tumult receives from its perpetual balance and falling this way and that to its level" (J, 225).

The Alpha of this unity was not in the things themselves, which are ever "falling away" into multiplicity and nothingness. The cosmos coheres in the immanent presence of the One. He is the Being described by "Parmenides the Great," as he is ac-claimed by Clement of Alexandria who then quotes the Greek philosopher's description of "the Word":

Entirely—since He is unborn and indestructible—
Whole, only-begotten, and immoveable, and unoriginated.
(*Strom.* 5. 14)

Being is worded in the universe, for "everything that exists pos-sesses gnosis." Hopkins noted: "All the world is full of inscape and chance left free to act falls into an order as well as purpose" (J, 230). Things think toward man, their target and inscape; he cannot be indifferent to any living thing: "The ashtree growing in the corner of the garden was felled. It was lopped first: I heard the sound and looking out and seeing it maimed there came at that moment a great pang and I wished to die and not to see the inscapes of the world destroyed any more" (J, 230). Man moves among the radii of Being; by his knowing, he creates a center of himself:

The earth and heaven, so little known,
Are measured outwards from my breast.
I am the midst of every zone
And justify the East and West;

The unchanging register of change
My all-accepting fixèd eye,

> While all things else may stir and range
> All else may whirl or dive or fly. (P130)

By 1866, the year this poem was written, the poet had already formulated the outline for his myth. The poem goes on to describe a swallow swerving about the observer as a fixed point, just as later the windhover turns overhead. Man forms "a little world made cunningly," as John Donne observed, or in a contemporary image, a nucleus of centrally charged and positive energy, massing reality within the mind, the focus of stress. The mind's perception of this convergence is inscape. The eye fixates change and chance in a timeless order, while instress fuses existence in thought and thought in existence. Gnosis not only recognizes oneness but creates oneness within itself; man makes his world in losing it and wins his life in sacrifice. "The earth and heaven, so little known" are known and measured from the cleave of Christ's breast, the heart and "fire's center." Each man is an "AfterChrist" who suffers and exalts his universe or, failing to be such, drags his world and himself into further chaos, the abyss of not-being.

The circle image also provided Hopkins with a traditional figure for the triune godhead:

> The Immortals of the eternal ring,
> The Utterer, Utterèd, Uttering. (P145)

Since only God himself is perfect completion, every finite sphere must show its imperfection of being in asymmetrical form. In addition, the circle in things is always in the process of becoming; it changes and holds true for a moment, then moves to rearrangements and fresh assumptions of the basic shape. The human mind, imitating the divine, fixes that shape and then focuses from new perspectives and angles. The ringed figure then is three-dimensional, seen in depth and motion, and the circles are really conical spheres, rounded and spinning. Hopkins notes, for example: "The 'pinion' of the blossom in the comfrey is remarkable for the beauty of the coil and its regular lessening to its centre" (J, 211). In elm trees he finds "beautiful inscape, home-coiling wiry bushes of spray touched with bud to point them" (J, 243). Weeds in wheels and whorled oaks spell out a similar action.

Another important illustration is found in the journal entry, dated April 29, 1871, which describes a whirlwind, with an accompanying drawing: "Just caught sight of a little whirlwind which ran very fast careering across our pond. It was made by conspiring catspaws seeming to be caught in, in a whorl, to the centre. There were of course two motions, the travelling and the rotation. The circle was regular and the drawing here bad. Each tail of catspaw seemed to fling itself alive into its place in turn, so that something like the scale ABCD was very rapidly repeated all round the ring—not a complete wall at once" (J, 208). One of the difficult words to fit into the poet's cylindrical system is "scale," which seems to imply a vertically static and hierarchical order. In the drawing, the scales are seen from above, converging inward at various regular points at the top, each flinging "itself alive into its place in turn." Exactly the same language is used to describe pitch and scale of being in the spiritual writings: "There is a scale or range of pitch which is also infinite and terminates upwards in the directness or uprightness of the 'stem' of the godhead and the procession of the divine persons" (S, 148). The stem of being in God is a dynamic axis and gyre of flowing, upturning stress. Lifted up, it draws all things to itself. The whirlwind is its counterpart in opposing miniature, a moving spiral which, active with freedom and restraint, turns inward on its axis to its own pivotal point. Seen from above, the whorl is round and its center has depth; it conforms to the circle figure we have studied in the other journal observations. Viewed from the side, it is a horn which the poet described as "a projection, a climax, a badge of strength, power or vigour, a tapering body, a spiral, a wavy object, a bow, a vessel to hold withal or to drink from . . . something sprouting up, something to thrust or push with" (J, 4). In one form or another the image of the horn reappears often in Hopkins's journals and poetry.

The action pictured here is the matrix of the poet's mythopoeic vision. "God gave things a forward and perpetual motion"; but Satan, his counterfeit image and Antichrist, projects a rival spiral or reverse movement which dissipates and draws toward non-being instead of mounting toward its target of truth: "A coil or spiral is then a type of the Devil, who is called the old (or original) serpent, and this I suppose because of its 'swale' or subtle and imperceptible drawing in towards its head or centre, and it is a type of death, of motion lessening and at last ceasing" (S, 198-99). Creatures are projectiles whirling out of themselves in "sakes" of being to and through man who turns this wheeling activity back to its source or, in evil perversion, makes himself a false drawing center. Sin is inscape gone awry, a self-centered enthronement of strange gods in one's own God-likeness. Self-defeating, it wears, wastes, and breaks down to ultimate immobility all the spiritual aspiration of man. Significantly, the journal entry on the whirlwind ends with the reflection: "I saw that there was something eery, Circe-like and quick about it" (J, 208). Sucking inward and swirling out, the spool of air simulates the up and forward movement of creation's return to Alpha and Omega. This dust devil is also an antitype of the devil's deceptive twisting of nature's dynamic, centripetal urge toward Christ, the cosmic centrifuge. For Hopkins, inaction and deadly silence issue from this demonic presence, just as motion and music spring from the Word of life. One lessens and dies, while the other "rings right out."

Instress then involves centrifugal motion from, and inscape centripetal motion toward, a center, a stem of force shooting outward or converging inward. In equilibrium, they are both "principle" (*arche* as origin and core) and "pressure" (energy and "the mark impressed": *OED*). Thus the poet pictures himself in the *Deutschland*:

> I steady as a water in a well, to a poise, to a pane,
> But roped with, always, all the way down from the tall
> Fells or flanks of the voel, a vein
> Of the gospel proffer, a pressure, a principle, Christ's gift.
>
> (P28, 4)

From the cone-shaped hill of Calvary rills of water and blood run down to the round well of the disciple's heart through the pierced heart of Jesus. Inscape always involves opening, a source from which stress flows and an entrance through which it eddies. The pomegranate has its cleaves and the olive its pores of ooze. This "proffer," the act or movement from the voluted source, is summed up in two elements that were favorites of Hopkins as they were of the pre-Socratics: fire and water. These traditional Hellenic and Christian symbols the poet used *in actu*, as generating light and force and as fountain of energy:

> Jesu, a springing well thou art,
> Daylight to head and treat to heart. (P167)

> Thee, God, I come from, to thee go,
> All dáy long I like fountain flow
> From thy hand out, swayed about
> Mote-like in thy mighty glow. (P155)

He sometimes fuses the two, as John Chrysostom does in calling Christ "a fountain of fire" (*In John.* 14), to create a startling inscape like that of the concluding coda of "Harry Ploughman": "With-a-fountain's shining-shot furls." With one stroke, he shows the wet, gleaming soil gyrating outward from under the racing plowshare. The line ingeniously frames a reference to earth in terms of water and fire, each caught in a flash of flowing identification produced by man's "hand to the plow."

Hopkins's dialogue "On the Origin of Beauty," written at Oxford and dated May 12, 1865, offers an invaluable clue to the development and definitive meaning of his mythopoesis. While discussing the nature of beauty, the speakers quickly agree that it is not absolute symmetry: "Complex beauty . . . is a mixture of regularity and irregularity" (J, 90). An inner law, or what the poet called "inlaw," is at work in nature and must be explored: "Then the beauty of the oak and the chestnut-fan and the sky is a mixture of likeness and difference or agreement and disagreement or consistency and variety or symmetry and change" (J, 90). Such an agreement of opposites is found in the two sides of a chestnut fan and the irregular radiation of the leaves. Then again the leaves of the fan differ from one another, although "they differ by a law, diminishing as they do towards the stalk," and the result is "more beautiful" by this stroke of symmetry. The conclusion is then drawn: "Although from their diminishing they do not form part of that most regular of figures the circle, yet in their diminishing they shape out another figure, do they not? partly regular, though containing variety; I mean that of a Greek Omega" (J, 92).

The Greek capital letter Omega exactly defines the figure we have been studying up to this point. It is a circular, rounded burl or ball shape, yet opens outward at its end. Like the pomegranate it is not a perfect sphere, but unlike the fruit its cleave is part of its form. Viewed in depth, Omega is the center of the vortex, the goal of all contraction, the coinciding point where the cycle spins to a close. Things themselves project Omega in their material form; their very shape impels the mind to seize the immanent, awaited end- and be-all of creation, the Lord who comes. As the monogram sign of Christ, Omega offered rich possibilities for Hopkins both in unifying his myth with tradition and in advancing his own love of innovation. The conclusion of the Apocalypse, itself the last book of the scriptural canon, rings with the claim of Christ: "I am the Alpha and the Omega, the first and the last, the beginning and the end!" (Apoc. 22:13). Revelation thus closes with the Word who called creation into being in the beginning; therefore, "the Word is called Alpha and Omega, of whom alone the end becomes the beginning, and ends again at the original beginning without break" (*Strom.* 4. 25). Here the poet's mythic quest terminates; for in Christ-Omega, "one term and part / Beyond" in "the arc where beauty shines" and the other one "within the looker's eye" fold in the center of the heart, there "to turn the compass on the all-starr'd sky" (P102, iii). The parabola and focal point of inscape, inclosed in the conic universe and heart, form Omega. "There must be one end (and only one) to which all the others are subordinate. The knowledge of it will give life an aim, σκόπον" (M2). That cosmic end is Omega.

For the student of Hopkins's myth, the most striking disclosure of Omega is that it unlocks—for it is also shaped like a keyhole—the Pauline mystery or secret of Christ. Its "diminishing" corresponds to the action of *kenosis*, the emptying and channeling downward of the Word's becoming man. Its curved globe, on the other hand, is the *pleroma*, the fullness of godhead dwelling bodily in Jesus as indicated by the suggested circle. In "The Windhover," for example, the curves of the bird's flight, in its circling climb of pursuit, culminate in the diapason of "Brute beauty and valour and act, oh, air, pride, plume," which are said to suddenly "Buckle!" At the instant the kestrel prepares to swoop, it turns on its side, draws in its wings, and assumes an Omega shape. In addition, "buckle" means "to bend into a bow under stress." Under longitudinal pressure a bar or column whose ends are fixed will bulge into an Omega figure.[2] Here the stress of Christ-being acts on the entire line from "Brute" to "here" with increasing tension, sounded in the verse by the accelerated crowding at the approach of the exclamatory, climactic verb. From the bottom to the top of the vertical line—between the animal "brute" and the angelic "plume"—the ejaculatory "oh" marks the exact midpoint where the tension gives way and buckling begins. An Omega shape only results if both ends are fastened; here both the falcon and the heart are lodged in Christ the creator-redeemer. To visualize the action, the poet has prepared a series of foreshadowing images in the octave: "rolling level," "rung upon the rein," "off forth on swing," and an explicit use of the Omega, "a bow-bend." Nature's Omegas are only figures of the actual "bow-bend" effected in man's heart through the atoning action of the great sacrifice. Like an instressed steel rod the lines of force meet, counterpoise, and give way in *kenosis*—and the *pleroma* bursts into being as Omega: the swooping kestrel; the plow held curved and tapering, plunged into the earth; and the rounded embers breaking open into flame. The Omega-flame that "breaks from thee then" is "a billion / Times told lovelier," the poet confides to his own ardent heart hidden in Christ, than the light of the Helios-king worded in the ecstatic falcon.

Instress may be further defined then as the literal exterior force (the "stress" of "stars and storms") which, delivered through the senses and converging on the mind, results in inscape, the shaping of fresh incarnation in the new man. As long as strain and steady pressure are exerted evenly along the line, a circular contour takes shape until it culminates in a final Omega-form; its end is equilibrium, wedding of opposite tensions and union of strengths. Psychologically, instress, "kept on the strain," not only initiates the action but is present finally, in the resultant forging of being and thought, as stasis, "the saying-*yes*" to Christ's configuration of the pliable heart.

In turn fullness, compressed, finds real and mental release in Omega, like the blowpipe flame of "To R. B." or the jetting waters in Hopkins's notes and drawings (see J, 176, 177, and Appendix i, nos. 12, 28, 31, 33). In pillowy clouds, falling stars, mountain ranges, and organ music, burliness forces out everything else and loads the eye and ear with inscape. The heart "is out with it": the breaking of the circle is Omega. Inscape will literally "explode" for man in touch with Being in nature and art.

Or to alter the analogy: inscape itself is both interior aim and objective mark. The bow, in archery, is drawn back with slow, graceful purpose and with the mark in the distance kept steadily in sight. The important motion is *back*, a word stressed, as we have seen, by Hopkins. The archer at the moment of release surrenders to the forward creep of the arrow, and almost without conscious intent, most taut and yet most relaxed, shoots. The bow, arched back attains its most perfect Omega-shape at the instant when the aim is set to sever its mark, when both are dynamically fused in the mind's eye of the bowman. The poet's most pertinent verse on this point is a fragment that puns on a man's name, but reveals some technical knowledge of the sport:

> Yet Arthur is a Bowman: his three-heeled timber'll hit
> The bald and bóld blínking gold when áll's dóne
> Right rooting in the bare butt's wincing navel in the sight
>   of the sun.[3]   (P143)

In play or in earnest man's actions "point to one end, which is always present." For, once it is hit, the goal will center all one's undertakings: it is the *sake* for which one acts and lives.

Another word linked to inscape is "hurl," which the poet seems to have taken from the game of hurling. Curiously enough, in the traditional form of play, as noted in the *Enclyclopaedia Britannica* (1960), "boughs of stripped wood bent to the form of a bow were used as goal posts." Note also that one of Hopkins's synonyms for "horn" is "a bow," that he connects "horn" with "curving" and "shooting up," and conjectures that "*grin* may mean to curve up the ends of the mouth like horns" (J, 4). The journal entry on "horn"—which also links it to "head" and "crown"—graphically shows us the poet in search of the shape of his myth.

More than a coincidence, perhaps, is Dante's use of the bow figure in canto 26 of the *Paradiso*. After confessing that "*Alfa ed O*" is the lesson love taught him to read, the poet is admonished by St. John, "*dicer convienti / chi drizzò l'arco tuo a tal berzaglio*" (26. 23-24), to tell who directed his bow to such a target. Dante replies that the secret, "*l'arcano*"—a pun on "*l'arco*"—was learned from the Johannine declaration that opens and closes the Apocalypse, "I am the Alpha and the Omega" (1:8; 22:13). The secret, the poet implies, was in the bow itself which drew him to Omega. In canto 29 of the *Paradiso*, Dante compares the action of the Trinity in creating to a triple-arrow shot from a three-string crossbow. In Christian art the bow and arrow, in the shape of miniscular omega, also symbolize the Trinity—the arrow being the incarnate Word.

The bow was likewise associated, as Hopkins the stargazer knew, with Sagittarius ("the Archer"), the southern constellation where lie the Omega nebula and the center of our spiral galaxy, the Milky Way. As a cosmic sign, Sagittarius, the centaur, embodies the whole man (animal-human-divine) and the arc of tension that links heaven and earth.[4] We have previously observed how the Victorian poet also identified the constellation Orion the hunter with Christ (P28, 21; P177; above, p. 174).

Hopkins's use of the bow figure aptly describes God's own movement "through the cycle of nature in a straight line towards the accomplishment of his end" (Plato's *Laws* 4. 715e). The cosmos, however, is not permanently fossilized but is in process of omnifariously rallying toward that end which transcends and yet materially draws on all creation. Hopkins marveled at the northern lights, "the crown of horny rays," the arched and concentrical "pulses of light." He reflected: "This busy working of nature wholly independent of the earth and seeming to go on in a strain of time not reckoned by our reckoning of days and years but simpler and as if correcting the preoccupation of the world by being preoccupied with and appealing to and dated to the day of judgment was like a new witness to God" (J, 200). While he may have remained chary of Darwin's theories on the struggle for existence and the origin of man, Hopkins's own outlook definitely supposes the evolutionary drift of the universe toward a final day of glory.[5] Opening to this strain in stars and auroras, the poet descried the inner beam or pulse of light that led on to the return of Jesus. "For as the lightning when it lightens flashes from one end of the sky to the other, so will the Son of Man be in his day" (Luke 17:24). "Thou art lightning and love, I found it," he confessed in the *Deutschland*.

Hopkins's fascination with coiled and forked lightning coincides with his Omega myth and the scriptural cast of his thinking. "Then shafts of lightning shall go directly from the clouds, as from a bow well bent, they shall be shot out, and shall fly to the mark" (Wisd. 5:22). Significantly, the same chapter of the Book of Wisdom joins the two inscapes of the arrow and the flight of a bird in a pair of similes for those who lack gnosis, knowledge of God, and the swift passing of their life:

> As when a bird flies through the air, of the passage of
> which no mark can be found, but only the sound of the
> wings beating the light air and parting it by the force of
> her flight; she moved her wings, and has flown through,
> and there is no mark found afterwards of her way; or
> as when an arrow is shot at a mark, the divided air presently
> comes together again, so that its passage is not known:
> so we also being born, forthwith ceased to be, and have
> been able to show no mark of virtue: but are consumed
> in our wickedness. Such things as these the sinners said
> in hell. . . . But the just shall live forevermore, and their
> reward is with the Lord, and the care of them with the
> most High. (5:11-14, 16)

In the midst of change the just man alone hits the mark of permanence traced in the "steady air" of a windhover's flight and buckled in the heart's acknowledgment of the Son who suffered and rose again: "I know that my Redeemer lives." Omega not only underlies reality, it is man's shield of defense against "outrageous fortune." "Therefore shall they receive a kingdom of glory and a crown of beauty at the hand of the Lord," the passage quoted above concludes, "for with his right hand he will cover them, and with his holy arm he will defend them" (Wisd. 5:17). The Lord draws home mankind to the curve of his embrace.

Man's submission to God is Omega. As John Ford employed the image in *The Witch of Edmonton*: "I am . . . like a bow—buckled and bent together" (2. 1), so Hopkins with his own metaphor of "doubling-over" describes his experience at Roehampton: "Thou knowest . . ."

> The swoon of a heart that the sweep and the
>   hurl of thee trod
>   Hard down with a horror of height:
> And the midriff astrain with leaning of, laced with
>   fire of stress.   (P28, 2)

Felix Randal, bent and "diminishing" in the exercise of his duty, labors over the "bright and battering sandal" that is itself Omega. Not only bowed in worship but intent on all his tasks, man is himself curve, his arms focused in work or play, his body channeled to action in the form of human Omega: "He of all," the poet claims for Christ, "can reeve a rope best." When he sees "somewhere some man do all that man can do," the Lord embraces and encircles him in his arms and cries: " 'O Christ-done deed! So God-made-flesh does too: / Were I come o'er again . . . it should be this' " (P63).

Man is identified with Jesus in Omega of "doing-be." "To lift up the hands in prayer gives God glory, but a man with a dung-fork in his hand, a woman with a sloppail give him glory too" (S, 241). Locked to the plow, Harry Ploughman's "hard as hurdle arms" fuse in one "sinew-service" and, like the blacksmith "at the random grim forge," define the contour of life's destination.

Even a sailor's "sea-corpse cold" retains the sign in his "lovely manly mould": "Look, foot to forelock, how all things suit! he / Is strung by duty, is strained to beauty" (P41)—like a bow not yet grown slack in spiritual death nor yet undone by the devil. Virtuous "strain" stretches back, tightens, and holds the arc of a lifetime of effort and determination; "O his nimble finger, his gnarled grip," his are the hands of a marksman.

Traditionally Omega, the last letter of the hornbook alphabet or Christ-cross-row, expresses finality, the end, purpose, and meaning: *telos*, of human acts and the cosmos. In Christian gnosis it is the perfection and completion the faithful steward of Jesus aims for and achieves through piety and learning. Hopkins wrote: "The multiplicity of ends converges in one end. Life is the sum of all actions; happiness of all ends" (G1). Christ's Spirit is above all the Comforter. Jesus as he has been historically shown to man is Omega, the "homecoiling" center of the Second Coming, the pole and final mark of creation in time. In preparation, his Spirit is at work in the world and in man, transmuting nature. All things are to be recapitulated in Christ, St. Paul—and Irenaeus after him—has stated; and in the last aeon or age, according to Origen and St. Gregory of Nyssa, the universe will attain its eternal transfiguration in subjection "under his feet." But the beginning is also present in the end, for the last has been made first. So in early Christian burial inscriptions the order of the two letters, Alpha and Omega, is frequently reversed to show the primacy and presence of Christ the Telos "in the beginning." For Clement of Alexandria and Tertullian, as previously quoted here (pp. 262–63 and 103–04), the last point joins the first to form the cosmic whole, "the finding and sake / And cipher of . . . Christ" (P28, 22).

Omega itself is shaped like a womb, pregnant with being, opening to birth. The figure is a recurrent one in Hopkins's poetry. For example, the dual action of the *Deutschland*, the nun's confession and the poet's proclamation of the origin of stress, are both seen as parturitions. "Warm-laid grave of a womb-life grey" knits beginning and end of salvation history. Jesus from the first is destined for the tomb; risen, he delivers mankind from "the womb-of-all, home-of-all, hearse-of-all night" (P61). The climactic lines: "Only the heart, being hard at bay, / Is out with it!" recalls the patristic idea of Christ's breast-womb, opened by the lance, giving birth to the Church, sprung like a second Eve from the side of the new Adam. The nun's inscape is "heart-throe, birth of a brain, / Word, that heard and kept thee and uttered thee outright." Her embracing of the martyr-master brings about another "storm-birth" of Jesus in space and time:

> Now burn, new born to the world,
> Double-naturèd name,
> The heaven-flung, heart-fleshed, maiden-furled
> Miracle-in-Mary-of-flame,
> Mid-numberèd he in three of the thunder-throne!
>
> (P28, 34)

Mary, the mother of Jesus, is the most perfect image of Omega, since by the Holy Spirit she conceived and bore him in her womb. Hopkins's devotion to the Immaculate Conception, her own initial identity from the womb with her Son, fits even more closely into the final emerging form of his myth. In Omega he found "the right metaphor of wholeness" for his theology and verse.[6]

The poet, as we saw in his sonnet "To R. B." (P76), depicted creative inspiration and composition as conception, gestation, and birth. The sonnet identifies the womb with "the mind a mother of immortal song." The same reference is made in "heart-throe, birth of a brain," in which the head-heart acts as one—the mind feels being and the heart harbors "the thoughts of the mind" (S, 103)—when man draws "Our King back" within himself. Omega is often in tradition symbolic of man as rational being. The eternal Reason or Logos is held in little within man's tiny span of brain. The Omega shape indicates the head, neck, and partial shoulders of man, his bust as the seat of cerebral activity which ranges from the perception of the five senses to judgment and abstract thought. In Greek and Russian iconography the image of Christ is strictly modeled on the Omega, sign of his full humanity united with the divine life. In some icons, in fact, within the halo with its usual inscription O ΩN ("Being"), the letter itself forms an explicit frame and outline for the holy face, the Icon of

God. Again, Omega as the womb of the mind is also associated with Jesus *in sinu Patris*, the bosom of the Father. Christ is thus frequently painted standing or seated within the mandorla of God's encircling embryo, "begotten, not made, of one substance with the Father," as the Creed declares. The *pleroma* is itself a womb of possible being in the divine mind. The creature shares that being by nature and by grace: "Christ as a solid in his member as a hollow or shell, both things being the image of God" (S, 195). Within the corporeal vessel (the *vas mirabile*) new life takes form, both the one image of Logos in man.

Omega: fullness at one pole, emptiness at the other; the round sea of Being flowing through the river of change: "The girth of it and the wharf of it and the wall" (P28, 32). Badge of the pilgrim in the shape of the scallop shell—the shell which, tradition says, once was held high in the Baptist's hand when he poured the water of the Jordan on the head of the God-Man: "The heavens were opened . . . and a voice from the heavens said, 'This is my beloved Son, in whom I am well pleased' " (Matt. 3:16–17).[7] Sign of eternity linked to the *extensio* of time; the One unfolded to the many; the Omega of man opened to the Omega of God.

> I am soft sift
> In an hourglass—at the wall
> Fast, but mined with a motion, a drift,
> And it crowds and it combs to the fall.   (P28, 4)

Omega: at one end the curve of godhead and at the other the extended right angles of man. Hermetically it becomes the secret talisman that holds the key to understanding the incomprehensible and seemingly irreconcilable paradox of God-made-man and man-made-God. Through it the *imago ignota* is made known. Inscape, "the *particularized, or 'individually distinctive' image of perfection*,"[8] is Omega, the *sake* or "being abroad" of God.

Dante, at the moment of the beatific vision, strains like a geometer to reconcile the human form with the divine essence until unexpectedly his mind is opened and he sees:

> Qual è 'l geomètra che tutto s'affige
> per misurar lo cerchio, e non ritrova,

pensando, quel principio ond'elli indige,
tal era io a quella vista nova:
veder volea come si convenne
l' imago al cerchio e come vi s'indova;
ma non eran da ciò le proprie penne:
se non che la mia mente fu percossa
da un fulgore in che sua voglia venne.[9]

Omega squares the circle; it is the principle that solves the impossible presence of divine and human natures in one person, a mystery known only to the Father who embodies it in the Son who reveals it to those he elects. Omega is the secret name, the pledge and omen inscribed on the stone, known only to the one who receives it (Apoc. 2:17). Watchword and countersign, it is Christ's inscape, the mark of him who is the aim of all.

Hopkins, who showed a familiarity with Oriental religions and shared in the new interest at Oxford in philology and comparative mythology, privately may have associated Greek Omega with the sacred syllable *Om*, uttered at the opening of each verse of the Vedas and used by Hindu priests in the offering of their sacrifices. The mystic syllable sounds the beginning, middle, and end of the universe, its essence and totality. *Om* is the center of man's contact with Brahman, the Self of all selves, as the *Mundaka Upanishads* declares: "Om is the bow, the Self is the arrow, Brahman is called its aim" (2.2.4).[11] By concentration, man may "hit the mark, as the arrow the target," and become one with Brahman. By sounding *Om* man can attain to the triune God, "the Utterer, Utterèd, Uttering" (P145), since the syllable expresses the cycle of waking-dream-sleep of cosmic life. The holy mantra is also described as the breath in the heart, the sun and shape of light, the lightning that illuminates the whole body, and the knowledge of the Highest Self. Originally *Om* seems to have meant *It* or *Yes*. "I did say yes / O at lightning and lashed rod," Hopkins writes in the *Deutschland*. He may also have linked *Om* with *home*: "Christ home" (P32), "come home" (P46), "bound home" (P48), "Fold home" (P60), "home-of-all" (P61).

Transliterated into English, Omega becomes long *O*, (actually the more ancient form of the Greek letter). In this shape it is the circle pattern with which we began. Omega is revealed as the Christic character of oaks, aureoles, moon, and "roundy wells"; it is the Word's homomorph throughout creation. Aside from its outward configuration, however, "O" is also the exclamation of wonder, appeal, lament, etc., which Hopkins uses in his poetry for a gamut of emotional responses. He seems to have distinguished it from "oh!" although Bridges's transcriptions of the poems present difficulties in establishing the poet's original intention in every particular case.[10] From the present text, however, we can assert his all-pervading purpose: "O" is the sign Omega, the secret Christogram of gnosis, in the tongue shape (in Greek: *scapos*) of man's confession of faith. The *Ah*'s and *O*'s with which Hopkins's poetry is so lavishly studded sound the full scope and meaning of his myth: Alpha and Omega—"But ah, but O thou terrible," Christ the creator and judge.

Hopkins's enigmatic note in speaking of the Gnostic heresies, that "the place of Sige, silence[,] should be remarked" (S, 200), refers, as we have seen, to the female aeon mentioned by Irenaeus in his *Adversus Haereses*. Her supposed revelations to the heretical Gnostic Marcus include an explanation of Omega "which sounds out the glory of Him who produced" the universe, the Word to whom "the glory of that sound is transmitted upwards." Iranaeus writes: "She asserts, moreover, that 'the sound of this uttering of praise, having been wafted to the earth, has become the Framer and the Parent of those things which are on the earth' " (*Adv. Haer.* 1. 14. 7). For proof, Marcus instances the cry of newly born infants, issuing from the womb:

> For this reason, too, David said: "Out of the mouth of babes and sucklings Thou hast perfected praise"; and again; "The heavens declare the glory of God." Hence also it comes to pass, that when the soul is involved in difficulties and distresses, for its own relief it calls out, "Oh" (Ω), in honour of the letter in question, so that its cognate soul above may recognize its distress, and send down to it relief. (*Adv. Haer.* 1. 14. 8)

Marcus goes on to identify Jesus, the Savior, with "the dove who is Alpha and Omega," by means of a numerological deduction. For the Victorian poet—despite Sige's questionable authority—these conjectures may have suited his mythopoeic purposes and provided material for his poems. He was, at any rate, ahead of his time in advancing from alphabet to sound, from a visual to oral-aural medium, for the communication of his meaning.

In his poetry, the interjection O declares the poet's inscape of Christ. In "The Windhover," for example, Hopkins calls on his heart-in-Christ: "O my chevalier," and cries: "Brute beauty and valour and act, oh! air, pride, plume . . . ," placing the "oh," as we have seen, precisely midway between the two sets of nouns, and thus preparing, at the critical point of maximum stress, for the Omega act of "buckling" which follows. The present reading in the fourth edition of the *Poems* gives "Oh, morning" in "God's Grandeur" (P31), which originally appeared as "O morning" in the copy of the poem sent to his mother shortly after its composition (L3, 145). Here Christ is the risen dayspring, the shining orb of sunlight "at the brown brink eastward." The *Deutschland's* first of many *overed* confessions is "O Christ, O God," and the nun's central cry: "O Christ, Christ, come quickly," inscapes the whole poem. The ode concludes with the wish: "Our King back, Oh, upon English souls!" where the Omega is positioned in the exact middle of the line, the center of England's return *back* to the true faith. Earlier the poet gropes for the right expression of the mystery: "Oh, / We lash with the best or worst / Word last!" The last letter of the Greek alphabet is "the best" sounding of the secret of the pierced side of Christ: Omega "Is out with it! Oh" (P28, 8). With the first letter, Alpha, voiced in the interjection "Ah!" each man's "heart right" gives utterance to the deepest chords of being. Thus, in "The Windhover," "O my chevalier" is rounded out with "ah my dear" to designate the heart's perfected praise.

Other pertinent examples can only be listed here: "O look" is the call to inscape in "The Starlight Night" (P32); "O maid's child" joins both Jesus and Mary in "Spring" (P33). Often "O" marks man's response as truth hits home: "O where it fails"

(P34); "O half hurls earth" (P38); "O Hero
on that path . . . O brace sterner that strail
dead then?" (P53); "O no there's none . . . O
(P59); "O marvellous! . . . O live air" (P6(
deed!" (P63); "O which one?" (P64); "O a
"O thou lord of life" (P74); and finally, the po

> O then if in my lagging lines you miss
>
> The roll, the rise, the carol, the creation,
> My winter world, that scarcely breathes that bliss
> Now, yields you, with some sighs, our explanation.

In each of these occurrences a case could be made for a hidden
dimension of meaning, or a clarification, only brought out by interpreting "O" as Omega. Sometimes the poet underlines his intention, as in the first lines of the *Eurydice*:

> The Eurydice—it concerned thee, O Lord:
> Three hundred souls, O alas! on board.

Here the interjection is first offered in worship, then made as a
cry of distress. In "Spelt from Sibyl's Leaves," the pivotal call:
"Our tale, O óur oracle!" directs attention to gnosis of Christ as
the rune to be read and properly spelt out. He is the hornbook
in which metaphysics and teleology are simply and exactly set
forth in epitome: read him rightly and live. Thus, in "To what
serves Mortal Beauty?" the enigmatic compound, "the O-seal-
that-so feature" from which "self flashes off," is explained by the
figure Omega as the shape of the head, "recapitulated" or "head-
ed again" in "the human form divine," the Word-made-flesh:

> . . . For Christ plays in ten thousand places,
> Lovely in limbs, and lovely in eyes not his
> To the Father through the features of men's faces.   (P57)

The poet's choice of the "Great O" antiphons for the subject
of his Christmas meditations (S, 257) indicates his awareness of
the tradition. These seven prayers, read at vespers during the
final week of Advent, are an excellent example of an imaginative

ical and poetic adaptation of the biblical heritage. The first, "O Wisdom," antiphon has been previously quoted in chapter 4 (p. 78); the second addresses Christ: "O Adonai, and Ruler of the House of Israel, You appeared to Moses in the fire of the burning bush, and on Mount Sinai gave him Your Law: Come, and with an outstretched arm redeem us!"[12] The third exclaims: "O Root of Jesse, You are an emblem of mankind," and the fourth: "O Key of David, . . . You open and no man closes, You close and no man opens." Hopkins must have particularly cherished the next: "O Dayspring, Radiance of Eternal Light and Sun of Justice, come and enlighten those who sit in darkness and in the shadow of death." Christ, "O Rising Dawn," appears in the poet's three best known works: "The Windhover," "God's Grandeur," and *The Wreck of the Deutschland*. Finally, the remaining "Great O" antiphons call on the Messiah to come, "O King of the Gentiles and the Desired of all" and "O Emmanuel, our King and Lawgiver, the Expected of nations and their Savior: . . . O Lord our God!" The seven antiphons show the roots and previous blossomings of Hopkins's mythic hymn to Christ Omega, the "Great O" (the literal meaning of *O-mega*), whose cosmic role is sounded in each of these magnificent prayers. No later writer, however, has matched the Jesuit poet in imaginative and exhaustive manipulation and application of this particular Christian inheritance. Even Rimbaud in "Voyelles" seems less avant-garde.

Hopkins found other insignia of Jesus in creation: the cross, star, fish, and chi-rho; but inscape was perception of Alpha-Omega, summed up in the circular print and script forms of the final letter. More specifically, inscape meant capital Omega, the Word's ideograph etched in the cosmos and the features of man, his sign as creator-redeemer. Evidence of its presence may be found in the journals, in the inscape of the bluebell, for example, of which Hopkins wrote: "I know the beauty of our Lord by it." The accompanying sketch shows an Omega-shaped flower, round, diminishing, and turning outward (J, 199). The spraying of fir and beech trees (J, 171), hands playing a musical instrument (J, 167), the sea "between the two cheeks" of a field (J, 251) are each illustrated with the discernible curve of Omega (see also J, Appendix i, figs. 1, 15, 16, 20; plates 10, 12, 24, 29, 31, and passim). The lovely "skeleton inscape of a spray-end of ash" with its "suggested globe" (J, 200), which has become famous as the dustjacket drawing for the third and fourth editions of the *Poems*, contains the globe and opening of capital Omega, as well as the distinct shape of the lowercase letter. Miniscular omega is also traceable in the drawing of ash trees (J, 182), heron (J, 225), and tiles (J, 255). The intent of the artist's eye and heart was always to catch in flight and to hold fast the "coinciding-point" of the world sweeping to its ever-present goal. Because he is beginning and end—Prudentius's "*fons et clausula*"—Jesus is now the existent-concrete, the opening wound of Being, "real inscape here seen descending and vanishing" (J, 175), then mounted and returned and made firm forever. Omega is not just a "still point," but the charge and circuitry of the universe, a center that stimulates and attracts the best of human energy. To borrow Pascal's definition, it is a point moving everywhere at an infinite speed, one and whole in every place. Hopkins's drawings—especially of clouds, trees, and water—catch Omega in "meaning motion."

With regard to the poetry, the sonnet form itself is a structure of unsymmetrical unity with its rounded octave and its diminished, concluding sestet. "Single sonnet-like inscape" in ash tree or verse is founded on a principle of nature that asserts irregularity in symmetry and directs limitation and finality to the perfection of a self-fulfilling circle. Sonnets too "shape out another figure, . . . partly regular, though containing variety; . . . that of a Greek Omega." In the poems themselves that figure is omnipresent. The "bent world," "warm breast" and "bright wings" of "God's Grandeur" are all suggestive of Omega. It may be also traced in the farmer's shining cragiron plowshare and the stacked crops of the harvest, when "the stocks rise / Around" and the heaped corn and wheat spell the Lord; for he who sows and he who reaps is the same creator-judge. Omega inscapes the billowy "silk-sack clouds" and shows how "the azurous hung hills are his world-wielding shoulder" raised and arched with the strain of moving the massive globe (P38). There the *Primum Mobile* is revealed through his eschatological mark. It becomes the "beetling baldbright" thunderhead that wrecks the Eurydice and is "a hood / All over" for the "bevy of eggs" that also shape the end in their beginning (P34). "Wherever an elm arches" or "the glassy peartree leaves and blooms," Christ-Omega is known by his fruit as "Trees by their yield / Are known" (P127); he touches heaven and thrusts downward to root deep in the earth. Water too utters the truth of its being in him, as the "darksome burn" of Inversnaid, for example, demonstrates in its race home to the lake:

> A windpuff-bonnet of fáwn-fróth
> Turns and twindles over the broth
> Of a pool so pitchblack, féll-frówning,
> It rounds and rounds Despair to drowning.   (P56)

In foam or in "cloud-puffball," the bright wind of the Spirit fills material creation with new epiphanies of Omega: "Breathe, arch and original Breath." Even the *Deutschland*'s demand to inscape the storm at sea,

> Strike you the sight of it? look at it loom there,
>   Thing that she,   (P28, 28)

defines the nature of the act in the verbs "strike . . . the sight" and "look at," and spells out in acrostic lettering the mark by which Christ cures "the extremity" of man's fate by transforming his end: "loOM therE, ThinG thAt." By a kind of telestich within these key lines, Hopkins indicates what "Thing" suddenly emerges into view with "despatch" and "doom." Omega and *Om, It* is the Self of all selves.

The heart, which plays as we have seen a central part in Hopkins's poetry, is representative of Omega. The Sacred Heart of Jesus, pierced by a stroke that "hearts are flushed by," opens to reclaim its own. Grace spurs on the mannerly hearts of the young to the goal; the winged heart dives to its nest. "*Home* at heart," man meets, and rests in, beauty and in "God's better beauty, grace" (P62). "A heart's-clarion," Being draws home to Being.

Omega is also the "colossal smile" of the great stormfowl which acts as the climatic inscape of "Henry Purcell" (P45) and the "smile" of joy that breaks spontaneously and "unforseen times" at the conclusion of sonnet 69. Just as Dante pictured the Eternal Light "smiling" upon itself (canto 33, l. 126: see above, p. 270), Hopkins views the smile as the joyous hornlike "grin" (J, 4) of Omega which "lights a lovely mile"—another inscape of the light held between the curving dip of two mountain slopes. We have seen how the poet prepares for the inscape of "Buckle!" by the previous bows and sweeps of the octet; so in "Henry Purcell" the "colossal smile" is foreshadowed by the "quaint moonmarks" of the bird's crescented plumage.

Hopkins's many observations of arches and arcs are an additional aspect of his Omega myth. Hence "so arch-especial a spirit as heaves in Henry Purcell" inspires the poet to praise him. In like fashion he exclaims at the critical point of defining, in the *Deutschland*, what the nun's cry meant by the resounding "O" that rang out over the storm:

> The majesty! what did she mean?
> Breathe, arch and original breath. (P28, 25)

The Spirit of the Word, breathed into man in the creation of Adam and again by the risen Christ when he breathed upon the apostles and said: " 'Receive the Holy Spirit' " (John 20:22), is invoked as the *arche*, the creative source and end of inspiration: "the searcher of hearts, our kind and, I might say, arch and gracious-minded master and king" (S, 229). A celebrated form of the arc, the rainbow, sign of God's covenant with man, is employed as an inscape of the resurrection of the body in "The Caged Skylark" (P39). The birdcage itself, the unifying image of the poem, suggests Omega. The "arch-inscape" (J, 245) of "Tom's Garland" (P70) is the gold and iron garlands, not a full circlet but an open-end wreath, that are "the visible badge of the place" the workers fill (L1, 273). Even the "manmarks" of footprints leave the human countersign for a moment in the "dough, crust, dust" (P72; see also 31 and 70). As a poetic summary, like the "enormous hat or skull cap" of "the vault of heaven" seen in miniature and made trivial, the "smooth spoons," which reflect the poet's *persona* for the last time in his verse, mirror "life's masque" (P75) in their shallow oval-shaped surfaces.

In the shape of a bell, Omega merits our final attention. The tall
nun on the foundering Deutschland summons the lost passengers to Christ, the Good Shepherd. His finger touches her, as it
did the poet in stanza 1, and she rings with his risen life:

> . . . lovely-felicitous Providence
> Finger of a tender of, O of a feathery delicacy, the
>   breast of the
>   Maiden could obey so, be a bell to, ring of it, and
> Startle the poor sheep back!   (P28, 31)

The interjected "O" signals the presence of Omega, who is here
sounded in the nun's "breast," the bell-shaped chest cavity or
pectus "of realer, of rounded replies" (P38). For the others she
becomes, as Father Boyle has noted, the sacring bell of the mass,
which calls men to worship and to receive the round host of the
eucharistic Sacrifice.[13] But she is also the ship's bell heard not
"in prayer apart," but in "danger, electrical horror"; she calls
out the distress signal and she embodies the rescue. One individual thus echoes the reverberation of the Word who creates
the universe and redeems mankind, whose name I AM from bluebell to "the orange pealing of Mitton bells"—all things chime
with and sing out: "each hung bell's / Bow swung finds tongue
to fling out broad its name" (P57). Omega is the bell of being
rung in each living creature and in the "bower of bone" that dies
in order to live, serves in order to reign:

> Not free in this because
> His powers seemed free to play:
> He swept what scope he was
> To sweep and must obey.
>
> Though down his being's bent
> Like air he changed in choice,
> That was an instrument
> Which overvaulted voice.
>   (P148, "On a Piece of Music")

Man turns to his daily tasks, to praise as best he can according to
his inscape. The martyr-master overbends and arches, like air and

sky, breath and melody, the harmonious return of the cosmos through man to its one chieftain and goal, "yonder" and within, present and to come, Jesus one and the same. Mark him:

> What makes the man and what
> The man within that makes:
> Ask whom he serves or not
> Serves and what side he takes.
>
> For good grows wild and wide,
> Has shades, is nowhere none;
> But right must seek a side
> And choose for chieftain one.

"One": man's ineffable power remains to choose between two; but only one, *ipse*, is real, the love and completion that is the aim of all desires and aspirations. The ultimate inscape of each is freedom not simply to choose but to sweep forward and upward, like a "music of the mind," to the mark of Christ's "bellbright" body, Omega. His "belled fire" is the torch that illumines every man who comes into the world and that judges each in the end, *per ignem*. "Till doomfire burn all" (P41), "million-fuelèd," shaped in the tongue of flame and torchlight of Omega, "nature's bonfire burns on" (P72). "I baptize with water, but one mightier than I is coming," St. John the Baptist announced. "He will baptize you with the Holy Spirit and with fire. His winnowing fan is in his hand, and he will clean out his threshing floor, and will gather the wheat into his barn; but the chaff he will burn up with unquenchable fire" (Luke 3:16-17). "The fan is a sort of scoop," Hopkins commented in his Dublin retreat notes, with "sides sloping down from the back forwards, and no rim in front" (S, 267). At the end of his life the same shape he had found in the chestnut fan reappears in the hand of Christ the winnower: "That my chaff might fly; my grain lie, sheer and clear" (P64). Its in-shape was inscape: "*scope, cope, scoop, scape, cap*" (L3, 285). "Meaning motion fans fresh our wits with wonder" (P45).

"There are certain forms," Hopkins observed in his Oxford essay on "The Probable Future of Metaphysics," "which have a great hold on the mind and are always reappearing and seem imperishable, such as the designs of Greek vases[14] and lyres, the cone upon Indian shawls, the honeysuckle moulding, the fleur-de-lys, while every day we see designs both simple and elaborate which do not live and are at once forgotten . . . —the forms have in some sense or other an absolute existence" (J, 120). Omega is that archetypal form, the lyre which is the attribute of the true Orpheus and the New Song: "And this deathless strain,—the support of the whole and the harmony of all, reaching from the centre to the circumference and from the extremities to the central part, has harmonized this universal frame" (*Protrepticus* 1). Clement of Alexandria continues: "A beautiful breathing instrument of music the Lord made man, after His own image. And He Himself also, surely, who is the supermundane Wisdom, the celestial Word, is the all-harmonious, melodious, holy instrument of God."[15] Horace avowed:

> Quodsi me lyricis vatibus inseres,
> sublimi furiam sidera vertice,

"If you seat me among the poets of the lyre, I shall strike my head against the stars" (*Odes* 1. l. 35). Poetry aspires to the condition of "immortal song," to enfold within its fragile lines "the roll, the rise, the carol, the creation" (P76).

Mythmaker, priest-poet, and Jesuit Gnostic, Gerard Hopkins discovered the arcane key that unlocked his universe. Hidden in the apostolic tradition, transmitted in enigmatic, apocalyptic imagery and language, the secret lay buried like a grail until the Ignatian knight, "God's own Galahad," went forth to find it. Discovering it, he used it with discretion and concealment as a lamp to light his private darkness and the Black Boreas riding through Victorian England. He traveled the obscure path alone, fearing only the enemy of misunderstanding and ignorance: "I earnestly asked our Lord to watch over my compositions, not to preserve them from being lost or coming to nothing, for that I am very willing they should be, but they might not do me harm through the enmity or imprudence of any man or my own; that he should have them as his own and employ or not employ them as he should see fit. And this I believe is heard" (S, 253-54). Had not Alfred Lord Tennyson in his *In Memoriam* asked the wild and happy bells to "ring the fuller minstrel in" for England's and for Christendom's sake?

> Ring out the darkness of the land,
> Ring in the Christ that is to be.[16]

And might not this prayer, yielding a hundredfold from a handful of seed, also be heard?

Perhaps in private conversations with close friends—all of whom seemed to possess the same trait of an "arch-especial" charisma of intellectual acumen joined to sensuous refinement—the poet revealed some of the buried recesses of his thought. His tutor and friend at Oxford, Walter Pater, probably gained as much intellectually as he gave in his long relationship with Hopkins. A journal entry for May 31, 1866, records their first acquaintance: "Pater talking two hours against Xtianity" (J, 138). Yet the bond between the two men strengthened and when the poet served as a parish priest at Oxford in 1880, he often visited with Pater (L3, 246). One may almost hear the voice of Hopkins in this description of the philosopher-king from Pater's *Plato and Platonism*:

> How could anything which belongs to the world of mere
> phenomenal change seem great to him who is "the spectator
> of all time and all existence"? "For the excellency" of
> such knowledge as that, we might say, he must "count all
> things but loss." By fear of punishment in some round-
> about way, he might indeed be compelled to descend into
> "the cave," "to take in hand the wrongs of other people
> to set them right"; but of course the part he will take in
> your sorry exhibition of passing shadows, and dreamy
> echoes concerning them, will not be for himself. You may
> think him, that philosophic archon or king, who in con-
> senting to be your master has really taken upon himself
> "the form of a servant"—you may think him, in our late
> age of philosophic disillusion, a wholly chimerical being.[17]

Pater goes on to show how Marcus Aurelius and Saint Louis of France both fulfilled the ideal; the important point for us, however, is the basically Pauline underthought of the whole passage, the use of phrases established with special force in Hopkins's myth, and the stress given to the higher "knowledge" or gnosis which "makes man like to God." The prototype of Plato and Pater's "philosophic archon or king" is Jesus of Nazareth, King of the Jews. Certainly, this is what Pater implies through his quotations and what Hopkins professed in and out of season in poem, sermon, and meditation.

Readers familiar with the writings of another Jesuit, Teilhard de Chardin, already will have been struck by the resemblances in insight and religious vision of these two *savants*, especially in the theory of reality's convergence in Omega, the person of Christ. Another poet, William Butler Yeats, also shows an affinity to Hopkins in his system of gyres, historical cycles, and mystical viewpoint. The cunning artifice of correspondencies that marks the fiction of James Joyce strangely resembles the complex intersecting of letters, sounds, words, and phrases that weave the fabric of the Jesuit's poetry. Yet none of these three later writers seems to have had the least interest in the Victorian poet's gnosis; nor could they have known much about it, embedded deep and securely in the heart of his personal writings. Most inexplicable of all, however, is the mysterious crossing of their paths in real and near encounters. Teilhard de Chardin studied theology from 1908 to 1912 at Ore Place in Hastings, near where Hopkins stayed on visits with his fellow poet, Coventry Patmore. At this theologate, modern Christology was initially reformulated in the first decade of this century through the work of the French Jesuits, Joseph Huby, Pierre Rousselot, and the other contributors to the volume *Christus*, first published in 1912. In his father's studio across St. Stephen's Green from the Jesuit's residence in Dublin, Yeats met Hopkins "on different occasions" after 1885 through the good offices of Fr. Matthew Russell, S.J., editor of *The Irish Monthly*. The "querulous, sensitive scholar," as Yeats later remembered him, discussed Bridges's verses and metrical theory with the twenty-year-old Irish poet.[18] Finally,

Joyce attended Jesuit schools in Ireland and the University College at Dublin where Hopkins had taught ten years before.

These points of tangency in thought, place, and time evince, I believe, the coinciding of consciousness in Omega. In Emily Dickinson's words:

> Each Life Converges to some Centre—
> Expressed—or still—
> Exists in every Human Nature
> A Goal—
>
> Embodied scarcely to itself—it may be—
> Too fair
> For Credibility's presumption
> To mar—[19]

In this study, however, we are concerned with the origins in tradition that met in the explosive genius of the Victorian poet. Behind him looms another genius, the man he referred to as "the Father," John Henry Newman. Hopkins at one time had hoped to write a commentary on *A Grammar of Assent*, but Newman did not feel the need for it, and added thoughtfully: "I could not, as a matter of conscience, allow you to undertake a work which I could not but consider at once onerous and unnecessary" (L3, 412). One would have wished, nonetheless, to possess Hopkins's reflections on this passage in which Newman draws his mental journey to its closing summary:

> A temporal sovereign makes himself felt by means of his
> subordinate administrators, who bring his power and will
> to bear upon every individual of his subjects who personally
> know him or not; the universal Deliverer, long expected,
> when He came, He too, instead of making and securing
> subjects by a visible graciousness or majesty, departs;—
> *but* is found, through His preachers, to have imprinted
> the Image or idea of Himself in the minds of His subjects
> individually; and that Image, apprehended and worshipped
> in individual minds, becomes a principle of association,
> and a real bond of those subjects one with another, who

are thus united to the body by being united to that Image;
and moreover that Image, which is their moral life, when
they have been already converted, is also the original
instrument of their conversion. It is the Image of Him
who fulfils the one great need of human nature, the Healer
of its wounds, the Physician of the soul, this Image it is
which both creates faith, and then rewards it.[20]

The "Image," as Newman defines it, is the "Thought of Christ,
not a corporate body or a doctrine" merely, but a life-giving presence, unifying and teaching from within. The Image is not an
abstraction or remote idealization, but the mind of Christ, the
existential being of Jesus himself, transmitted by human voices
through which the Spirit works.[21] This presence is the real meaning of the human Lord, the concrete apprehension of his historical reality. Man, from a mere notional assent to him, is changed
by this knowledge into giving real assent in the act of faith.
Transformed in Christ, man then remembers and discovers that
the source of all his present goodness and happiness was also
the cause of his first turning to the iconic Word. The Image is
then both the Alpha and Omega of man's experience of God, the
impetus and end of his search.

The way of opinion, as Parmenides intended long before, is
thus replaced by the Way of Truth. For Hopkins, gnosis, the
faculty of identification and apprehension of the concrete, would
have equated Newman's Image, "apprehended and worshipped
in individual minds." It binds men not only to Christ but to one
another as "a principle of association," becomes "their moral
life" in deeds of love, and "fulfils the one great need of human
nature," the need to know. It is inscape "called out everywhere
again" to join men in common praise, reverence, and service. For
Gnosis, Image, Icon, Inscape are *epinoiai* of the Son of God, the
Word-made-flesh.

One hundred years after, readers have difficulty in sensing the
revolutionary character of Newman's theology and preaching
and the effect it must have had upon the impressionable Hopkins.
We cannot conceive, for example, that words like the following
had not been heard for centuries in the pulpits of Christendom:

> Christ came to make a new world. He came into the world
> to regenerate it in Himself, to make a new beginning,
> to be the beginning of the creation of God, to gather
> together in one, and recapitulate all things in Himself.
> The rays of His glory were scattered through the world;
> one state of life had some of them, another others. The
> world was like some fair mirror, broken in pieces, and
> giving back no one uniform image of its Maker. But He
> came to combine what was dissipated, to recast what was
> shattered in Himself. He began all excellence, and of
> His fulness have all we received.[22]

With fire such as this, kindled from within years of patient poring over long-forgotten texts, Hopkins himself gathered the live flame and forged a new shape for Omega; in the smithy of his soul the poet "didst fettle for the great grey drayhorse his bright and battering sandal!"

"Nature never set forth the earth in so rich a tapestry as divers poets have done; neither with pleasant rivers, fruitful trees, sweet-smelling flowers, nor whatsoever else may make the too much loved earth more lovely. Her world is brazen, the poets only deliver a golden."[23] In his *Apology for Poetry* Sir Philip Sidney thus set forth the ideal he so beautifully carried out in practice. Renaissance man, the most misunderstood figure in the cultural history of the West, was in earnest about his gentlemanliness; his knowledge, as Castiglione envisioned it, mounted through spheres of more perfect love. The dream Erasmus cherished, when the "pure and simple Christ" would be mined by the scholar in his library and sung by the plowboy in the fields, has never been more clearly defined than by the humanist of Rotterdam: "What is the philosophy of Christ, which he himself calls *Renascentia*, but the insaturation of Nature created good?—moreover, though no one has taught us this so absolutely and effectively as Christ, yet also in pagan books much may be found that is in accordance with it."[24] But the dream galled in Erasmus's own lifetime. Its embers continued to smolder, however, and to "gash gold-vermilion" in men and women who searched their own classical and Christian past to light their present "winter world."

Rembrandt, Calderón, Milton, Pascal, and Dostoevski represent, each in his own chosen field of knowledge, the recurrent sunburst of biblical revelation in the art, drama, poetry, philosophy, and fiction of Western man.

With these and other dreamers of the real, Hopkins takes his place. They, like him, were all doomed to failure, for none have turned the course of Christianity back into the mainstream of learning and life. But the Master himself—inexplicable irony— "was doomed to succeed by failure." Therefore, we can justly consider Hopkins, despite his lack of "bulk," as one raised to the blessed circle "of those who were truly great," since, in Pater's famous maxim: "To burn always with this hard, gem-like flame, to maintain this ecstasy, is success in life."[25] Gerard Hopkins so maintained it that the fire glows more brightly for the "burning witness" which he freely gave "To Christ our Lord."

With the Church's ministers before and after him, lighting the pascal candle with fire struck from stone and initialing it with the sacred letters AΩ—the ancient ritual repeated on the vigil of Easter Sunday down through the centuries—his poetry joins in the prayer:

> Christ yesterday and today
> The beginning and the end
> Alpha and Omega
> His are the seasons and the ages
> To him glory and dominion
> Through endless ages. Amen.[26]

The priest and poet speaks with one voice from the same deep resources of his own and the Church's heart. His myth is her myth, her rubrics are his: "When the procession enters the church, the priest carrying the candle lifts it aloft and sings, 'Lumen Christi.' All present immediately genuflect toward the candle and sing the response, 'Deo gratias.'" Each Easter vigil the light of Christ, borne by priests like Hopkins, winds up the darkened aisles, "a beacon, an eternal beam" that gives promise and comfort of the resurrection. And the congregations light their candles from the flame.

The prayer of another great Jesuit seer of the modern age, Père Teilhard de Chardin, may serve as a proper *nunc dimittis* to this book's pilgrimage. In *La Vie Cosmique*, written in 1916, he prayed for men of this century: "Lord Jesus, you are the centre towards which all things are moving: if it be possible, make a place for us all in the company of those elect and holy ones whom your loving care has liberated one by one from the chaos of our present existence and who now are being slowly incorporated into you in the unity of the new earth."[27] Gerard Manley Hopkins was one of those elect and holy ones, and his poems already share—even as they announce—the unity of the new earth. "Human nature in these men," Hopkins himself wrote, "saw something, got a shock; wavers in opinion, looking back, whether there was anything in it or no; but is in a tremble ever since" (L2, 147-48). To read Hopkins's poetry and prose is to see with new eyes and to hear a new tongue; to feel, in a word, something of that tremble ever since.

APPENDICES

NOTES

SELECTED BIBLIOGRAPHY

INDEX

The connection of Mythology and Philosophy

With the Greeks mythology gave rise to poetry, history, and philosophy. It was, as Grote says, to the ages before literature the whole result of what now takes the form of literature, and the whole field and interest of the minds which would now enjoy poetry, science, history. Its bearing on philosophy can be understood only by asking first what mythology in itself was and what the process of mind which created it or allowed and accepted it.

Two valuable theories of the rise of mythology have been made by modern criticism and may be used to supplement one another, that of the comparative Mythologists and that of those who like Grote on *a priori* grounds trace the state of mind in which mythology was thrown out. Combining them we explain mythology thus. Two stages can be seen in it. In the first there is the least possible power of generalisation in the mind of man, nothing but the common objects of life and the common beasts of the field have connotative names, and even here where the work of any craftsman is unusually elaborate and remarkable it receives a denotative name and is thought of almost or quite as a personal thing. Such is Arthur's sword Excalibar and all the multi-

---

This Oxford essay, previously unpublished, is one of the general essays Hopkins wrote for Robert Scott, Master of Balliol, probably in 1865. The second essay, also printed for the first time, was written in 1866 or 1867 as a Greats essay for Robert Williams, Fellow of Merton College. I have followed the precedent set by Humphry House and Graham Storey in their edition of the *Journals* and lengthened abbreviations in the texts of the notebooks.

tude of famous arms and attributes of heroes. This state of mind comes less of excessive imagination than of defective science. We see it in children and in madness—"Cry you mercy, I took you for a joint-stool"—, and that ships and steam-engines, things that are very organic, are called *she* is a remnant of the same attitude. Those things which like the common chattels of the house are in the control of man entirely and offer no resistance except weight become generalised, that is cease to have individuality or personality, but all things which by their freedom from man's control, their irregular and unaccountable sequence, and their influence on man himself most of all, look like persons and seem to have will of their own, these receive only personal names and according to their greatness become the important figures in mythology. This state of mind, imaginative from want of reasoning and so without the art value of imagination, offers material to poets and men of real imagination. These describe the shows of morn, night, evening, storm, sea, spring, rain, and the rest under language personal as in the earliest stage but definite and interesting, and the words they use are taken up and become the stock of mythes in any people.

At the time philosophy began in Greece the mythes had lost their meaning as accounts of the sights of the earth and sky and were believed in as history. There had also been what may be called the cosmogonical stage, the last of mythology and the foreshadowing of philosophy, in which an attempt is made to explain the creation of the world and the fatherhood of the best known nations. From this latter kind comes the cosmological philosophy of the Ionians, prepossessed by mythology with the idea of some unity, a historical unity perhaps, in the world and substituting for that a scheme of its physical unity. This the less important side of Greek philosophy wins its proper development in science. The more important side springs from the personifying frame of mind which has been spoken of. As the people who produced the mythes found personal *action* in the process of nature so the philosophers, all more or less but more prominently Anaxagoras, Socrates, Plato, were engaged in finding the results of mind in the order, both the standing constitution and the process that is, of nature. They begin with the belief that it is there. The Pythagoreans try to see the numerical relations of nature, taking up the science which being most abstract most represented pure intellect with themselves. Heraclitus, who felt beyond any of his predecessors the chaos, uncertainty, and illusion of all things, spoke nevertheless of a rhythm, something imposed by mind as an air on the notes of a flute. Finally Plato, with whom nature has retired into unimportance, in the doctrine of ideas tries to find in the most recondite and elastic and subtle scheme the existence of mind, that is either at once or by deduction personality, behind the confused and provoking field of natural sights and events as yet almost untouched by science.

Connection of Aristotle's metaphysics with his ethics

There are three stages in the conception of all Being—the potential, the actual, and the passing from the one to the other: these answer to the Not-being, Being, and Becoming which appear in various philosophies from Heraclitus to Hegel. The passing over or becoming is called by Aristotle κίνησις, defined as ἐνέργεια τοῦ δυνάμει ᾗ δυνάμει.

Withdraw these conceptions from the field of the purely abstract: in the world subject to our reason we have three conceptions answering to them—pure matter, which in itself is negation and cannot be known by us but also is a cloud of possibilities; pure form, which as unrealised in matter also cannot be known by us; and the concrete world inner and outer, which is matter in various degrees of form. The change or passing from the one to the other is motion and its meaning is form [,] the realisation of form in matter.

There are then, it follows, two arch-sciences, physics of matter, metaphysics of form. These two meet preeminently in man, whose essence is a body of matter informed by a soul.

The study of physics ends in man as the highest piece of organisation in the world, in other words the highest realisation of form. The same principle is carried into any science which deals with man only: the science as a science will concern itself with finding the highest degree of form attainable by man in that particular field, but the thing will not stop there: action will follow, in which man will realise the form proposed.

Matter, form, and motion have been spoken of: it is necessary to mention the fourth cause which throws the three things into relation with each other: this is the efficient or spring of motion, ἀρχὴ τῆς κινήσεως.

With reference to the efficient we give new names to form and motion: form is called the end or final cause, motion is called the outworking or ἐνέργεια.

Now all through nature we have found the action of some efficient cause which drove matter towards its fullest or highest form, the fullest or highest that is of which the particular matter was capable. Can this principle fail in man? On the contrary as man is the highest organisation of nature it must be eminently true of him.

Man is himself an agent, an efficient cause; his own action therefore must realise his proper end.

What is his end?—the end, it has been said, is the form. That property plainly which is not common to trees or beasts. This is mind. And so Aristotle incidentally says in his Ethics that the mind is the man.

But all this is in the field of the concrete. It is not possible to realise his end in one leap, by one act of thought. It is thus we come to the concrete science of morals. The complexity of matter (and man is the most complex of all matter) makes it possible to realise the end with endless degrees of completeness and of directness and allows of an absolute or primary and of a secondary and a tertiary and so on.

It has been already implied what is the absolutely highest end of man; it must be the fullest action of his mind—that is contemplation, and that on the purest attainable forms, namely what is eternally and unchangeably true. But for many reasons this is only possible to a few and we must enquire the secondary realisation of the end.

Now man is a sheaf of faculties, capacities, or potentialities, each having its own form or end the realisation of which is its virtue, and man has as many virtues as he has faculties. But how is their right form to be known? It is found by right reason, for the mind being the form of the man and reason being the action or process of mind reason must necessarily impose the forms on the faculties—besides that the Greek language allows Aristotle to force a conclusion, for to deny this would be to maintain a contradiction. But what is the right form of the mind, what is right reason? We reach two questions of psychology at last—What is the nature of man's faculties? and what is the nature of his reason?—and here the *a priori* enquiry ends.

Notes

INTRODUCTION: *Myth and Gnosis*

1. "Homily 7 on Philippians 2:5-11," in *Nicene and Post-Nicene Fathers: First Series*, ed. Philip Schaff (New York, 1894), XII, 216-17. See L1, 177.
2. This figure is also used by Fr. Robert Boyle, S.J., in his *Metaphor in Hopkins* (Chapel Hill, 1961), pp. 172–204. His book does employ biblical and doctrinal material in studying the poems, but with method, scope, and result quite removed from those found here. Alan Heuser, *The Shaping Vision of Gerard Manley Hopkins* (London, 1958), offers still another, brief but helpful, view of Hopkins's intellectual development.
3. Elisabeth Schneider, *The Dragon in the Gate: Studies in the Poetry of Gerard Manley Hopkins* (Berkeley, 1968), pp. 26–31. Her arguments first appeared in "*The Wreck of the Deutschland*: A New Reading," *PMLA*, 81 (1966), 116-18. Even so sensitive a critic as Paul Mariani accepts her theory (*A Commentary on the Complete Poems of Gerard Manley Hopkins* [Ithaca, 1970], p. 67). For my reasons against this reading of the poem, see below, p. 148 and chap. 7, n. 6.
4. John L. McKenzie, S.J., *Myths and Realities: Studies in Biblical Theology* (Milwaukee, 1963), p. 183.
5. *In the Human Grain* (New York, 1968), p. 123.
6. See, for example, Hopkins's handling of the Perseus myth in his "Andromeda" (P50). Mariani's critique of this sonnet is indispensable (*Commentary*, pp. 150-55).
7. *The Dialogues of Plato*, trans. B. Jowett (New York, 1937), II, 487.
8. "Holderlin and the Essence of Poetry," trans. Douglas Scott, in *Existence and Being*, 2d ed. (London, 1956), p. 310.
9. All quotations of Clement's *Stromata* (hereafter abbreviated as *Strom.*) are from *The Ante-Nicene Fathers* (New York, 1885), II, 299-567.
10. *Essay on the Development of Doctrine* (London, 1903), p. 365.
11. See, for example, Hopkins's explication of Thucydides' *History of the Peloponnesian War*, bk. 2, l. 90, with elaborately detailed maps and commentary, in Todd K. Bender, *Gerard Manley Hopkins: The Classical Background and Critical Reception of His Work* (Baltimore, 1966), pp. 52–56.

CHAPTER 1: *The Making of a Myth*

1. For a recent look at the main interpretations of *inscape*, see Adrian J. McCarthy, S.M., "Toward a Definition of Hopkins' *Inscape*," *University of Dayton Review*, 4, (1968), 55–68. He concludes: "Inscape is a concept that reconciles individual distinction with cosmic unity" (p. 67). W. A. M. Peters sees it as "the outward manifestation of this intrinsic principle of unity" (*Gerard Manley Hopkins: A Critical Essay towards the Understanding of His Poetry* [London, 1948], p. 3).

2. See C. N. Luxmoore's letter to Arthur Hopkins in L3, 394-95.

3. *The Divinity of Our Lord and Saviour Jesus Christ*, 14th ed. (London, 1890), p. 232. See also Jean-George Ritz, *Le Poète Gérard Manley Hopkins, S.J., 1844-1889: L'Homme et L'Oeuvre* (Paris, 1963), p. 113.

4. Liddon, *Divinity*, p. 369.

5. See Morse Peckham, *Beyond the Tragic Vision: The Quest for Identity in the Nineteenth Century* (New York, 1962), p. 96.

6. The best (indeed, the only) full treatment of the crucial place of Parmenides in Hopkins's poetic development is found in J. Hillis Miller, "The Univocal Chiming," in *Hopkins: A Collection of Critical Essays*, ed. Geoffrey H. Hartman (Englewood Cliffs, N.J., 1966), pp. 107–10. The essay is from Miller's book, *The Disappearance of God: Five Nineteenth-Century Writers* (Cambridge, Mass., 1963), pp. 276–317.

7. *Ancilla to the Pre-Socratic Philosophers*, trans. Kathleen Freeman (Cambridge, Mass., 1966), p. 42. Excepting those made by Hopkins, cited translations of Parmenides' text are taken from this edition, hereafter cited as *Ancilla*.

8. Hopkins quotes from Max Müller's essay "The Veda and Zend-Avesta" in *Chips from a German Workshop* (London, 1867), I, 70. Müller's text goes on to say that "the sun is called the Self of all that moves and rests" (pp. 70-71). A renowned philologist, translator, and scholar of comparative religions, Friedrich Max Müller taught at Oxford during Hopkins's matriculation there. The poet mentions "Max Müller" in a reading list for August-September 1864 (J, 36).

9. Todd K. Bender notes the connection between the Greek imperative σκοπή ("look!") and Hopkins's "scope-scape" but dismisses it as "idle conjecture" (*Gerard Manley Hopkins: The Classical Background and Critical Reception of His Work* [Baltimore, 1966], p. 40, n. 21).

10. *The Mind's Road to God*, trans. George Boas, The Library of Liberal Arts (New York, 1953), p. 35. This and the following three quotations are from chap. 5, sec. 3. See also pp. 37-38.

11. Ibid., p. 42. See the discussion in note 16 below on the six leaps described in Cynewulf's *Christ*.

12. *The Basic Works of Aristotle*, ed. Richard McKeon (New York, 1941), pp. 755-56.

13. Ibid., p. 645.

14. *Parochial and Plain Sermons* (London, 1901), VI, 242.

15. The interpretation that follows is based on my article " 'Altar and Hour' in *The Wreck of the Deutschland*," PLL, 5 (1969), 73-79.

16. Cardinal Newman's motto. The first movement of the *Deutschland* is reminiscent of the six leaps of Christ's incarnation, from his descent "to the spotless Virgin" to his ascent into heaven, as described in Cynewulf's *Ascension*, ll. 718-43. The Christian in turn must leap up to his God:

> As here on earth's soil   God's Son Eternal
> Mounted by leaps   above the high hills,
> Bold on the mountains,   so we mortal men
> In our hearts' musings   must mount by leaps
> From strength to strength,   and strive for glory,
> That we may ascend   by holy works.   (ll. 744-49)

(*Early English Christian Poetry*, trans. Charles W. Kennedy [London, 1952], p. 106.)

17. See Emile Bougaud, *Life of Blessed Margaret Mary Alacoque* (New York, 1890), pp. 163-79.

18. Cited in Edgar Hennecke, *New Testament Apocrypha*, ed. Wilhelm Schneemelcher (Philadelphia, 1963), I, 303.

19. *Lectures and Essays in Criticism*, vol. 3 in *The Complete Prose Works of Matthew Arnold*, ed. R. H. Super (Ann Arbor, 1960–), p. 201. Hopkins listed Arnold's essays among books to read in February–March 1865 (J, 56).

20. From St. Ignatius's autobiography, as quoted by James Brodrick, S.J., *Saint Ignatius of Loyola* (New York, 1956), p. 108.

21. *Ancilla*, p. 45. I have taken the liberty of substituting "resplendent" for "destructive" in Miss Freeman's translation, as this word would be closer to the version of the passage available to Hopkins.

22. *The Friend*, ed. Henry Nelson Coleridge, vol. 2 in *The Complete Works of Samuel Taylor Coleridge*, ed. W. G. T. Shedd (New York, 1856), pp. 466–67.

CHAPTER 2: *The Meaning of St. Paul*

1. See, for example, Piet Schoonenberg, " 'He Emptied Himself'—Philippians 2:7," in *Who Is Jesus of Nazareth?* (New York, 1966), vol. 2, *Concilium*, pp. 47-66; Oscar Cullmann, *The Christology of the New Testament* (Philadelphia, 1963), pp. 174-81, 217-18, and passim; and Lucien Cerfaux, *Christ in the Theology of St. Paul* (New York, 1959), pp. 374-97. For a useful nineteenth-century commentary on the text, see J. B. Lightfoot, *St. Paul's Epistle to the Philippians*, 6th ed. (London, 1881), pp. 110-15; and for a suggestive homiletic reading, see Henry Parry Liddon, "The Humiliation of the Eternal Son," *Passiontide Sermons* (London, 1890), pp. 18-33.

2. See Michael Lieb, "Milton and the Kenotic Christology: Its Literary Bearing," *ELH*, 37 (1970), 342-60.

3. Notebook 42, quoted in J. Robert Barth, S.J., *Coleridge and Christian Doctrine* (Cambridge, Mass., 1969), p. 138. Coleridge's grandson, Ernest Hartley Coleridge, was a close friend of Hopkins and may have shown him the notebooks.

4. Pierre Benoît, "Corps, Tête et Plérôme dans les Epître de la Captivité," *Exégèse et Théologie*, 2 (1961), 151.

5. *The Divinity of Our Lord and Saviour Jesus Christ*, 14th ed. (London, 1890), p. 324. For Liddon's discussion of St. Paul's Christology, see pp. 306-59.

6. Ibid., p. 9.

7. F. R. Webber, *Church Symbolism*, 2d ed. (Cleveland, 1938), p. 78.

8. Cited by Sir James George Frazer, *The Golden Bough*, pt. V: "Spirits of the Corn and of the Wild," vol. 1, 3rd ed. (London, 1912), p. 14. Clement also notes the use of the pomegranate in the Eleusinian mysteries (*Protrepticus* 2).

9. See *From Glory to Glory: Texts from Gregory of Nyssa's Mystical Writings*, eds. Jean Danielou, S.J., and Herbert Musurillo, S.J. (New York, 1961), pp. 230-32.

10. "Of the Inconstancie of our Actions," *The Essayes of Montaigne*, trans. John Florio (New York, n.d.), p.297.

11. Cited by George A. Maloney, S.J., *The Cosmic Christ: From Paul to Teilhard* (New York, 1967), p. 181.

12. "The full procession of the whole of restored Humanity" with Christ at its head is also elaborately pictured by Hopkins's contemporary, Joseph Rickaby, S.J., in his retreat commentary, *Waters That Go Softly* (London, 1907), pp. 150-52. Besides his frequent reliance on the Greek philosophers, church fathers, and Cardinal Newman, Rickaby is notably Pauline in his thought. See, for example, his remarks on the *pleroma*, pp. 165-66.

13. *The Works of George Herbert*, ed. F. E. Hutchinson (Oxford, 1945), p. 91. See L2, 23-24.

14. *Lectures and Essays in Criticism*, vol. 3 in *The Complete Prose Works of Matthew Arnold*, ed. R. H. Super (Ann Arbor, 1960–), p. 230.

CHAPTER 3: *The Person of Christ in the Synoptic Gospels*

1. *Parochial Sermons* (London, 1901), VI, 59.

2. Ibid., III, 169.

3. The only full treatment of Hopkins as a preacher is by John McLaughlin, S.J., "The Pulpit Rhetoric of Gerard Manley Hopkins," Diss. Columbia 1967.

4. *The Literary Remains*, ed. Henry Nelson Coleridge, vol. 5 in *The Com-*

plete Works of Samuel Taylor Coleridge, ed. W. G. T. Shedd (New York, 1856), pp. 83-84.

5. Cited by Joseph A. Fitzmyer, S.J., in "The Oxyrhynchus *Logoi* of Jesus and the Coptic Gospel according to Thomas," *Theological Studies*, 20 (1959), 539.

6. See Robert Boyle, *Metaphor in Hopkins* (Chapel Hill, 1961), pp. 45-70.

7. "The Risen Life," in *Sermons Preached Before the University of Oxford, First Series*, 6th ed. (London, 1876), p. 271. Hopkins would have heard this remarkable sermon, which affirms the risen life as a present principle of spirit and energy, when it was "preached at St. Mary's on the Second Sunday after Easter, April 30, 1865."

8. Ibid., p. 259.

9. *Parochial Sermons*, V, 139.

CHAPTER 4: *The Word of St. John*

1. On Jesus' use of the divine name, see Raymond E. Brown, S.S., ed., *The Gospel according to John (I-XII)*, vol. 29, *The Anchor Bible* (Garden City, 1966), pp. 533-38. In quoting the Gospels, I have capitalized the divine name.

2. *Paradise Lost*, ed. Merritt Y. Hughes (New York, 1962), p. 171. In keeping with Hebrew tradition, Milton pictures the kenotic Word ordering chaos rather than creating out of nothing.

3. *Ancilla to the Pre-Socratic Philosophers*, trans. Kathleen Freeman (Cambridge, Mass., 1966), pp. 24-25, 29.

4. Ibid., p. 28.

5. See J. Hillis Miller, "The Univocal Chiming," in *Hopkins: A Collection of Critical Essays*, ed. Geoffrey H. Hartman (Englewood Cliffs, N.J., 1966), pp. 89–116.

6. *Sartor Resartus*, ed. Charles Frederick Harrold (New York, 1937), p. 263.

7. *William Shakespeare: The Complete Works*, ed. Alfred Harbage (Baltimore, 1969), p. 169.

8. Notebook 42, quoted in J. Robert Barth, S.J., *Coleridge and Christian Doctrine* (Cambridge, Mass., 1969), p. 138.

9. *The Divinity of Our Lord and Saviour Jesus Christ*, 14th ed. (London, 1890), p. 233. For Liddon's treatment of the Logos, see pp. 63–70.

10. See below, pp. 113 and 184 ("Pied Beauty").

11. Hopkins stopped copying the sermon just as he was about to reveal "that great and profound change" which took place between the Middle Ages and "the age we live in." I believe the difference he would have found is that observed by the Sacred Heart according to St. Margaret Mary Alacoque: Jesus complained to her that "hearts have now grown cold." See *Sermons*, pp. 104 and 282.

12. *Ode on Intimations of Immortality*, in *The Poetical Works of Words-worth*, ed. Thomas Hutchinson and Ernest de Selincourt (New York, 1950), p. 460. For Hopkins's high opinion of the ode, see below, p. 145.

13. *Parochial Sermons* (London, 1901), III, 278.

14. *The Works of George Herbert*, ed. F. E. Hutchinson (Oxford, 1945), p. 174.

15. *The Literary Remains*, ed. Henry Nelson Coleridge, vol. 5 in *The Complete Works of Samuel Taylor Coleridge*, ed W. G. T. Shedd (New York, 1856), p. 113.

16. *The Hero With a Thousand Faces*, 2d ed. (Princeton, 1968), p. 249.

CHAPTER 5: *The Fathers of the Church*

1. Hopkins's reading of patristic texts would have involved J. P. Migne's *Patrologiae cursus completus: Series Latina* (Paris, 1844–55), 221 volumes, and *Series Graeca* (Paris, 1857–66), 161 volumes. Translations available included *Library of the Fathers*, ed. Pusey, Keble, and New-man (Oxford, 1838–88), 45 volumes, and the Edinburgh edition (1866–72) of the translations used in this present study. The latter, published in New York between 1884 and 1886, includes vol. I: apostolic writers, Justin Martyr, Irenaeus, and Polycarp; vol. II: Clement of Alexandria; and vol. IV: Origen and Tertullian's *De Monogamia*.

2. *Early Christian Writings*, trans. Maxwell Staniforth (Baltimore, 1968), p. 119.

3. Besides the pomegranate and sloe, Hopkins links "fruit" with Christ's passion and the Eucharist in several of his early poems (P6 and P7).

4. In chapter 56 of the *Trypho*, Justin argues that "He who appeared to Abraham, Jacob and Moses is distinct from God the Father." See also chaps. 56-63 and H. P. Liddon, *Divinity of Our Lord and Saviour Jesus Christ*, 14th ed. (London, 1890), pp. 52-60.

5. In 1865 Hopkins wrote that Savanarola is "the only person in history (except perhaps Origen) about whom I have a real feeling" (L3, 17). These two examples of religious nonconformity placed in the service of a purer canon of teaching and practice seem to have whetted the poet's own peculiar zeal and independence of spirit. Curiously, Origen is not otherwise referred to in Hopkins's extant writings.

6. This quotation is from *On First Principles*, trans. G. W. Butterworth (New York, 1966), p. 248. As a key text to prove how all things will be subjected to God through Christ, the Philippians hymn (2:5-8) also proved invaluable to Origen who made extensive use of it. He writes: "He first fulfilled in himself what he wished to be fulfilled by others" not only through his obedience on the cross but by his own future sub-jection to the Father "at the consummation of the ages" (*First Prin.* 3. 5. 6, p. 242).

7. Ibid., p. 153.

8. Cited by Jean Danielou, *Origen* (London, 1955), p. 295.

9. *Causes of the Rise and Successes of Arianism* in John Henry Cardinal Newman, *Tracts, Theological and Ecclesiastical* (London, 1902), p. 201. *Causes* appears in this volume, hereafter cited as *Tracts*, between pp. 137 and 300.

10. The homilies on the Gospels appear in *Nicene and Post-Nicene Fathers: First Series*, ed. Philip Schaff (New York, 1894), vol. 10; those on St. Paul, in vol. 12.

11. *The Works of George Herbert*, ed. F. E. Hutchinson (Oxford, 1945), p. 21.

12. The homilies on St. John's Gospel are found in the *Nicene Fathers*, vol. 14, and in *The Fathers of the Church*, vol. 33 (New York, 1957), and vol. 41 (New York, 1960).

13. *The Confessions of St. Augustine*, trans. Edward B. Pusey (New York, 1951), p. 213.

14. Ibid., p. 237. See the discussion on Philippians 3:13-14 below, p. 271.

15. *Four Quartets*, in *The Complete Poems and Plays (1909-1950)* (New York, 1952), pp. 122, 139.

16. See Jerome H. Buckley, *The Triumph of Time: A Study of the Victorian Concepts of Time, History, Progress, and Decadence* (Cambridge, Mass., 1966), pp. 129-30, 139-40.

17. *Selected Treaties of St. Athanasius*, trans. John Henry Newman (London, 1900), I, 178.

CHAPTER 6: *Scotus and the Scholastic Tradition*

1. The tradition at times found an exceptional spokesman, like Cardinal de Bérulle in the seventeenth century. In his tenth discourse on the "condition and dignities of Jesus" after his resurrection, the cardinal writes that Jesus received from the Father a body "far more glorious than the sun," a body that "contains within its immense grandeur both earth and sun, all the stars and all the expanse of the heavens, a body that rules all bodies and all heavenly spirits." In his *Life of Jesus*, he prays: "Earth and Heaven, Grace and Nature, look to you and tend towards you, as to their whole and their Centre" (both quotations from Henri de Lubac, *Teilhard de Chardin: The Man and his Meaning* [New York, 1967], p. 57). Pascal also wrote movingly of the "Mystery of Jesus" and of his sufferings "until the end of time." Especially does he link man's knowledge and Jesus: "We not only do not know God except through Jesus Christ, but we only know ourselves through Jesus Christ. We only know life and death through Jesus Christ. Except in Jesus Christ, we do not know the meaning of life or our death, or God or ourselves" (*Pascal's Pensees*, trans. Martin Turnell [New York,

1962], p. 287). Nevertheless, Pascal's approach to Christ is moral and personalistic rather than cosmic and mythopoeic.

2. R. V. Seller's translation in his *The Council of Chalcedon* (London, 1953), p. 210.

3. *The Literary Remains*, ed. Henry Nelson Coleridge, vol. 5 in *The Complete Works of Samuel Taylor Coleridge*, ed. W. G. T. Shedd (New York, 1856), p. 209.

4. See Cyril L. Shircel, O.F.M., *The Univocity of the Concept of Being in the Philosophy of John Duns Scotus* (Washington, D.C., 1942), pp. 45-59.

5. In the realm of beings there actually exists a being that enjoys primacy of causality and preeminence: this being is infinite, Duns Scotus argues. "This notion of God as an infinite being is the most perfect absolute concept we can have of him" (*Philosophical Writings: A Selection*, trans. Allan Wolter, O.F.M., The Library of Liberal Arts [New York, 1962], p. 80).

6. *The Confessions of St. Augustine*, trans. Edward B. Pusey (New York, 1951), p. 195.

7. Ibid., p. 178.

8. See Karl Rahner, *Mission and Grace* (London, 1963), I, 60.

9. *La Divina Commedia*, ed. Guiseppe Vandelli (Milan, 1955), canto 32, ll. 85-87, p. 908. "Look on that face most like to Christ's, for only its brilliance can prepare you to gaze on Christ" (my translation).

10. Ibid., p. 900. "My Lord Jesus Christ, true God, was this how you once looked?"

11. *Nature*, in *Selected Prose and Poetry*, ed. Reginald L. Cook, 2d ed. (New York, 1969), p. 37. Although Hopkins never refers to Emerson, his myth and *Nature* dovetail on a number of salient points. Robert Frost, for example, remarks that for Emerson, "ideally in thought only is a circle round. In practice, in nature, the circle becomes an oval" (*The Selected Prose of Robert Frost*, ed. H. Cox and C. Lathem [New York, 1966], p. 118).

CHAPTER 7: *Inscaping* The Wreck of the Deutschland

1. The distinction between inscape as artifact and object in nature has been noted by J. Hillis Miller, "The Creation of the Self in Gerard Manley Hopkins," *ELH*, 22 (1955), 310. See also Virginia C. Byrne, "The Creator and the Maker in the Aesthetics of Gerard Manley Hopkins," *McNeese Review*, 14 (1963), 60-73.

2. *Gerard Manley Hopkins (1844-1889): A Study of Poetic Idiosyncrasy in Relation to Poetic Tradition*, 2d ed. (London, 1958), II, 128-34.

3. See Bell Gale Chevigny, "Instress and Devotion in the Poetry of Gerard Manley Hopkins," *VS*, 9 (1965), 141-53.

4. The ratio is noted by Alan Heuser, *The Shaping Vision of Gerard Manley Hopkins* (London, 1958), p. 110.

5. See Oscar Cullman, *The Christology of the New Testament* (Philadelphia, 1963), pp. 208-15.

6. *The Dragon in the Gate: Studies in the Poetry of Gerard Manley Hopkins* (Berkeley, 1968), pp. 26-31. Miss Schneider argues that "fetched" implies a miraculous event, but see the last line of *The Loss of the Eurydice* and Gardner's note on the nautical meaning of "fetch" (P, p. 262).

7. See above, pp 52, 99. In his published Bampton lectures, H. P. Liddon also lays great stress on the martyrs' confession as part of the traditional teaching of Christ's divine nature (*The Divinity of Our Lord and Saviour Jesus Christ*, 14th ed. [London, 1890], pp. 406-11, 414-18).

8. Wendell Stacy Johnson, *Gerard Manley Hopkins: The Poet as Victorian* (Ithaca), 1968, p. 69.

9. On the heart image in Hopkins's poetry, see Robert Boyle, S.J., *Metaphor in Hopkins* (Chapel Hill, 1961), pp. 71–110. See also Hopkins's sermon on the Sacred Heart (S, 100-04) and above, p. 29.

10. For Origen's concept of the *epinoiai*, see above, p. 109.

11. *The Poems of Prudentius*, ed. and trans. H. J. Thomson, The Loeb Classical Library (London, 1949), I, 76-77. Thomson translates: "Born of the Father's love before the world's beginning, called Alpha and Omega, He is both source and end of all things that are or have been or hereafter shall be. He gave the word and they were created, He spoke and they were made—earth, heavens, the deep sea, the threefold fabric of the world, and all that lives in them under the lofty globes of sun and moon. He put on the shape of mortal body, members doomed to die, so that the race that sprang from the first man's stock should not perish though the law of sin had plunged him deep in hell. O blessed birth, when a virgin in labour, having conceived by the Holy Spirit, brought forth our salvation, and the child who is the world's Redeemer revealed His sacred face!" A verse rendering of the hymn may be found in *The Poems of Prudentius*, trans. Sister M. Clement Eagan, C.C.V.I. (Washington, D.C., 1962), vol. 43 in *The Fathers of the Church* (New York, 1947–), pp. 56-69.

12. The connection between *ipse* and *Colossians* is also noted, but not developed, by John Keating in *The Wreck of the Deutschland: An Essay and Commentary* (Kent, Ohio, 1963), p. 94.

13. Patristic references for "the Divine Hand" are found in Newman's *Selected Treatises of St. Athanasius* (London, 1900), II, 142.

14. *The Epistles to the Colossians and to Philemon*, 3rd ed. (London, 1879), p. 155. Lightfoot's commentary on verses 15-20 is found on pp. 140-58.

15. Sister Mary Adorita Hart, B.V.M., views the mystical body of Christ as the subject of the entire poem; see her "The Christocentric Theme of

Gerard Manley Hopkins' *The Wreck of the Deutschland*," Diss. Catholic University 1952, pp. 6–9, 21, 171.

16. *Parochial Sermons* (London, 1901), VI, 254.

17. *The Mind's Road to God*, trans. George Boas, The Library of Liberal Arts (New York, 1953), p. 31. Among his extant papers is a passage Hopkins has copied from St. Bonaventure's *Life of St. Francis*.

18. On the *apocatastasis*, see above, p. 110.

19. *The Complete Poetical Works of John Milton*, ed. Douglas Bush (Boston, 1965), p. 147.

20. The source is noted by Brother Adelbert Scheve, "*The Wreck of the Deutschland*, Stanza 33," *The Explicator Cyclopedia*, vol. I: *Modern Poetry*, ed. Charles Child Walcutt and J. Edwin Whitesell (Chicago, 1966), 172-73. The Christmas liturgy applies this psalm to Christ, the Sun of Justice.

21. *The Presocratics*, ed. and trans. Philip Wheelwright (New York, 1966), pp. 72, 88.

CHAPTER 8: "*Let him easter in us*": *Sonnets of 1877*

1. Hopkins fully expected the fourth year of study (see L1, 30; L3, 58, 122, 242). I cannot agree with Alfred Thomas that reasons of health may have barred him from the Long Course (*Hopkins the Jesuit: The Years of Training* [London, 1969], pp. 181-82.). See Father Devlin's comments in *Sermons*, p. xiii.

2. *Poems* 177. Gardner offers the following translation: "O heavenly Jesus, you who gather up in your hand us men and these lofty stars, all things come from you: I pray that the year too may take its beginning from you; it will (then) be a good year. All things are in you: may our race (also) live in you because we are your limbs: all the breezes that we enjoy and the sky to which we look up have, I assert, been granted to us (for use), but many, indeed, have no gratitude; yet even if gratitude is lacking, gracious nature, bountiful nature is also at hand to help all men; nature, to whom that provident hand of yours is stretched out everywhere" (P, p. 336).

3. In his seventh Bampton lecture, H. P. Liddon quotes from this prayer of "the perfect Gnostic" (*The Divinity of Our Lord and Saviour Jesus Christ*, 14th ed. [London, 1890], p. 395).

4. *Macbeth*, ed. Kenneth Muir, Arden Shakespeare Series (Cambridge, Mass., 1957), p. 72.

5. *Dialogues of Plato*, trans. B. Jowett (New York, 1937), I, 770.

6. For a literal reading of the sonnet, see F. X. Shea, S.J., "Another Look at 'The Windhover'," *VP*, 2 (1964), 219-39. Father Shea, however, entirely ignores the *volta* which separates the octave and sestet, the *blason* and consequent reflection.

7. *Selected Writings of Francis Bacon*, ed. Hugh G. Dick (New York, 1955), p. 244. On the Renaissance view of poetry and reason, see my articles, "The Songs in *Astrophil and Stella*," *SP*, 67 (1970), 178-200; and "The 'Baiser' Group in Sidney's *Astrophil and Stella*," *Texas Studies in Literature and Language*, 12 (1970), 381-403.

8. Ronald Bates, " 'The Windhover'," *VP*, 2 (1964), 63-64.

9. *Causes of the Rise and Successes of Arianism*, in John Henry Newman, *Tracts, Theological and Ecclesiastical* (London, 1902), p. 203. See above, p. 113.

10. Ibid., p. 203.

11. Ibid., p. 205.

12. *The Complete Poetical Works of John Milton*, ed. Douglas Bush (Boston, 1965), p. 147.

CHAPTER 9: *Poems of the Apostolate*

1. See Richard J. O'Dea, " 'The Loss of the Eurydice': A Possible Key to the Reading of Hopkins," *VP*, 4 (1966), 291-93.

2. This feat of multiple exposure of scriptural verses has long been explored by Christian preachers and artists. It is found for example in Rembrandt's *Hundred Guilder Print* where four episodes from Matthew 19 appear in the one scene of Christ healing the sick.

3. *Enchiridion*, trans. Wynkyn de Worde (1553), quoted by James Brodrick, *Saint Ignatius of Loyola* (New York, 1956), p. 160.

4. See George A. Maloney, S.J., *The Cosmic Christ: From Paul to Teilhard* (New York, 1967), pp. 156-57. Also pp. 47 and 246-47 of this volume.

5. *The Symposium*, trans. Michael Joyce, *The Collected Dialogue of Plato*, ed. Edith Hamilton and Huntington Cairns, Bollingen Series, vol. 71 (New York, 1961), p. 562.

6. On the historical background of the poem, see Alfred Thomas, "Hopkins's 'Felix Randal': The Man and the Poem," *TLS*, March 19, 1971, pp. 331-32. The original Felix Spencer died at age thirty-one.

7. Compare this passage from Ecclesiasticus 38:29-30: "Here is the blacksmith sitting by his anvil, intent upon his iron-work, cheeks shrivelled with the smoke, as he battles with the heat of the furnace, ears ringing again with the hammer's clattering, eyes fixed on the design" (Knox's translation, quoted by Thomas, ibid., p. 332).

8. *Marius the Epicurean* (London, 1910), II, 71.

9. "The Image and the Word," *Month*, n.s. 3 (1950), 197.

10. Cited by Devlin, ibid., p. 197.

CHAPTER 10: *"In a Whirlwind"*: *Last Poems*

1. "Day of wrath, that day will loosen time into ashes: thus witness David and the Sibyl. How great will be the dread when the Judge

comes to take a strict account of all" (my translation). The musical setting of this chant must also have been in Hopkins's mind when writing his sonnet.

2. Canto 33, ll. 85-87 (quoted below, p. 327, chap. 12, n. 1).

3. *Sartor Resartus*, ed. Charles Frederick Harrold (New York, 1937), p. 258. See also Carlyle's comments on the Sibylline leaves, pp. 77-78.

4. See W. H. Gardner, *Gerard Manley Hopkins (1844-1889): A Study of Poetic Idiosyncrasy in Relation to Poetic Tradition*, 2d ed. (London, 1958), II, 310-12. The Virgilian parallels, however, as Norman White shows, are problematic and less convincing than the poem's use of the Sibylline Odes composed by the Jews and early Christians in the form of apocalyptic foreshadowings ("Hopkins' 'Spelt from Sibyl's Leaves'," *VN*, no. 36 [Fall 1969], pp. 27-28). White offers a striking quotation from the Second Book of the Oracles. See also St. Augustine's *City of God*, bk. 18, chap. 23.

5. Hopkins copied out a passage from Coleridge's *Biographia Literaria*, chap. 6, which is also pertinent here: "This fact [the delirious girl who talked Latin, Greek, Hebrew, etc.] contributes to make it even probable that all thoughts are in themselves imperishable and that if the intelligent faculty should be rendered more comprehensive it would require only a different and apportioned organisation, *the body celestial* instead of the *body terrestrial*, to bring before every human soul the collective experience of its whole past existence. And this, this perchance is the dread book of judgment, in whose mysterious hieroglyphics every idle word is recorded."

6. *Sermons Bearing on Subjects of the Day* (London, 1902), p. 10.

7. For the allusions to Scripture in this poem, as well as to Greek initiation rites, see J. Angela Carson, "The Metaphor of Struggle in 'Carrion Comfort'," *PQ*, 49 (1970), 547-57.

8. See Sister Mary Humiliata, "Hopkins and the Prometheus Myth," *PMLA*, 70 (1955), 58-68. Gardner (*Hopkins: A Study*, I, 176 ff.) traces the underthought to *King Lear*.

9. For other meanings of "fell," see Paul L. Mariani, *A Commentary on the Complete Poems of Gerard Manley Hopkins* (Ithaca, 1970), p. 219.

10. *Paradise Lost*, ed. Merritt Y. Hughes (New York, 1962), p. 84. Compare also *King Lear* (IV, 1, 27-28): "And worse I may be yet; the worse is not / So long as we can say 'This is the worst'" (cited by Mariani [*Commentary*, p. 228] in connection with "No worst, there is none").

11. Noted by Elisabeth Schneider, "My own heart let me more have pity on," *The Explicator Cyclopedia*, vol. I: *Modern Poetry*, ed. Charles Child Walcutt and J. Edwin Whitsell (Chicago, 1966), 163.

12. Gardner, *Hopkins: A Study*, I, 164-65.

13. *The Christian Image: Studies in Religious Art and Poetry* (Pittsburgh, 1966), p. 19.

14. "There is a significant poetic yield in declaiming the preposition 'Across' slowly so that what is suggested is 'a cross' shining in the dark to the speaker" (Mariani, *Commentary*, p. 285).

15. *The Great Catechism* in *Nicene and Post-Nicene Fathers: Second Series*, ed. Philip Schaff and Henry Wace (New York, 1893), V, 482. The potsherd also recalls Job 2:8 and Psalm 21:16.

16. On the *lapis-Christus* parallel, as well as the "diamond body," see Carl G. Jung, *Psychology and Alchemy*, trans. R. F. C. Hull (London, 1953), vol. 12, *The Collected Works*, pp. 407-08. Jung concludes that the ultimate aim of alchemy was really "to produce a *corpus subtile*, a transfigured and resurrected body" which was "at the same time spirit" (p. 408). In "The Alchemist in the City," Hopkins pictures the alchemist himself hungering for personal transformation. This will be found in "the wilderness" and "after the sunset" by piercing "the yellow waxen light / With free long looking, ere I die" (P15). Twenty years later the "yellow hornlight" of evening reappears in "Spelt from Sibyl's Leaves." The *lapis philosophorum* was also likened to wax and horn. The poet's father, Manley Hopkins, identified the stone with the salutary thought of death in his book of verse, *A Philosopher's Stone*, published in 1843 (see Gardner, *Hopkins: A Study*, II, 3).

17. "Heraclitus says that both life and death exist in our state of life and in our state of death alike; that during life our souls are dead and buried within us, and that when we die our souls revive and live" (Sextus Empiricus, *Outlines of Pyrrhonism* 3. 230). "Heraclitus the philosopher says that the soul is a spark of starry essence" (Macrobius, *Commentary on the Dream of Scipio* 1. 14). Translations are by Philip Wheelright, *The Presocratics* (New York, 1966), pp. 87, 89; see also pp. 82-83 on "the road up-down."

18. *Paradise Lost*, ed. Hughes, p. 5. See Robert B. Clark, "Hopkins's 'The Shepherd's Brow'," *VN*, no. 28 (1965), pp. 16-18.

19. First noted by Gardner, *Poems*, p. 297, and Paul L. Mariani, "The Artistic and Tonal Integrity of Hopkins' 'The Shepherd's Brow'," *VP*, 6 (1968), 63.

20. See Joseph Campbell's valuable discussion of Schopenhauer's analogy of anamorphosis in *The Masks of God: Creative Mythology* (New York, 1968), pp. 194-95.

CHAPTER 11: *Poetry and Gnosis*

1. Besides the original Greek text and Latin translation in Migne, the English version, used here, by William Wilson in the *Ante-Nicene Christian Library*, vol. 4 (Edinburgh, 1868), was available to Hopkins.

2. *The Divinity of Our Lord and Saviour Jesus Christ*, 14th ed. (London, 1890), p. 389.

3. *The Arians of the Fourth Century* (London, 1901), p. 48. See also pp. 49, 67-68, 73-74, 81, 83, 87-89. A Jesuit priest informed Newman that what was taught in Roman seminaries was eclectic, "like St. Clement's Stromata" (*The Letters and Diaries of John Henry Newman*, ed. Charles Stephen Dessain [London, 1961], XI, 279).

4. In this connection, Father Devlin's voucher for the Scotist position should be quoted: "Documentarily speaking, there are only four significant places in GMH's spiritual writings where he certainly refers to Scotus. From these, as from four small bones of a prehistoric monster, must be reconstructed the skeletal outline of the undoubted relations between the two men" (S, 338). Many of Hopkins's papers disappeared after his death; he seems mainly to have guarded those that would aid his teaching of the classics and his professional work as a priest.

5. Hopkins cites only the Greek, which I have translated.

6. *The Dialogues of Plato*, trans. B. Jowett (New York, 1937), I, 750-51.

7. Rudolf Bultmann, "Gnosis," in *Bible Key Words*, ed. Gerhard Kittel (New York, 1958), II, 36.

8. *Sermons Preached Before the University of Oxford, First Series*, 6th ed. (London, 1876), p. 128. See also Hopkins's notes for Liddon's course on 1 Corinthians, above, p. 5.

9. See C. H. Dodd, *The Interpretation of the Fourth Gospel* (Cambridge, 1953), pp. 151 ff.

10. *Divinity of Our Lord*, p. 303.

11. Ian A. Richmond, *Archaeology and the After-Life in Pagan and Christian Imagery* (New York, 1950), p. 57.

12. *Tracts, Theological and Ecclesiastical* (London, 1902), p. 238.

13. *Idea of a University* (London, 1902), pp. 137-38.

14. *Apologia Pro Vita Sua*, ed. David J. DeLaura, Norton Critical Edition (New York, 1968), p. 34. DeLaura's essay on Newman (pp. 482-503) offers a wise and fresh approach to Newman which can be validly applied to Hopkins: "Newman sought nothing less than an entrance into the buried springs of morality, perception, and feeling in the reader. The implicit object is a transference of values, and a transformation of the reader, effected by Newman's conveying to him and acting out before him a special and intense way of looking at things which in his view is the uniquely personal context for the 'habit' of supernatural faith" (p. 494). Despite his seeming indifference to an audience, Hopkins by writing was intending to communicate, not to a wide circle of readers, but ultimately to those ready to receive his gnostic "way of looking at things."

15. See David A. Downes, *Victorian Portraits: Hopkins and Pater* (New York, 1965), pp. 68-83.

16. *Lectures and Essays in Criticism*, vol. 3 in *The Complete Prose Works of Matthew Arnold*, ed. R. H. Super (Ann Arbor, 1960–), p. 34.

17. *1000 Years of Irish Poetry*, ed. Kathleen Hoagland (New York, 1947), p. 14.

18. For a perceptive critique of this passage, see Francis Fike's "Gerard Manley Hopkins' Interest in Painting after 1868: Two Notes," *VP*, 8 (1970), 319–20.

19. Robert J. Dilligan and Todd K. Bender, *A Concordance to the English Poetry of Gerard Manley Hopkins* (Madison, Milwaukee, and London, 1970), pp. 136-37, 303.

20. *A Greek-English Lexicon of the New Testament and Other Early Christian Literature*, ed. William Arndt and F. William Ginrich (Chicago, 1957), γνῶσις.

21. *An Apology for Poetry*, ed. George Shepherd (London, 1965), p. 100.

CHAPTER 12: *Inscape and Omega*

1. *La Divina Comedia*, ed. Giuseppe Vandelli (Milan, 1955), canto 33, ll. 124-32, pp. 922-23. Charles Eliot Norton translates: "O Light Eternal, that sole abidest in Thyself, sole understandest Thyself, and, by Thyself understood and understanding, lovest and smilest on Thyself! That circle which appeared in Thee generated as a reflected light, being awhile surveyed by my eyes, seemed to me depicted with our effigy within itself, of its own color; wherefore my sight was wholly set upon it" (*The Divine Comedy*, trans. Charles Eliot Norton [Boston, 1941], pp. 256-57). Earlier in the same canto Dante says that his vision has fled, as "by the wind, on the light leaves, was lost the saying of the Sibyl" (ll. 65-66, p. 254). In the Eternal Light, he writes, "I saw that in its depth is enclosed, bound up with love in one volume, that which is dispersed in leaves through the universe" (ll. 85-87, p. 255). "Spelt from Sibyl's Leaves" also uses the underthought of scattered pages and of the one tale and oracle written in the life of Christ (see p. 218 of this study). On the cosmic book of nature in Dante and other writers, see Ernst Robert Curtius, *European Literature and the Latin Middle Ages*, trans. Willard R. Trask (New York, 1953), pp. 319-47. Curtius notes that according to Hugh of St. Victor both creation and Christ are "books" of God (p. 320).

2. See F. R. Shanley, *Strength of Materials* (New York, 1957), pp. 575-76, figures 24.8 (c) and 24.9.

3. Behind these virile lines lie the philosopher's gold that fulfills life and the bow and arrow which, as the attributes of Apollo, were associated with the sun. The Delphic *Omphalos* ("navel") was an ovoid stone in the temple of Apollo and supposedly marked the center of the earth. In his unpublished Dublin notes on Homer's *Iliad*, Hopkins wrote that the "silver-bowed Apollo" (bk. 5, l. 449) was "as true to Aeneas as his arrows to the mark." The literal and figurative meanings again suggest the moral gloss.

4. A happy pause at this point in our argument—one too good to resist—
is offered by Carlyle's comic description of "the Bag *Sagittarius*" filled
with Sibylline fragments and scraps of his hero's writings: "So enigmatic, so chaotic we have always found, and must always find, these
scattered Leaves . . . all blown together as if by merest chance . . . to
decipher therein any illustrative primordial elements of the Clothes-
Philosophy becomes such a problem as the reader may imagine" (*Sartor Resartus*, ed. Charles Frederick Harrold [New York, 1937], p. 108).

5. On Hopkins and Darwinism, see L3, 128, and L1, 281; also Walter
Ong, *In the Human Grain* (New York, 1968), pp. 119-23. Hopkins
wrote approvingly of St. George Mivart's *On the Genesis of Species*
(London, 1871) which attempted to reconcile evolutionism with Catholic doctrine. As proof of their accord, the chapter on "Theology and
Evolution" cites the authority of St. Augustine, St. Thomas Aquinas,
and Suárez to show how tradition upholds the idea of divine concur-
rence through all stages of creation. Nature and miracle synchronize
in a "continuously-operating law" that tends toward a forseen goal,
and the whole course still shows "the unmistakeable impress of Divine
volition" (p. 291). A saltationist, Mivart attacked Darwin's theory of
natural selection and proposed that species originate through an innate
force or tendency that transforms them by working out new and sudden designs. In the sixth edition of *On the Origin of Species* (1872),
Darwin added a lengthy refutation of Mivart's conclusion. (The Catholic biologist's later controversy with Cardinal Vaughan, who excom-
municated him two months before his death, had nothing to do with
his views on evolution.) Hopkins must have responded to the breadth
and detail of Mivart's claim: "The Christian system is one which puts
on the strain, as it were, *every* faculty of man's nature" (p. 286), since,
through the evolution of his body and the creation of his soul—the
concurrent action of nature and grace—man himself becomes "not only
the head and culminating point of the grand series of organic Nature,
but in some degree *a new and distinct order of being*" (p. 301). The
"just man" in limbs and features "keeps grace" and deals out that
"being-indoors" that inscapes, aims at, Christ.

6. Here the poet's and the reader's quest meet: "The problem with each
poet is to find the right metaphor of wholeness, one that will grasp
but not deform the full range of the poetry, holding it firmly in its
implicit shape" (Balachandra Rajan, *The Lofty Rhyme: A Study of
Milton's Major Poetry* [Coral Gables, 1970], p. 3).

7. See Hopkins's discussion of this "shell or scoop" and the winnowing
fan in his last retreat notes on Christ's baptism (S, 267-68); also note
the "*scoop, scape*" parallel (L3, 285) and the chestnut fan that shapes
out a Greek Omega (J, 92). A scoop fan or basket was used in the

Eleusinian mystery rites (*Protrepticus* 2). In P10 and P25, St. Dorothea carries such a basket of blossoms and fruit from heaven.

8. Adrian J. McCarthy, S.M., "Toward a Definition of Hopkins' *Inscape*," *University of Dayton Review*, 4 (1968), 67.

9. *La Divina Comedia*, canto 33, ll. 133-41, pp. 923-24. Norton translates: "As is the geometer who wholly applies himself to measure the circle, and finds not by thinking that principle of which he is in need, such was I at that new sight. I wished to see how the image was conformed to the circle, and how it has its place therein; but my own wings were not for this, had it not been that my mind was smitten by a flash in which its wish came" (*The Divine Comedy*, p. 257).

10. For some reason one concordance lists "oh" but not "O" (Robert J. Dilligan and Todd K. Bender, *A Concordance to the English Poetry of Gerard Manley Hopkins* [Madison, Milwaukee, and London, 1970], p. 182). It notes that "ah" occurs 28 times, "oh" 12 times. The other concordance omits these but lists 100 occurrences of "O" in the poems (Alfred Borrello, *A Concordance of the Poetry in English of Gerard Manley Hopkins* [Metuchen, N.J., 1969], pp. 407-09, 706).

11. *The Upanisads*, trans. F. Max Müller (New York, 1962), II, 36. For Hopkins's quotation of Müller, see above, p. 17.

12. See Pius Parsch, *The Church's Year of Grace*, trans. William G. Heidt (Collegeville, Minn., 1957), I, 178-80. The translations, partly used here, and the commentaries on all seven "Great O" antiphons appear in vol. I, 176-83, 187-91.

13. *Metaphor in Hopkins* (Chapel Hill, 1961), p. 15.

14. In the original opening lines of his presentation poem "Ad Episcopum Salopiensem" (P173), Hopkins draws an elaborate analogy between a revolving urn (a Roman "face-pot") and the turning constellations and seasons (P, pp. 329-31).

15. Hippolytus writes that "the lyre is a musical instrument fashioned by the Logos. . . . It consists of seven strings signifying by these seven strings the entire harmony and construction of the world as it is melodiously constituted. For in six days the world was made and the Creator rested on the seventh" (*Philosophumena* 4, 48). Athanasius describes the Wisdom of God "holding the universe like a lyre" and harmonizing earth and heaven in one world order (*Contra Gentes* 41). Earlier, Heraclitus identified harmony as a union of opposing tensions: "There is a harmony in the bending back, as in the cases of the bow and the lyre" (*The Presocratics*, ed. and trans. Philip Wheelwright [New York, 1966], pp. 79). Hopkins himself may have linked the lyre with the horn, which he defined as both "a bow" and "an instrument of music," since the lyre reproduces sound through the horns that form its two sides.

16. *Poems of Tennyson* (Oxford, 1921), stanza CVI, p. 385. See also Eugene R. August, "Tennyson and Teilhard: The Faith of *In Memoriam*," *PMLA*, 84 (1969), 217-26.

17. *Plato and Platonism* (London, 1910), p. 265. See also David Downes, *Victorian Portraits: Hopkins and Pater* (New York, 1965), pp. 106-07, for parallels in the two men's theory of knowledge.

18. See *The Oxford Book of Modern Verse*, ed. W. B. Yeats (New York, 1936), p. v, and *The Letters of W. B. Yeats*, ed. Allan Wade (New York, 1955), p. 281. Also see L3, 373-74, 430.

19. *The Complete Poems of Emily Dickinson*, ed. Thomas H. Johnson (Boston, 1960), p. 337.

20. *A Grammar of Assent* (London, 1902), p. 464.

21. On Christ as Image, see also Newman's *Selected Treatises of St. Athanasius* (London, 1900), I, 178-83.

22. *Sermons Bearing on Subjects of the Day* (London, 1902), p. 61.

23. *An Apology for Poetry*, ed. George Shepherd (London, 1965), p. 100.

24. Quoted by Johan Hulzinga, *Erasmus and the Age of Reformation* (New York, 1957), p. 110.

25. *The Renaissance: Studies in Art and Poetry* (London, 1913), p. 236. The question that evokes this famous response is also worth quoting: "How shall we pass most swiftly from point to point, and be present always at the focus where the greatest number of vital forces unite in their purest energy?"

26. *The Liturgy of Holy Week* (Collegeville, Minn., 1966), p. 106.

27. *Hymn of the Universe* (New York, 1965), p. 76.

Selected Bibliography

This bibliography must of necessity be limited to the secondary
literature on Hopkins. Primary sources may be found in the list
of abbreviations at the beginning of this book. Although no attempt is made here to provide bibliographical material for the
biblical, classical, and patristic background of Hopkins's intellectual growth, I must acknowledge a debt to the following works
which have not previously been mentioned: W. K. C. Guthrie,
A History of Greek Philosophy, 2 vols. (Cambridge, 1965); John
Burnet, *Early Greek Philosophy*, 4th ed. (London, 1930); *The
New Catholic Encyclopedia*, 15 vols. (New York, 1967); *The
Jerusalem Bible* (Garden City, N.Y., 1966); Aloys Grillmeier, S.J.,
*Christ in Christian Tradition: From the Apostolic Age to Chal-
cedon*, trans. J. S. Bowden (New York, 1965); Emile Mersch, S.J.,
The Whole Christ, trans. John R. Kelly, S.J. (Milwaukee, 1938);
Berthold Altaner, *Patrology*, trans. Hilda C. Graef (New York,
1960); and Johannes Quasten, *Patrology*, 2 vols. (Westminster,
Md., 1950). An additional bibliography on recent biblical and
dogmatic studies may be found in *Theology in Transition*, ed.
Elmer O'Brien, S.J. (New York, 1965).

In the list that follows I have not given separate mention to
articles that occur in collections and critical anthologies, such as
The Explicator Cyclopedia and Geoffrey H. Hartman's edition,
Hopkins, in the "Twentieth Century Views" series, an uneven but
valuable *vade mecum* for readers of Hopkins. Since no collection,
nor even the present list, can do justice to the wealth of secondary
material, I have chosen those books and articles that were of particular help to me. For a full-length bibliography, the reader is
referred to Edward H. Cohen's *Works and Criticism of Gerard
Manley Hopkins: A Comprehensive Bibliography* (Washington,
D.C., 1969). The Hopkins Society also publishes an annual bibli-

ography in *The Hopkins Research Bulletin*. There are now two computer-produced concordances: Alfred Borrello, *A Concordance of the Poetry in English of Gerard Manley Hopkins* (Metuchen, N.J., 1969), and Robert J. Dilligan and Todd K. Bender, *A Concordance to the English Poetry of Gerard Manley Hopkins* (Madison, Milwaukee, and London, 1970).

Andreach, Robert J. *Studies in Structure: The Stages of the Spiritual Life in Four Modern Authors*. New York, 1964.

August, Eugene R. "The Growth of 'The Windhover'." *PMLA*, 82 (1967), 465–68.

——. "Hopkins' Dangerous Fire." *VP*, 1 (1963), 72-74.

Barry, Paul J. *Mary in Hopkins' Writings and Life*. Rome, 1970.

Bates, Ronald. "Hopkins' Ember Poems: A Liturgical Source." *Renascence*, 17 (1964), 32–37.

——. " 'The Windhover'." *VP*, 2 (1964), 63–64.

Bender, Todd K. *Gerard Manley Hopkins: The Classical Background and Critical Reception of His Work*. Baltimore, 1966.

Bischoff, D. Anthony, S.J. "The Manuscripts of Gerard Manley Hopkins." *Thought*, 26 (1951), 551-80.

Boyle, Robert R., S.J. "Duns Scotus in the Poetry of Hopkins." In *Scotus Speaks Today*, pp. 297-319. Southfield, Mich., 1969.

——. *Metaphor in Hopkins*. Chapel Hill, 1961.

Brinlee, Robert Washington, Jr. "The Biblical underthought of Hopkins' 'terrible' sonnets." In *Literature and Theology*, ed. Thomas F. Staley and Lester F. Zimmerman, pp. 12-22. Tulsa, 1969.

——. "Hopkins' Reconciliation of Religion and Poetry: Its Critical History and Its Implications for the Christian Imagination." Diss. Missouri 1969.

Byrne, Virginia C. "The Creator and the Maker in the Aesthetics of Gerard Manley Hopkins." *McNeese Review*, 14 (1963), 60-73.

Carson, J. Angela. "The Metaphor of Struggle in 'Carrion Comfort'." *PQ*, 49 (1970), 547-57.

Charney, Maurice. "A Bibliographical Study of Hopkins Criticism, 1918-1949." *Thought*, 25 (1950), 297-326.

Chevigny, Bell Gale. "Instress and Devotion in the Poetry of Gerard Manley Hopkins." *VS*, 9 (1965), 141-53.

Clark, Robert B. "Hopkins's 'The Shepherd's Brow'." *VN*, no. 28 (1965), 16-18.

Cohen, Selma Jeanne. "The Poetic Theory of Gerard Manley Hopkins." *PQ*, 26 (1947), 1-20.

Collins, James. "Philosophical Themes in Gerard Manley Hopkins." *Thought*, 22 (1947), 67-106.

Cotter, James Finn. " 'Altar and Hour' in *The Wreck of the Deutschland.*" *PLL,* 5 (1969), 73-79.

──────. "Inscaping *The Wreck of the Deutschland.*" *Renascence,* 21 (1969), 124-33, 166.

Devlin, Christopher, S.J. "The Image and the Word." *The Month,* n.s. 3 (1950), 114-27, 191-202.

Downes, David A. *Gerard Manley Hopkins: A Study of his Ignatian Spirit.* New York, 1959.

──────. "The Hopkins Enigma." *Thought,* 36 (1961), 573-94.

──────. *Victorian Portraits: Hopkins and Pater.* New York, 1965.

Driskell, Leon V. "The Progressive Structure of 'The Windhover'." *Renascence,* 19 (1966), 30-36.

Duncan, J. E. "The Catholic Revival and the Metaphysicals." In *The Revival of Metaphysical Poetry: The History of a Style, 1800 to the Present,* pp. 91-192. Minneapolis, 1959.

Eleanor, Mother Mary. "Hopkins' 'The Windhover' and Southwell's Hawk." *Renascence,* 11 (1961), 21-27.

Explicator Cyclopedia, The. Vol. 1: *Modern Poetry.* Ed. Charles Child Walcutt and J. Edwin Whitsell. Chicago, 1966.

Fike, Francis. "Gerard Manley Hopkins' Interest in Painting after 1868: Two Notes." *VP,* 8 (1970), 315-33.

Frost, David L. " 'The Windhover': A Commentary." *Theology,* 72 (1969), 10-13.

Fulweiler, Howard W. "Gerard Manley Hopkins and the 'Stanching, Quenching Ocean of a Motionable Mind'." *VN,* no. 30 (1966), 6-13.

Gardner, W. H. *Gerard Manley Hopkins (1844-1889): A Study of Poetic Idiosyncrasy in Relation to Poetic Tradition.* 2 vols. 2d ed. London and New York, 1958.

Graves, William L. "Gerard Manley Hopkins as Composer." *VP,* 1 (1963), 146-55.

Grennen, Joseph E. "Grammar as Thaumaturgy: Hopkins' 'Heraclitean Fire'." *Renascence,* 15 (1963), 208-11.

Hallgarth, Susan A. "A Study of Hopkins' Use of Nature." *VP,* 5 (1967), 79-92.

Harrison, Thomas P. "The Birds of Gerard Manley Hopkins." *SP* (1957), 448-63.

Hart, Sister Mary Adorita. "The Christocentric Theme in Gerard Manley Hopkins' 'The Wreck of the Deutschland'." Diss. Catholic University 1952.

Hartman, Geoffrey H., ed. *Hopkins: A Collection of Critical Essays.* Englewood Cliffs, N.J., 1966.

Heuser, Alan. *The Shaping Vision of Gerard Manley Hopkins.* London, 1958.

Hill, Archibald A. "An Analysis of 'The Windhover': An Experiment in Structural Method." *PMLA*, 70 (1955), 968-78.

Holloway, Roberta. "Some Effects of Classical Study in the Work of Hopkins." Diss. University of California at Berkeley 1945.

Holloway, Sister Marcella Marie. *The Prosodic Theory of Gerard Manley Hopkins*. Washington, D.C., 1947.

Hufstader, Anselm. "The Experience of Nature in Hopkins' Journal and Poems." *Downside Review*, 84 (1966), 127-49.

Humiliata, Sister Mary. "Hopkins and the Prometheus Myth." *PMLA*, 70 (1955), 58-68.

Jennings, Elizabeth. *Every Changing Shape*. Philadelphia, 1962.

Johnson, Wendell Stacy. *Gerard Manley Hopkins: The Poet as Victorian*. Ithaca, 1968.

Jordan, Frank, Jr. "Hopkins' 'The Caged Skylark'," *Explicator*, 28, no. 9 (1970), item 80.

Keating, John E. *The Wreck of the Deutschland: An Essay and Commentary*. Research Series 6. Kent, Ohio, 1963.

Kenyon Critics, The. *Gerard Manley Hopkins*. Norfolk, Conn., 1945.

Lawler, Justus George. *The Christian Image: Studies in Religious Art and Poetry*. Pittsburgh, 1966.

Litzinger, Boyd. "The Pattern of Ascent in Hopkins." *VP*, 2 (1964), 43-47.

McChesney, Donald. *A Hopkins Commentary: An Explanatory Commentary on the Main Poems, 1876-89*. London, 1968.

MacKenzie, Norman H. *Hopkins*. Writers and Critics Series. London, 1968.

McLaughlin, John, S.J. "The Pulpit Rhetoric of Gerard Manley Hopkins." Diss. Columbia 1967.

McNamee, Maurice B., S.J. "Mastery and Mercy in 'The Wreck of the Deutschland'." *College English*, 23 (1962), 267-76.

Mariani, Paul L. "The Artistic and Tonal Integrity of Hopkins' 'The Shepherd's Brow'." *VP*, 6 (1968), 63-68.

————. *A Commentary on the Complete Poems of Gerard Manley Hopkins*. Ithaca and London, 1970.

Martz, Louis L. *The Poetry of Meditation*. New Haven, 1954.

Mathison, John K. "The Poetic Theory of Gerard Manley Hopkins." *PQ*, 26 (1947), 21-35.

Miller, Bruce E. "On 'The Windhover'." *VP*, 2 (1964), 115-19.

Miller, J. Hillis. "The Creation of the Self in Gerard Manley Hopkins." *ELH*, 22 (1955), 293-319.

————. *The Disappearance of God: Five Nineteenth-Century Writers*. Cambridge, Mass., 1963.

————. " 'Orion' in *The Wreck of the Deutschland*." *MLN*, 76 (1961), 509-14.

Milward, Peter, S.J. *A Commentary on G. M. Hopkins' 'The Wreck of the Deutschland'*. Tokyo and London, 1968.

————. *A Commentary on the Sonnets of G. M. Hopkins.* Tokyo, 1969.

Montag, George E. " 'The Windhover': Crucifixion and Redemption." *VP*, 3 (1965), 109-18.

Morris, David. *The Poetry of Gerard Manley Hopkins and T. S. Eliot in the Light of the Donne Tradition.* Berne, 1953.

Nassar, Eugene Paul. "Hopkins, *Figura*, and Grace: God's Better Beauty." *Renascence*, 17 (1965), 128-30, 136.

Noon, William T., S.J. *Poetry and Prayer.* New Brunswick, N.J., 1967.

Ochshorn, Myron. "Hopkins the Critic." *Yale Review*, 54 (1965), 346-67.

O'Dea, Richard J. " 'The Loss of the Eurydice': A Possible Key to the Reading of Hopkins." *VP*, 4 (1966), 291-93.

Ong, Walter J., S.J. *In the Human Grain.* New York, 1968.

Peters, W. A. M., S.J. *Gerard Manley Hopkins: A Critical Essay towards the Understanding of His Poetry.* London, 1948.

Phare, E. E. *The Poetry of Gerard Manley Hopkins: A Survey and Commentary.* Cambridge, Mass., 1933.

Pick, John. "Gerard Manley Hopkins." In *The Victorian Poets: A Guide to Research*, ed. Frederic E. Faverty. 2d ed. Cambridge, Mass., 1968.

————. *Gerard Manley Hopkins: Priest and Poet.* London, 1942.

————. "Hopkins' Imagery: The Relation of His Journal to His Poetry." *Renascence*, 7 (1954), 30-38.

Pitchford, Lois. "The Curtal Sonnets of Gerard Manley Hopkins." *MLN*, 67 (1952), 165-69.

Rader, Louis. "Hopkins' Dark Sonnets: Another New Expression." *VP*, 5 (1967), 13-20.

Richards, I. A. "Gerard Hopkins." *The Dial*, 81 (1926), 195-203.

Ritz, Jean-Georges. *Le Poète Gérard Manley Hopkins, S.J., 1844-1889: L'Homme et L'Oeuvre.* Paris, 1963.

————. *Robert Bridges and Gerard Hopkins, 1863-1889: A Literary Friendship.* London, 1960.

Schneider, Elisabeth. *The Dragon in the Gate: Studies in the Poetry of Gerard Manley Hopkins.* Berkeley, 1968.

Schoder, Raymond V., S.J. " 'Spelt from Sibyl's Leaves'." *Thought*, 19 (1944), 633-48.

Shea, F. X., S.J. "Another Look at 'The Windhover'." *VP*, 2 (1964), 219-39.

Thomas, Alfred, S.J. "Hopkins's 'Felix Randal': The Man and the Poem." *TLS*, March 19, 1971, 331-32.

————. *Hopkins the Jesuit: The Years of Training.* London, 1969.

Weyand, Norman, S.J., ed. *Immortal Diamond: Studies in Gerard Manley Hopkins.* New York, 1949.

White, Gertrude M. "Hopkins' 'God's Grandeur': A Poetic Statement of Christian Doctrine." *VP*, 4 (1966), 284-87.

White, Norman, "Hopkins' 'Spelt from Sibyl's Leaves'." *VN*, no. 36 (Fall 1969), 27-28.

Wolfe, Patricia A. "The Paradox of Self: A Study of Hopkins' Spiritual Conflict in the 'Terrible' Sonnets." *VP*, 6 (1968), 85-103.

Wooton, Carl. "The Terrible Fire of G. M. H." *Texas Studies in Literature and Language*, 4 (1963), 367-75.

Zoghby, Sister Mary, R.S.M. "The Cosmic Christ in Hopkins, Teilhard, and Scotus." *Renascence*, 24 (1971), 33-46.

Index

Like the *Poems, The Journals and Papers* and *The Sermons and Devotional Writings* are listed here according to contents. For words like *epinoiai, kenosis, sake,* etc., the first entry contains a definition or description of its meaning.